FACING FORWARD

*Edited and with an Introduction
by Leah D Frank*

BROADWAY PLAY PUBLISHING INC.

56 E 81st St., NY NY 10028–0202
212–772–8334/FAX 772–8358

FACING FORWARD
© Copyright 1995 by Broadway Play Publishing Inc

First printing: May 1995
ISBN: 0-88145-112-6

Book design: Marie Donovan
Word processing: Microsoft Word for Windows
Typographic controls: Xerox Ventura Publisher 2.0 PE
Typeface: Palatino
Printed on recycled acid-free paper and bound in the USA.

CONTENTS

INTRODUCTION

American theater, mostly melodramas at the turn of the last century, concerned many of the same passionate topics included in this anthology: adultery, the American Dream, abusiveness, drunkenness, love, and betrayal. There are major differences, however. For one, the plays a hundred years ago were written almost exclusively by men, which meant among other things that "bad" women characters died or were killed while the "good" women got married, or at least engaged. Augustin Daly's UNDER THE GASLIGHT, Bronson Howard's popular SHENANDOAH, and Dion Boucicault's POOR OF NEW YORK are typical of the nineteenth century popular theater, filled with stock characters and plots in which social order is restored. David Belasco's GIRL OF THE GOLDEN WEST and MADAME BUTTERFLY are two of the better of this genre in that the women are not totally one-dimensional characters, although they both follow the dictates of strictly defined social mores. Of course, the moral imperatives in drama were assigned by men who—apparently unlike the women of those days—understood the concepts of good and evil. All these melodramas reflected American society in the early nineteen-hundreds.

Times have certainly changed during the twentieth century, haven't they? At least in the American theater? The answer is: Not necessarily. As recently as 1980, testimony at the Congressional Hearing for The National Endowment for the Arts showed that only seven percent of the federally funded theaters across the nation produce plays written and directed by women. There are still very few women drama critics analyzing new plays, and only a handful of women directors interpreting new plays by either men or women. All of this means that our theater is still a male-dominated art form and, in light of the recent studies in the difficulty of intergender communication, one gender's voice is still not fully represented on the American stage. Yet at the same time that nothing has changed, everything has changed—as the plays in this anthology indicate.

"Are plays by women somehow different from those by men?"is one of the most frequently asked questions concerning gender in theater. It is probably a question that has no definitive answer—how simple the world would be if there were clear distinctions to complicated issues! However, one of the answers often heard is that plays by men are about important issues and are filled with dramatic action, whereas those by women are diminutive both in subject and stage action.

The idea that male authors are authoritative is long-standing throughout literary history. Writing in 1886 about his theory of poetry, Gerard Manley Hopkins explained that the artist's"most essential quality is masterly execution, which is a male gift, and especially marks off men from women, the begetting of one's thought on paper, on verse, or whatever the matter is....The male quality is the creative gift." The belief that a penis is the first gift of a master writer is still prevalent over a century later.

Our language also reflects these mistaken gender assumptions. A male critic, for example, is considered knowledgeable, insightful, and usually accurate. A women who criticizes is known as a nag at best, a bitch at worst. Fortunately, these attitudes are slowly changing. Men are beginning to work with women as equal partners in law, business, and in the arts. There are more women historians bringing back into the mainstream the work of women artists, writers, poets, and playwrights so that we can understand that the foundation of women's art already exists—and it is strong. Women are moving to the forefront of every field, from politics to art to religion. It is no longer uncommon for women—like the very uncommon Wendy Wasserstein—to win a Pulitzer Prize for drama.

It also is not uncommon for plays at this point in the twentieth century, like Ms Wasserstein's WORKOUT, to be either highly political or to be presented, as WORKOUT was, to benefit a women's rights political agenda. Karen Sunde's HAITI (A DREAM) explores not only the tragedy of the Haitian boat people, but the tragedy of all women refugees who have one foot anchored in the mud of the past while the other foot seeks a toehold in a new era. Judy GeBauer looks at America's role as world leader in THE NIP AND THE BITE. Megan Terry explodes gender roles in BREAKFAST SERIAL while also addressing the appalling social issue of child abuse.

The personal is also political, as Lynda Sturner points out in THE DEATH OF HUEY NEWTON, which compares a contemporary relationship with its beginnings during the political idealism of the 1960s. The gap between the financially well-off and a growing community united by poverty is the issue Y York looks at in her poignant LIFE GAP. Personal experience as a metaphor for life—as in"How do I get through this mess?"—occupies Lenore Bensinger's harried writer in A GHOST STORY, Christina Cocek's analysand in STEPPING OFF A CLOUD, and the patients in Lee Hunkins' THE BEST OF STRANGERS.

Reading the plays here collected shows that women are more diverse, interesting, and talented now than they have ever been. Facing forward into the twenty-first century with that idea in mind, I think we can begin to believe in the possibility of a positive social change for women.

One more thing strikes me: Equal is not Same—the one-acts in this
volume are equal to any by men, but they have been written by beings
with different hormones, different physiologies, different experiences,
and unequal educations and expectations. Vive la difference!

Leah D Frank

Leah D Frank has been a drama critic for twenty years. For ten years she
was a regional theater critic for *The New York Times* Long Island Edition,
where she became the first woman to write drama criticism for the *Times*.
She currently writes feature stories and criticism on theater, film, and
television for publications such as *The New York Times, The New York Daily
News, Elle, Travel and Leisure, New York Theatre Review, Soho Weekly News,
The Stamford Advocate, the Staten Island Advance,* and *Contemporary
Dramatists.* She was the founding editor of *Other Stages,* a biweekly
newspaper of Off and Off-Off Broadway Theater and Dance. She has been
an actress and stage manager, and studied voice, acting, and the fine arts
before beginning work on her PhD in American Theater and Film History at
Columbia University, where she is a doctoral candidate.

67201

Adele Edling Shank

Adele Edling Shank has written numerous plays, five of which have
premiered at the Magic Theatre in San Francisco. Her work also has been
seen at the Actors Theatre of Louisville (once as the co-winner of the Great
American Play Contest), in Los Angeles, San Francisco, New York, and in
England. Her full-length works include six plays—SUNSET/SUNRISE,
WINTERPLAY, STUCK: A FREEWAY COMEDY, SAND CASTLES, THE
GRASS HOUSE, and TUMBLEWEED—a series of independent but
interconnected plays set in various California locations, with one or
more characters appearing from a previous play. Other full-length plays
include WAR HORSES, ROCKS IN HER POCKET, and a new play entitled
SINGING IN THE WILDERNESS.

She is the recipient of numerous awards including an NEA Playwriting
Fellowship, Rockefeller Playwrights-in-Residence Grant, and a Dramatists
Guild/CBS Award. Most of her plays have been published by the Theatre
Communications Group in their *Plays in Process* series and in *West Coast
Plays*. She is a professor and head of the playwriting program at the
University of California, San Diego.

67201 premiered in June 1991 at the University of California, San Diego,
as part of the larger piece I'M A STRANGER HERE MYSELF.

MIKE . . . . Steven Pearson
LOIS . . . . Robyn Hunt

Director . . . . Theodore Shank

"All the Way from Wichita" was composed by Melissa McCracken.

(*An absolutely ordinary motel room with nothing in it that gives away its geographic location. It could be any city in the United States.* MIKE *is sitting at a table and using glue and small bits of wood to build a replica of a building. He has a tourist brochure with a picture of the building he is replicating. Country music comes from a radio.* MIKE *looks at his watch. The song ends.*)

RADIO D J: And that was poor 'ole Willie Nelson singing "If You've Got the Money, I've Got the Time." And that makes it 1:56 on this gorgeous Saturday afternoon in…

(MIKE *leaps for the radio and turns the volume down. He looks at his watch, keeping track of the time that is passing. When he turns the volume back up, the radio is again playing music.* MIKE *goes back to work.*)

(LOIS *comes in, carrying a brown paper bag.* MIKE *doesn't hear her above the radio. She goes behind him and covers his eyes.*)

MIKE: Miss Wichita?

(LOIS *laughs and releases him.*)

MIKE: Hi.

LOIS: Hi.

MIKE: (*Looking at watch*) You cut it pretty close.

LOIS: Yeah... Mike, I'm sorry. There was this tiny little emergency….

MIKE: Hey!

LOIS: OK, OK. So uh…well, see what happened is…I got stuck in this really horrendous traffic.

MIKE: And where was this really horrendous traffic?

LOIS: Ummmm. It was over by Century II, the pride of Wichita, a modernistic convention and cultural complex. That was some mean traffic.

MIKE: Well, you made it. With seconds to spare. Every second matters, you know that don't you, every second we have matters to me.

LOIS: Well, sure, Mike.

(MIKE *looks at his watch and is startled by the time. He takes two cans of beer out of his paper bag and pops both open. He hands one to* LOIS *and they stand waiting.*)

RADIO D J: Listen up cowpokers and pokees, it's our Saturday special. To Lois with love from Mike. Boy, these guys sure do get around. Today it's "All the Way from Wichita." Had to dig for this one, Mike. Hope she likes it.

("All the Way from Wichita" *plays on the radio as* MIKE *and* LOIS *toast with their beer cans.*)

MIKE and LOIS: To Wichita.

(MIKE *and* LOIS *dance.*)

MIKE: Does she like it?

LOIS: You bet she does, cowpoker.

MIKE: Pokee.

LOIS: You know, I just can't get over how tiring all that sight-seeing is. I do declare I'm just plain tuckered out. *(She starts to unbutton his shirt.)* And I was wonderin' if it wasn't maybe about time to tuck ourselves in.

MIKE: Don't you want to see what I'm making?

LOIS: Maybe it could wait a little while?

(MIKE *starts to unbutton her shirt. She notices his wedding ring.*)

LOIS: Mike!

(LOIS *covers her eyes with her hands and points at the wedding ring on his finger.*)

MIKE: *(Taking off ring and putting it in a pocket)* Oh geez! Man, I'm sorry Lois, I....

LOIS: Shhhh! Safe?

MIKE: Safe.

LOIS: Now where were we?

MIKE: So what'd you see that pooped you out so much?

LOIS: I checked out the speech and hearing rehabilitation center....

MIKE: Owwww hot stuff.

LOIS: *(Lying down on the bed)* You bet. Then I walked around the "cow-town" restoration. What'd you do?

MIKE: *(Indicating his replica)* Central Presbyterian Church.

LOIS: Nice. That's all?

MIKE: I suppose not.

LOIS: So?

MIKE: I guess I looked in on an oil refinery and checked out a flour mill.

LOIS: Owwww hot stuff. *(Silence)* Mike? *(Points to her shoes)*

(MIKE takes her shoes off.)

LOIS: So where'd you have lunch?

MIKE: *(Caught without an answer, he finally comes up with...)* McDonald's.

LOIS: McDonald's! Oh that's really weak, Mike. Can't you do better than that?

MIKE: What's the matter with McDonald's? Every town's got a McDonald's.

LOIS: That's what's wrong with McDonald's.

MIKE: OK smarty, where'd you eat?

LOIS: I just happen to have had an absolutely scrumptious lunch at the River Front Inn, so there.

(The song fades out.)

RADIO DJ: That's about enough of this Saturday's special. Listen Mike and Lois, you have a good one. This is Frightfully Friendly Freddie coming to you from....

(MIKE lunges at the radio and turns it off quickly. With a gesture LOIS invites MIKE to the bed. MIKE returns to the table and picks up the brochure.)

MIKE: Did you know that we are "at the confluence of the Arkansas and the Little Arkansas Rivers. Wichita is the chief commercial and industrial center of southern Kansas and the seat of Sedgewick County."

LOIS: This comes later, Mike.

MIKE: Here's the good stuff. "Wichita is located on the site of a village (1863) inhabited by Wichita Indians who had been driven out of Oklahoma and Texas for their Union sympathies during the Civil War." Did you know that, that there were Indians that had Union sympathies during the Civil War?

LOIS: They probably also had women that told 'em to shut up and come to bed.

MIKE: *(Taking a piece of paper from his pocket)* I checked up on them Wichita Indians. They belonged to a group called the Caddo Indians. These guys were agricultural and they "lived in villages of thatched houses. In general, they were intermediate between the settled tribes of the lower Mississippi and Gulf states and the moving bison hunters of the Plains." They were "semi-sedentary". *(Demonstrates)*

LOIS: What's the matter Mike?

MIKE: I'm semi-sedentary.

LOIS: You know what I mean.

MIKE: They left a whole mess of artifacts.

LOIS: We seem to have a problem here.

MIKE: I thought you liked artifacts.

LOIS: In their proper place. Sex first, then artifacts.

(MIKE *goes to the table and starts to work on his model. Silence.*)

MIKE: Want another beer?

LOIS: You brought four?

MIKE: Six.

LOIS: What's up?

MIKE: Nothing's weird about six. Six is normal.

LOIS: So is sex, but it looks like we aren't having any. *(Silence)* Wichita's going to be a bummer isn't it? I had a feeling last Saturday, when you jabbed down on Wichita, I had a what a ya call it, a premonition, Wichita was going to be a bummer. *(No response)* But hey Mike, we take what the finger of fate gives us and we don't complain, right? Of course Wichita does put a certain pressure on that philosophy. We'll have better luck next week. *(Silence)* I said, we'll have better luck next week.

MIKE: I'm not the one's complainin' about Wichita.

LOIS: Statement, not complaint.

MIKE: Sounded like a complaint to me. Enjoy the present.

LOIS: I always do, Mike. You're the one seems to be having a bad time.

(*Silence.* LOIS *takes from the paper bag a scrapbook and a large map of the United States which she opens and spreads on the bed.*)

MIKE: Hey, what are you doing?

LOIS: What's it look like?

MIKE: But it isn't four o'clock yet!

LOIS: So we bend the rules. I thought it might cheer you up to know where we're going next week. In fact, why wait until next week. Let's just scrap this dumpy town and spend the afternoon in, let's see where....

(*With her finger pointed down at the map, she closes her eyes and circles her arm above the map.*)

MIKE: Lois! This is all wrong, we haven't done any research, we can't do that! *(As her finger jabs down on the map)* Don't tell me!!

LOIS: Okay okay okay okay, we'll stay in Wichita. Baby? Come on sweetie. Come to Lois.

(MIKE *goes to her.*)

LOIS: Good boy. So tell me, what have you dug up on dinner, huh? What's the hottest spot in Wichita?

MIKE: The Chow Down Steak House.

LOIS: Sounds Chinese.

(MIKE *laughs.* LOIS *rubs his neck.*)

LOIS: That's better baby. Owwww, knots. Terrible knots. We're goin' a hafta try some desperate means to unkink them knots. Too many hours at the sorting machine, that's the trouble. I told you last week you should stop taking the overtime.

MIKE: I'm not in a position to say no, unlike some people.

LOIS: Mike.

MIKE: I'm not the one who brought up the post office!

LOIS: Jeez. Sorreeeee.

MIKE: Dad blast it. Automate the sorting and what happens. What'd the union rep tell us, huh, if we went along with the new machines?

LOIS: I don't remember anyone askin' our permission. I'm sorry I brought it up. Let's not talk post office now, this is....

MIKE: We've got to talk about it, Lois. But I can't figure out when, not without breaking the rules.

LOIS: We can talk Monday, we can talk post office on our coffee breaks for pete's sake. Mike, nobody's going to think we're screwing just because we talk post office on our coffee break. 'Course, spin the bottle, that'd be a different matter.

(*He doesn't respond to her joke. He goes to the table and starts working on his model. He tries hard to focus on what he's doing.* LOIS *gets up off the bed and buttons her blouse.*)

LOIS: What's the matter? Wrong time of the month?

MIKE: Ha ha.

LOIS: Your...your...what's-her-face found out!?

MIKE: Shut up Lois!

(LOIS *puts on her shoes and heads for the door.*)

MIKE: Where you goin'?

LOIS: I'm going home. I'd just about as soon listen to my husband snore in front of the baseball game as fight with you.

MIKE: Great, now you've blown it!

LOIS: Who cares!

MIKE: Well jeez, all week I've been trying to figure out how to talk to you without breaking the rules and you blow them off without half a thought.

LOIS: Damn the rules. Talk to me.

(Silence)

MIKE: You're gonna have to start up with the bowling team again.

LOIS: Yeah, why's that?

MIKE: To fill up your Saturday afternoons.

LOIS: Your wife did find out!

MIKE: No. I'm being transferred.

LOIS: Transferred?

MIKE: Transferred.

LOIS: Transferred! When?

MIKE: Wednesday.

LOIS: Wednesday? What Wednesday?

MIKE: Next Wednesday.

LOIS: Saturday, Sunday, Monday, Tuesday, Wednesday? Five days!

MIKE: From today.

LOIS: When'd you find this out?!

MIKE: A while ago.

LOIS: Nothing?

MIKE: I didn't want things to end before they had to. And I figured once I told you it'd be the end.

LOIS: Where they moving you to anyway? And how come you're getting transferred?

MIKE: They said because of the automation they don't need as many employees at our substation, so they're transferring me to a town that's growing.

LOIS: But they've been having you on overtime!

MIKE: I know, it doesn't make sense. Does that really surprise you?

LOIS: You going far?

MIKE: Yeah. Too far. *(He puts his arms around her.)* I've been thinking about it for three weeks now and I can't figure any way we can keep this up. It's hard enough with us in the same town.

LOIS: No, no, there's got to be something.... We'll have to really travel, that's all. We'll have to pick some place that's half way. It'll be all right, Mike, we'll just meet in the middle.

MIKE: Lois, we've only got two hours. It's too far.

LOIS: Why are they moving you so far away!?

MIKE: They say it's the only job open for me.

LOIS: You've got options. You just won't admit to 'em that's all.

MIKE: How's that?

LOIS: Don't go.

MIKE: No choice.

LOIS: Quit.

MIKE: Get real.

(Silence)

LOIS: I guess this is where we say we always knew it was going to end sometime.

MIKE: Somewhere.

LOIS: Who'd a thought it'd be Wichita.

MIKE: It's a beautiful word, Wichita.

LOIS: Charleston. Remember Charleston?

MIKE: Ummm. Settled in 1670.

LOIS: The Magnolia Plantation.

MIKE: Santa Fe was the first. The Chapel of San Miguel.

LOIS: St Petersburg.

MIKE: San Antonio.

LOIS: Savannah.

MIKE: Syracuse.

(They look at the scrapbook together.)

LOIS: Our "Dickensian Christmas in Nantucket." You read the Tiny Tim book to me.

MIKE: Pretty weird, huh. 79401.

LOIS: Lubbock. 70802.

MIKE: Owww, Baton Rouge. Remember 97625? It rained all afternoon.

LOIS: Klamath Falls!

MIKE: 80914. *(Colorado Springs)*

LOIS: Ummm. 34233. *(Sarasota)*

MIKE: 55403. *(Minneapolis)*

LOIS: 05753. *(Middlebury, Vermont)*

MIKE: *(Putting the Wichita brochure in the scrapbook)* 67201.

(Silence)

LOIS: Wichita is a hundred miles from the geographic center of the United States.

MIKE: Yeah?

LOIS: So are we going to do this end business well, or are we going to do it badly?

MIKE: You do everything well. Pain, you know, pain is O K if you understand it.

(Silence)

LOIS: What are we going to do with the scrapbook?

MIKE: You take it. I've got the models.

LOIS: Where do you keep 'em anyway?

MIKE: In the garage. Plain sight. Never occurs to anybody to wonder.

LOIS: I don't think I can stand to keep the scrapbook. Maybe we should bury it. No, leave it here maybe, for someone to find. Our artifacts.

MIKE: You could just leave it in the P O box.

LOIS: No.

(Silence)

LOIS: They got P O boxes in every P O, right?

MIKE: Sure.

LOIS: You could get a P O box, right, in your new post office?

MIKE: Yeah.

LOIS: So, maybe we could write.

MIKE: Write?

LOIS: Sure, like letters.

MIKE: I was never very good at writin'. Essays, an' stuff, they weren't my thing.

LOIS: But letters. Like lovers write each other.

MIKE: Lovers don't write, they telephone.

LOIS: Well they used to write. We could write like they used to write in the old days.

MIKE: What would we say?

(Silence)

LOIS: We could maybe be them, we could be old lovers.

MIKE: What's so great about being old lovers?

LOIS: I mean real old, like in dead. It'd be like the towns, see, we'd study up. Then we'd write like we were them. We'd have to get a book to choose them from, a sort of map of famous lovers, there's gotta be a book listin' lots of lovers. Well, maybe not.

MIKE: You really are a wacko lady, you know that.

LOIS: We'd each have to have a copy of the same book. The phone book! No, then all we'd have is a name and you can't do research on just anybody. It's gotta be dead famous people who've gotten written about. The Bible. No, with our luck we'd hit Job every time.

MIKE: Lois…

LOIS: I remember, in high school there was this book of quotations, pear something? Bartlett! *Bartlett's Quotations*!

MIKE: We're supposed to write each other quotations?

LOIS: No, silly! Each quotation's got the name of the person who said it. See, say I go first.

MIKE: Say right.

LOIS: So I close my eyes and open the book and jab my finger down on a quotation and I've got the name of a famous person and that's who I'll be.

MIKE: Come again?

LOIS: I'll write you as if I were that person. A love letter. To your P O box in your new P O.

MIKE: Say maybe like, Lady Godiva?

LOIS: Yeah.

MIKE: But you don't know anything about Lady Godiva.

LOIS: Of course not, we'll have to go to the library on our lunch hours and find out, just like we've been doing with the towns!

MIKE: *(Unsure)* Ohhhkay. But what if you jab down on somebody that's a man?

LOIS: Well that's O K, I can pretend to be a man! And you can pretend to be a woman if you have to.

MIKE: Oh I don't know.... And what if it's...say Einstein?

LOIS: What about it?

MIKE: Well, I mean you'd have to write about science and stuff.

LOIS: No I wouldn't! See, I'd find out what his wife's name was and then I'd write you like, well..."Dear Mary, I sure hope your mother's better soon. I miss you something awful. I think it's because you aren't with me that my science isn't going too good. I love you precious babykins, with every one of my sixteen zillion brain cells."

(MIKE *laughs.*)

LOIS: Well, I'd do better than that 'cause I'd find out more, like did they have kids, and what her mother's name was and where they lived, stuff like that to make it real. It's not so hard, it just might take more than one lunch hour.

MIKE: So I get this love letter from Einstein to his wife....

LOIS: I guess you're right, that's kind of kinky. We better stick with our own sexes. So if I jab down on Einstein, I'll become Mrs Einstein writing to Mr Einstein.

MIKE: So if I happen to jab down on Mata Hari I write to you like I'm... Mr Mata Hari.

LOIS: That's it. You game?

MIKE: Sure. Why not. Beats bowling.

LOIS: Great! Jeez, three-thirty!

MIKE: What's the hurry?

LOIS: I wanna stop at the book store. Besides, last times are never any good. We don't want to have a last time, do we?

MIKE: No.

LOIS: I can give you your *Bartlett's* Monday at the post office. Pretty strange farewell present, but nobody's going to think we're screwing just because I give you a *Bartlett's*.

(LOIS *puts the scrapbook under the mattress.*)

MIKE: Lois. I love you.

LOIS: Me too. And we'll say it over and over again. Lots of different ways. Oh yeah, sexy, huh, make some of 'em really sexy O K?

MIKE: I'll try.

LOIS: I'm gonna get one of those thesaurus things too, there's gonna have to be a whole lot of new word learning. New words, maybe even new languages. Arrivederci.

MIKE: Arrivederci.

(MIKE *watches* LOIS *leave. He looks at his watch. He turns on the radio and sits down to finish the model. The song on the radio ends.*)

RADIO DJ: Welcome back cowpokers and pokees. This is Frightfully Friendly Freddie saying get outside man, it's too nice an afternoon, we've got a beautiful seventy-two degrees in downtown Chicago and the Cubs are hot in Wrigley Field!

BLACKOUT

THE BEST OF STRANGERS

Lee Hunkins

Lee Hunkins is a New York playwright whose works include FREEDOM IS MY MIDDLE NAME, produced by The Open Eye: New Stagings; SEQUESTERED, also produced by the American Folk Theatre; ANYBODY I WANT TO BE and JUST ONE STEP, produced by Plays For Living; REVIVAL, produced by Family Classic Theatre of San Francisco; and THE DOLLS, produced by the Afro-American Total Theatre. Her television script HOLLOW IMAGE was selected for the National Playwrights Conference at the Eugene O'Neill Theatre Center. In connection with the conference, the play won the A B C Theater Award, and the two-hour drama was a Titus Production, A B C-T V.

THE BEST OF STRANGERS was presented at the American Folk Theatre, Inc, Artistic Director Dick Gaffield, in New York City on 9 October 1985, with the following cast and creative contributors:

SYBIL MOSS . . . . .Helena de Crespo
AMY . . . . Sheila Linnette
TISHO ANDERSON . . . . Hope Clarke
SAM COLEMAN . . . . .Frank Adu
DR CAVENDISH . . . . .Janne Peters
ARTHUR MOSS . . . . .Arthur French

Director . . . . Henry Miller
Assistant director . . . . Louise Mike
Stage manager . . . . .Audrey James
Scenic and costume designer . . . . Felix E Cochran
Lighting designer . . . . Tony Giovanetti

CHARACTERS

SYBIL MOSS: *White female in her early fifties. Hospital patient.*

AMY: *Black female in her mid-twenties. A nurse.*

TISHO ANDERSON: *Black female in her early forties. Hospital patient.*

SAM COLEMAN: *Black male in his late forties.* TISHO's *boyfriend.*

DR CAVENDISH: *White female in her thirties.*

ARTHUR MOSS: *Black male in his mid-fifties.* SYBIL's *husband. Speaks with a slight West Indian accent.*

DEDICATION

To Anne McGravie, a friend and fellow playwright who understands

Scene One

(Sunday afternoon. A semi-private hospital room in New York City. Two beds are down center. Near each one is a chair, night table, telephone, and overhead reading light. A dresser for storing linen is up center. A basket of fruit is on a night table. A bouquet of roses and get well cards are on the dresser. Buzzers are attached to each bed. A curtain separates the two beds. A television is mounted on the wall. A window and air conditioner are up left. The bathroom is down right. When the door is open, the sink and mirrored medicine cabinet can be seen. The closet and door leading to the corridor are down left. A chart is hooked on the front of SYBIL's bed.)

(SYBIL MOSS is propped up in the bed nearer to the bathroom. Adjusting her half glasses, she studies the Times *crossword puzzle. AMY enters, carrying the meter used in measuring blood pressure.)*

AMY: *(Taking SYBIL's pressure)* How's my favorite patient doing?

SYBIL: Pretty good today.

AMY: Pain easing up a little?

SYBIL: Oh yes, definitely!

AMY: Then why'd the night nurse have to give you a sedative to help you sleep?

SYBIL: You've got spies reporting my activities to you!

AMY: Highly paid spies at that. Can't trust you to tell me what's going on.

SYBIL: I drank too much coffee. Had a bit of insomnia, that's all.
(AMY writes the pressure on SYBIL's chart.) Amy, you're a born worrier. Really, I'm all right. But you don't look so good.

AMY: *(Flopping down in a chair)* My feet are killing me. Wish I could trade them in for a new pair.

SYBIL: And recycle the old ones?

AMY: Yeah. Just imagine thousands of feet all crunched together. Bunions, callouses, and corns tumbling around in a giant cookie jar. Oh God, I need a vacation!

SYBIL: A cruise might be nice.

AMY: No way. My boyfriend gets seasick in the bathtub. Funny thing is he loves to swim. Tells me that's different. It's got something to do with motion. You ever been on a cruise?

SYBIL: Arthur and I celebrated our twentieth anniversary on the high seas.

AMY: Sounds romantic.

SYBIL: He went to bed at nine o'clock every night.

AMY: You devil you! That was romantic!

SYBIL: You're not listening. I said *he* went to bed. The sandman usually mugs him about nine, and the cruise was no exception.

AMY: That must have slowed you down a bit.

SYBIL: Like hell it did. I drank champagne two glasses at a time, one for me and one for Arthur. After about six glasses, I held my own hand in the moonlight and whispered sweet nothings to lifeboat number seventeen.

AMY: Mr Moss seems like a nice man.

SYBIL: He is. If I could just get him to loosen up a bit.

AMY: It could be worse. Suppose he was one of those guys who runs around at parties with a lamp shade on his head.

SYBIL: If I thought he'd do it, I'd buy him the damn shade! *(Looking at the puzzle again)* I need an eight-letter word meaning, "Bantu language".

AMY: You're sure it's eight letters?

SYBIL: *(Counting the spaces)* Yep.

AMY: That's too bad.

SYBIL: What word were you thinking of?

AMY: *(Getting up and crossing to the door)* Didn't have a thing in mind. I just refuse to be intimidated by the *Times* crossword puzzle. Oh, almost forgot. You're getting a new roommate. She's on her way up from emergency now.

SYBIL: Hallelujah! This isn't the liveliest place in town to begin with, but on the weekend you could get more action out of King Tut's tomb.

AMY: *(Exiting)* I wish the week had seven Sundays.

SYBIL: *(Calling after her)* By the third day of Sundays, you'd be bored to tears!

(SYBIL takes a hand mirror off the night table and looks at her face. Putting the mirror down she begins combing her hair and fluffing it up. She's not a vain woman, but does take an honest pride in her hair. Except for writing, she does everything with her left hand. She holds her right arm across her mid-section as if it were in a sling. Looking at her bed, which is covered from one end to the other with sections of the Times, *she tries to gather them up, but using her left hand is*

tiresome and she gives up on the neatness idea and goes back to her crossword puzzle. TISHO ANDERSON enters. AMY is pushing her in a wheelchair. She's followed by SAM COLEMAN. He's carrying TISHO's personal belongings. AMY attempts to help TISHO into bed.)

TISHO: I can manage.

(AMY stands behind her. TISHO raises up out of the wheelchair. Her legs are unable to support her and she starts to fall. SAM moves forward, but AMY catches her.)

TISHO: Did you reach my doctor?

AMY: We left a message with her service.

(AMY opens the night table door looking for the bedpan. It's not there. SYBIL gets out of bed and crosses to the bathroom.)

AMY: Oh Mrs Moss, this is Miss Anderson.

SYBIL: If you only knew how miserable I've been with no one to talk to. Greetings Miss Anderson, and may I extend a warm welcome to room two eighteen!

(After curtseying SYBIL flounces into the bathroom and closes the door. TISHO is taken back by the dramatics.)

AMY: She's very nice. I'm sure you two are going to hit it off fine.

TISHO: Look, I just want to find out what's wrong with me. I didn't come in here to make friends!

AMY: Excuse me? We ask patients not to leave valuables around, and only keep about ten dollars on hand. We're not responsible if anything is stolen.

(TISHO ignores her. AMY's fuse is getting short.)

SAM: I'll take care of it, thanks. *(AMY exits. SAM, indicating her clothes and purse.)* Where should I put these?

TISHO: In the closet, I guess.

SAM: Looks like my locker at the gym. Not much room for two people.

TISHO: I didn't check into the Waldorf, it's a hospital! They just have to fix me up and let me get out of here, so how much room do I need for that?

(SAM looks at her. She closes her eyes. He hangs her clothes in the closet and puts her purse in the night table. TISHO opens her eyes and holds out her hand. He takes it.)

TISHO: Do me a favor?

SAM: What's that?

TISHO: If I verbally assault anybody else, put a gag in my mouth.

SAM: I'm seriously thinking of having you declawed.

TISHO: Then how will I scratch your back?

SAM: You're a very imaginative woman, you'll think of something. *(They look at each other and smile, sharing a private moment.)* Is there anything you want me to take home?

TISHO: No, I'll keep my watch on, and I've only got a few dollars with me.

SAM: *(Jotting down her phone number)* I'll call you in the morning. Bring over whatever you need, okay?

(TISHO nods her head. Now that he's leaving, she's frightened.)

TISHO: *(Lightheartedly)* It can't be anything too serious. They didn't put me in the intensive care ward. It's probably the same old problem.

SAM: You're gonna be just fine. Nothing can happen to my lady... I won't let it. *(Kissing her gently)* Now get some rest.

(He crosses to the door.)

TISHO: *(Loud, frightened voice)* Sam! *(Softly)* Call me.

SAM: First thing.

(SAM exits. TISHO looks around the room. She begins to tremble, and pulls the covers closer. SYBIL comes out of the bathroom. She picks up the basket of fruit.)

SYBIL: Hello again.

TISHO: Hi.

SYBIL: Would you like an apple, Mrs Anderson?

TISHO: It's Ms and no thank you.

SYBIL: A banana perhaps, Ms Anderson?

TISHO: No thanks.

SYBIL: I have a container of milk left over from lunch. It's a little warm, but...

TISHO: What is it with you? I don't want bananas, apples, or chit chat. I just want to be left alone!

SYBIL: *(Peeling a banana)* I admire your physical stamina.

TISHO: What?

SYBIL: It can't be easy carrying your ass on your shoulders all day.

TISHO: It's my ass, okay? Just because we're stuck in here together, doesn't mean we have to become sorority sisters!

SYBIL: A civil attitude would be sufficient.

TISHO: That I can manage.

SYBIL: I'm thankful for small blessings.

(Both women turn on their sides, backs to each other. AMY enters, carrying a bedpan and chart. She puts the chart on the front of the bed.)

AMY: *(Indicating the bedpan)* You'll have to use this.

TISHO: I can walk to the bathroom.

AMY: *(Elevating the foot of the bed)* Your doctor called. You're to stay in bed with your legs elevated. Can I get you anything?

TISHO: A blanket, I feel cold. Will I see her tonight?

AMY: *(Getting a blanket from the dresser and putting it over TISHO)* I doubt it, but she'll be here in the morning.

(AMY exits. TISHO throws back the covers, and attempts to get out of bed.)

SYBIL: That's not a good idea.

TISHO: *(More to herself, than to SYBIL)* It's ridiculous to use that thing. The bathroom's only a few feet away.

(SYBIL goes back to her puzzle. TISHO stands up near her bed. She's weak, and as she makes the first step, a sharp pain causes her to double up and gasp. SYBIL rushes over and helps her back to bed.)

SYBIL: Take it slow…that's it…easy now.

(AMY enters, carrying a small cup with two pills in it.)

AMY: What happened?

(TISHO looks at SYBIL and shakes her head.)

SYBIL: Well…she got a sharp pain and grabbed her stomach. I was just going to ring for you.

(AMY closes the curtain, as SYBIL steps back to her side.)

TISHO: *(Indicating her pelvic area)* It hurts…right here.

(AMY gently touches the area. She gives her the pills and water. SYBIL waits anxiously. AMY pulls the curtain back, and fixes the covers.)

AMY: She'll be all right.

SYBIL: Well that's my excitement for the evening.

AMY: Thought you said Sundays were dull.

SYBIL: A lot I know.

AMY: The pain should ease up soon. Any problem, just press the buzzer.

TISHO: Thank you.

(AMY exits. A sharp pain causes TISHO to cry out. SYBIL crosses to her.)

SYBIL: Do you like old movies?

(TISHO *doesn't answer.*)

SYBIL: Well do you?

TISHO: Yes.

SYBIL: Then you're in for a treat. *Now Voyager* is coming on in a few minutes.

TISHO: Whoopee.

SYBIL: It's a classic! Bette Davis goes on a cruise, calling herself Camille Beauchamp. She comes down the gangplank wearing that smart-looking suit, the white hat tilted over one eye. I've seen the picture a dozen times, but that scene still gives me goose pimples. How did it end?

TISHO: I don't know.

SYBIL: What kind of movie buff are you?

TISHO: *(Still in pain)* Not a very good one it seems.

SYBIL: Think! She's on the balcony with Paul Henreid, and....

TISHO: He lights two cigarettes, and gives her one....

SYBIL: Right, and then she says?... Come on, what did she say?

TISHO: Why ask for the moon...something about the stars...
I can't remember. (*The pain subsides a little;* TISHO's *body relaxes.*)

SYBIL: Feel better?

TISHO: Yes...the pain's almost gone.

SYBIL: Good, then I can stop all this trivia crap and go back to bed.
If you decide to get up again, wait 'til I'm asleep.

TISHO: It was a stupid thing to do. Guess my nerves are on edge.
I've never had to stay in a hospital before. Thanks for not snitching on me.

SYBIL: *(Gangsterlike manner)* When you're doin' time sister, you learn that stool pigeons die young, know what I mean?

(TISHO *laughs weakly.* SYBIL *starts brushing her hair.*)

SYBIL: I had surgery a while back, and they won't let me wash my hair.
It's beginning to smell like old turnips.

TISHO: It doesn't look too bad, Mrs?...

SYBIL: Moss, but call me Sybil.

TISHO: Mine's Tisho.

SYBIL: Tisho Anderson, now that's a nice name. I've always hated mine.
First it was Sybil Quimby, then I got married and it became Sybil Moss. I

went from a Dickens novel to a tropical fungus. *(As patient)* Oh doctor, what is this strange green stuff growing out of my ears? *(As doctor)* I'm sorry to inform you that you have a severe case of Sybilmoss. We'll have to quarantine you on Devil's Island. *(As patient)* Oh no doctor! Anything but that!

(TISHO and SYBIL are laughing, as AMY enters.)

AMY: Let's have a little hospital decorum in here. Don't have to ask how you feel.

TISHO: A lot better.

AMY: Would either of you like some juice?

TISHO: Nothing for me.

SYBIL: I have a yen for Moo goo gai pan.

AMY: Will you settle for apple juice?

SYBIL: Moo goo gai pan or nothing.

AMY: One order of nothing with duck sauce coming up. 'Night, ladies.

SYBIL: Goodnight.

TISHO: Amy, I'm sorry I snapped at you.

AMY: *(Exiting)* As long as you don't bite.

TISHO: For someone who just had an operation, you're pretty energetic.

SYBIL: Minor surgery.

TISHO: But you said you've been in here a while.

SYBIL: They're probably trying to get more money out of my insurance company. What about you?

TISHO: Pains in my stomach…I don't think it's serious.

SYBIL: Maybe you lifted something heavy and pulled a muscle.

TISHO: Could be. Think I'll take a nap.

SYBIL: *(Turning on the TV)* You're going to miss *Now Voyager*. I'll turn it down low.

TISHO: *(Turning out her overhead light, and getting bedpan)* The sound won't bother me.

SYBIL: I know the dialogue by heart anyway. (SYBIL *goes back to her crossword puzzle, and glances up at the screen.* TISHO *screams.* SYBIL *jumps out of bed and rushes to her.)* What's the matter? Should I call Amy? (TISHO *shakes her head "No".)* Then what is it?

TISHO: *(Voice quivering)* The bedpan is so cooooold!

SYBIL: I almost popped my stitches leaping over here, and for that you owe me. What's an eight-letter word for the Bantu language?

TISHO: Angolese.

SYBIL: *(Writing it in)* That's it! I've been mulling over that word all day and you just roll it off the tip of your tongue.

TISHO: Sitting on this bedpan must have charged my brain waves.

SYBIL: I wouldn't be a bit surprised. When your ass made contact with the cold metal that stimulated your nervous system, which in turn accelerated the messages transmitted to your brain. Makes damn good sense to me!

(TISHO stares at her in disbelief. Then puts the covers over her head. The music in "Now Voyager" begins. SYBIL turns it up. TISHO slowly comes from under the covers to watch.)

SYBIL: I knew you couldn't resist.

(SYBIL hums along with the melody as the lights fade.)

Scene Two

(The next morning. TISHO is sleeping. SYBIL comes out of the bathroom carrying her towel and toiletries. She puts them away and gets into bed. AMY enters, carrying items to change the dressing on SYBIL's chest.)

SYBIL: Good morning! Aren't you off duty yet?

AMY: Your doctor is in surgery, so I have the honor of changing your dressing.

SYBIL: *(Disappointed)* Oh.

AMY: *(Pulling the curtain for privacy)* I can see you're thrilled by that bit of news.

(SYBIL sits on the side of the bed, blocking the audience's view of the right breast area. She takes down her gown and covers her left breast with the sheet. AMY removes the bandage from under SYBIL's arm. SYBIL looks straight ahead. TISHO stirs, looks at her watch, and stretches lazily.)

SYBIL: It's always good to see you. I'm so use to Dr Jarvis bouncing in here, just as I put the first spoonful of cereal in my mouth.

AMY: And far be it from him to come back later.

SYBIL: So I can eat my breakfast while it's hot? Heavens forbid!

AMY: Are you exercising your arm?

SYBIL: When my social calendar permits. I'm so popular that....

AMY: I'm not joking, Mrs Moss.

SYBIL: Forgive my silliness. I know I don't exercise enough. I make a few circles or raise it a little, but I figure it's too late to close the barn door now.

AMY: Your emotional adjustment is great, but let's face it. You've had a radical mastectomy and if you don't exercise every day, the fluid will build up and they'll have to drain it. I don't want you to go through all that.

(TISHO *sits up, surprised at what she hears.*)

SYBIL: Amy my girl, it's a promise. Every day from now on, one for me... *(Raising her right arm, wincing and lowering it)* And one for Amy. *(Raising her right arm again, higher this time, and lowering it)*

AMY: That's more like it. *(Writing on* SYBIL's *chart)* You may be leaving on Friday.

SYBIL: So soon?

AMY: I thought you'd be glad to get out of here. It's been almost a month.

SYBIL: I am. Be it ever so humble, there really isn't any place quite like home...is there?

AMY: *(Pulling the curtain back)* You're gonna be okay. Just take it one step at a time, and exercise that arm or else!

SYBIL: Aye aye Captain Amy! Raise the right arm or walk the plank of the good ship lollipop. 'Tis a hard woman ye be!

(AMY *exits.* SYBIL *gets out of bed and does one or two arm exercises.* AMY *enters with two breakfast trays.* SYBIL *takes hers.* AMY *puts the other on* TISHO's *table.*)

SYBIL: I didn't hear Lenny in the hall.

AMY: *(Crossing to the door)* You were too busy walking the plank. I'll see you this evening. Tell Sleeping Beauty hello.

SYBIL: Find out when I can wash my hair.

AMY: *(Exiting)* Will do.

(TISHO's *phone rings.*)

TISHO: Hello... Hi Sandy...not too bad... Sam's bringing over some things. Oh, remember to call Mr Hewitt and tell him about the change in air fare. He's going to complain, but it can't be helped...well do your best...all right, I will. Don't let them get to you now. Bye. *(Hanging up the receiver)* Good morning.

SYBIL: Morning. Did you sleep well?

TISHO: So so. Heard you moving around a bit.

SYBIL: When I'm home I get up around two in the morning and bake bread or polish furniture. I seem to come alive at night. Maybe I'm a vampire. *(Inspecting her breakfast)* Oh, I hate prunes!

TISHO: So don't eat them.

SYBIL: This is not by choice. Amy was here.

TISHO: I know.

SYBIL: I gather you heard our conversation?

TISHO: You gather right. I thought you had a routine operation. Since when is a mastectomy considered minor surgery?

SYBIL: There wasn't any point in giving you the gruesome details.

TISHO: That's fine! You don't know me and you didn't have to tell me anything, but you didn't have to lie either!

SYBIL: I didn't lie. As far as I'm concerned, it is minor. Most people take life too seriously. I was raised in a house where no one ever cried.

TISHO: Oh come on…

SYBIL: No matter how bad things got we always found something to laugh about.

TISHO: I can't find any humor in having a breast removed.

SYBIL: It isn't a laughing matter, but the trick is to take a part of the illness and make it less frightening.

TISHO: You're jumping the track again, Sybil.

SYBIL: Now hear me out. We can't take away an illness, but we can take the fear out of it. Look at the medical terms they use…radical mastectomy… sounds like something a mad scientist is working on.

TISHO: I know I'm going to be sorry I asked, but what would you call it?

SYBIL: *(Thinking about it for a second, a broad smile crosses her face)* A rainbow special!

TISHO: I hate to be the one to tell you this, but your elevator does not go to the penthouse.

SYBIL: My elevator doesn't go to the?… *(Laughing)* I love it!

TISHO: It's good you're not feeling sorry for yourself, but to think that a word can change your outlook on an illness…

SYBIL: I know it sounds crazy, but Tisho we're stuck with boobs, broads, frigid, and fucked up. What do men say if we've got a really terrific body? What are we built like?

TISHO: A brick shit house!

SYBIL: Of all the buildings a woman could look like. We don't resemble the Taj Mahal or the Eiffel Tower.... Just a smelly brick shit house!

TISHO: Point made! *(Raising her coffee cup)* To rainbow specials!

SYBIL: *(Raising her cup)* And my elevator's stuck between the first and second floor.

TISHO: Amy said you might be leaving on Friday?

SYBIL: Yes, just when I was beginning to like this place. Food's lousy, but it beats dishes and homework.

TISHO: You have children?

SYBIL: One boy, Philip. He's eleven. How about you?

TISHO: Not yet, too busy getting my career off the ground.

SYBIL: Don't wait too long. Tell your hubby that tempus is gonna stop fugiting pretty soon. Got a peek at him last night...he's a good-looking man.

TISHO: Sam and I aren't married.

SYBIL: I just assumed...oh...I see.

TISHO: What do you see?

SYBIL: Well he's either somebody's husband or he's got a fetish for wedding bands. I spotted it when he was standing by my bed.

TISHO: So we don't play twenty questions, he's married and we've been lovers for over ten years.

SYBIL: Oh dear.

TISHO: Does that rub your morality the wrong way?

SYBIL: I am a bit old-fashioned, but it's really none of my business. I must admit, I've never understood triangles. It's like starting a novel, knowing how it's going to end.

TISHO: It's not as cut and dry as all that.

SYBIL: I suppose not. Are you happy?

TISHO: I think so. Why do you ask?

SYBIL: I seem to detect a sadness in your voice.

(AMY enters with a wheelchair.)

SYBIL: I thought you went home.

AMY: They won't let me out of this place. Every time I say I'm leaving, they give me something else to do. *(To TISHO)* How are you feeling this morning?

TISHO: Much better.

AMY: Good. They want you up in X-ray.

TISHO: Can I shower first?

AMY: There's no time.

TISHO: But I feel cruddy....

AMY: The X-ray machine won't know the difference. Put on your slippers.

(TISHO *puts on her slippers and gets into the wheelchair.*)

TISHO: Don't go dancing.

SYBIL: I'll try to restrain myself. (AMY *and* TISHO *exit.* SYBIL's *telephone rings.*) Hello?... Hi dear... Yes I'm coming along. How are you?... That's too bad. Maybe you sat in a draft.... Did you put a lot of epsom salts in the water?... Arthur, it's not the end of the world, it's just a backache.... Mrs Sellinger? I don't want that woman to set foot in this hospital!... Because she's a nosy ass busybody! Arthur don't be naive. She's not coming here because she's concerned. She wants to look me over and rush home to tell the neighbors I'm dying.... I'm not being crotchety! This conversation is tapping a nerve.... I know you don't mean to upset me...all right...yes... See you then. (*Hanging up the receiver*) Mrs Sellinger! If she crosses that doorsill, I'll break her kneecaps! (*She is upset and stands up, not realizing the breakfast tray is not centered on the table, and it falls on the floor, the contents scattering about.*) Damn it!

(*She bends down and starts putting things back on the tray.* SAM *enters. He's carrying a small tote bag and a rose wrapped in green tissue*)

SAM: Let me give you a hand.

SYBIL: Thanks. (*Wiping the floor with a napkin as* SAM *picks up the remaining items*) Phew! That should do it. (*She flops back on the bed, exhausted.*)

SAM: Are you okay?

SYBIL: A little winded. (*Extending her glass*) Could you get me some water, please?

SAM: (*Crossing to the bathroom*) Where's Miss Anderson?

SYBIL: Up in X-ray.

SAM: (*Giving her the water*) Did something go wrong? Is her doctor here? Why...

SYBIL: She's fine. It's just routine.

(SYBIL *watches him closely. He's uncomfortable under her steady gaze. He takes a plastic cup, fills it with water, and puts the rose in.*)

SYBIL: It's lovely.

SAM: She's never liked a lot of flowers…just one rose.

SYBIL: A woman with simple taste…rare in this day and age….
You're a lucky man.

SAM: I know.

SYBIL: What do you do?

SAM: I'm a consulting engineer.

SYBIL: That's nice, but what do you do?

SAM: Well, I work with air conditioning systems. If something goes wrong a company calls me in and I tell them how to fix it. I'm like a trouble shooter.

SYBIL: I like trouble shooter. Consulting engineer is too stuffy.

(There's an uncomfortable silence.)

SAM: Well, I'd better be going. Would you tell her to beep me if she needs anything else, and I'll be back this afternoon.

SYBIL: Be glad to.

SAM: Goodbye Mrs…?

SYBIL: Moss. Sybil Moss.

SAM: *(Extending his hand)* Sam Coleman.

SYBIL: *(Giving him her left hand)* I've got a thing about names. Yours is strong and direct. Are you a direct man Mr Coleman?

SAM: I try to be.

SYBIL: I'm glad to hear that.

SAM: Well…so long.

SYBIL: Goodbye Mr Coleman.

(SAM exits. SYBIL looks at the rose. She picks it up and inhales, enjoying the sweet fragrance.)

(The lights fade.)

Scene Three

(Later the same day. SYBIL is sitting in a chair watching a game show on television. The master of ceremonies, the contestant, and the audience are prerecorded voiceovers. The audience can be heard shouting answers to the contestant. TISHO is in the bathroom with the door partially open. She's washing her face.)

VOICEOVER: *(M C)* So what's it gonna be Karen? We need a bid, and we need it now!

SYBIL: Twenty-one thousand, you dumb dumb!

VOICEOVER: *(M C)* What are we doing, audience?

VOICEOVER: *(Audience)* We're waiting, Karen!

VOICEOVER: *(Contestant)* Now let's see. I'd say it's worth…that includes the hot tub, right?

VOICEOVER: *(M C)* Right. Now give us an answer!

VOICEOVER: *(Contestant)* I'll say…twelve thousand dollars.

(SYBIL falls back on the bed. A buzzer sounds indicating the contestant is wrong. TISHO dries her face and watches from the doorway.)

VOICEOVER: *(M C)* Too bad Karen. The correct answer is twenty-one thousand dollars!

SYBIL: I told her what it was, but did she listen to me? No! *(Imitating the contestant)* "I'll say twelve thousand." She must be sitting on her brains.

TISHO: You've got all the answers, why don't you try out for the show?

SYBIL: *(Turning down the volume)* With ten million people watching me, I'd probably be as dumb as she is. Should you be standing so long?

TISHO: I got permission to walk around, if I don't overdo it.

SYBIL: Your doctor was here.

TISHO: Saw her upstairs.

SYBIL: Did she say what's wrong with you?

TISHO: *(Meaning "Yes")* Mmmmm mmmm.

SYBIL: You don't have to tell me if it's too personal.

TISHO: *(Peeking out from the bathroom)* It's too personal.

(TISHO ducks back inside. SYBIL is offended and sticks out her tongue in the direction of the bathroom. TISHO peeks out, almost catching her.)

TISHO: She wants me to have…a hot fudge sundae.

SYBIL: A what?

TISHO: Didn't you say medical terms were obsolete? Well, I'm substituting a hot fudge sundae for a hysterectomy.

SYBIL: Oh Tisho…

TISHO: I knew I had fibroids, but this is the first time they've given me so much trouble.

SYBIL: It's a warning. Time to take care of it.

TISHO: I will, but I have to wait.

SYBIL: For what? I felt a lump in my breast…it was smaller than a green pea. I figured I'm getting older, my body's changing. By the time I got the courage to face my fears, it was too late…please…don't put it off.

TISHO: But I'm only forty-one. I've got about four or five years before I lose my option.

SYBIL: What option?

TISHO: Whether to have a child.

SYBIL: Oh for God's sake, you've had ten years to get pregnant! The man was there, the age was right, now suddenly it's pitter patter time! Your eggs are old almost enough to file for social security!

TISHO: You've got one hell of a nerve! I didn't ask for your advice!

SYBIL: You didn't have to!

TISHO: I'm quite capable of making my own decisions.

SYBIL: I think you want more from that man than a child.

TISHO: And what do I want?

SYBIL: A commitment.

(TISHO *glares at* SYBIL *and strides into the bathroom, slamming the door. The sound of water can be heard. The water stops.* TISHO *comes out, drying her hair. She watches the television.* SYBIL *turns around. When she notices what* TISHO *is doing, she snaps off the television.*)

TISHO: I was watching that show.

SYBIL: I know you were.

TISHO: You may be paying for the set, but that was very rude!

SYBIL: I intended it to be. Just because we had a difference of opinion is no reason for you to be vindictive!

TISHO: What did I do?

SYBIL: *(Crossing to the bathroom)* Don't play Miss Innocent with me. You know how miserable I am about this… *(Indicating her hair)* and you washed your hair!

(SYBIL *goes into the bathroom and slams the door.* TISHO *is dumbfounded. She shrugs it off and puts cold cream on her face.* DR CAVENDISH *enters.* TISHO *gets into bed, and reads a magazine.*)

DR CAVENDISH: Mrs Moss?

TISHO: In there.

DR CAVENDISH: (Sing-song voice) Mrs Moss, I'd like to talk to you about your treatments.

SYBIL: (OS, sing-song voice) I'd rather not discuss it now.

DR CAVENDISH: Would you please come out?

(SYBIL comes out of the bathroom.)

DR CAVENDISH: I'm Dr Cavendish. I believe you know why I'm here.

SYBIL: Yes, and I told Dr Jarvis I need time to think about it.

DR CAVENDISH: You waited a year before deciding to see a doctor, and now you want to wait again? Time is your worst enemy, Mrs Moss. I suggest you take the bull by the horns immediately.

SYBIL: I'm not a matador Dr Cavendish. I'm a woman who's had a breast removed, and wonders if that isn't enough.

DR CAVENDISH: I'd like to examine you now.

SYBIL: Dr Jarvis looks in on me every day.

DR CAVENDISH: I'm sure he does. (Examining the bandaged area) Any soreness here?

SYBIL: No. (DR CAVENDISH examines the other breast.) There's nothing wrong with that breast!

DR CAVENDISH: I have to check it. (Touches a spot and SYBIL winces.) Is it tender?

SYBIL: A little.

DR CAVENDISH: Did you mention this to Dr Jarvis?

SYBIL: No. I assume it's sore from the operation.

DR CAVENDISH: I'm going to schedule you for a mammogram.

SYBIL: There's no need for that.

DR CAVENDISH: Just a precaution. Now let's talk about chemotherapy.

SYBIL: Let's talk about the side effects.

DR CAVENDISH: Mrs Moss, if you decide to take the treatments, and I think you should, I'll have to try a number of drugs and hormones to determine which has the least toxic side effect. The most important thing is to prevent the cancer from spreading.

SYBIL: Spreading? I thought they got it all.

DR CAVENDISH: We can never be a hundred-percent certain.

SYBIL: Are you telling me there are more cancer cells in my body?

DR CAVENDISH: Let me put your mind at ease. The survival rate has risen to seventy-two percent, so there's a good chance that …well.…

SYBIL: That I'll survive.

DR CAVENDISH: Based on the percentages, an excellent chance.

SYBIL: Will I lose my hair?

DR CAVENDISH: There's a ninety-six percent chance you will.

SYBIL: Seventy-two percent survival, ninety-six percent bald eagle.

DR CAVENDISH: They have wonderful wigs now. You can hardly tell it's not your own hair.

(SYBIL *puts her head down and laughs.*)

DR CAVENDISH: You find that amusing?

SYBIL: *(Still laughing)* Not amusing, ridiculous.

DR CAVENDISH: *(Looking at* SYBIL'*s chart)* Blood pressure's good…temperature's normal. You've been having irregular bowel movements. Have they given you anything to relieve the problem?

SYBIL: So far, just prunes. I hate laxatives.

DR CAVENDISH: Well I think we're going to have an enema tonight.

SYBIL: We are?

DR CAVENDISH: That's right.

SYBIL: Are we taking this enema because there's a seventy-two percent chance that I'm constipated? Or a ninety-six percent chance that you're full of shit?

(TISHO *laughs.* DR CAVENDISH *looks at her, and she puts the magazine over her face.*)

DR CAVENDISH: That's not a proper attitude, Mrs Moss. *(Striding to the door)* I'll drop in to see you tomorrow.

SYBIL: *(Calling after her)* Don't bother! (TISHO *applauds and* SYBIL *takes a bow.*) I promised Arthur I wouldn't use any profanity, and I haven't stopped cursing since I got here. Can you believe her? Why in God's name would they give me a therapist who's about as sensitive as Jack the Ripper?

TISHO: Are you going to take the treatments?

SYBIL: I honestly don't know. I guess I should and my doctor is in favor of it, but he's not going to have the side effects and neither is Cavendish. My hair is one of the few treasures I have left. *(Getting a tea bag and cup)* I'll be back. I need a strong cup of tea.

TISHO: It's going to work out.

SYBIL: *(Crossing to the door)* To bald or not to bald. That's one hell of a question, isn't it?

(SYBIL exits. After a few seconds, ARTHUR enters, carrying a newspaper.)

ARTHUR: Good afternoon.

TISHO: Can I help you?

ARTHUR: I was looking for Mrs Moss.

TISHO: She just went down the hall for a cup of tea.

ARTHUR: I'm a cocoa man myself. *(Uneasy...not sure what to say to TISHO)* Do you like cocoa?

TISHO: Love it. Too many calories, though.

ARTHUR: You should taste the raw chocolate from the West Indies. It's rich and pure...nothing like the junk they sell here. I didn't know Sybil had a new roommate.

TISHO: I came in last night.

ARTHUR: I see. Would you like the paper? I'm through with it.

TISHO: Thank you.

(SYBIL enters, carrying a cup of tea. ARTHUR is relieved. He kisses her on the cheek.)

SYBIL: You're early.

ARTHUR: Didn't feel like taking the subway, so I drove in.

SYBIL: And you found a parking space?

ARTHUR: I was lucky for a change. A delivery truck was just pulling out.

SYBIL: Did you meet my husband?

TISHO: We've been chatting, but we haven't really met.

SYBIL: Arthur, this is Ms Anderson.

ARTHUR: It's a pleasure to make your acquaintance.

TISHO: Same here. Excuse me.

(TISHO partially closes the curtain. ARTHUR sits down as SYBIL turns on the television and gets into bed. SAM enters. He nods to SYBIL and ARTHUR and crosses to TISHO. He kisses her and sits very close. ARTHUR's chair is facing the television. The voices on the television are not audible. For the rest of the scene between the two couples, when one couple is speaking, the other couple will mime conversation, not

heard by the audience. During these times SYBIL *and* ARTHUR *say very little to each other.* TISHO *and* SAM *are more animated.)*

ARTHUR: How are you feeling?

SYBIL: About the same. Didn't expect to see you.

ARTHUR: Why is that?

SYBIL: You said your back was bothering you.

ARTHUR: Have I ever missed a day?

SYBIL: No.

(She smiles at him and puts her hand on his arm. He pats her hand comfortingly, then as if embarrassed by the gesture, takes his hand away.)

SYBIL: Philip over at Michael's house?

ARTHUR: Yes. I'll pick him up on my way home.

SYBIL: Nice of them to look after him.

ARTHUR: We'd do the same if the situation was reversed. I told Mrs Sellinger you couldn't have any visitors, except the family. She was very disappointed.

SYBIL: I bet she was.

ARTHUR: They've postponed the rent strike.

SYBIL: Why?

ARTHUR: Landlord wants to negotiate.

SYBIL: That's a good sign.

ARTHUR: A very good sign.

*(*SYBIL *and* ARTHUR *watch television.)*

SAM: Come on now, I can't believe all that.

TISHO: It's true. A woman next door started screaming, and doctors and nurses were running up and down the hall. Then somebody turned over a cart. If you want peace and quiet this is not the place!

SAM: *(Meaning* SYBIL*)* And she didn't hear any of it?

TISHO: Slept like a baby.

SAM: Now, about you. Did the bleeding stop?

TISHO: Yes, but the tumors have to come out.

SAM: Is it risky?

TISHO: I don't think so. I'm going to see if I can put it off for a while.

SAM: You were in pretty bad shape last night. You don't want that to happen again.

TISHO: It's not just the tumors, she might have to do a hysterectomy.

SAM: So you have it done right away. I tell you what, soon as the doctor says you can travel we'll go to Negril. It's quiet there. A good place for you to recuperate.

TISHO: Sam, you don't understand.

ARTHUR: They closed down Vinnie's supermarket.

SYBIL: Why?

ARTHUR: Health inspector found rat turds on the cabbages.

SYBIL: Rat turds...on the cabbages? (*She puts her hand over her mouth, trying to hide the smile on her face.*)

ARTHUR: I am only relating to you what was told to me. If you choose to find humor in a rodent's indiscretion, that is your prerogative.

(*SYBIL can't hold it back any longer. She slides under the covers, and puts the sheet over her head.*)

ARTHUR: Come out from under there, and stop acting the fool!

(*SYBIL's hand comes out, swinging a tissue as if offering a truce. ARTHUR snatches the tissue, hoping no one comes in and catches SYBIL. She peeks from under the covers still laughing, tears streaming down her face.*)

ARTHUR: Sybil, you are a most trifling woman.

(*SYBIL knows he's not really angry. As they watch television, she peeks at him. He smiles, but refuses to look at her.*)

SAM: What's on your mind?

TISHO: I'd like to have a baby.

SAM: Aw Tish!

TISHO: Aw Tish what? All you have to do is donate a few sperms, what's the big deal?

SAM: I thought we both decided...no children.

TISHO: I changed my mind.

SAM: I'm almost fifty years old, and you want me to play daddy again. What's your doctor going to say about this?

TISHO: I don't know.

SAM: And you don't care, right? I mean, why the hell should you care what she says? You've got the fibroids, you keep hemorrhaging, but you want to put your life on hold to get pregnant. Woman, you are driving me straight up the wall!

TISHO: When you left last night, I was frightened. For the first time in ten years...I felt...alone.

SAM: Honey, there's no reason to feel that way, you've got me.

TISHO: I've got you the day after Thanksgiving, the day after Christmas, and the day after New Year's Eve. Sam, I'm tired being the day after yesterday!

(SAM *gets up and turns away from her.*)

ARTHUR: Did they say when you'd be coming home?

SYBIL: Not yet.

ARTHUR: Thought it was the end of this week?

SYBIL: It's not definite.

ARTHUR: I finished the last of your homemade bread. Now I'll have to make a big to-do over Pepperidge Farm. I hate store-bought bread.

SYBIL: You'd better get use to it. I won't be able to do any of those things for a while.

ARTHUR: Dr Jarvis told me it was important that you resume your normal life.

SYBIL: I think he was referring to things like sex more so than homemade bread.

ARTHUR: (*Flustered*) Oh...well...we'll cross that bridge when we get to it.

(ARTHUR *nervously cleans his glasses.*)

SYBIL: (*Taking his hand*) Arthur?...

(*He looks at her, hoping she's going to open up, but her mood quickly changes and she pulls her hand back and smiles.*)

SYBIL: Know what I'd like to have?

ARTHUR: A new washing machine.

SYBIL: A telescope.

ARTHUR: Going to be a star gazer now?

SYBIL: I want to discover a comet. I read somewhere that if you spot one, they name it after you. When I die only a few people will know that I ever existed. I would have come and gone without so much as a ripple. Don't you see, Arthur? If they name a comet after me, somewhere in the sky there'd be a ball of fire called Sybil and my tail would be spinning around this universe forever!

TISHO: Guess I threw you a curve.

SAM: You've never made any demands before. This must be important to you.

TISHO: Important to us.

SAM: Right. Let me think about it, okay?

(She nods her head. He kisses her lightly.)

SAM: See you tomorrow.

(SAM exits.)

ARTHUR: I'd best be leaving. It's almost your dinner time.

SYBIL: Give Philip a kiss for me.

ARTHUR: He won't like that. Says he's not a baby anymore. Sybil?... Just hurry and get well.

(He moves her table closer to the bed. Kisses her on the forehead and crosses to the door. He waves goodbye to TISHO and exits. The women turn away, each in her own thoughts. AMY enters, carrying two brown bags.)

AMY: Rise and shine ladies! *(Giving each woman a bag)* Go ahead open them up.

SYBIL: I know what it smells like.

TISHO: Shrimps in lobster sauce! How'd you know what to get me?

AMY: Met your friend coming in and asked him.

SYBIL: Moo goo gai pan, bless you my child!

AMY: You're not on restricted diets, so I said to myself, why not give the ladies a break.

TISHO: Your timing is perfect. How much do I owe you?

AMY: *(Crossing to the door)* Give me a blank check when you're leaving!

(AMY exits.)

TISHO: This is delicious. Amy is all right.

(They eat in silence for a few seconds.)

SYBIL: Did you tell him about your plans?... The baby?

TISHO: I don't think he wants to play daddy, and then of course it's the old he loves me, he leaves her not.

SYBIL: But you must have known this from the beginning.

TISHO: I met him over fifteen years ago. I was in my twenties and he was that elusive knight in shining armor. I had stars in my eyes as big as saucers. At forty-one, the stars are all gone, and I don't even know when they left.

SYBIL: Arthur refuses to discuss my surgery. We can talk about cabbages, rent strikes, and homemade bread...but not my operation.

TISHO: You seem so happy-go-lucky, maybe he's just following your lead.

SYBIL: Could be. Were you surprised to see a gentleman of color?

TISHO: A little.

SYBIL: Met him while I was vacationing in Jamaica, that's his home. Personality wise we're complete opposites. He's shy and reserved, basically a very quiet man, and I don't have to tell you how much I gab. We found we had a lot in common. Music, books...ideas...what we wanted out of life. I came back to the States and told my family I was in love with a black man. My mother almost fainted and my father seemed to go into a catatonic state. They made it quite unpleasant for me, but I loved Arthur, and I wouldn't give him up.

TISHO: What about his parents?

SYBIL: His father took it quite well, but his mother didn't exactly turn cartwheels. She had a nice sweet Jamaican girl picked out for him and I was upsetting her plans. To top it off, she wanted to know if I was a virgin. I said I was because I felt pure in heart, and I wasn't because I'd had one prior disturbance. Then she screamed at me... *(West Indian accent)* "My son should marry a virgin, and a virgin you will be!" She goes out into the backyard and gets this root and boils it up. She pounds it into a powder and I have to use it as a douche three nights in a row before the wedding. I thought it would burn my insides out!

TISHO: Oh my God, she gave you that alum stuff. I've heard about women doing that, but I thought it was an old wives' tale. And it burns that much?

SYBIL: Set me on fire! But I must admit, if it was a virgin he wanted... a virgin is what he got.

TISHO: It really tightens up your.... It just snaps back into place? *(Shaking her head doubtfully)* I find that hard to believe, Sybil. I mean, when it's gone...it's gone.

SYBIL: A hot price to pay for chastity, but it worked. That was thirty years ago. I can laugh about it now, but at the time...not so funny.

TISHO: I imagine the families have mellowed a bit.

SYBIL: Arthur and my father go fishing, and both mothers adore their grandson. I have one sister who hasn't spoken to me since the day of the wedding, but I figure that's her problem, not mine. Things have changed somewhat, but people still look at us in restaurants, or when we go on vacation. The best part is that Arthur and I have never seen each other as black and white. If anything...we're both a very unusual shade of lavender.

(Lights fade.)

Scene Four

(A few days later. AMY's *in the bathroom washing* SYBIL's *hair.* TISHO *is writing a letter.)*

SYBIL: *(OS)* That's it, pour it on! Water, water everywhere!

AMY: *(OS)* Stop moving around, I'm getting soaked!

TISHO: Hey, pipe down! There's a sick woman in this room!

*(*AMY *and* SYBIL *enter.* SYBIL *has a towel on her head. She sits on the end of the bed, and tries drying it, but* AMY *hits her hand, and does it for her.)*

SYBIL: Ohhhh my head feels so gloriously clean! I'm a new woman! Thanks for taking your own time to do this.

TISHO: How come you're working a double shift?

SYBIL: She's dedicated.

AMY: I'm broke, and my car needs new tires. There, you look gorgeous!

*(*AMY *takes the towel back to the bathroom.* SYBIL *combs her hair.)*

AMY: You're part owner in a travel agency, right?

TISHO: *(Meaning "Yes")* Mmmmm...mmmm.

AMY: Must be a good feeling to be your own boss.

TISHO: It's a lot of hard work, I can tell you that.

SYBIL: I've always wanted to go to Greece. Drink a little ouzo...dance along the beach.

*(*SYBIL *snaps her fingers and does a bit of the dance from "Zorba." She hums and twirls around the room.* AMY *and* TISHO *clap in time with the tune and cheer her on.* DR CAVENDISH *enters with a wheelchair.* AMY *stops clapping.* SYBIL *whirls around and faces* DR CAVENDISH. *The fun and laughter stop abruptly.)*

DR CAVENDISH: *(Looking at* AMY*)* Roseland Ballroom, perhaps? You're setting a fine example, nurse.

AMY: I'm sorry, Dr Cavendish.

DR CAVENDISH: *(To* SYBIL*)* I've scheduled you for a mammogram.

SYBIL: Right now?

AMY: I'll take her over.

DR CAVENDISH: That won't be necessary.

SYBIL: No matter.

(SYBIL *refuses to let the doctor dampen her spirits. She snaps her fingers and humming again, dances over to the wheelchair and sits down. She smiles mischievously at* TISHO *and continues to sing as* DR CAVENDISH *wheels her out.* AMY *straightens out* SYBIL'*s bed.*)

AMY: The dragon lady strikes again.

TISHO: Is that what the nurses call her?

AMY: We've got names for all the doctors, but she's our favorite.

TISHO: What's with Sybil?

AMY: How do you mean?

TISHO: She won't talk about her operation…just laughs it off.

AMY: She's not laughing.

TISHO: Amy, I share this room with her, and she's never down. She told me her husband doesn't mention it either.

AMY: I see it all the time. It's a game called, if we don't talk about it, maybe it'll go away. I've got to admit, she plays the game harder than most.

TISHO: But eventually they'll have to deal with it.

AMY: Sure, but in the meantime they push it in a corner. Leave it in some dark place. Guess we've all got a corner like that.

(SAM *enters.* TISHO *is surprised to see him. He nods to* AMY, *who exits.*)

TISHO: Playing hooky today?

SAM: I'm going in this afternoon. How do you feel?

TISHO: Okay.

(*Uneasy silence*)

SAM: So…your doctor been by?

TISHO: Yes.

SAM: It's not going to work Tish. When that child is fourteen I'll be sixty-three, if I live that long. It's a selfish thing to do to a child.

TISHO: You're thinking about your father. You were twelve years old when he died, and you've never forgiven him for that.

SAM: For what?

TISHO: Leaving you.

SAM: That's not true.

TISHO: You don't want to admit it. Sam, there's a part of you that I've never been able to reach. You've closed it off from me and probably everybody else in your life. As far as a child...it's the chance we take.

SAM: *(Holding her)* Baby I love you, but...

(She eases back from his arms.)

SAM: I can't do it.

TISHO: You'd better go.

SAM: Try to understand...

TISHO: Just leave me alone.

(SAM tries to find the right words, but failing...exits. A few seconds later, SYBIL rushes in.)

TISHO: How'd you make out?

SYBIL: Don't know yet. She's studying the X-rays. I'm particular about the company I keep, so when she wasn't looking I got someone to wheel me back.

TISHO: Dr Cavendish has taken a special interest in your case and that's the thanks she gets. Shame on you Sybil.

SYBIL: I've taken a special interest in her too, that's why I'm going to treat her to an obscene phone call.

TISHO: I don't like mammograms. All that cold metal, and they pick up your breast and plop it down like it's a lamb chop.

SYBIL: At least you have something to put up there. I'm so small I almost have to throw my whole body on the machine, and the technician is saying, "Raise it up Mrs Moss" and I'm stretching and pushing. The things we go through. Did your friend call?

TISHO: He came by. Says it's too late in life for more children.

SYBIL: Arthur and I tried for years to have a child. I even subjected us to some silly method of taking my temperature every hour to hit a fertile peak.

TISHO: Then you'd put your libido on hold until he got home.

SYBIL: It doesn't work that way. I'd hit a peak, call him and he'd rush home and try to.... Oh God, I hate to think about it. Your first lesson in sexual myths. A man cannot have an erection because his wife's temperature happens to be ninety seven point three. We gave up on that idea then bingo!

Pregnant at the over-riped age of forty-one. Should have named him Bingo instead of Philip.

(DR CAVENDISH *enters, carrying a clipboard.*)

SYBIL: Just the person I wanted to see. I wonder if I could have your telephone number.

(TISHO *starts laughing.*)

DR CAVENDISH: *(To* TISHO*)* Would you mind sitting in the lounge for a few minutes? I'd like to talk to Mrs Moss alone.

(TISHO *gets up to leave.* SYBIL *doesn't take her eyes off* DR CAVENDISH.)

SYBIL: Stay, please.

DR CAVENDISH: This is very personal.

SYBIL: Ms Anderson can hear whatever you have to say.

DR CAVENDISH: The X-rays show a tumor on your breast.

SYBIL: Where's Dr Jarvis? Why isn't he telling me this?

DR CAVENDISH: He had an emergency. He'll be down shortly.

SYBIL: Has he seen the X-ray?

DR CAVENDISH: Of course. He's scheduled your surgery for tomorrow morning.

SYBIL: What surgery? Why are you telling me these things?

DR CAVENDISH: Mrs Moss, it's the same procedure as before. We'll take a biopsy and the results will determine what has to be done.

(DR CAVENDISH *holds out the clipboard. There's a form attached to it.*)

SYBIL: And what's this?

DR CAVENDISH: A release form…in case the breast has to be removed.

(SYBIL *looks at* DR CAVENDISH, *then flings the clipboard to the floor, and rushes into the bathroom.* DR CAVENDISH *picks up the clipboard.*)

TISHO: Lady, what is your problem? You don't know what kind of tumor it is. It may not even be malignant, but you've already got her signing papers and losing her other breast!

DR CAVENDISH: It's hospital procedure! When a mammogram indicates…

TISHO: *(Cutting her off)* I don't want to hear that crap! Don't you feel anything for that woman?

DR CAVENDISH: I have to deal with this type of situation every day. I can't allow myself the luxury of sympathizing with each patient.

TISHO: What do you mean luxury? Sybil's a human being. She needs to know you people are there for her!

DR CAVENDISH: I've seen what happens to doctors who get emotionally involved. If I start losing sleep over every cancer patient, I won't last very long. I've gone through six years of medical school, and a four-year residency. Now, I specialize in people like Mrs Moss. I have a long way to go, and I can't have patients taking bits and pieces of me. I've got to be a survivor, Ms Anderson. If that means not letting women like her cry on my shoulder, so be it.

TISHO: Being an eternal optimist, I can only hope that one day you end up in a hospital bed, and a cold-blooded bitch who's gone through six years of medical school and a four-year residency, pulls out your IV and says, "Dr Cavendish I think you're dying, and who gives a shit?"

(DR CAVENDISH *puts the clipboard on* SYBIL's *bed and exits.*)

TISHO: All clear! Typhoid Mary's gone!

(SYBIL *comes out of the bathroom.*)

SYBIL: She'll be back.

TISHO: Not tonight.

SYBIL: What did you say to her?

TISHO: Nothing much.

SYBIL: *(Looking at the form)* I'll sign this after I've talked to Dr Jarvis.

TISHO: I read something about reconstruction…lots of women have it done.

SYBIL: *(Nervously)* You know they can even salvage the nipple. They graft it to another part of your body…that's all I need…can you picture me with a nipple on my elbow?

TISHO: Sybil…

SYBIL: I'm glad you're a travel agent. I'm seriously thinking about a trip to Greece. If Arthur can take his vacation in July, then Philip will be out of school, and it should work out perfect. Just as well give our business to you. *(Getting up and dancing around)* Soon I'll be dancing near the ocean…with the sand tickling my toes.…

(SYBIL *dances and sings with lots of energy.*)

TISHO: Sybil…stop it.

SYBIL: You're as bad as Arthur, loosen up sweetie!

(TISHO *steps in front of her.*)

TISHO: You can't make it go away. Aren't you tired of the game?

SYBIL: Children play games. I am a dancer!

TISHO: Damn it, woman, be realistic for a change!

SYBIL: Well fancy that. The pot calling the kettle a dreamer. You feel a maternal tug on your fibroids and suddenly you want to be mother of the year!

TISHO: At least I've seen both sides of the coin, but you can't get out of never-never land!

SYBIL: I won't let this drag me under, and you have no right to pass judgment on me! Do as you please with your life, but stay the hell out of mine!

(SYBIL *rushes into the bathroom.* TISHO *is angry. She picks up a magazine to read, but slams it down.* SYBIL *comes out of the bathroom, she crosses to the night stand and rummages around looking for something.* TISHO *crosses to the bathroom. The door is ajar. She is about to enter when* SYBIL *spots her.)*

SYBIL: *(Almost screaming)* Don't go in there! *(Smiling nervously)* I want to wash up.

TISHO: I'll be right out.

(TISHO *turns to go in as* SYBIL *rushes over, trying to get in the bathroom first.)*

TISHO: Woman, what is the matter with you?

(TISHO *steps inside and* SYBIL *crosses back to her bed and sits down. She is on the verge of tears.* TISHO *pushes back the door, and looks at the towel draped over the mirror of the medicine cabinet. She crosses to* SYBIL.)*

TISHO: Why's the towel over the mirror?

SYBIL: I'm eccentric. I don't like mirrors. But I forgot you have to be rich to be eccentric.... I guess that makes me just plain crazy, but you knew that all along.

(TISHO *looks at her, searching for the truth.* SYBIL *turns away.)*

SYBIL: What do you want from me?

TISHO: All this time, the laughs...the jokes. Oh Sybil...Sybil...there's no more magic...you've got to face it.

SYBIL: I can't.

TISHO: You have to try...you have to look at yourself.

SYBIL: And what am I suppose to see? Puckered skin? Damaged tissue? An ugly scar where my delicate breast use to be? I've tried.... If I don't look at it, then my world is still right side up.... I'm still a whole woman.

TISHO: If you don't deal with this now, and they have to remove the other breast...you're not going to be able to handle it.

SYBIL: *(Lightly)* That's tomorrow morning. *(Realizing the decision is now)* Oh Tisho...I'm so afraid. I don't think I can look at it.

TISHO: You've got to try. I'll be right outside the door, if you need me.

(SYBIL steps inside. She takes her arm out of the gown and slips on her bathrobe. TISHO leans against the outside wall praying that SYBIL finds the courage to look at her chest. SYBIL takes the towel off the mirror and opens her bathrobe. She steps back quickly, startled by what she sees. Stepping forward again, she touches the area, and starts to whimper...softly. She looks down at her chest, still touching the area and shaking her head as if denying what she can feel and see. She leans against the wall, her left hand gripping the door frame. She moans in one continuous sound...almost like a chant. TISHO turns slightly and reaches for SYBIL's hand. She remains outside the door, but holds SYBIL's hand tightly.)

(Lights slowly fade)

Scene Five

(The next day. ARTHUR is sitting in the room alone. TISHO enters.)

TISHO: Oh Mr Moss.

ARTHUR: *(Getting up quickly)* I didn't mean to startle you. Lots of people in the lounge...thought I'd wait here, if you don't mind.

TISHO: Of course not.

ARTHUR: You've helped Sybil a great deal. When she called to tell me about the tumor and the surgery, she was so calm about it. Usually when it's bad news, she gets real hyper. She's finally making peace with herself, and I thank you for that.

(TISHO smiles, embarrassed by his gratitude.)

ARTHUR: I went to work this morning, but I couldn't stop thinking about the operation. If they take the other breast...she won't want to live.

TISHO: She's a strong woman, and she's got you and Philip.

ARTHUR: We may not be enough. Once she bought a roasting chicken. When she opened the package, a wing was missing. She held the bird up and studied it, and the tears streamed down her face. She cried, Miss Anderson...cried at the imperfection of a lowly bird.

(AMY enters, pushing SYBIL on a gurney. ARTHUR jumps up, as AMY transfers SYBIL to her bed. SYBIL smiles weakly.)

SYBIL: The score is one out...one still on base.

(ARTHUR *slumps down in a chair and covers his face.*)

SYBIL: *(To* TISHO*)* We'll throw away all those sick words, but I think we'll keep benign.

(TISHO *squeezes* SYBIL's *hand. She and* AMY *exit.*)

SYBIL: I'll be coming home on Friday. Will you be able to pick me up?

ARTHUR: Of course.

SYBIL: If I'm not too tired, maybe I'll bake some bread over the weekend. You'll have to help me knead it. *(An uneasy silence)* I feel guilty that you have to be a part of this. For better or for worse shouldn't mean....

ARTHUR: *(Cutting her off)* We have a lot to be thankful for.

SYBIL: We're going to have to talk about it.

(ARTHUR *nods in agreement.* SYBIL *holds his hand.*)

SYBIL: It's not a pretty sight. Arthur, I don't want you to see it.

ARTHUR: Understand me Sybil. I didn't marry a breast.... I married a warm and generous woman. You are the same woman you were four weeks ago. When everything has settled down, I will look at your scars.... I will touch your scars...and from that day on, we will share the pain.

SYBIL: It's so wrinkled, and that side is as flat as a pancake.

ARTHUR: Have I ever intentionally hurt your feelings?

SYBIL: No.

ARTHUR: But I always speak my mind?

SYBIL: Always.

ARTHUR: Then I have to be honest and tell you that you really didn't have that much to begin with.

SYBIL: Well I never! After thirty years! How come you're telling me this now?

ARTHUR: Just come right out and say, Sybil, you're flat-chested. Do I strike you as a man with a death wish?

SYBIL: You strike me as the man I love so very much.

(SYBIL *leans against him and* ARTHUR *puts his arm around her shoulder.*)

(*Lights fade*)

Scene Six

(Friday morning. TISHO is reading. SYBIL is not in the room. SAM enters.)

SAM: Hi honey.

TISHO: Thought you deserted me.

SAM: Had a job upstate. Tried to call, but your line was tied up.

TISHO: Been on with Sandy. She's having problems with tickets and airlines.

(SAM walks around. TISHO watches him.)

SAM: I want us to get married and have the child.

TISHO: What changed your mind?

SAM: It's the right thing to do.

TISHO: I pushed you on this one, didn't I?

SAM: You know me better than that. I've been thinking about my marriage. Even when the love is gone, you keep goin' through the motions…hanging on. Well, it's time for me to let go.

TISHO: Thank you, Sam.

SAM: For what?

TISHO: Caring. A few minutes later and you might have missed me. My operation is scheduled for this morning.

SAM: What about the baby?

TISHO: A child isn't the answer.

SAM: We'll still get married.

TISHO: If it was as simple as a divorce, and running down to City Hall, we would have done that a long time ago.

SAM: There's no right way out, is there?

TISHO: Doesn't seem to be.

(SYBIL rushes in. She's wearing street clothes)

SYBIL: Dr Jarvis says I can.… Oh hello, Mr Coleman.

SAM: Looks like you're bailing out of here.

SYBIL: Today is the day! Didn't think I'd be this excited.

SAM: Well good luck, and I hope everything works out for you.

SYBIL: And for you too.

(SYBIL *starts removing the things from her night table.*)

SAM: Think I'll call the job and tell them I won't be in. I'd like to be here when you come down.

TISHO: No, you go to work. I'll probably be groggy all day. Don't look so worried, I'll be fine.

SAM: I know that, but maybe I should stay and....

TISHO: Go to work. I'll see you this evening.

SAM: You got my beeper number?

TISHO: Yes.

SAM: And the office number?

TISHO: Goodbye Sam!

SAM: Okay...goodbye Mrs Moss.

SYBIL: Bye.

(SAM *exits.*)

SYBIL: Wish I could stay around to make sure you're all right, but eleven o'clock I either check out or get thrown out. Maybe I'll wait in the lounge.

TISHO: I'm sure Arthur will love that. Don't worry, I'll send you a postcard from the operating room.

SYBIL: As long as it doesn't say, wish you were here.

(AMY *enters with the gurney.*)

AMY: *(Helping* TISHO *on the gurney)* All aboard the Orient Express!

TISHO: *(To* SYBIL*)* Well this is it, huh?

(AMY *moves aside, giving them a little privacy.*)

TISHO: You take care of yourself, and keep in touch.

SYBIL: Maybe one day when you're not busy, we could have lunch. We'll meet at the Plaza and have tea sandwiches filled with salmon and parsley.

TISHO: And jasmine tea, with just a pinch of sugar...yes, I'd like that.

(AMY *pushes the gurney towards the door.* TISHO *grabs* SYBIL's *hand.*)

TISHO: To rainbow specials.

SYBIL: And hot fudge sundaes. Good luck Tisho.

(TISHO *and* AMY *exit.* SYBIL *checks the closet and dresser to make sure she hasn't forgotten anything.* ARTHUR *enters.*)

ARTHUR: Ready to go?

SYBIL: Just about.

(ARTHUR *hands her an envelope. She opens it and takes out a certificate.*)

SYBIL: The Star Makers Society?

ARTHUR: It's an organization that studies the galaxy and finds new stars. They're legitimate. I went over to Jersey and checked them out myself.

SYBIL: *(Glancing over the certificate)* I have a…star…named after me?

ARTHUR: That's right.

SYBIL: It's called, Sybil Moss?

ARTHUR: That's your name, isn't it?

SYBIL: I can't believe it. Thank you Arthur.

(*He picks up her bag and crosses to the door.*)

ARTHUR: Did you remember to get Miss Anderson's phone number?

SYBIL: I wrote it down.

ARTHUR: And she has ours?

SYBIL: Yes, but I doubt if we'll see each other again.

ARTHUR: I thought you became such good friends.

SYBIL: We certainly did.

(ARTHUR *shrugs his shoulders and exits.* SYBIL *picks up her basket of flowers and starts to leave. She turns back and puts the basket on* TISHO's *bed. Not satisfied with the placement, she thinks a second then gets* TISHO's *bedpan. She puts it in the middle of the bed, places the basket of flowers in it and smiles. She looks around the room, and takes a deep breath. Now that she's leaving, she's afraid. She remembers the certificate in her hand, and laughs.*)

SYBIL: Hot damn Tisho, I'm a star!

(SYBIL *regally makes her exit.*)

THE END

BOARDERS
Three Short Plays with an Epilogue by the Landlady

Constance Congdon

BOARDERS
© copyright 1995 by Constance Congdon

Constance Congdon's most recent well-known play, TALES OF THE LOST FORMICANS (published by Broadway Play Publishing Inc), has had over forty productions, and was most recently produced at The Oregon Shakespeare Festival as part of their 1994 season. Congdon's plays also have been produced in Moscow, Helsinki, Hong Kong, Edinburgh, and London. Her CASANOVA was produced at the New York Shakespeare Festival in 1991. She has just completed a commission from that theater, a play called DOG OPERA. LOSING FATHER'S BODY received its premiere at the Portland Stage Company in April 1994. Congdon wrote the libretto for a new opera by Peter Gordon, THE STRANGE LIFE OF IVAN OSOKIN, which opened at La Mama Annex in April 1994. She also works with composers Ronald Perera and Mel Marvin, and has written seven plays for The Children's Theater of Minneapolis, one of which she co-wrote with Mark Strand, with sets and costumes designed by the inimitable Red Grooms. She has received Rockefeller, N E A, and Guggenheim playwriting grants, and was awarded New York *Newsday*'s Oppenheimer Award for the best new play in New York (1990) and the Arnold Weissberger Award. She is a member of New Dramatists.

CHARACTERS

APARTMENT #1 (Play #1): SUSAN, *thirty-two*; BUNNY, *forties*; BUCKY, *thirties*

APARTMENT #2 (Play #2): JEFF, *twenty-eight*; SANDY, *twenty-eight*

APARTMENT #3 (Play #3): LEONARD, *twenty-three*; JULIE, *twenty-two*; GRAM, *seventies*

APARTMENT: THE LANDLADY'S (Play #4—Epilogue): MRS LUCY, *sixty-one*

SETTING

This play takes place in an apartment house in a once-nice neighborhood in a medium-sized city in the northeastern part of the U S. The time is late fall, the present.

DEDICATION

To Betty Osborne (1941-1993)
who named and directed these plays
and who is missed, very much,
by her friend, Connie

APARTMENT #1

(Time: 5:30 p.m.)

(The scene is a one-room apartment in a seedy area of a large eastern city. The furniture consists of a bed, a couch, an end table, and a treadle sewing machine with a long piece of cloth in it. There is a chair by it. There are two "collections" of cardboard cartons, stacked on one another. One of them has clothing in it and has large flowers drawn on the side in red Magic Marker. The other stack is empty and undecorated. There is a kitchen area with an old refrigerator and another box with very few things in it. There is a large window, uncurtained. There are old magazines stacked near the bed and the couch.)

(SUSAN is thirty-two and the inhabitant. She is lying on the couch, reading a magazine. A faint knock, then a pounding is heard. She jumps up, runs to window, looks out, opens door.)

SUSAN: *(Shouting, friendly)* Yeah! It's not locked! Come on up!

BUNNY: *(Starting up stairs)* Don't you lock the door in this neighborhood?

SUSAN: It doesn't lock.

BUNNY: *(In the doorway, out of breath)* Oh! Well, look at this. It has lots of light, doesn't it? Well, how are you? *(Hugs SUSAN)* Are you sure this is all right?

SUSAN: Sure. Of course. Do you want a Coke or something?

BUNNY: No. I'll have something on the plane.

SUSAN: Oh—you going back today?

BUNNY: I've used all my vacation time. So—

SUSAN: So! Well! Do you need any help? Here, my shoes are here somewhere. *(Looks for them, finds them, etc.)*

BUNNY: *(Rummages in her purse. Pulls out a paper bag, stapled with a ticket, from a pharmacy.)* Give him one of these a day absolutely. And there are others in here—the directions are on the bottles. He's used to going for a walk at about four p.m.

SUSAN: *(Taking bag)* Okay. No problem. It'll be good for both of us.

BUNNY: Make sure he eats. You can put food out for him, but you have to see that he eats it. *(Pause. She begins to show some emotion.)* You understand why I can't keep him.

SUSAN: Of course. I know.

BUNNY: *(Begins to cry. Hugs SUSAN)* Thank you, Susan. There was no one. I had no one.

SUSAN: I know.

BUNNY: Well. *(Regaining composure, gathering her things)* I'll go down and get him.

SUSAN: Do you need any—

BUNNY: No. I'll just get him out of the cab.

SUSAN: Okay. *(BUNNY starts out the door.)* Bunny, he'll be fine. He'll be fine here.

(BUNNY exits. We hear the bottom door open and close. Then, a minute later, open and close again. SUSAN goes to landing, looks down, smiles.)

SUSAN: There's Bucky.

BUNNY: Come on. That's it. *(To SUSAN)* There's paraphrenalia here.

SUSAN: I'll get it.

(BUNNY leads in BUCKY, a man, thirty-five, wearing sunglasses, and walking slowly, almost stiffly. He is silent and does not react to anything.)

BUNNY: Here we go. Where should I put him?

SUSAN: Er—on the couch.

(BUNNY sets him down.)

BUNNY: Now, Bucky, I'm leaving. You've got all clean laundry. Susan has your Triavil and the others. Please take them.

SUSAN: I'll go down and get the bags. *(Exits)*

BUNNY: Goodbye, Bucky. *(Pause)* This was the last time.

(BUNNY touches BUCKY on the head. She goes to the door, turns to say something, changes her mind, leaves quickly. We hear her say goodbye to SUSAN on the stairs. Door opens, closes. SUSAN appears on landing with a beat-up suitcase and a half-full laundry bag. BUCKY hasn't moved. SUSAN stands and looks at him.)

SUSAN: *(Still on landing)* Do you want to play a game? *(No answer from BUCKY)* Okay. *(She carries his stuff in, puts it down, goes to her bed, brings back with her a magazine with two cards marking a place. The cards, we discover when she takes them out, have string on them so they can be worn around the neck.)* Now, this is called the Get-acquainted game. On this card, as you can see,

I've printed your name. Bucky. See? *(Holds in front of him)* And on this card, I've printed my name. Susan. Now, each of us writes things about him or herself on the card and then we wear it, you see, like this. *(She puts it on to demonstrate and takes it off again.)* Why don't I go first? Good. *(Reads)* "'In the upper right-hand corner, write your favorite color." Oh, that's easy—green. I love green. (BUCKY *does not move. She writes.*)

G-R-E-E-N. Green. "In the lower right-hand corner, write the name of your favorite song." That's a hard one. There are so many. I've always had a secret passion for 'Surfer Girl'. "Above your name, write the name of the person who most influenced your life." God, these are getting harder. Well, I can't think of anybody. We'll have to come back to that one. "Below your name, write the name of the thing you would rescue first if your room was burning." I assume they mean besides yourself. Humm. *(Looks around the room)* Not much here. My sewing machine. But of course it's got curtains stuck in it now. The needle won't go in or come out. So they're just sort of nailed there. Do you know anything about sewing machines? "In the upper left-hand corner—your favorite movie." I don't know, *The Miracle Worker*? I know. *(Sings)*
I'm singing in the rain,
Just singing in the rain.
What a glorious feeling,
I'm happy—

"What do you want to be when you grow up?" What magazine is this? *(Looks at cover)* Oh, *Tiger Teen*. Well, I haven't the faintest idea. I'll put happy, I guess. There. Oh, I almost forgot, "the person who most influenced my life." Gee, there's so many letters in Annette Funicello's name. *(She laughs.)* You remember her. We're the same age I think. All three of us. We'll do yours now. *(Hands him the name tag and the pen. He doesn't take them. She puts them in his lap and reads from the magazine.)* "In the upper right-hand corner, write—" *(Sees that he is doing nothing, puts magazine down, takes the card and pen.)* That's okay. No problem. I will write. Bucky—favorite color? These aren't that hard, really. *(Silence)* Tell you what, we'll just put our name tags on. *(Puts his over his head)* Now if it gets real crowded in here, we'll be able to find each other. Ah! Why don't I unpack all this stuff? That'll make you feel more at home. Looks like all this will have to be folded. That's all right. Don't mind. We here at Sunrise Towers aim to please. Now, Bucky, this is your dresser. No, you might say. No, Susan —*(She points to her name, as if trying to help him read it.)*—that is merely a pile of cardboard boxes. And then I would say, "Why Bucky, it is one of a matched set." *(Indicates her dresser)* The only difference being a subtle decorative motif which I can duplicate—if the Magic Marker hasn't dried up. So, shirts *(Puts away)*, underwear *(Puts away)*, socks *(Puts away)*, pants *(Puts the one pair of pants away)*—there must be more in there. *(She looks in*

*laundry bag, then empties it on couch. There are just a few things, which she folds
and puts away. Bathrobe. Pajamas. The pajamas are hospital issue.)* They let you
bring these home with you? Well, all done. *(Folds bag, puts it in the suitcase,
takes toilet items out, shuts case)* Let's see, toothbrush, comb, electric razor.
(Pause. To herself:) Damn! I thought I told her. *(To* BUCKY*)* Mrs Lucy,
downstairs, thinks the rats chew the wires and suck all the electricity out.
How does one explain deterioration to someone who's a bit deteriorated
themselves? See, she has to believe that the rats do it because time is a lot
scarier. You know? Well, no matter. Not to worry. I've got a razor I shave
my legs with. The blade's a little dull. *(Pause. She comes close to him.)* It's okay
for you to have a razor blade, isn't it?

*(*BUCKY *reacts slightly to this remark. This takes* SUSAN *aback. There is a long
pause. She goes to her bed area, looks for something, finds it, puts it in her right
hand, and, concealing it, crawls to the couch from behind. A hand puppet appears
over the back of the couch, at* BUCKY's *shoulder. It talks in a high voice, and moves
to different places around* BUCKY *to get his attention. He stares straight ahead.)*

Hi Bucky! My name is Elliot the Elephant. Susan is taking a little nap right
now, but she asked me to give you a tour of the apartment. This is the
kitchen. Nothing in it works, but the refrigerator keeps the roaches out. The
bathroom's down the hall. You have to use a flashlight at night, so you can
see where to go. Ha! Ha! That's a little elephant joke. Hey! Guess what!
You're sitting on your bed. It's a fold-out bed. It used to be Susan's bed
when Barbara lived here. Because Barbara had a boyfriend and they needed
the bed to make rude noises in. Even elephants don't make noises as rude as
that. "Stop making those rude noises!" said Susan. "I can't live with a
thirty-year-old virgin!" replied Barbara, slamming the door. Susan's
forgotten, but I remember. Because an elephant never forgets. *(Elliot
disappears, but we don't see* SUSAN. *She is quiet for a long pause.)*

SUSAN: *(From behind the couch)* And you know what really makes me mad?
She took the goddamn television with her. And the curtains. The electricity
was working pretty well then. *(She gets up.)* I was the one that used to watch
it. The TV, not the electricity. I would expect electricity's pretty boring to
watch. It doesn't move. It just sits there in the hall, waiting. *(She sits on the
couch.)* I liked the *Late Show* and the *Late, Late Show*. Sometimes even the
Early Show. I watched whatever I wanted. I had complete control. I loved
those talk shows with their beautiful furniture. They'd sit up there in that
little box and somehow you'd begin to feel that you were in their living
room instead of the other way around. And *One Life to Live* and *Days of
Our Lives* and *The Edge of Night* and all those really beautiful people in living
rooms and hospital rooms with tubes going in and out and nothing ever
resolved but all the movements so beautiful and careful and the beautiful
clothes and the clean beautiful living rooms. Now I'd even like to see the ad
for the Miracle Brush or the Miracle Knife or Miracle Glue or even that thing

that makes mounds of carrot salad. I was working three days a week then. I was sure they were going to hire me on permanent. *(Pause)* But there'll be something— Hey! I know what this party needs! *(Just remembers something)* Oh! Perfect, perfect! There's someone you haven't met. *(Goes to her bed area)* We're going to be living together for a while, so— *(Brings out, with some ceremony, a large stuffed panda bear, holds him in front of* BUCKY, *extending his paw to shake hands)* Bucky, this is Sir Tedrick. Tedrick, this is Bucky.

Let's see *(Looks at window)*, it's past tea time, oh, and walk time for you Bucky, but let's have a party instead.

(She pulls the end table around in front of BUCKY, *sets Tedrick in the chair by the sewing machine, after placing it beside the table. When it is time,* SUSAN *will sit on the floor. Gets a Coke out of the fridge. It's the only thing in it. Finds two teacups and a small glass, puts them on the table. Pours the Coke into the cups and glass.* SUSAN *gives the glass to herself, giving the teacups to* BUCKY *and Tedrick. She sits and sips her Coke.* BUCKY *does not participate.)*

Oh! I think I've got something else. *(Gets up, finds some cellophane-wrapped crackers from a cafeteria)* There. *(Puts them on the table. Pause.)* I don't know which one of you is enjoying your tea more. *(Pause. Suddenly, she seems to feel silly on the floor and sits up on the couch. Long pause.)* It's getting darker earlier. Winter. *(Pause. Then suddenly:)* I'd better get to the store. There's not a thing in the house to eat. *(Standing up)* Bucky, I'll — I'll have to bother you for that money. *(*BUCKY *begins to react.)* I don't have a cent. She didn't mention anything—she seemed upset— I just assumed she gave it to you.

*(*BUCKY *hits the table with his fist. Some of the Coke spills.* SUSAN, *alarmed, removes her panda and then begins to wipe up the spill.)*

It's all right, Bucky. Really. If you don't have it, we'll manage. Tell you what, I'll call Bunny collect, tomorrow, from the drug store. So it's just a matter of getting through tonight. No problem. Okay? For that matter, I could always hock the sewing machine. It might be worth something, particularly with a perfectly good curtain stuck in it. And then Bunny could pay me back when she sends for you.

*(*BUCKY *sighs deeply and slumps over slightly.)*

You're not feeling well. Gee, I've just been jabbering on. I didn't think. Where's your medicine? *(She finds the Rx bag, tears it open.)* Damn! Child-proof top. There. *(Hands him the bottle)* Oh. You need some water.

(She goes to sink for water, returns to see BUCKY *pouring contents of the entire bottle of medicine— pills— into his mouth. She drops the water, races to him and grabs his hands, reaches into his mouth to get as many of the pills as she can claw out. His sunglasses fly off in the scuffle. She grabs the container to read the label for how many pills were in the prescription.)*

Twenty. *(She grabs all the pills she can find and counts them frantically.* BUCKY *has buried his head in his arms.)* Let's see— goddamit! One two three— *(She begins to cry.)* —eight, eleven, thirteen—GODDAMN you, Bucky! There's three more. Well, guess what? Guess what, you sonofabitch! You're going to LIVE! *(She slaps him.)* How dare you! HOW DARE YOU! *(She stands before him, trembling with rage, still crying. After a moment, she softens and touches* BUCKY *tentatively on the head.)* Bucky, I'm sorry, Bucky. Please forgive me. I'm sorry, Bucky. *(He lifts his head out of his arms, but doesn't look at her.)* It's just that—life isn't like that. It's never that bad—really. *(*BUCKY *sits up slowly and looks her straight in the eye. After a moment, she turns away. She begins glumly puttering, absently clearing up.* BUCKY *looks at her, now and then. She glances at the window and then goes to the kitchen area and brings out a couple of candles on old saucers, puts them on the table in front of* BUCKY, *lights them. As she leans over to do this, she notices her name tag and takes it off. She won't look at him, but he looks at her.)*

BUCKY: I'm cold.

(This stops SUSAN *for a moment. Then she goes to her bedroom and returns with two blankets, both off her bed. She puts one around him, and then one around herself. She sits on the couch and opens a package of crackers from the table.)*

BUCKY: Thank you.

*(*SUSAN *looks at him, hands him one of the crackers. He takes it and eats it.)*

BLACKOUT

APARTMENT # 2

(Time: 11:30 p.m.)

(JEFF knocks on door, waits, then again. SANDY is asleep on the fold-out bed. She's in her nightgown, with a book. The light is on. Upstage right is a small table filled with food, all set for a dinner; two dinner candles are entirely burnt down. On the second knock, SANDY mumbles "What?" JEFF opens door gently, sticks his head in.)

JEFF: Are you in bed?

SANDY: *(Sitting up)* Oh—oh, it's you, Jeff. That's all right, come in.

JEFF: I know it's late, but the light was on.

SANDY: Will you get in here?

JEFF: Oh good. *(Enters quickly)* I didn't see his car outside, so I figured—

SANDY: Yeah. He went out with her.

JEFF: *(Winces in pain)* Ooooo.

SANDY: Yeah. He called Mrs Lucy because right at 7:45 she opens my door—

JEFF: She opened your door?

SANDY: Opened it right up. *(Puts hand to mouth as if to announce)* "Your boyfriend can't come. He has to go out with his wife." Slams door, stomps downstairs.

JEFF: Well, he called in the middle of *The Newlywed Game*. You think *you* were mad? So—?

SANDY: So I'm sitting here. Dinner all ready. Candles lit. Wine open. Music on the stereo. My best dress.

JEFF: Which one?

SANDY: The green one.

JEFF: The Qiana one?

SANDY: Yeah.

JEFF: That's a terrific dress.

SANDY: I know.

JEFF: So how did we get here? *(Motions to bed)*

SANDY: Well, I sat like Miss Havisham for a bit. The candles all burned down. The stereo turned itself off. The food got cold.

JEFF: A pathetic sight.

SANDY: Indeed.

JEFF: And then what did our heroine do?

SANDY: Our heroine got up, taking off the terrific green Qiana dress and the special one-piece undergarment with no seams and the panty hose, also with no seams, turned her back on the tawdry scene, put on her flannel nightie—

JEFF: With lots of seams.

SANDY: —and went to bed to read.

JEFF: And what are we reading?

SANDY: Flannery O'Connor.

JEFF: Oh good. That should cheer us right up. Be out on the window ledge soon.

SANDY: I'm not the window-ledge type.

JEFF: Oh? What type are we?

SANDY: I don't know.

JEFF: *(Sits on bed on something that crunches, discovers candy wrappers)* Oh— I do. "I'm sorry, Jeff. It was an overdose of peanut butter cup. There was nothing we could do—it clogged the stomach pump."

SANDY: It was some candy I bought for the little boy upstairs—for Easter.

JEFF: Oh, Sandra, the depths you have sunk to. I'll have to watch you like a hawk all through April. I'll find you in the gutter with pieces of plastic grass in your hair and I'll know you've been out mugging bunnies. We won't be able to set foot in Woolworth's. The shame of it.

SANDY: *(Miserably)* Oh, Jeff.

JEFF: Tell him to fuck off, Sandy, just tell him to fuck off.

SANDY: Jeff, I love him.

JEFF: Shit, yeah.

SANDY: I do.

JEFF: Well, I don't know why.

SANDY: I don't know why, either. I hate being in love. I have always hated being in love. It's like a disease. I am not myself. It's like there are two people living in my body. One is perfectly sane—not enough to be boring—but sane, you know. Adult, even. And then there's this other one, who's about fourteen years old—a total ninny. I don't know, I wish I could take a cure, a shot. It's like just at the beginning, it's so sweet. There are these parts of you that are aching with it.

JEFF: It.

SANDY: Like I read this kid—he had this accident—he was burned on his legs very badly. And when he stood on them for the first time after being in bed for months, the blood forced itself through his veins. And it hurt so much, but it was wonderful. And he went on to become a great runner.

JEFF: While the rest of us just get burned. And limp home.

SANDY: I mean, Jeff—I mean, I just feel if we could break out of living this moment-to-moment way we do. Like the moment Mrs Lucy came up and told me, you know, he wasn't coming—that was painful, and this moment, here, right now, isn't as much.

JEFF: Well, that's good to hear.

SANDY: But what I mean is, if we could just see the whole picture, and this moment here or there as part of a big whole picture that is our lives—

JEFF: And what would it look like over the couch. That's the important question.

SANDY: Why did you come over? Did't you have a date with whatshisname—Brian, tonight?

JEFF: Whatshisname.

SANDY: Well?

JEFF: Well, I went to the bar, all dressed up. And I sat. And then I sat some more. My aftershave began to fade. And I began to get those little wrinkles in my trousers—those unattractive ones around the thighs? So when you stand, they make a kind of wing formation around your naughty parts? (*After their laughter fades*) So. He went to the market. And the lamb chop wasn't there.

SANDY: Lamb chops are like that.

JEFF: I know. I used to be one.

SANDY: When was this? Y camp?

JEFF: I was a major lamb chop for several years.

SANDY: Oh? And what are we now?

JEFF: We are leaving— (*Starts to exit, stops at door, unable to really leave, looks back at* SANDY. *They giggle.*) Well, look at all this food just lying about gathering botulism and God know what else—a regular cockroach convention center. Suzy Homemaker will have to get on this. (*Gets food wrap, etc., begins wrapping up food, putting it away. Pauses over one of the dishes.*) This looks yummy.

SANDY: Yeah.

JEFF: (*At refrigerator*) Looks like I could clean this refrigerator out again. (*Lifts lid on something*) This look familiar. (*Shows her something*) Sandy, what was this?

SANDY: A hamburger patty.

JEFF: It's furry, it looks like a dead hamster, and I'm throwing it away. (*Dumps it in the trash*)

SANDY: I haven't been too hungry lately.

JEFF: Oh, you just sleep with peanut butter cups, hmmmm? Very kinky.

SANDY: That's not food.

JEFF: (*Finding something*) Sandy, is this my moussaka? Is this what you think of my moussaka? (*Shows her*)

SANDY: Oh Jeff, I love your moussaka, and you know it. I was just so stuffed that night, I couldn't look at it again,

JEFF: It was too greasy, wasn't it.

SANDY: No, it was fine.

JEFF: I should have drained the meat better.

SANDY: Jeff, it was fine. It was perfect. I loved it.

JEFF: Are you sure, Sandra? You can tell me the truth.

SANDY: (*Getting out of bed, coming to him*) Do you want me to show you? Do you want me to prove it to you? Give it to me. Give it to me. (*Taking it from him, grabbing a utensil*)

JEFF: Sandy, don't eat it!

SANDY: It's your moussaka, and I love it!

JEFF: (*Grabbing it from her*) It's green, for Christ's sake! Give it to me! (*Throwing it in the garbage*) Do you want to die?

SANDY: No. (*She laughs.*) No.

JEFF: My god, she walks! Look at her, she's standing! (*They laugh. It dies down. Pause.*) I should go. It's late.

SANDY: Oh—don't go.

JEFF: I'll miss the last bus. *(She goes back to the bed, sits quietly.)* You know, Sandy. I've been thinking. You know, with our two salaries, we could get a really good apartment together. Two bedrooms. A bathroom actually in the apartment instead of down the hall. A phone?

SANDY: Jeff, you know that won't work. Everyone will think we are living together.

JEFF: Well, we will be.

SANDY: You know what I mean. They'll think we're a couple. Unless you wear a big sign that says, "I'm gay."

JEFF: I need a sign?

SANDY: You know what I mean. If we had someone living with us, then it would look different, but a couple is a couple.

JEFF: Sandy, nobody cares.

SANDY: I'm not talking about caring! I'm talking about knowing, understanding. In the grocery store, we'd be together. We could never go out together, especially to places where we might get a date.

JEFF: We don't go to the same places to get a date.

SANDY: In the world? Look, my mother still thinks we're the perfect couple. She refuses to accept it. Face it—except for a handful of people who know us well, male and female in the same residence equals a unit. Your mother will be bringing us Tupperware.

JEFF: I like Tupperware.

SANDY: How about celibacy?

JEFF: Not as much. Although the way things have been going lately— *(Pause)* You don't want to live together because of what he'll say— tell the truth.

SANDY: I don't give a damn what he says.

JEFF: Uh-huh. And by the way, this lamb chop is rump-roast, well aged.

SANDY: Why do you talk about yourself that way? I wish you wouldn't do it.

JEFF: Why?

SANDY: Because it depresses me, that's why.

JEFF: More than usual?

SANDY: All right! It makes you sound like a hustler!

JEFF: Well, I am a hustler, Sandy. And let me tell you something—so is anyone. Take a look at yourself, or me, or anyone, all dressed up, waiting. Doesn't have to be a street corner.

SANDY: Jeff!

JEFF: Well, talk about your big picture—let's take a look at it! Let's have a bird's eye view of Sandy on that street corner—the longer she stands there, the more she's willing to put up with. He can have a wife—it's amazing what we'll settle for.

SANDY: Brian, of course, is a great prize.

JEFF: I don't care about Brian.

SANDY: Oh, I see. It's not cheap if you don't care. You can still keep your standards, right? That superb taste of yours won't be violated. You won't have spoiled yourself for Prince Charming— somewhere out there spraying his apartment and himself all over with Givenchy. George Benson on the stereo. And himself, Mr After-Dark, in a Halston caftan and some of that Italian underwear with no seams, putting satin sheets on the bed just for you.

(JEFF *stares at her a moment, then grabs his jacket and stomps out.* SANDY *doesn't know what to do. Just as she's about to go after him, he comes back in.*)

JEFF: Hello. I don't have cab fare.

SANDY: I do. Just a minute.

JEFF: Sandy, fact is, I just can't go home tonight.

SANDY: You can stay here. (*They touch awkwardly.* SANDY *gets into bed with her book. He begins getting undressed.*)

JEFF: There's a James Dean festival at the Paris Cinema. (SANDY *stares straight ahead, holding the book.*) We could go to Kramer's and laugh at the furniture. (*She looks at him and smiles. He climbs into bed.*) Read me a story.

SANDY: Not tonight, dear, I have a headache.

JEFF: I'll get the light.

SANDY: (*In darkness, after* JEFF *gets into bed*) Jeff?

JEFF: Uh-hum?

SANDY: Tomorrow we'll get a paper. And we'll look. And we'll talk about it. Okay?

JEFF: He won't like it.

SANDY: I know.

JEFF: You don't really hate Tupperware, do you, Sandra?

SANDY: No, course not.

JEFF: Well, it's the only way to get it—without going to those stupid parties.

SANDY: Good night, Jeff.

JEFF: Good night, Sandy.

BLACKOUT

APARTMENT #3

(Time: 1 a.m.)

(A young man,. LEN, sits in bed, a fold-out couch, in his underwear, waiting. JULIE, a young woman dressed in a bathrobe and carrying a towel, comes out of a nearby room, shutting the door behind her.)

LEN: Julie?

JULIE: *(Whispering)* Just a minute, Leonard. I have to go to the bathroom.

LEN: I thought that's where you were.

JULIE: *(Whispering)* No, I was checking on my roommate.

LEN: Is she awake?

JULIE: No. *(She starts out the apartment door.)*

LEN: Where are you going?

JULIE: The bathroom's down the hall. *(She exits.)*

(LEN sighs, chews on cuticle. Decides to take off his undershirt, does so, folds it up and hides it in the pillowcase. He expands his chest and lowers the sheet until his navel is just uncovered, but this also exposes his jockey shorts a bit so he tries to lower the elastic. He finally decides to remove them and also stuffs them in his pillowcase. JULIE enters and turns off light.)

LEN: Julie?

JULIE: I'm coming, Leonard.

LEN: Where are you?

JULIE: I'm coming, Leonard.

LEN: Julie?

JULIE: Here I am.

LEN: Ahhhh.

JULIE: Leonard! You're—you're all ready!

LEN: I know. Come here—ow! What was that?

JULIE: I'm sorry—my hairbrush in my pocket.

LEN: You still have your bathrobe on?

JULIE: And my nightgown, but you can take them off me.

LEN: Okay.

JULIE: What's wrong?

LEN: I can't undo the knot. There. No.

JULIE: Leonard, what are you doing?

LEN: Trying to get—trying to get this with my teeth. Damn!

JULIE: Now it's all wet.

LEN: I know— Just slip it off.

LEN:	JULIE:
Here—get your arms out. No The other one. Yeah. Here, I'll—well, here—we'll just move this around and just slip it—I'll hold—sorry.	Okay. No—you move this. Oh! Okay, hold. Leonard! I don't bend that way. Oh, I see. No, wait. That's the nightgown sleeve. Okay. Yeah. I'll get out of it. Here. Let me stand up. Okay

JULIE: There. I'm cold. Can we get under the covers?

LEN: You bet. *(Sounds of beginning lovemaking)*

JULIE: You can't stay all night.

LEN: It's all right. It only takes a few minutes.

JULIE: What?

LEN: I mean, however long you want me to stay, I'll stay.

JULIE: Okay. *(Passion)*

(GRANDMA *enters in dark, sits on edge of bed.*)

JULIE: What's wrong.

LEN: Do you have a cat?

JULIE: No.

LEN: *(Whispering)* I think someone is sitting on the bed.

JULIE: Oh no. Where's my nightgown? Oh, I'll never find it in that mess. Here.

LEN: Julie, what are you doing?

(JULIE *gets out of bed, goes to light, turns it on—she is wearing pillows, one in front, one in back.*)

JULIE: *Debbie*, what are you doing? This is my roommate, *Debbie*. Debbie, this is Leonard.

LEN: Hello.

(GRANDMA *turns around to acknowledge him—he sees that she is old.*)

JULIE: I'm just going to throw something on.

LEN: *(Reaching around the bed, trying to find something to put on)* Julie! Julie, wait a minute! *(Finds his undershirt, puts it on as pants under the covers, gets out of bed with his legs through the arms of his undershirt)*

JULIE: I'll only be a second, Leonard.

LEN: *(Whispering to* JULIE*)* Julie, this Debbie is an old lady.

JULIE: Shhh. *(Exits into bedroom)*

(LEONARD *pauses, not knowing what to do, finally approaches* GRANDMA.)

LEN: How are you?

GRAM: I'm having a heart attack.

LEN: What?

GRAM: I'm having a heart attack.

LEN: Oh my god! *(Runs to bedroom door)* Julie! Julie!

(JULIE *enters, carrying the pillows and wearing something she's thrown on.*)

JULIE: What are you up to, Debbie?

GRAM: I'm having a heart attack.

JULIE: No you're not.

LEN: How can you tell?

JULIE: Leonard, look at her. Does she look like she's having a heart attack?

LEN: I don't know—

JULIE: Leonard, she looks like she's waiting for the bus. Come on, we're going to put her back to bed. *(Comes down to* GRAM, *takes her elbow and begins to lead her to the bedroom)* Debbie, we're going back to bed now.

GRAM: I could hear it beating.

JULIE: That's good.

GRAM: Oh. *(As she passes* LEONARD*)* Hello.

LEN: Hello.

GRAM: *(As she gets to the bedroom door,* GRAM *turns to* LEONARD.*)*
You know what would be good right now? A jelly donut.

JULIE: *(To* GRAM*)* You didn't take your medicine, did you? *(Turning her over to* LEONARD*)* I'll get it. *(Exits into bedroom)*

GRAM: Would you like a jelly donut? *(Starts toward kitchen)* Let's see if I can find something.

LEN: No. No, that's all right. I'll get it. You stay there. *(Indicating couch. He goes to kitchen area, opens a few cupboards, talking while he does.)* You know, it must be nice for Julie—to have someone here, you know, to eat with and just be in the apartment. I room with a guy at work. He's all right. Here are some cookies—I'll put them on a napkin here.

(While he has been at the cupboards, GRAM *has tipped over until the top part of her body is lying on the bed, but her feet are still on the floor. Her eyes are closed.* LEONARD *returns with the cookies to see her collapsed. He looks with horror, afraid to get too close to touch.* JULIE *enters. Just then,* GRAM *snores.)*

JULIE: She's asleep, right? Let's get her to bed. Here, you help.

(They gently remove GRAM*, help her to the bedroom.)*

GRAM: *(Waking up a bit)* The sheet was cold. Everybody was gone.

JULIE: Everybody's here now. And we're all going to bed.

GRAM: Are you sure?

JULIE: I'm sure.

GRAM: *(From the bedroom)* That young man—he's wearing a shirt where he's supposed to have trousers.

JULIE: Good night.

GRAM: Okay.

*(*JULIE *enters, breathes a sigh of relief, then approaches* LEONARD *sexily, kisses him, etc.)*

LEN: Wait a minute, Julie. Hold it—let's just keep my shirt on for a minute.

JULIE: Okay. What?

LEN: What?! Well, I think you could explain a few things.

JULIE: Okay. She's my grandmother.

LEN: You called her Debbie. How could anyone call their grandmother Debbie?

JULIE: It's her name. I do usually call her Grandma.

LEN: I should hope so.

JULIE: You sound annoyed.

LEN: You told me she was your roommate.

JULIE: Well, she is! Temporarily. Look, if I had told you that Grandmother was staying here, would you have come home with me?

LEN: No!

JULIE: See?

LEN: Are you sure she's all right?

JULIE: Yes. Look, the other night, Mr Vogel was on his roof fixing his T V antenna and she thought Venutians had landed. She's thought her bathrobe was a prowler twice. And I had to get rid of the houseplants temporarily—can you imagine what she'd make of a big Swedish ivy in a hanging planter on a dark night?

LEN: Okay. Okay. I'll get the light. *(Crosses to light)*

JULIE: You should wear a tie with that, it would be cute.

(LEONARD turns off light, comes to bed, lovemaking starts up.)

(Light comes on again, catching LEONARD and JULIE in a heavy clinch. GRANDMA is right at the bed, smiling down at them.)

GRAM: Would you like some cocoa?

JULIE: Not now, Grandma.

GRAM: What about you, young man?

JULIE: I don't think he cares for any just now.

GRAM: Okay. *(Goes to kitchen)*

JULIE: Grandma, where did you put your medicine?

GRAM: *(Not looking at JULIE)* I don't like that medicine very much.

JULIE: *(Getting up, putting on a nightgown)* It helps you sleep.

GRAM: We—I, I don't like to sleep quite like that.

JULIE: Like what?

GRAM: Like a rock.

JULIE: Well, rock or no rock, we'd better take a pill tonight. *(Starts toward bedroom, stops, goes to LEONARD, harried)* Talk her out of the cocoa—it gives her diarrhea. *(Exits into bedroom)*

(LEONARD gets up, wrapping blanket around him.)

LEN: Are you sure cocoa agrees with you?

GRAM: Of course.

LEN: *(Seeing her about to drink a cup)* Well, I changed my mind—I think I will have a cup.

GRAM: Oh good. (*Hands him her cocoa*) You know, you have real interesting clothes.

LEN: Thank you. (*Sees her start another cup*) You know, I think Julie would like one, too.

GRAM: Oh good! We'll have a party. (*Continuing to talk as she starts another cup, this third one for herself*) She won't find that medicine. I threw it out.

LEN: Why?

GRAM: I don't like the way it made me feel. I don't like to sleep like that. I kept having this dream. I'd wake up at home in bed. In my house. In the middle of the night. And Richard wasn't there beside me. The sheet was cold where he was supposed to be. And I didn't know where he was. I couldn't remember. So I got up— I could feel the carpet under my feet— it was so real. And I ran to the children's rooms, but they were empty. So I ran all over the house, calling for them, and for him. But nobody came. Nobody answered. That medicine—it was like being put in a sack and dropped in the ocean. What am I doing? This kind of cocoa gives me the runs. But real cocoa made with real milk doesn't. (*She starts gathering stuff for real cocoa.*)

(JULIE *enters.*)

JULIE: I can't find it anywhere. Where did you put it?

GRAM: In the toilet.

JULIE: You mean you left it in the bathroom.

GRAM: No.

LEN: She means she put it in the toilet. (*To* GRAM) Isn't that right?

GRAM: (*Surprised and pleased*) Yes! That's right! Now, we get rid of all this nasty instant cocoa and I'll make us all some real cocoa.

JULIE: (*Going glumly to bed*) I give up.

GRAM: Oh. Oh, what am I doing? I'm keeping you up! We can do this again—sometime. I'm going to bed now. (*She begins her exit.*)

(JULIE *is delighted, signals to* LEONARD. *He is torn—watching* GRANDMA.)

LEN: Grandma?

GRAM: Yes?

LEN: (*After a moment*) Good night.

GRAM: You're a nice boy, you know that? (*She exits.*)

JULIE: Leonard, get the light. Leonard?

(LEONARD *follows* GRAM *into the bedroom. After a moment, he comes out.*)

LEN: She's already asleep. I turned off her light. *(Turns off the livingroom light. Comes to bed.)* Julie, can I stay all night?

JULIE: Sure, now it doesn't matter. Grandma would love it.

LEN: Good. Good night, Julie.

JULIE: Good night, Julie?

LEN: Yes, I'm a little tired. But I had a good time. Good night. *(Turning over and then back to her)* She called me a nice boy. Can you beat that? *(He turns over, going to sleep.)*

JULIE: *(Still sitting up in bed)* Evidently not.

LEN: Humph?

JULIE: Goodnight, Leonard.

LEN: Hmm.

BLACKOUT

EPILOGUE

(Time: 5:00 a.m.)

(Dark. Bedside lamp is turned on by MRS LUCY. *Lying flat in bed, she reaches for her electric alarm clock and brings it right down on top of her eye to see the time.)*

MRS LUCY: Well the rats have sucked a good two hours out of this clock. *(Puts it back on the bedside table. Turns her head to talk to the space beside her on the double bed.)* Bob? *(No answer. She turns the lamp off, then on again, after a second.)* It's still dark. *(To herself)* I don't know what the world's coming to. *(Turns off lamp. A few beats. She sighs. She turns on the lamp, sits up, puts on glasses.)* I give up. Yes, yes, yes. *(She gets out of bed, puts on robe, slippers, goes immediately to chair, sits in it.)*

Well, I'm up. Bob? You up? I'm up. I couldn't sleep a wink. I don't know what they could have been doing—ha! Like that little snip of some kind of doorstep missionary asking me all kinds of personal questions, acting like she discovered Jesus! Well, girlie, I said. Are you listening, Bob? Well, Miss Sainthood, Jesus and I were loving each other when you were still carrying a load in your pants. I don't expect her back. It's still my house. Someday I'm gonna kick them all out. And fix up Irene's room the way it used to be. In case she wants to come and stay. And David's room, too, even though... *(Looks at floor)* What? You want to go out? *(Stands up, talking to an imaginary dog)* You want to go out? It's awful dark out there. Well, come on, Dinah. Here we go. Here we go. *(Opens door)* Well, you better get going. There you go. *(Shuts door. Goes to heat up water for coffee.)* Well, let's get serious, then. I know I cannot go back to sleep. I'm fixing you coffee, Bob. *(To herself)* That always does it. *(Goes to window)* Hmmmm. No extra cars. They must have come in taxi cabs. All I know is nobody went home! Now Irene and David were never like that. Listen to me—I'm talking about Irene as if she were in the past. She's not, she's just in Seattle. You know, I think she's going to call today, Bob. I think that's why I'm thinking about her so much. You know we always had that special communication, Irene and me. I could just call her, of course. But it's her turn. It's her turn. Even if I have to wait another month.

Dinah? Is that you? *(Gets up, goes to door, opens it)* You didn't stay out very long. Did the bad dark scare you? Well, you settle down. That's right. *(Looks toward the window)* The sky's starting to change, I think. Bobby, have you heard anything I've been saying here?

I don't understand it. Every weekend's the same. Pairing up like they're getting ready for the flood. Like the flood's coming. I swear that's all they think about. I think they'd do anything just to keep from being alone. Where is their pride? Is what I want to know. Pride is what makes us different from apes. And horses and cattle, too, are like that. Well, I don't mean to judge. They're all God's children.

Why, Bob, we never needed that—all that stuff. That much. Oh, you'd turn to me in the dark sometimes. You'd just turn to me and slide my nightgown up. I never needed to touch you—there or anything like that. I'd stare up in the dark at the light fixture. It had a piece chipped out of it. All those times were exactly the same. They were like one time. I'd get up and go to the bathroom and come back to bed and listen to you snore until I fell asleep. Usually when I was feeling lonely, I'd just go in and check on Irene and David in their beds. Just fixing the covers would make me feel better. But after those times—those times with you, Bob, I couldn't look at the children just then. I stood in the doorway of their rooms a few times, feeling like a stranger. I don't know why. If they'd listen to me, I'd tell them upstairs. Look, it just makes you lonlier. A good conversation—a good talk—that's better. Just having someone to talk to. (*Goes to get coffee—two cups—looks out window*)

Wouldn't it be funny if it never came up? We'd all just sit in the dark, trying to go back to sleep, I guess. Coffee's ready!! (*Goes to other side of the bed, where Bob should be sleeping*) Come on, Bob. Time to get up. (*Takes framed photograph of a man from under the covers, sets it on the table, and puts a cup of coffee in front of it. She sits down and takes a sip of coffee.*)

There go the birds. They always know. Before they can see any light, they start to sing. That's faith all right. That's what I should have told that little doorstep missionary when she asked. I feel—we should sing a little song, Bobby. I feel like singing a morning song. Like we sang a long time ago. We sang morning songs, didn't we? A long time ago? (*Holds cup up, prepared to sing. Long pause. No song, puts cup down.*) Well, no matter. (*About the sun*) It's coming up anyway. (*Suddenly*) Here. (*Puts cup up to toast, and sings*) You deserve a break today, So get out and get away— (*Can't remember or doesn't think the rest is appropriate. Drinks the toast. Puts cup down. Picks up Bobby's picture, wipes the fog from the glass.*) I believe Irene is going to call today. (*Puts picture back down carefully*) Yes.

BLACKOUT

BREAKFAST SERIAL

Megan Terry

Megan Terry is the author of more than sixty published plays. She has been changing the face of the American theater for four decades with transformation plays, the formalization of theater games into play structures, docudramas, "theatre verité", and performance art. She is called the "mother of feminist theater" by Helene Keyssar in her book *Feminist Theater*. Ms Terry, a founding member of the famed Open Theater, revolutionized the American theater when she developed this country's first rock musical, VIET ROCK.

Leading critics have compared Terry's work to O'Neill, O'Casey, D H Lawrence, Kafka, Lorca, and Brecht. Ms Terry has been awarded National Endowment for the Arts, Rockefeller, and Guggenheim Fellowships; the Stanley Drama Award; and Office of Advanced Drama Research grants. Articles or chapters on Ms Terry's work are featured in major books on the American theater.

Ms Terry is deeply involved in the national theater scene. She has served on several National Endowment for the Arts panels; the Theater Communications Group board of directors; the New Dramatists committee selection panel; the A S S I T E J-U S A board; and the Rockefeller Foundation theater panel. She was recently honored by being elected to the College of Fellows of the American Theater. Installation into this lifetime society took place at the Kennedy Center of Performing Arts in Washington, D C in recognition of her "Distinguished service to the profession by an individual of acknowledged national stature."

Megan Terry also tours as a performer with the Omaha Magic Theater. Nebraska Governor Ben Nelson named her 1992 Nebraska Artist of the Year. Her book of photographs, *Right Brain Vacation Photos*, was nominated for the Barnard Hewitt Award for the best theater history text of 1993.

CHARACTERS

KORD, *a strong, clean-cut, twenty-year-old man*

JEFF, *a boy of fourteen, played by a woman over eighteen*

MIKEY, *a boy of thirteen, played by a woman over eighteen*

ROYCE, *played by a woman over eighteen (This character is a woman masquerading as a boy of twelve.)*

SETTING

A road and a small clearing in a grove of trees near a river

TIME

Early Sunday morning. The present.

(A suburban road. Dawn.)

(JEFF walks along, shivering. KORD flies by on his motorcycle. KORD returns from the other direction, gunning his cycle, then stops. Looks at JEFF.)

KORD: Where ya goin'?

JEFF: Get m' papers.

KORD: Wanna git there fast?

(JEFF shrugs.)

KORD: Hey, I'll get you to your papers, help you fold 'em. We deliver them on the bike, and then I'll take you to a party.

JEFF: On Sunday morning?

KORD: You like parties?

JEFF: I like parties.

KORD: Hop on.

(JEFF hops on and they're off, fast.)

(A small grove of trees. KORD helps JEFF fold papers very fast.)

JEFF: Where are we?

KORD: I come here to party.

JEFF: Girls coming?

KORD: *(Nods)* You party with your friends?

JEFF: We have Robitussin parties.

KORD: Cough syrup?!

JEFF: Better high than Scotch Guard.

KORD: Scotch Guard fries yer brains.

JEFF: We don't do that any more. Save up for "robe parties."

KORD: What's the "robe" high like?

JEFF: *(Trying to act cool)* Cross between booze and psychedelic.

KORD: Where'd you get your hands on acid?

JEFF: Richie's brother made some.

KORD: Fer sure?

JEFF: He said witches in the olden times got high by eating the mold off their old rye bread. They'd get higher than kites and then put spells on people. People'd come down with bad sickness, get mad at the witches, and then burn 'em at the stake or drown 'em in the river.

KORD: Platte River's right over that hill.

JEFF: Hey, I'm too far from home. My mom'll kill me.

KORD: We won't tell her, will we?

JEFF: Let's go. Some a my route get up early on Sunday—they want the sports pages right away.

KORD: We'll go on your route right after you take off your clothes.

JEFF: What?

KORD: You heard me.

(JEFF *looks at* KORD *and flinches.*)

KORD: I told you to take your clothes off.

JEFF: I don't dig guys.

KORD: Me neither.

JEFF: Why'd you bring me here?

KORD: To make you take off your clothes.

JEFF: People don't get their Sunday paper they'll call the paper, then they'll call the cops.

KORD: Nobody's up.

JEFF: The old guys are up. The fishermen, they're up.

KORD: Maybe they'll come looking for you. Would you like them to see you tied up? Would you like them to see you tied up with no clothes on?

JEFF: What do you get out of this?

KORD: You. I got you.

JEFF: But you said yourself...you don't want me, in...in like in that way.

KORD: What way?

JEFF: SEX.

KORD: You want sex?

JEFF: No. God no. I don't want nothin' from you.

KORD: NOT EVEN THIS? *(He shows him knife.)*

JEFF: Who are you?

KORD: Who are you?

JEFF: This isn't funny anymore.

KORD: But it's fun.

JEFF: I'm going.

KORD: *(Slaps him)* Good clean fun.

JEFF: What do you want?

KORD: *(Slaps him again)* I got what I want.

JEFF: I gotta go. *(Starts to run)*

KORD: *(Grabs him)* You'll go when I tell you.

JEFF: You bastard. Let go of me.

KORD: You got a dirty mouth. You know what we do with dirty mouths? We fill them with dirt. *(Forces JEFF 's head down on ground)* Take a big bite. Take a nice big bite of nice clean dirt. It'll clean out yer dirty mind.

JEFF: Don't hurt me. Please.

KORD: *(Kicks him)* I can't stand begging. Plead for your life like a man.

JEFF: I got money saved for college. If you let me go, I'll give it to you. All of it.

KORD: Take 'em off. I wanna see you do that.

JEFF: Then can I go?

KORD: Hey, you're late fer work. You better get started. Huh? Huh? *(Pokes him with knife)*

JEFF: I'm not gonna do it.

KORD: Oh no? How far do you think your blood can spurt? As far as you can pee? Let's see how far you can pee. Oh oh—you smell! I smell you from here. You shit yer pants. I can smell it. You have to take them off. Yer Momma will bop you—you come home with shitty pants. Won't she? Won't she? And she'll get Dad to beat you, too. Won't she? Won't she?

JEFF: No. No. My Mom's nice. She won't do that.

KORD: No, she won't. Because she'll never see you again, if you don't do exactly as I say. I mean exactly.

JEFF: They'll be looking for me.

KORD: People're too lazy, kid. My name's Kord, what's yours?

JEFF: You're crazy.

KORD: You're the one's crazy. You came with me. You don't know me. But I know you. I know you'll end up doing exactly what I say. *(Swipes at him with knife)* Name?

JEFF: Stop it! My name's...my name's Jeff.

KORD: How old are you Jeff?

JEFF: Yer not much older'n me. Why are you doing this to me?

KORD: You'll do as I say. Exactly. *(Swipes at him and nicks him. JEFF screams.)*

JEFF: *(Breaking)* Please, please. Please don't hurt me. *(Falls to ground and puts arms around his knees)*

KORD: You're scared shitless, aren't you? Take off your clothes or I'll cut 'em off. Jeff?

JEFF: *(Pulls off shirt)* There.

KORD: Stand up! I can't see. Get the rest off.

JEFF: *(Pulls off jeans)*

KORD: Get out of the dirt you little shit.

(JEFF gets up on knees, falls back on ground, and takes off shoes.)

KORD: I'm getting mad, and it's interfering with what I can see. Get up and get the rest off!

JEFF: *(Takes off socks)* There. Now can I go? I'm cold. It's cold out here.

KORD: *(Puts knife under JEFF's nose)* You can't stand up to us, can you Jeff? *(Swipes knife at JEFF's legs, draws blood)* Take 'em off.

(JEFF screams and starts to pull off shorts as lights blackout.)

(The woods: KORD confronts a half-dressed new boy. He's a bit younger than JEFF.)

KORD: *(Brandishing knife)* You heard me. Quit stalling!

MIKEY: Why you wanna do this, man? Did Pink Kopeckney put you up to this, man? He's kinda jealous of me cuz LaVonne Hamberger's nice to me. Even tho' I'm younger than her. And he'd kind of like to get next to her but she likes me, I think she does. If it was Pink made you do this to me, man, l can straighten it all out. I'll take him over to her house, too. The both a you. Ain't that a deal? It'll be cool man. LaVonne Hamberger, she's got, you know, out to here. Triple D at least. That's what the guys say. Triple D. Can you imagine what that would feel like? Wouldn't you rather see her than me?

KORD: You're made in God's image.

MIKEY: Huh?

KORD: Didn't God say he made men in God's own image?

MIKEY: He did? When? Hey, we're all the same, man.

KORD: Are we?

MIKEY: This isn't fun anymore.

KORD: When was it fun?

MIKEY: When you said we could get high.

KORD: I'm getting high. *(Swipes knife toward boy's shorts)* Jackpot!

MIKEY: If I take off all my clothes will you put away the knife?

KORD: Take a risk.

MIKEY: I'm tired and hungry.

KORD: You should eat a big breakfast before going off to work.

MIKEY: *(Breaking down)* Didn't have no food in the house.

KORD: *(Cutting his shoulder with knife)* Don't mock me? Get the job done!

MIKEY: You made me bleed.

KORD: You made me mad.

MIKEY: You're crazy.

(KORD cuts him again.)

MIKEY: *(Screams)* Don't! Don't! *(He breaks all the way down and screams.)* Please don't cut me again!

KORD: There are a few things I want to know about you.

MIKEY: Why? What?

KORD: What you'll do when you have no clothes.

MIKEY: This is as far as I go.

KORD: *(Raises knife)* I'm prepared to kill you if you don't take everything off.

(MIKEY takes off undershirt as lights blackout.)

(The woods: KORD and ROYCE , a hyper boy of twelve, are there. ROYCE paces and jumps about.)

ROYCE: Hey, this's no party! This's the dumb outdoors. Hey, I'm gone. It's too noisy.

KORD: We're just a little early.

ROYCE: You said at the 7-11 we were going to a party where this dude had a lot of free video games. I'm into action. I can't stand listening to birds and bees. *(He runs around kicking at dirt.)*

KORD: Don't dig up the dirt. Creatures live under the dirt.

ROYCE: *(Digging faster)* Where, where? I'm hungry. Help me, puke head, help me, grunt nose. Can't you see? *(Screams)* I'm starving!

KORD: What's your problem?

ROYCE: Don't you understand English? You wouldn't, you're from Mars. But I'm a Martian detector. I seen you, when you didn't seen me.

KORD: You talk too fast.

ROYCE: Too bad for you boo-ga-loo. Listen faster. I don't like it here and I don't like you and I hate being hungry. And I hate liars!

KORD: Don't call me a liar, you little jerk-off!

ROYCE: That's fun, isn't it? You ever jerk off in a circle? I beat everyone. Can you beat that? *(Laughs and hits himself)*

KORD: *(Cuffs ROYCE)* Shut up!

ROYCE: I won't shut up. I'm up all the time. I'm always up ain't I little pup? *(Pats his crotch)* I'm going to have you arrested. I don't dig people hitting people!

KORD: You're gonna what?

ROYCE: You got a lower I Q than worms. And speaking of worms, I could eat a plateful. Let's go back to the 7-11 and you can buy me a red hot chili burrito for taking up my time.

KORD: You're a pisser. Where'd you come from?

ROYCE: You said you needed some extra guys for a party. You can't remember nothing. I'm going to report you.

KORD: Shut up or I'll draw and quarter you!

ROYCE: Your head's in quarters, dick nose.

KORD: I can't stand you. Get out of here!

ROYCE: I don't know where I am so how can I get out of here?

KORD: You're totally crazy.

ROYCE: My mother thinks so, too.

KORD: Fer sure!

ROYCE: She took me to the nut inspector and they inspected my nuts and said my nuts were fine, but my mind needed to be refined. I'm gonna get locked up, Tuesday.

KORD: Get lost, ding-a-ling.

ROYCE: I'm Royce! The wrecker! I'll cut off your pecker.

KORD: You gnat, you couldn't cut my nails. You've wasted my time. I can't do anything with a crazy.

ROYCE: I'm going to report you to the thought police. You definitely need some Thorazine.

KORD: You are a total waste! I'm not getting what I want! *(Pulls knife)*

ROYCE: Little pricks like you don't know how to play with knives. Give it to Daddy Royce and I'll cut your hair for the electric chair.

KORD: I can't get worked up.

ROYCE: I want that knife!

KORD: *(Puts knife away)* I'm not gonna show you what my knife can do because you're nothing but a pinball. *(Turns away from* ROYCE*)* I want kids to pee their pants when they see a knife.

ROYCE: *(Pulls a blackjack out of crotch of her pants and slugs him over and over)* Kids like Jeff! Kids like Mikey!

KORD: Get out of my face! I'll kill you, you jerk off!

ROYCE: Not if I kill you first. *(She beats and kicks him down into the dirt. Pulls out cuffs and cuffs his wrists.)*

ROYCE: *(Pushes some buttons on her wrist watch, talks to watch)* Officer Royce reporting in. Yeah... No... Better an ambulance. The scumbag tripped on his own knife. (KORD *moans and stirs. She kicks and slugs him.)* Somebitch! You don't deserve to live on this planet! You don't lie still you'll hurt as bad as you hurt those boys! *(Speaking back into watch radio)* S'okay, I just had to give 'im another tranquilizer. You bet it worked. Shakespeare was right. *(Kisses blackjack)* A codpiece of generous weight and size will rivet gaze and addle judgment every time.

BLACKOUT

BRUSSELS SPROUTS

Janet Neipris

BRUSSELS SPROUTS
© copyright 1995 by Janet Neipris

Janet Neipris's plays have been produced at Arena Stage, the Goodman,
Circle Repertory, Milwaukee Rep, the Women's Project, Philadelphia
Theatre for New Plays, Annenberg Center, Center Stage, and the Manhattan
Theatre Club. She is the author of STATUES, EXHIBITION, THE BRIDGE
AT BELHARBOUR, THE AGREEMENT (P B S Radio, Earplay, Best Short
Plays, 1987), THE DESERT, SEPARATIONS, OUT OF ORDER, ALMOST IN
VEGAS, NOTES ON A LIFE (book, music, and lyrics), 703 WALK HILL,
and A SMALL DELEGATION (W. Alton Jones Production Award, 1992).
For television she has written THE BAXTERS and C B S and A B C pilot
series. She is the recipient of a Shubert Fellowship, an N E A Playwriting
Grant, and a Rockefeller Grant. Chair of the dramatic writing department
at New York University, Tisch School of the Arts, she is a member of PEN,
American Academy of Poets, The League of Professional Theater
Women/NY, the Writers Guild of America, and the Dramatists Guild.

BRUSSELS SPROUTS was originally produced by the League of
Professional Theater Women and published in *The Kenyon Review*.

CHARACTERS

ELLIE BURNS: *Early thirties, a college professor*
BILLY WESTERMAN: *Early thirties, a Sikh*

TIME

Early morning. The present.

(An office in the English department of Harvard University, Cambridge, Mass. ELLIE BURNS sits at her desk, reading a biography of Virginia Woolf, taking notes. The sun streams in the window. The desk is covered with layers of paper— administrative memos, students' work. There are posters on the walls and diplomas. Mozart plays on an old radio on the bookcase. The intercom buzzer sounds twice, startling ELLIE from her reading.)

ELLIE: *(Into the phone)* Is that him? Is that Mr Westerman, my nine-thirty? *(Beat, taking a breath)* You can send him in.... Wait a minute! No! Take three minutes...wait...after five minutes, send him in...wait a minute...God!... Oh, boy! No.This is it. Wait until I buzz you, then send him in. And I won't open the door like I sometimes do. You open the door and I'll be sitting... NO. When the door opens, I'll come out from behind my desk, greet him, then you'll ask if we'd like any coffee.... Oh shit! Just wait for my buzz!

(Hanging up the phone, using the window as a mirror, taking out her lipstick, applying it carefully, when the door opens. Enter BILLY WESTERMAN, dressed in traditional Sikh clothing—white turban, white tunic, leggings, and sandals. He carries a briefcase. The briefcase is the only thing that isn't white.)

ELLIE: My God! I was going to buzz! *(Dropping the lipstick)* BILLY! Is that you?

BILLY: I told your secretary we were old friends, and no, I didn't want a seat. I wanted to see you.

ELLIE:Well I am in total shock

BILLY:Well it's me.

ELLIE: I see it's you. You jerk. You could've written more in five years. Oh God, I feel awful saying "jerk" to you dressed like that. Oh fuck... Oh, I'm sorry.... Jesus!... Wow, God, can I say "Jesus"? *(Beat)* I'm sure "fuck" is out of the question

BILLY: You can say "Buddha" if you want. You can say whatever you want to say. *(Beat)* Why don't you start by asking me to sit down.

(ELLIE gestures to the seat, still in shock, and turns off the radio. He follows her every motion.)

BILLY: You look super. I see a new calmness in your face.

ELLIE: You see shit. You see a wreck. The English department's a pressure cooker. Everyone's writing, publishing, giving papers, being goddamn brilliant. It's insufferable. *(Beat, pointing to his outfit)* What is this? Come on.

BILLY: I'm a Sikh. I finally found my center, El. I found peace.

ELLIE: I thought you were working for *Readers Digest.*

BILLY: Well I was.... But then I did this last year, and when I came to work dressed—as you can see—it didn't wash. Conservative three-buttoners. No imagination there. "Imagination," Einstein said, "is more important than knowledge."

(Silence, then ELLIE holds up a dish of withered grapes on her desk.)

ELLIE: Would you like a grape? I'm afraid they're left over from the faculty meeting. We had cheese and Danish salami too, but all that's left are the grapes.

BILLY: Thanks. It's a little early for me.

ELLIE: *(Nervously eating one withered grape after another)* You know, I can't talk to you looking like this. It's making me very uncomfortable. You mind me saying it's ridiculous for a thirty-three-year-old man.... *(Pointing to his outfit)*

BILLY: I don't mind your saying anything. I don't take offense, nor do I accept flattery. I just like the sound of your voice. *(Beat)* See, same old Billy, same old B S. Be reassured. *(Looking out window)* Hey! You have a view of Memorial Church!

ELLIE: Can you believe I'm too busy to look? *(Beat)* God, that sounds pompous. I mean I adore being dean. You get to take taxis.... What I'm saying is—if I could afford it, I mean I'd chuck it!... Though it's a very solid job. *(Pointing to the desk)* It just involves a lot of paper.

BILLY: Your choice.

ELLIE: I'm not into passing a tambourine in the streets.

BILLY: Those are the Hare Krishnas. The Sikhs believe in hard work. We're farmers and soldiers. We have stores. We sell sandals. Voila! *(Picking up his feet, showing his sandals)* We have a restaurant.

ELLIE: *(Interrupting)* Are you back in Boston for good?

BILLY: They assigned me here. They felt the spirit of the city was in harmony with me. I said it certainly was, when I was in graduate school here in the seventies.

ELLIE: Yes...

BILLY: Memorial Church will never be the same.

ELLIE: No...

BILLY: Not after us.

ELLIE: No…

(Pause)

BILLY: *(Taking some papers out of his briefcase)* I've come about a teaching job in the English department. *(Handing them to* ELLIE*)* My résumé.

ELLIE: *(Taking the résumé without looking at it)* When I was in New York last year, for a conference, I called you at work. You were out for lunch. I left a message. You didn't call back. So I called you at home. A woman answered.

BILLY: Kim.

ELLIE: I don't care who it was. I thought I had the wrong number. I called your parents. I caught your father in. He'd just come from the hospital. He, incidentally, was very nice. He sent me a card after the accident.… I was in a car accident.

BILLY: He told me.

ELLIE: He always liked me, you know.

BILLY: My father has great taste.

ELLIE: The point is, you didn't call back.

BILLY: I had nothing to say.

ELLIE: Well if you had nothing to say, at least you could have said it. *(Beat)* I sent you a real Burberry scarf for your birthday. Not even a thank you.

BILLY: This makes me sad.

ELLIE: Could you not talk like that…like a guru.

BILLY: *(Pause)* I love the scarf. I don't let anyone else wear it.

(Beat)

ELLIE: Who the hell is Kim?

BILLY: The "Struggle and Change" woman. The one who drove up to Seabrook with us, who drew all the signs.

ELLIE: Her! The one who thought she knew me from another life! (BILLY *nods in acknowledgment.)* If you didn't like me anymore, you shouldn't have strung me along with those letters. And then, not even telling me you turned into an Indian!

BILLY: It's not a case of liking. I like carrots, I like Brussels sprouts.…. I just like carrots more

ELLIE: Oh…and I'm the Brussels sprouts.

BILLY: I thought we were pals.

ELLIE: You usually screw around with your pals?... Oh, excuse me...your Brussels sprouts.

BILLY: We made love fifty-three times, before we got caught in the back pew. I said we were praying. The janitor did not believe us.

ELLIE: You counted...but you don't like Brussels sprouts.

BILLY: No! I *like* Brussels sprouts. That's what I'm trying to say.

ELLIE: *(Sarcastically)* But I'm not a carrot. Gee, if I knew you wanted a carrot, I would have tried harder.

BILLY: It has nothing to do with trying. Either you are a carrot, or you are a Brussels sprout. Look, let's not get into it. Just cool it. God, I'm sorry I started with all these vegetables. *(Pause)* I didn't call because I was getting married.

ELLIE: Oh...

BILLY: And we were in the middle of wedding plans. It was a complicated wedding.

ELLIE: I wouldn't know. Your father didn't say a word on the phone.

BILLY: My father wasn't invited.

ELLIE: Boy, you really closed out everyone. *(Pause)* It makes me sad.

BILLY: I wish you wouldn't talk like a guru. *(Beat)*

ELLIE: *(Looking out the window)* Snow... They said flurries this morning.

BILLY: I hope we have a Goddamn blizzard.

ELLIE: I bet Gandhi never said "Goddamn."

BILLY: What I wish is, the snow would come and come and come.

ELLIE: The way storms used to in the old days.

BILLY: Exactly. And we'd be snowed in.

ELLIE: Like in an Emerson essay or a poem by Whittier.

BILLY: Something like that. And then we'd go across the yard to the Church, and we'd open the door, lift the latch, and go around the stairs to Appleton Chapel. The bell would be ringing the hour. We go to the back pew, and the seat is still covered in red velvet.

ELLIE: Thank God for small acts of grace, for something that *hasn't* changed.

BILLY: Then I unbutton your blouse and put my hand...first I take off my turban.

ELLIE: You can do that?

BILLY I can do whatever I want…. And we go back to a place where it was all okay. *(Beat)* Give me a kiss, El. I need a kiss. *(She hesitates.)* Come on.

ELLIE: I'll give you a hug.

BILLY: I don't want a hug. I want a kiss

ELLIE: Well I don't.

BILLY: Well I do.

(He grabs her and kisses her. ELLIE doesn't resist, but there is an absence of passion from her. She pulls away, goes back to her desk, puts on her glasses, and starts reading BILLY's résumé. BILLY speaks as she reads.)

BILLY: Been a long time.

ELLIE: *(Continuing reading)* Eons…much water under the bridge…accidents real and imagined.

BILLY: I'm looking for a position as an instructor in freshman English. You can see by my résumé, I've taught a course at Staten Island Junior College. Also, an editor at *Readers Digest*. After that, I was a driver for one of the carriages in Central Park. Only, my horse died on the hottest day of the summer, ninety-eight degrees. His name was Maggio. They said it was my fault for not feeding him, which you know is ridiculous. I gave him plenty of water and all the carrots he wanted.

ELLIE *(Putting down the résumé)* Listen, Bill. *(Hesitating)* We had three hundred applications last year for two openings in Expo. Our budget's been cut by five percent for next year. *(Pointing out window to main buildings)* And the administration…well, they insist on a PhD. I mean, it *is* Harvard.

BILLY: I know. I identified it by all the ivy. *(Beat)* Well, lucky I'm in the process of completing my thesis

ELLIE: *(Surprised)* On what?

BILLY: *(Pointing to the book on Virginia Woolf)* Well it's quite a coincidence…Virginia Woolf.

ELLIE: I thought you hated Virginia Woolf.

BILLY: I'm working on liking her. *(Beat)* I'm working on a lot of stuff…. Maybe, if you don't have a job, you could at least give me a recommendation on your Harvard stationery. *(Pointing to a pile of stationery on her desk)*

ELLIE: But I don't even know your recent work

BILLY: Then vouch for my character. Say things like "articulate" and "responsible" and "has integrity." …How about "highly original"? *(ELLIE doesn't answer.)* I see success has made you selfish.

ELLIE: Just cautious. *(Pause)* Bill, I have another meeting.

BILLY: You didn't even read my whole résumé.

ELLIE: *(Putting the résumé in her drawer)* I have no job. All the positions are filled. I'll keep it on file. Sometimes people pull out at the last minute, just like that, *(Snapping her fingers)* I really have a ten o'clock appointment with a student.

BILLY: Let the student wait. *(Beat)* I missed you for a long time after we graduated.

ELLIE: Me too… You, too… I like to be punctual. I know it's neurotic. I get so crazy when I run late.

BILLY: Is it because I'm dressed like this?

ELLIE: *(Shaking her head)* It's like…you're carrots, and I'm Brussels sprouts, and more Brussels sprouts is what I need here, which says nothing bad about carrots. *(Beat, making it clear the interview is over)* If you're ever in town… Oh God, you are in town. Well, I'd like to meet Kim…oh God, I have!

BILLY: *(Finally standing, looking out the window)* We're separated.

ELLIE: I'm sorry.

BILLY: No. It's good. *(Nodding to outside window)* End of flurries… No old-fashioned New England blizzard after all.

ELLIE: No. *(The ten o'clock chapel bell begins to ring)* It's ten o'clock.

BILLY: Not till the last bell.

ELLIE: Right. *(Beat)* Not until the very last bell. *(Beat)* I'm sorry. I'm really sorry.

(BILLY stands and waits until the tenth bell rings, and then stops. He starts walking to the door as the lights fade.)

CURTAIN

THE CORD AND THE TRACK

Helen Duberstein

THE CORD AND THE TRACK
© copyright 1988 by Helen Duberstein

Helen Duberstein lives and works in Westbeth Artists Housing in New
York City. Her plays have been performed Off-Off Broadway and in
universities and alternative spaces in the USA, South America, and
Germany. She has been Playwright in Residence with the Circle Repertory
Theater Company and Artistic Advisor to The Theater for the New City.
As president of the Playwrights Group, Inc, she coordinated two festivals of
experimental theater in New York City. She has published essays, reviews,
short stories, and poetry. The working script of MADAM AXE or HOW WE
CREATE will be published by Applause in the *New Radical Theater Notebook*
edited by Arthur Sainer. She is currently at work on a performance piece
with music by Cengiz R Yaltkaya, based on her recently published volume
THE SHAMELESS OLD LADY, selected poems of 1963-1983.

THE CORD AND THE TRACK was first produced by Mark J Roth of the
Westbeth Resident's Performing Arts Center in 1988. It was directed by
Helen Duberstein, and featured Jack Davidson and Jerome Weinstein.

CHARACTERS

BENJAMIN: *A stocky man with a peppered black beard, in his early fifties*

JOE: *A thin man, who is nearly bald; what hair he has is gray.*

SETTING

A table in a deserted diner

JOE: The thing, Benjamin, is the way people look at Celeste and me, not the way I feel, when we walk down the street and my arm is around her.

BEN: Joe, I tell you, I followed, I only followed, the cord into my daughter's room. I had to make a phone call and the phone was in Anna's room. She talks so much and has so many secret things, you know, talks on and on with her girlfriends and all of it so secret it has to be in her room, with the door closed.

JOE: Celeste invited me to her parents' house in Long Island for Thanksgiving dinner.

BEN: Going?

JOE: Of course.

BEN: Of course, you are, you old son of a…Anna's breast was exposed. I couldn't help it. Here. Her left breast. Here. I saw it. It was in my line of vision, where the phone was.

JOE: I told Celeste we could only shake hands in greeting in her parents' home.

BEN: I promised myself I wouldn't look again on my way out.

JOE: Celeste said, You're crazy, Joe. Why? She asked me, why.

BEN: I looked. I haven't seen a breast as beautiful in the twenty years I've been married.

JOE: Jeez, Ben! I have a daughter thirty years old. Celeste's nineteen. She's crazy about me. She lives in Boston and has a boyfriend. You know, I'm glad she lives in Boston and has a boyfriend. I'm glad about that. You know. Really, glad.

BEN: Talk about the boyfriend, Joe.

JOE: Huh?

BEN: Talk about the boyfriend. To the parents. You know. At the dinner. Talk about the boyfriend. Find out, get a line on what they think about the boyfriend.

JOE: Good.

BEN: I mean it.

JOE: I mean it. I'm glad you said it. I'm glad you said that, you know, I'm glad you said that. That's what I'll do. Exactly what I'll do. I'll talk about the boyfriend. I was wondering what to do. Now, I know exactly what I'll do. I'll talk about the boyfriend. Get them to open up.Their opinion of him will give me a line on what to do, how to proceed, what they expect for their little girl. The look she gave me, when I said we'll shake hands. Like this? she said, looking so mock serious I just had to grab her and kiss her right there, right then, right there right then right on the street right on the lips. It's not how I feel, it's how they look. They stare at us, walking so happy, arm in arm. Truth is, I'm glad. I'm glad she has a boyfriend and lives in Boston. Truth is, I don't know what I'd do if she did not have a boyfriend and lived in New York. I love her so. You know, I want a baby. How about that? It just struck me, I want a baby.

BEN: A baby? By Celeste? What about the boyfriend? When are they due to get married? Aren't they...? Joe?

JOE: Not particularly. Not particularly by Celeste, Ben, but a baby. It just struck me, came over me, how wonderful to have a baby, start from beginnings again, wouldn't it be lover—ly? To have a baber—ly?

BEN: Yes. Yes. A brand new baby, a wonderful new wife, Joe, one who makes things so comfortable and sweet when the day's work is done. When you come home, so smiling and cheerful, not that nag who screams and her breasts, ugh.

JOE: Hey, snap out of it, Benjamin. Out of the glow. Out of the dream. God, snap out of it, man, I say. Hey, you complain about supporting those three at home. You showed how your jacket is torn in the lining under the arms and they have everything just so fine.

BEN: The jeans are new. Everything on the bottom is new. Shoes, socks, underwear, just the top of me could do with something new. I'm getting there. Working my way up, ha! ha! My daughters say I'm mean to their mom, Joe.

JOE: Mean to their mom? Mean to their mom? With the phone in her room? Building up the bills? Which is Anna, with the exposed breast. What's the other? What's she like?

BEN: Anna is allowed to sleep without a bra if she wants to. I told my wife Anna can sleep anyway she wants to. The phone has a long cord that stretches into both of their rooms. Anna doesn't have to drag it into her room to talk when she knows I have early morning business calls to make. God, what a breast. For such a breast. The other? The other? What's she like? Gwendolyn is always screaming about borrowing Anna's hair dryer, or her mother's. I ought to buy her one of her own, I guess. Each one is entitled to their own hair dryer, I guess, otherwise there's a lot of quarrelling as to which bedroom the hair dryer is in and when I have to start looking for the hair dryer in my daughters' room, that will be the last straw.

JOE: You have a hair dryer of your own?

BEN: I didn't say that. But, looking for Celeste's hair dryer in Gwendolyn's room...

JOE: Celeste?

BEN: Anna. I mean Anna, of course. Anna, all along.

JOE: Celeste.

BEN: Celeste?

JOE: Yes, you're right. She wants me to meet her parents, for God's sake. I'll ask them how they like the, her fiancé. That's a good ploy. That way I can get to know....

BEN: Trim your beard.

JOE: No. No. I'm going just the way I am.

BEN: It's gray, and you're bald. If you shave your beard....

JOE: I'm going just the way I am. That's what Celeste says, what she likes about me, that I'm so real.

BEN: You gonna shake hands?

JOE: Yeah. Yeah. That's what I said, what I told her. As to Celeste's parents. Yes. At her parents' house, with her fiancé there, we'll shake hands, Hello, and we will shake hands, Goodbye, when I leave.

BEN: She'll giggle and throw herself into your arms.

JOE: She won't. Celeste won't.

BEN: You'll see.

JOE: You think so? Maybe. Giggle, yes, but start mauling me, you mean, right there, with the old folks... Nah.

BEN: I can see it. I can just see the scene. Old folks, not so old folks, she's nineteen, you say.

JOE: Christ, I have a daughter almost twice Celeste's age. It's not the way I feel, you know. That's OK. It's the way people look at us. Christ! Her parents. She insisted. They're both alcoholics. What a thing, and me ten years sober, me. What a scene. Picture it. One hundred miles out on the Island. Shake her hand. Hello, good night, goodbye.

BEN: You should stay the night.

JOE: They asked me. But, no. No. Even if she looks at me, you know, that way, and I'm all melted up inside of me. You know. Like, I'm off, crazy, you know. She's so mad about me. Can't keep her hands off me.

BEN: Oh?

JOE: No. Oh, no. She's sweet, I tell you. Very, very sweet. Sweet. On me. She loves me. Wanted me there. At the table. One hundred miles out, on the railroad track, choo choo choo. What a thing. What a place. Picture it, me, there, beard just the way you see it, me so real, so real, she keeps saying, I'm so real.

CURTAIN CALL

Roma Greth

CURTAIN CALL

Roma Greth is not only a playwright and novelist, she is an accomplished writer of short stories, articles, and advertising copy. She is a member of the Writers Guild, The Dramatists Guild, Theater Association of Pennsylvania, Mystery Writers of America, and the American Crime Writers League. Her published mystery novels are NOW YOU DON'T and PLAIN MURDER. Her plays have been widely performed at theaters such as Syracuse Stage; Academy Theater in Atlanta; Washington, D C and Los Angeles feminist theaters; women's prison and drug rehab programs (with inmate participation); Second Stage, L A; and A D T Theaters in L A. In New York City her work has been seen at WPA, IRT, Playwrights Horizons, Shelter West, and Playwrights Preview Productions, among others.

Honors and awards include a fellowship at the O'Neill Theatre Conference, the Aspen Playwrights Conference, and the Erie, PA Playwrights Festival. She is a winner of the Scene Award, University of Miami Playwrights Award, Bicentennial Playwrighting Award of Washington-area Feminist Theatre, and three Pennsylvania Council for the Arts grants. Her play, WINDFALL APPLES, is published by Broadway Play Publishing.

CURTAIN CALL was originally produced at the WPA Theater, NY NY, in 1982.

CHARACTERS

RUTHIE MILLAY: *A late-middle-age actress*

VOICE

(The scene is a dressing room of a sterile and new theater, in some center city art complex built of cement and tiles. There is a phone, dressing table, a few chairs, perhaps a chaise. And somewhere a persistent leak that drips from the ceiling. There is a commotion outside this room, in the corridor, beyond a door with a gold star on it. These are the sounds of reporters and fans. RUTHIE comes bursting into the room, escaping the confusion outside. She is an energetic woman wearing a wig of long curls, heavy theatrical eyelashes, a star-shaped beauty spot, and other makeup. All this is professionally applied, plentiful, and does its job of simulating youth as well as it can. Her figure is still good. Her outfit is expensive, modern, flamboyant. She is speaking as she comes on stage.)

RUTHIE: Oh. There's a show they're just begging me to do…a Broadway revival nobody's thought of in years. But it's much too early to talk about that, darling—What?— So if my last husband turns out to be the producer what's wrong with that?— I have absolutely nothing against him or any of my husbands— My TV series was not cancelled by the network! I bowed out because I wanted room to expand my talents— No. No! Sorry, but I haven't had a minute to myself in weeks!— Cocktail parties—interviews— I need an hour to myself before it's time to get ready for the show!

(RUTHIE slams shut the door and leans against it; sounds outside fade away; for an instant she seems in a state of collapse, then slowly straightens. Her eyes wander about the room, coming to rest on the dripping water, regular as a clock. She goes to the drip, looks up, cannot see what is causing it.)

Somebody's fucking toilet is overflowing.

(She spots the phone and stalks to it, dials impatiently.)

Hello, darling. This is Ruthie Millay in the star dressing room.…
Oh, did you! It was one of my best performances, don't you think? …
Listen, darling, I have a leak.… In my dressing room… If I want a shower, I'll use the bathroom. So will YOU get a plumber upstairs to see what is wrong up there? …What? …Ten million dollars to build this Civic Center Art Complex and the fucking fountain on the patio leaks? …Well, put me in another room. It doesn't have to have a star on the door.… You mean all the dressing rooms leak? …The reflecting pool extends over the entire length of the dressing room area and it seeps through …Well. why don't you people fill in the damn thing? It's full of litter anyhow!... You'll send down a bucket? Thanks, maybe I will have to throw up before I get out of here.

(Hangs up the phone)

I don't know—maybe it's me. It can't be the whole rest of the world.

(Gets a flask out of her bag)

That thing is like a Chinese water torture.

(Takes a small swig, then the flask is empty)

Oh. crap.

(At the phone again)

Hello again, darling. This is Ruthie. Listen, does anybody around here know where I can get a drink? I think my flask has sprung a leak too.... I mean, I want a bottle...as soon as possible, sonny.

(Hangs up)

At least it's good to know they speak English. I wasn't sure they did this far from New York.

(Looking at drip)

I wouldn't mind if it were Scotch.

(Testing the depth of the puddle on the floor)

I could drown before show time.... I wouldn't mind if it were Scotch. Concentrate, Ruthie. On something else. Then you won't even notice it.

(Into mirror)

Because you, Ruthie, can do anything, girl. Imagination, go to work! There is no drip here.

(She looks, it is still dripping; she closes her eyes, gestures theatrically.)

There is no drip. I will not see a drip. I will not see it.

(She opens her eyes; the drip stops.)

Aha! Told you there was no leak in here!

(She turns away, the drip starts again; turns back, pointing a finger at it.)

Stop! I command you—cease. Desist!

(The drip continues.)

How dare you? Don't you know we of the theater create fantasies— miracles are part of our everyday lives. Well...the old miracles have been sort of—tired—lately. And the old magic went to Off Off Broadway or someplace. Sure as hell hasn't been with this show.

(She gets a rosary from her bag and hangs it over the mirror.)

The best song in the whole damn show didn't even go over in Louisville. What's wrong? What—the—hell—is—wrong?

(She does a little "da-dum" singing and practices a few dance steps.)

Maybe if I play right to the audience like Ann-Margret does— Chees, maybe if I had the shape Ann-Margret has... Oh, well.

(At phone)

Hello? Sonny, any musicians around here that I can use for half an hour? ...I mean, that could help me go over that first act finale ... Well, besides a seventy-nine-year-old drummer and a piano player with missing teeth... Forget it.

(Hangs up)

So who needs them? I was the greatest camedienne—What am I saying! I *am* the greatest comedienne ever reviewed in *Variety*! Momma thought she was teaching me to be a tight rope walker.

(Walking an imaginary rope)

But what she was really teaching me was to be—funny.

(She carries on, out of balance, nearly falling. She dials an imaginary phone.)

Hey, Daddy, it's your little girl. I'm tired of Momma and the circus, so how about taking me along on your next gig?... I may be young but I'm funny! Ruthie, girl comedienne!

(She winds down, wanders to the mirror.)

Okay, Ruthie. So the TV series bombed—you've bombed before. Remember how the elephants in the circus hated your act? You've still got your health and your looks. Hey—get a load of that shape. Well, maybe a sexpot you ain't but in a one-woman show who's going to compare? If this tour's a success you can play the Palace in New York. "Ruthie at the Palace." Original cast album. The Palace is still there, Ruthie—and so are you, my girl. So get it together!

(Picks up phone)

Sonny, get me an outside line. You find a bottle yet? ...Well, keep looking.

(Dials a long-distance number)

Hello. This is your Garage Door of the Month Club. If you had answered this phone with any four-letter Anglo-Saxon expletive you'd have won a garage door a month for twelve months, in different designs of your choice, plus twelve free garage doors, plus a two-transistor radio made in New Jersey...You guessed... You were going to call me? It's my E S P thing, Freddy—goes along with my imagination.... Well, I have this terrific idea! I mean, the boondocks are okay when you're on your way up but this is the kind of place where I stand up and I'm overdressed in a denim bathing suit so—I think we should come into New York. Play the Palace! Garland did it before she died so why not me?... What?... Listen, I'm the one who's supposed to be cracking the lousy jokes...it's no joke? Freddy, you can't cancel my tour! Think of all the tickets that have been sold... There were no tickets sold?... Listen, it's the promotion! People know me—from my T V series.... Okay, so it only lasted a month, maybe they'll bring it back. Maybe... Who told you audiences have been walking out on me?... Oh, she did? Well, some stage manager she is. All she does is stand around making anti-nuke signs with her knuckles.... But, Freddy; what am I going to do?... I divorced him.... So what if he was making a fortune selling furniture for hotels, restaurants, and shoe stores, I didn't want alimony.... I want my career!... Freddy, go fuck yourself... Don't worry about me. I can take it. I get pimples, but I can take it.

(Slams down phone)

Boy, I'd better be able to take it. There's a lot of it here.

(Going to drip)

It wouldn't be so bad if the water were leaking from a pipe up there. I could throw a rope over the damn thing and hang myself. Boy, what a fate. To end up in Georgia under a leaky fountain. Somehow it lacks the dignity that usually closes a great career. Where's the curtain call? At least Judy Carne used to get buckets of water thrown at her on *Laugh-In*. All I get is a small drip... *Laugh-In*!— What made me think of—? Does anybody still remember *Laugh-In*? My God... Show business is so—transient.... Oh, shit... Hey, Ruthie Girl, did you hear the one about...the one about...the...wow. I—Damn you all to hell. Freddy—you cancelled my tour! It was the only thing left. Oh...it's not Freddy's fault. It's just—Ruthie in her wig and her ten-ton eyelashes ain't got her ratings no more. Girl Comedienne Lays Egg.

(Gets a chair and places it directly beneath the drip. She sits.)

They say water wears away the hardest rock. So maybe it'll do something for my head. I think I'll just sit here until the drip kills me.

(She sits still for a second, then rises and pushes away the chair.)

It ain't funny, Ruthie! The schtick ain't funny no more!

(She takes her rosary.)

Hail, Mary...Holy Mary, Mother of God... Help! Look, I've always donated. I mean, us women got to stick together. You know? You must have been through plenty in your time. What did those guys know? Joseph and the boys and the Disciples. You had your share of lumps. I don't even think Mary Magdalene was much help. Oh, you know what I mean. I am one girl in trouble, Mary, or I wouldn't bother you. Who else can I talk to?

(The door opens and closes without anyone entering. RUTHIE stares, dumbfounded. Her eyes follow an unseen presence to a chair.)

Wow…what'll I do now? I mean, you invite some people, you don't
expect them to show up. Uh… Well…hi! I mean, hello. How's the family?—
I didn't mean that the way it sounded maybe. I'm sure the family's okay—
I mean, that's what heaven's all about, right? Hey, what'll I call you?…
When I prayed, I always called you "Mary" but somehow in person like
this…. Come to think of it, I don't even know your last name. Look, if you
want to say something to me I'll gladly shut up and listen. You're not—
going to just sit there and stare at me, are you? You are.

(There is a knock on the door.)

Oh, my God!—No. No! I didn't mean that. Not God. This isn't even a
church. It looks more like a mausoleum.

VOICE: Miss Millay, here's your bottle.

RUTHIE: You're bringing holy water around? Oh—my bottle!

(Opens door and takes a bottle of Scotch)

Thanks. Can't talk now. Got company.

(Slams shut the door)

Uh….

(Holds out the bottle to Mary, then quickly brings it back again)

Gee, I'm sorry. I…

(She puts the bottle in a drawer of the dresser.)

Guess I don't really need any more of that. Well. Now. You sure don't look
like I thought you would. I always sort of pictured you—more like a statue.
You're a lot heavier and darker. Uh, don't get me wrong. Nothing's the
matter with being dark complexioned. And you're not fat. God, no. Heaven,
no. Uh—no. I like your outfit. I thought it would be blue but prints are nice,
too…. Well. You want to hear about it? After all, I did pray.

(Looking)

Okay. You know who I am? Maybe you don't, huh? Compared to some of
the superstars you know I guess I'm— Well, I've been in show biz for a long
time. Little Ruthie, Girl Comedienne? Maybe you saw me on those feminine
protection commercials. It's my whole life—not feminine protection! I don't
expect you to understand that—except you understand everything, don't
you? You know, I wish you'd say something. Feel like a jerk standing here
talking to you like this. Aren't you going to say anything? You talked to St
Bernadette and to St Joan. I know those times you appeared in London you
didn't say anything—but I thought maybe that was because— Well, you
know how the British are. A little hard to talk to. Like my agent.You should
try getting something across to him. Listen, you need an agent, let me give

you sane advice. Don't get Freddy. He couldn't book you into Bethlehem for a one-night gig. It was a guy like Freddy probably took care of your hotel reservations for your trip. Listen to me. I'm telling you. I don't want to be telling you. I want you to tell me. You get to a point you need somebody to tell you what to do. Like you. Or even Buddha, I guess, if he's what you're into. Oh. I'm sorry— Guess I shouldn't have mentioned another act like that. I keep saying such dumb things to you. You know...you're really beautiful. I mean that. You're older than I thought you'd be but you're very...l don't know—your face. Those eyes... Please don't keep staring at me like that. Like if I don't get hold of myself I might not make it out there on stage tonight for my last show. I might just lock myself in here—just you and me and the waterfall—until they come and get me out and haul me off to the great big playpen— Will you stop staring at me! What's the matter with me?... My wig? Don't you like my wig? Well...maybe it's not the greatest—but believe me, it wasn't cheap!

(Removes the wig and puts it aside)

Is that better? No? Well, now what? —You don't like my false eyelashes?

(She peels off the eyelashes.)

Now why'd I do that? You're ruining my looks! I'm not going to talk to you anymore. Because I'll tell you a secret. You're not there. I know you're not really there, so quit staring at me.

(Speaking into an imaginary mike)

This is Ruthie Normal, girl guide, speaking to you from down here in the sewer pipes under your civic center. Our next point of interest, ladies and gents, will be the grotto built in honor of Our Lady of Urban Decay.

(Rushing to Mary and kneeling)

I'm sorry! I didn't mean it. It's just.... Well, they cancelled my T V show. And my tour. But I'm not ready to pack it all in, Mary. They want to bury you before you're dead in this country! Everything comes with the word "young" in front of it. What're you staring at now? This? Oh. It's just a beauty spot—supposed to highlight my best feature.... Well, everybody used to wear them.

(She removes the beauty spot, looks at Mary, then goes to her mirror. During the following, she removes her makeup.)

Listen. You know what I used to do when I was a kid? Used to think up stories. About this big collie dog. "If Christ Had a Collie" I called them. I can see it. Walking on the water— He'd reach back and pick up the collie and carry him. And the fishes and loaves of bread story. The collie'd carry the basket in her teeth. It'd have to be a collie, you know. That's the only kind of dog Christ would have. When He prayed in Gethsemane the collie'd be sitting very still beside Him and He wouidn't have been so alone.... And then on the way to Calvary, the collie'd be walking along beside the cross He had to carry—I'm sorry! Look, I didn't mean to upset you. Please, He's not here on earth any more. All that was over a long time ago.... Boy, really said it, didn't I? "It was over a long time ago."'

(She observes herself closely in the mirror.)

But I—Mary, I look so old. Nobody's going to recognize me! I mean, I'd have to get a new routine. Old jokes. Well, new old jokes. I'd have to get a whole new stage personality. I'd have to get their sympathy for—older people. I'd have to admit to myself and everybody else that I'm not a kid anymore! Maybe—even tell them how old I am ... I can't do it!... Can I?—Mary...? Where is she? Hey, you can't just walk out like this! I know they must keep you pretty busy but— She reminds me of my audiences lately.

(Slowly RUTHIE *picks up her imaginary microphone.)*

Hello again. This is Ruthie Millay, woman.

BLACKOUT

THE DEATH OF
HUEY NEWTON

Lynda Sturner

THE DEATH OF HUEY NEWTON
© copyright 1992 by Lynda Sturner

LYNDA STURNER began as an actress in the theater, appearing in OLIVER
on Broadway and THE EFFECTS OF GAMMA RAYS ON MAN-IN-THE-
MOON MARIGOLDS Off-Broadway. She is the founder and producing
director of Playwright's Forum Inc, and produced THE JUNIPER TREE
and SEPARATES Off-Broadway. She teaches an acting workshop for writers
in N Y C and Truro, MA. She is vice-president of the board of directors of
Music Theatre Group and past co-president of the League of Professional
Theatre Women. She was graduated from Boston University's School of the
Arts in 1963. Her plays have been read at The Women's Project, The Actors
Studio, Circle Repertory, Playmarket, and The Provincetown Art
Association. Ms Sturner is currently working on a full-length play called
ALMOST SISTERS. She lives in New York City.

THE DEATH OF HUEY NEWTON is one in a series of ten-minute plays written under the title TEN-MINUTE COUPLES. Another play from that series, OATMEAL, was part of short play festival benefit for Broadway Cares, Equity Fights AIDS, in May 1993 at the Marymount Theatre.

THE DEATH OF HUEY NEWTON was presented as a reading by the Women's Project and Productions at La Mama Galleria on 24 April 1994, as part of a series called "Relative Strangers".

SUZANNA . . . . .Jacqualine Knapp
MICHAEL . . . . .Jack Davidson
Director . . . . Bryna Wortman

CHARACTERS

SUZANNA: *A forty-nine-year-old psychologist. She had been part of the radical student movement at Berkeley in the sixties. She is now the mother of an eighteen-year-old girl named Starshine and married to* MICHAEL.

MICHAEL: *A fifty-three-year-old successful artist. He had been* SUZANNA's *art teacher at Berkeley. They have been married for twenty-two years.*

TIME: The present

PLACE: A Soho loft in New York City

(Music plays "Good Morning Starshine".)

(SUZANNA and MICHAEL are having breakfast in their Soho loft. They each have their own New York Times. *MICHAEL is reading the front page. SUZANNA pours him coffee and watches him reading his paper; she is working up the courage to speak.)*

SUZANNA: Where were you last night?

MICHAEL: *(Tenses, looks at her, then looks down at the paper)* Did you see this? Huey Newton died.

SUZANNA: He died...

MICHAEL: Huey P Newton...it's right here in the paper...front page of *The New York Times.*

SUZANNA: No. How he'd die?

MICHAEL: Wait a minute...I'm still reading.

SUZANNA: I can't believe Huey Newton's dead. How'd he die?

MICHAEL: Would you let me finish the article please. You can read it yourself. You've got your own paper.

SUZANNA: Oh, right... *(She looks at her paper.)* Where is it?

MICHAEL: Weren't you listening? I said the front page... bottom left hand...*(She looks right.)* left Suzanna.

SUZANNA: Oh...they have a picture...it's a nice picture. I forgot what he looked like...it says, he was shot to death early yesterday at the age of forty-seven on a street in Oakland, California.

MICHAEL: Forty-seven years old. Huey Newton was forty-seven years—

SUZANNA: Did you know he had a PhD in social philosophy from the University of California at Santa Cruz?

MICHAEL: I'm trying to read about it right now.

SUZANNA: I wonder if I still have my Free Huey button. I voted for him in 1968. Remember when he ran for president?

MICHAEL: You didn't vote for Huey Newton...it was Bobby Seale.

SUZANNA: You're right...no, it was the other one...what was his name? He wrote the book.

MICHAEL: What book?

SUZANNA: The book about the Black Panthers. You know…BURN THIS.

MICHAEL: That was Abbie Hoffman.

SUZANNA: No it wasn't. Abbie Hoffman wrote STEAL THIS BOOK. Remember they were afraid to put it in the stóres.

MICHAEL: Abbie Hoffman also wrote BURN THIS.

SUZANNA: No…Jerry Rubin wrote BURN THIS.

MICHAEL: Abbie Hoffman's dead too, you know.

SUZANNA: I thought he was working on Wall Street.

MICHAEL: That's Jerry Rubin. Abbie Hoffman committed suicide.

SUZANNA: So who wrote that book that I can't remember the name of?

MICHAEL: I don't know what you're talking about.

SUZANNA: We voted for him for president…you know…in 1968… instead of Hubert Humphrey…afterwards you said it was like a vote for Nixon voting for…you know…what's his name? Is it warm in here ?

MICHAEL: I'm freezing. You have the air conditioning on high again.

SUZANNA: What was his name? I can't remember anything anymore.

MICHAEL: You have to stop taking Halcion.

SUZANNA: Then how do you suggest I get to sleep at night?

MICHAEL: Eldridge Cleaver…that's the one you're thinking of.

SUZANNA: Right. And he wrote SOUL ON ICE. What an incredible title. SOUL ON ICE. Huey Newton's dead. Remember that rally?

MICHAEL: We never made it to the rally.

SUZANNA: I wanted to go.

MICHAEL: You didn't tell me that.

SUZANNA: I was shy. I didn't know you that well then.

MICHAEL: We had just spent a week together. We never left the studio. Shy was not the word I would use to describe you that week.

SUZANNA: I was just getting to know you. I mean I didn't want to hurt your feelings…. If you thought that I felt that the demonstration was more important to me than being with you…

MICHAEL: Give me a break Suzanna… You hardly let me get up to go to the bathroom that first week.

SUZANNA: Yeah...well...sure...ah...yeah...that was a great week.

MICHAEL: Remember that poster of him...sitting in that big wicker chair with a gun in one hand and a spear in the other.

SUZANNA: ...The Huey Newton Chair. But I liked the poster you designed for the march better.

MICHAEL: You seduced me into designing that poster.

SUZANNA: You got me stoned. I was an eighteen-year-old freshman asking my art teacher to help us...

MICHAEL: You came into my studio carrying the biggest joint I'd ever seen in my life...rolled in American flag paper. You said it was Acapulco Gold.

SUZANNA: Did I?

MICHAEL: Don't you remember?

SUZANNA: Sort of.

MICHAEL: You moved in.

SUZANNA: You asked me to.

MICHAEL: God you were beautiful...

SUZANNA: Then...

MICHAEL: Don't finish my sentences for me please, Suzanna. You're still a good-looking woman.... You could lose a few pounds. I don't look the way I did twenty-three years ago either.

SUZANNA: It's not fair. You got better looking.

MICHAEL: Twenty-three years.

SUZANNA: You never actually said will you stay. But you didn't tell me to leave either. I mean if you wanted me to leave you could have said something.

MICHAEL: And lose my Acapulco Gold connection...are you kidding?

SUZANNA: I had a dream the other night that we were never married. That we'd just been living together all these years.

MICHAEL: We were married.

SUZANNA: I know that. I was talking about a dream.

MICHAEL: Suzanna... *(With great difficulty starts to tell her, but* SUZANNA *doesn't want to hear it)*

SUZANNA: So...Huey Newton's dead.

MICHAEL: Dead. *(Silence)*

SUZANNA: Think they'll have a memorial service?

MICHAEL: I don't know.

SUZANNA: They have to do something.

MICHAEL: Who's they?

SUZANNA: What does it say?

MICHAEL: You've got the article right in front of you...you tell me.

SUZANNA: It says he's survived by his wife, a son, two daughters, three brothers, and three sisters. They'll have to do something.

MICHAEL: You want to call his wife and invite yourself? Tell her you're sorry you missed the march but you're available for the funeral.

SUZANNA: We could take Starshine with us.... She has freshman orientation next week. Stanford is right across the bay from Oakland...we could all fly out early.... You could come too.

MICHAEL: She asked us not to call her Starshine any more. You know how she feels about her name.

SUZANNA: I can't get used to...to calling her Jane. I understand why she wanted to change it. I know that but...why not Jennifer, Melissa, or Vanessa even...

MICHAEL: You had your shot at naming her. Let go of it now. You can never let go.

SUZANNA: I let go...I've let go of a lot of things...all these years. Believe me there's not much left that I'm holding on to.

MICHAEL: Now what am I being blamed for?

SUZANNA: I'm not blaming you. I'm talking about Huey Newton, Bobby Seale, and all the others who opened our lives.....made us believe things were going to change. When Lyndon Johnson passed the Civil Rights bill we thought blacks and whites were finally...were going to be able to relate to each other as people.

MICHAEL: Huey Newton said, "We do believe in self-defense for ourselves and for black people" He's quoted right here in *The New York Times*. I don't see him saying anything about blacks and whites relating. But anyway nothing's changed. What's changed?

SUZANNA: The way we think about things has changed. Star...Jane...Jane has opportunities it took me years to take advantage of. I didn't....

MICHAEL: Jane has obligations. She's working so hard she never has time for anything. She doesn't read for pleasure or go to a museum...she's a beautiful young girl...she should be out having fun. She spent four years in high school buried in books so she could get into college where's she's going to have to do the same thing for another four years...and maybe graduate school. When she's gonna get a chance to have a life?

SUZANNA: This is her life...her work...she enjoys....

MICHAEL: She's only eighteen years old. I see her taking on...she's shouldering all the unbearable responsibilities I've been carrying all my life....

SUZANNA: What are you talking about? What do you want for her?

MICHAEL: It has nothing to do with what I want. She's driven...she has to become someone...do something with her life.

SUZANNA: What's so wrong with that. I did...so did you.... You managed to do what you wanted...you're an artist...we both work...we did it.... You're not a lawyer or an accountant or any of those other things your father wanted you to be.

MICHAEL: No. But I always felt that I should...that somehow I was shortchanging you and Jane by doing...a grown-up man doesn't play with paints.

SUZANNA: But you love your work.

MICHAEL: I don't love my work. You love being married to an artist.

SUZANNA: You were an artist before I met you.

MICHAEL: I was a graduate student. I didn't know what I wanted. I had a small talent and managed to get a job as a teaching assistant. It was a way of avoiding the draft...and going to Viet Nam. I never considered this would be my life's work. You saw my studio and fell in love with me. No girl had ever looked at me like that before. I was afraid I'd lose you if I told you I wasn't really a painter.

SUZANNA: And now you're no longer afraid of losing me.

MICHAEL: You're putting words in my mouth again Suzanna.

SUZANNA: It's not my fault, Michael, that you're an artist.

MICHAEL: I didn't say it was. I was trying to explain to you some of my feelings...you always accuse me of being so closed off. So I'm doing that sharing stuff you think is so important Suzanna...as you say in your profession I'm...

SUZANNA: Oh...so that's what you're doing, sharing...I see....

MICHAEL: I was trying to talk to you.... I was very struck by the way you told me you wanted to go to that rally. Why did it take you twenty-three years to tell me that?

SUZANNA: It didn't take me twenty-three years to talk about this. I didn't spend twenty-three years of my life brooding over that I never got to go to the Free Huey rally. I'd forgotten about it until this morning when I...when you showed me the paper. I'm not the one who...oh shit...Michael...I... why is it that I feel somehow responsible...and what are we talking about. You've had a...have a successful career. You're represented by one of the most important galleries in New York...you're an artist, Michael. You want to tell Mary Boone that you'd rather be an orthodontist?

MICHAEL: Why do you turn everything I say into a personal attack?

SUZANNA: Because you just told me that I made you become an artist... that if it hadn't been for me and my needs you...

MICHAEL: I was telling you how much I loved you then. How I felt about you when you walked into my studio that day asking me to design a Free Huey poster.

SUZANNA: That day...then...oh.

MICHAEL: I was.

SUZANNA: Oh I see.... I didn't hear that.

MICHAEL: You weren't listening. People pay you lots of money to listen to them. I thought that was one of your skills. It's late. I have to get to the studio. The morning's....

SUZANNA: Did you wake Jane?

MICHAEL: No...did you?

SUZANNA: Shit...she has to get to work. I better wake her.

(SUZANNA *walks to the door.*)

MICHAEL: I have to run. I'll probably be working late tonight. I'll call you.... Don't sing "Good Morning Starshine" to her... it drives her her crazy.

SUZANNA: I don't do that anymore.

MICHAEL: Did you hear me say I'll probably be working late tonight?

SUZANNA: I heard you. I was listening Michael.

MICHAEL: Are you going to tell her about Huey Newton?

SUZANNA: She doesn't know who he is. Besides...what's the point... Huey Newton's dead.

(*Music cue: Judy Collins sings "Suzanne".*)

CURTAIN

DRY SMOKE

Adele Edling Shank

DRY SMOKE
© copyright 1995 by Adele Edling Shank

Please see page 2 for a bio of Adele Edling Shank.

CHARACTERS

MAN
HELEN

(A woman sits on a chair near a desk. She appears calm. A man in an ordinary suit sits at the desk. Among the clutter on the desk are a cassette tape recorder, newspaper, steno notebook, and pencils. The tape recorder is playing and the MAN *and* WOMAN *are listening. He is watching her. She is not looking at him.)*

HELEN'S RECORDED VOICE: I don't know why I couldn't sleep. I don't sleep well, I never have really, not since I was a child.

(The MAN *stops the playback by pushing the "Stop" button, then the "Fast Forward", then the "Stop" button, then the "Play" button.)*

HELEN'S RECORDED VOICE: …very stuffy. I can't be sure what woke me, but I think it was just the heat. You see, I hadn't opened my window because I thought it was going to rain. I got out of bed and went to the window. No, first I put on my bedroom slippers. Not my robe, because it was so hot. I opened the window about six inches and then I took off my slippers and laid down. I didn't even get under the sheet. The pale blue sheets with the bright blue cornflowers embroidered on the hem. My sister did them just before she died. Some of the stitches were off because her hands were so shaky. She always did such….

(On the tape HELEN *realizes she is digressing. There is a pause.)*

HELEN: *(Live)* I don't understand what you want me to say. I've already….

HELEN'S RECORDED VOICE: I know. I'm sorry. After I opened the window, I laid down again and I must have dozed off. I remember I heard Frank walking downstairs and that usually means that I've been dozing. When I'm half asleep I often hear him in the kitchen. Or on the stairs. So I can't be sure how I first knew something was wrong. Whether it was Frank I heard, or whether I smelled something.

HELEN: Yes. Yes, I see what you mean. But that's not what I meant. I didn't mean to say that there was someone else in the house, that someone… I mean, I thought I heard Frank in the kitchen. But as soon as I thought I heard him, I knew it couldn't be him. I mean, if you know when you think you hear something that that's impossible, then it's not the same thing as…. *(Trailing off)* It's not as if…

(The MAN *shuts off the tape recorder.* HELEN *sighs, tries to order her thoughts, and starts again with renewed commitment. The* MAN *turns on the tape recorder when she speaks.)*

HELEN: I mean if you think you hear something, and at the same time you know you don't really hear it, then it's not the same…I don't see what difference it makes anyway. It's not as if I'm trying to blame someone, to say it was someone's fault. It wasn't. I know that. I…I didn't hear anyone. Just Frank. It's…I'm not really being as silly as it sounds. It's that… You see, sometimes I really do hear Frank. *(Looking at her hands)* I mean, he walked in the kitchen, up and down those stairs, so many times. So many pick up the foot, put it down, all over that house, so many years. It's like there's a kind of ghost of the sound.

(Pause. HELEN studies her hands. The MAN turns off the tape recorder and waits. HELEN sighs.)

HELEN: All right. But you have to understand. We lived there thirty-seven years. He's only been gone…a long time, thirty-seven years. It was a long time.

(Silence. The MAN leans back in his chair. HELEN looks at him.)

HELEN: But I don't see why I have to keep going over and over this.

(The MAN leans forward again.)

HELEN: *(A little angry)* I was dozing. I heard Frank.

(The MAN turns on the tape recorder and HELEN speaks in a rush.)

HELEN: I woke up. I smelled the smoke. I got out of bed, I went downstairs, and I left the house.

(The MAN turns off the tape recorder. He picks up a newspaper and leans back in his chair and starts to read. HELEN looks at him helplessly. She regains her control.)

HELEN: All right. I woke up. It took me a minute or so to realize that what I was smelling was smoke.

(The MAN turns on the tape recorder. He puts his newspaper aside and looks at HELEN as she speaks. She describes the destruction without sentiment.)

HELEN: It smelled funny. Peculiar. Not like smoke when you burn the trash. Like vaporized dust. I suppose it was because everything was so old. Very old. The house was so full of…my nephew calls it the museum. It wasn't a large house really, not large enough for all…you could hardly move around. I kept…they kept leaving…leaving things to me. The things my grandmother brought over with her on the boat. My mother's things. My sister's things. Everything old. The smoke was light, not heavy like burning damp leaves, but light like dust. Light and dry. I could hear the fire crackle even before I was out of bed. I put on my slippers. I don't know why. Habit I suppose. Anyway, I put on my slippers and I went downstairs. I was…too late. The fire was eating everything. The sideboard with the silver and china. The chest where all the linens were. The table and the

chairs with mother's needlepoint seats, and the desk my father made. He was a cabinet maker you see, after he left the farm. He made all the furniture in the house. Enough for three houses really. All old. Except the television. That was almost new. But it's gone too. It's all gone. It's not red you know. Did you know that? The flames aren't red. I always thought they would be. But they aren't. No color really. Except around the edges. I suppose it sounds as if I were standing around watching it all. I didn't of course. I just took one look to see if there was anything I could do and of course I saw right away that there wasn't and I'd better get out of there. I should have gotten out sooner, I could have been.... So I ran out in front...yes I did have on my robe then,
I don't know why, I guess it was habit. I ran out in front to get help and my neighbors were coming from across the street. They said they had already called the fire department.

(The MAN *reaches toward the pile of tape cassettes on the desk.)*

HELEN: Yes, I know my neighbors said that they heard a kind of explosion, a sort of pouf! But I don't know what that could have been. I certainly didn't hear anything. I was lying on my bed. I was asleep. I didn't hear anything. And I didn't have the light on! Why would I have the light on, lying on my bed asleep. The fire was so bright, it lit everything with white hot light. It shattered the glass on the photographs and all those dead faces disappeared. It melted the wax on the furniture and blistered the finish, wax swam on the blisters. There were thousands of little pops as the teacups cracked. All the china shattered. And the silver, molten silver dripped off the tea service. It was just plate you know. Mother always claimed it was solid sterling, but it wasn't. I put on my slippers and I went downstairs and everything was flame. It was too late when the fire department got there. They just sprayed water on the burning timbers. It's all gone. All my mother's things, all my sister's things, the things my grandmother brought over on the boat, all those things they left me to take care of. Heirlooms. Everything's gone. My neighbors have been very kind. Everyone's been very kind. Except I don't understand why you keep me here, what you want from me. It was an accident, everyone knows that.

(The MAN *looks at her with surprise.)*

HELEN: Well, not exactly an accident. It must have been the wiring or something. An old house like that, you have to expect. I suppose you think I was...negligent in some way. I assure you, I have never been careless. I've always taken great care of everything. It was all properly looked after. And I always kept the oily dust rags in a sealed jar. I never hung the pot holders near the stove burners. I was always very careful. Even when I... if I....

(HELEN silently looks at her hands. The MAN shuts off the tape recorder. HELEN looks up at him, at the tape recorder, then speaks defiantly.)

HELEN: I've been thinking a lot about time. I mean trying to. It's hard for me to understand things. I mean, I try but...see, it puzzles me. My hands are here, you see, in the present. My hands that have dusted and washed all those things that are gone now. No trace. Except in the cracks and callouses on my hands. And here they are in the present. They have been in the past and now here they are in front of me. And they will continue. Until I die. And that will finally be the end of all the things I've touched and cared for that aren't there anymore. I'm tired. I want to go.... My neighbors have been very kind. I'm staying with them until the furniture for the apartment arrives. I've ordered...beautiful things. Clean, bright, new things. A twenty-five inch color television. RCA. All new things. A wonderful bed with an extra thick mattress. Frank always wanted a hard mattress. Like sleeping on an ironing board. Now I'll sink down. It's important to me you see. I don't sleep well. I read at night. Sometimes almost all night. I don't really sleep at all. Just doze. I listen to the trains go through. The fast freight. And I hear Frank. In the kitchen, on the stairs. *(Looking at her hands)* They used to touch Frank. And they're here and he's not. It's all gone now. In the apartment there will be no sound of trains, no cut glass bowls, no lace cloths...and no sound of Frank. *(Slow fade)* In the kitchen. On the stairs.

FADEOUT

FOOD

Neena Beber

FOOD
© copyright 1995 by Neena Beber

For all rights please contact Broadway Play Publishing Inc.

Neena Beeber's plays include THE BRIEF BUT EXEMPLARY LIFE OF THE LIVING GODDESS (Magic Theatre, directed by Marcus Stern); THE COURSE OF IT (Missing Children/Ohio Theatre, Chicago's Mettle Theater, South Coast Repertory's California Play Festival); EASY JOURNEY TO OTHER PLANETS (New Georges/Samuel Beckett Theatre, BACA Downtown); and TOMORROWLAND (developed at Audrey Skirball-Kenis Theater and the Drama League). Other work has been produced by En Garde Arts, Cucaracha's Underground Soap, One Dream, and Circus Minimus. She recently completed a short film, *Bad Dates* (Disney, directed by Des McAnuff), and premiered a new play, FAILURE TO THRIVE, at the 1994 Padua Hills Playwrights Festival. She has taught playwriting to children, has written about the theater for *Performing Arts Journal, American Theater,* and *Theater* magazines, and is a recipient of MacDowell Colony and Paulette Goddard Fellowships.

FOOD was first produced by the New Works Project at the Public Theatre on 4 February 1992.

ANNE HARRIS . . . . .Mary Schultz
MISS FRANCES . . . . Adrienne Shelly

Director . . . . Beth Schachter

An earlier version of ANNE HARRIS was performed by Nela Wagman in OCCASIONAL GRACE, produced by En Garde Arts (Anne Hamburger, Artistic Director), directed by Bill Rauch.

Special thanks to Dr Robert Barr, Morgan Jenness, and L A T C's Women Artists Group.

CHARACTERS

ANNE HARRIS
MISS FRANCES

Production notes: In the production directed by Beth Schachter, MISS FRANCES referred to a journal in which she was writing. Eventually, she tore out strips of paper and ate them. ANNE HARRIS revealed gold sweat on her palm at the play's close. This effect can be achieved by attaching gold leaf to the palm with hairspray.

MISS FRANCES: The children in the kindergarten class I teach have begun to eat unusual things. During recess several of them graze the playground, bowing their heads to the grass. At the end of the day I notice their desktops are damp with little pools of saliva, the color of lettuce. Alphonso eats crayons. He peels the labels off as if they are fruit rinds. When his stomach heaves he tells me it's the brown ones that make him sick, only the brown ones.

ANNE HARRIS: It started when I was about twelve. Shortly before my twelfth birthday.

MISS FRANCES: I don't understand what is happening to the children I teach. I bring in apples, cupcakes, potato chips, but even the Ring Dings and Cheez-Its fail to distract them from their mania. The children's faces no longer comfort me. They drink Paint 'n Glow instead of milk.

ANNE HARRIS: At first it was just from my neck, from the back of my neck. I thought it was sweat, but when I wiped the back of the neck with my hand, my hand was covered with flecks of gold. I was afraid, I didn't tell anybody, and after awhile it went away.

MISS FRANCES: When I look at the faces of the children I teach, I fear that everything in the world is wrong. I call up Robert, who works in radiology. He's in a lab at the VA, studying an X-ray of a man's stomach bloated with fuzzy round objects—tumors the size of apricots. He spots what looks like a mouth on one of the tumors, then imagines eyes.

ANNE HARRIS: Many years later it started again, not just from my neck but now from my palms...and belly...and face—the right side of my face—and from the soles of my feet. The material has been analyzed and it is, in fact, gold— a gold-based substance. I'm no longer afraid of it. This is coming from my body, and I have learned to accept it as a blessing— I do see it as a blessing of some sort. I don't know what else I can say about it. God sends messages in strange ways and leaves it to us to interpret them. I don't know why I've been chosen in this way —God has never spoken to me before, and my life has been ordinary in all other respects.

MISS FRANCES: Alphonso holds onto his crayons long enough to draw a picture. He draws himself, a small brown figure with a belly the size of a beach ball. He fills the belly with colored squares. "Toys," he tells me, "Wrapping paper." Yesterday Alphonso did eat a toy, a shiny plastic robot called Transformer Man. I think it was already broken when he ate it. Later

Robert calls to tell me that the blobs in the man's stomach are not tumors after all, but heads of Barbie Dolls. The man swallows the doll heads whole, then waits for them to pass through his system. I picture the little plastic heads floating in the toilet bowl, their perfect blond features stained with excrement.

ANNE HARRIS: Specialists have begun to test me, to look for a "scientific" explanation; I don't believe they will find one. Many kinds of people come to see me and find comfort in my situation, it seems to give them some sort of comfort.

MISS FRANCES: I am afraid it is something I am doing. Something I should know not to do. Mildred sprinkles swirls of glitter onto construction paper, cuts the paper into bite-size strips. She chews slowly, offering me a taste. Glitter freckles her chin. If it were just Mildred, or any one of them, I would call in the school psychologist to analyze the aberrant behavior, he would administer a series of test, study the home environment. He would write his report and whatever it was she was doing, he would make it go away. But it is not just Mildred. Everyone in my class is hungry in new ways.

ANNE HARRIS: I'm saving the gold to make a cross for my church.

MISS FRANCES: I cannot tell anyone about my class until I have corrected whatever it is I am doing wrong.

ANNE HARRIS: I've never considered myself to be especially religious, but I do believe that once in a while God causes something like this to happen if only to suggest the possibility of miracles.

MISS FRANCES: Robert calls: the Barbie Doll man is back, plastic heads clogging his intestines. I study Alphonso's drawing as if it is an X-ray: I check the face to make sure it has ears, eyes, a mouth; I look for the hands. If these things were missing, I would have some idea how to help. But the boy is whole, he is smiling, even. He looks like he is about to give birth. I take a pair of stubb-ended scissors and cut. I crumple the strips into my mouth, suck the paper hard. I keep sucking, trying to absorb something more than crayon, more than vitamins—starving for whatever it is that might somehow fill me.

END

A GHOST STORY

Lenore Bensinger

A GHOST STORY
© copyright 1995 by Lenore Bensinger

For all rights please contact Broadway Play Publishing Inc.

Lenore Bensinger is a resident of Seattle, where she received her M F A in
playwrighting from the University of Washington. Over the past decade she
has written numerous plays, including comedies and musicals. Much of her
work is concerned with environmental issues, and the role and
responsibilities of women in society. She also is actively involved in
producing new plays by upcoming playwrights, and she is in exploring the
medium of film.

A GHOST STORY is the winner of the 1991 Northwest Playwrights' Guild
Award. Its first production was as a staged reading in 1991 at Seattle Group
Theater.

CHARACTER

LENA

(LENA *is in the kitchen, chopping veggies for spaghetti sauce while she listens to the news on the radio. When music resumes, she turns down the volume.*)

I'm an ex-ghostwriter. But you already know that, that's why you're here. Ghostwriters Anonymous, first Seattle branch, dedicated to the pursuit of a credit line with one's own, real name. After my last job with those jokers in L A, I figure I never even want to use my nickname again. Noonie—short for "No One". —The way I see it, Shakespeare was all wrong about that rose. By any other name, it's a kosher deli in New Orleans, the smell of a hydrangea, or the name of the woman who put the make on my husband.

The Boys were pretty happy, at first, when I quit the ghostwriting business.
"'Mom, that's great. I need thirty dollars for the football banquet."
"The Mommy is going to stop crying all the time."
"She'll find something else to cry about."
"Dad, that's mean."
"Then how come I bought her flowers?"
"They were on sale."
"That's really mean."
"'Mommy, did you hear what Daddy said about you?"
That night, we checked into a motel with a waterbed. I hid my copy of *The Writer's Marketplace* in the drawer with the Gideon Bible. It's never too soon to start look for work.

I've been ghosting so long, it feels funny to me to sign my name on a letter. Lately, I've been writing to congressmen, senators, and other public figures. I get the idea for most of my letters from newspapers or from the radio. When I was working all the time, ghosting, I never knew there were so many problems in the world. I try to stay current now. See those wires up near the ceiling and out the door. I put them up. When I'm done, the whole house will be patched into an intercom with a programmable recording and playback system. Radio ghosts in every room. An electronic antidote to loneliness.

I went to a psychic advisor today.... For the first time. Conch shell lights and wind chimes. Incense. All for five bucks.

"You must be a writer."
"How can you tell?"
"The bump on your finger."
"Oh, that. Read my life line."
"A lot of strife in the South."

"Is that bad? I've got to get another job."

"It could be good and it could bad. Tell me, what are your connections to the South?"

"My mother. I was born and raised here."

"The New South will rise again for you today?"

"What's that mean?"

"Don't question your fate. It's dangerous."

"Just give me one clue. I can't afford to miss an opportunity."

"Ghosts. That will be two dollars extra."

Atlanta. Savannah. Charlottesville. I don't know anyone there. Never even sent a résumé south of the Mason-Dixon line since I moved west, unless you'd call L A the South. L A, that's it, dreamland of the New South. Sounds like bad news to me. I'd better stay close to home today and wait for my fate.

My mother made me eat too much liver so I tried to join a circus, posing as a dwarf. I was seven. The carney boss read my palm, line by line. "It's not in your fate today," he said, "Maybe someday, when you're all grown up. And by the way, I like tall women." He kissed my hand, bowing at the waist. And I fell in love with him, truly, madly, deeply. Come Halloween, I filched twenty-nine cents from my mother's pocketbook and bought a jar of Dixie Peach hair pomade to mold my fleecy hair into sticky ringlets, like I'd seen the black girls do downtown. My dress was a pale pink sheet twisted tight 'round the waist with a watermelon-colored belt. In the costume parade I sang, "Home, Home on the Range". It sounded 'bout as old as the Civil War and just as sad. The judge who was really a lunchroom lady said I was the most perfect ghost she'd ever seen. I won first place and all for him, the carney boss who read my palm.

Most people don't like to hear bad news, unless it's gossip about movie stars and old boyfriends or outright gruesome, like mass murderers or freak floods. That's why T V news is so popular. You can get it all in less than fifteen minutes, without getting upset. It's like watching a travelogue transmitted from a rocketship.

"USS Martian to Ground Control. This is Captain Holmes with our last views of the western hemisphere before we leave earth's atmosphere. Looks like a slow news day. Dense cloud covering in the Northeast, lots of traffic jams in the Southland— Who's got the peanut butter? Sooty smoke blacking out the Amazon. What's new? Wait, signs of warfare west of the rising sun. Too late. It's out of sight. Over and out."

Me, I'm just the opposite. I'd rather hear the news than see it. Maybe that's because I'm the child of a tone-deaf mother. Back then, she'd wear bright Chinese red-orange lipstick. Lying on my back in my crib, like a beetle in a

cage, I'd watch her vivid lips form the words "Home, Home on the Range."
But the sound in her throat came from a time long before women invented
bone needles or drums, back to when America belonged to the deer and the
antelope. In my mother's lullabyes, I could hear the howl of the wind on the
range and the first yips of newborn wolf pups. That's why I love the radio.

"Mom. When is dinner going to be ready?"
"Soon. Soon."
"Mom, can I move your newspapers and make myself a peanut-butter
sandwich?"
"Just a minute. I'll help you."
"We're starving."
"Leave them alone. They're in a special order."
"Mom, please. We've got hunger headaches."
"Eat some raisins!"
"We know, they're good for you. So's peanut butter."
" Boys, I have some friends here. Colleagues, actually. We're talking
business."
"She doesn't have any colleagues anymore. She's unemployed."
"Shhhh. Daddy said we're not supposed to say that."
"Do you see any friends?"
"I don't see any friends. Do you?" "No, they must be ghosts."
"She could be seeing things."
"Or nuts."
"She's nuts."

I like ghosts. Or, at least the idea of ghosts. There must be dozens of kinds,
not counting angels and graveyard haunts. Even when I was a little girl,
I always wanted to see one. So I made a ghost trap out of nylon stockings
with seams and feathers for lures. I'm not alone in the yearning to see a
ghost. Here's what a friend wrote me on the bottom of a holiday card:
"My father, poor soul, longed to see a ghost so much he joined a ghost club,
through which he visited all the haunted houses in England—to no avail."

You can never tell when something sets off inspiration…. This stack of
newspapers goes back to August. I have another pile of magazines that
dates back to last Christmas. Magazines take much longer. If I like an article,
I cut it out, staple it together, and stick it on the refrigerator with a magnet
to reread while I am cooking. When the refrigerator is covered in newsprint,
I recycle some stories. My boys say it's like a ghost hotel in the the kitchen,
the luminous newsprint faces staring out at them from the refrigerator door.
I think it's more like information salad, edible at room temperature.

"Hey boys, you telling me you don't stare?"
"That's different, Mom. We look at real people."
"They speak to me collectively, like a mini oratorio."
"I say it's time some folks have a chance to stare back."

"She's cutting out more clippings."
"Yeh, that's her collection."
"Hey, there's some in the drying rack today."
"And some in the pasta pot."
"No spaghetti tonight."
"That's what you think."
"She's weird."
"Yeh. What kind of collection is that?"

Is that the phone? Do you hear the phone ringing? No, not next door!
I'm sure I heard the phone ringing. I've been waiting for a call all day.
Especially after the psychic advisor. I've got it. Oh, it's a wrong number.
Lately, I've been looking for stories about women who are shaking up the
planet. Women you have to reckon with. When I went to school, it wasn't
the style to have seminars about women so I've got a lot of catching up to
do. Some of the things you learn about your own gender reading the
newspapers and, especially, listening to the radio knock my socks off. You
get their voices, too, the way they sound in real life. It's a lot different from
what you can hear on the telephone. Did I mention that I loathe and detest
the telephone? Don't let anyone tell you otherwise about me. The phone is
my ball and chain. We have five telephones and one telephone number in
this house. When the phone rings, everyone jumps to answer it, When I
want to talk to one of my boys about something important, I go next door
to my neighbors and call home. When I want to tell my husband I love him,
I call him at work. He goes into his back office and really speaks to me,
saying each syllable of every word.

But we were talking about women on the radio. This morning, I heard a real
kicker. The engineer driving a transcontinental cargo train somewhere in
the midwest stops to catch some shuteye. And when he wakes up, there's
a dozen women or so chained to the wheels of his train. Why? To stop the
train from moving, according to the reporter. He interviews one of the
women. It's hard to make out what she is saying over the train whistle.
Something about the cargo. Maybe it's perishable. Tomatoes or pears.
They go bad in two or three days. Then I hear police car sirens. I think
they're going to saw the women off the trains. I mean saw the chains off
the women on the trains. The engineer is very upset. I can see his point.
What good are rotten tomatoes. You can't even put them in canned
spaghetti sauce. All that fuss over rotting fruit. It doesn't compute.
What if there's an accident? It's enough to make you sick just thinking
of women twisted up in rusting iron chains. Don't go! We won't discuss
the train anymore. Stay, please. I really need the company. The boys are
avoiding me. They watch Monday night football in the basement on the
black and white T V. You'll love my spaghetti sauce. No kidding. Just a
second while I chop some more onions. There it goes, the phone, again. You

can count on it—as soon as you build up a good head of steam, it rings, cutting a road of ruination in its wake,
like Sherman's army. The garlic scorches in the pan. Grilled cheese turns to charcoal. I'd let it ring if I wasn't looking for a job. Hello, hello. Who's there? Say something or I'm going to hang up. Mom? Mom! Oh, hi, Mom. It's my mother, three thousand miles away in the other Washington. She's hard of hearing. So, I am yelling and crying because of the onions and the long way my voice has to travel.

"The boys are fine, Mom. Really." I reach for a Kleenex and knock over my bowl of chopped plum tomatoes; juice spatters on my journal.
"I can hear in your voice something's wrong."
"I got a speeding ticket this morning. The kids were late to school again. Seventy-six dollars"
"Always blaming, just like when you were little. What are you doing with your life?"
I daub at the stain with a tear-soaked Kleenex. The words disappear under red.
"The same cop pulled me over this afternoon for a burnt-out brake light. He didn't recognize me."
"You'd feel better if you threw out some of that trash in the kitchen."
"I told you it's research for a new project."
"From old newspapers? How's your hubby?"
"Very busy..."
"He's a good man. And a good father. You should thank your stars."
"Listen, Mom, ever since I quit ghosting I've been feeling like I'm becoming invisible, a spook in my own house. The boys wouldn't notice if I disappeared entirely."
"You don't know what it's like to be alone...," she howls.
The line goes dead. God, those onions are strong.
"MOM...Mom..."
The words "I miss you" bounce off a communications satellite traveling over Kansas and echo, echo, echo into space.

What am I doing with my life? Making spaghetti sauce from scratch, working with my hands for inspiration. I just sent out a trillion resumes. And now I'm waiting for that phone to ring and for a voice on the other end to say, "I need a freelance writer, A S A P. Any chance you could spare me some time?"

"A watched pot never boils," my favorite teacher, Mrs Georgianna K Yuni, always used to say along with a lot of other useful things, like how to roll clay snakes to ward off shaking fits in the face of demons. That's how come I'm cutting the tomatoes, the green peppers, and the onions into just the right-sized pieces, with ninety-degree corners.

My first encounter with the Ghostwriter Demon happened in the winter of my tenth year. I'm Mrs Yuni's pet. Straight As, class president, and patrol captain. Life is perfect. Then Elaine enrolls in my school and shares my locker, she'll do anything to be Mrs Yuni's pet. My life is ceaseless toil, keeping ahead of her. We both get perfect scores on every math test but she writes hers with an ink pen, the kind you can never, ever erase. She sits next to me on the school bus, shining her Mary Jane patent leather flats. "Your saddle shoes suit you," she says, and I want to die. I see myself shrinking into a miniature me, becoming too little, too invisible for Mrs Yuni to see with her bifocals.

One dark and wet December day just like this, Mrs Yuni summons us into a magic circle on the floor, "Boys and girls, I have a grand surprise for you. The brand-new Maryland State Christmas card contest for fifth graders. I know someone in my class will win the blue ribbon prize—a whole day at the governor's mansion in Annapolis. This is a fine chance for all of you to show your best inspirational writing, and do me proud." Oh yes, it's going to be me for sure, eating southern fried chicken in Betsy Ross' chair and signing autographs for handsome senators. I, the author of the longest spelling word story in the history of my school, am favored to win by a country mile. Even Mikie says so, who swears he's going to drown me in crab pickling brine for giving him 16 demerits in one day. I wait at my mirror for inspiration until midnight but for the first time ever, nothing comes to me. The next morning, Elaine, looking all rested, is shining her shoes on the school bus. She says her Christmas card is ready. I fall out of my black leatherette seat when the driver sets the brake. My pleated, plaid skirt rips. My saddleshoes instantaneously stretch into mammoth gunboats. Elaine says, "They suit you better than ever," and steps gracefully out of the bus. I wait until the nine o'clock bell rings to go to my locker—alone. And there it is, the Ultimate Shapeshifter, the Ghostwriter Demon, in the form of a note, written in lemon ink on the folded tonsils of a cootie-catcher, advertising the services of one A Spook: "Timeless poems for all occasions. Never plagiarized. Ghostwritten. Be assured of absolute confidentiality."
How dare you?
Take that! And that!
Here's one for you, Elaine, and you too, Mikie!
I can make up my own poems!

Twenty-eight fifth-grade students are singing "God Bless America" when I arrive. Mrs Yuni holds up her right forefinger and twenty-eight students put their hands on their desks. "What's the matter with you?" I moisten my lips to say 'I'm...sorry...I...I...but a thundering hippopotamus holler comes out instead. "Oh my, this is serious. What you need is a hobby to take your mind off yourself." And off she goes—faraway— to the supply cabinet. Elaine peeks at me and titters. My hand, in a fist, finds the wadded cootie catcher in my pocket. I let the power of the Ghostwriter Demon enter me and in a golden haze, I see my Maryland Christmas card. Cover art inspired by the great seal of the Black-eyed Susan State and inside, A Winter Ode to an Oriole. I see Mrs Yuni pinning the blue ribbon to the blouse of a girl who looks like me with a Ghostwriter Demon living inside her shell. She wipes away a tear and I know she sees what's happened to me. It's two years later. I sell my words to other classmates for a pat on the head and two dances with the cutest boy at the sock hop. It's much easier writing for someone else, no stakes, no shakes. until one day, you're on the phone with your mother and it goes dead. I think maybe the line is bugged.

"Mom...Mom!" "This will calm you down."
"Mrs Yuni?"
"Just roll the clay between the palms of your hands until it turns into a snake. Like this. We're goddesses now, aren't we, making new life with our hands." "No, I'm a golem."

The phone is working again.
"I'm worried you're disappearing. Are you eating right?"
"You hurt me, Mother."
"I can't lie to my own child. You'd feel much better if you threw out all of that trash in your kitchen."
"I can't believe you're saying that, my own mother. I have to go."
"Your voice, it sounds terrible."

At last, I'm on the verge of making her repent. And then I hear it, the beep of another call on the same line. I have to answer it. It could be my last chance to stop myself from fading into nothingness in a car with no doors in the carpool lane. I click the phone button into another reality.

"I'm a friend of a friend of a friend."
"Can I call you back? I have someone on the other line."
"Do you know who this is?"
"Wait...I know. Your voice is really familiar."
"Who am I?"
"A personality."
"Who isn't, nowadays. Guess."
"I think I heard your voice on an ad for a broadcast school."
"You've got to be kidding. Now guess where I'm really from."
"The C I A?"
"Hey, that's not funny."
"Sorry."
"Keep it that way if you want to find work in Hollywood."
"Sure. Do you want me to keep on guessing who you are?"
"Give me a break."
"What do I dare do next?"

"Maybe I called at a bad time."

"No, this is a great time. I was just talking to a ghost…"

I follow the electrons from my lips to his through the receiver, up the telephone pole, and through the wire under crows' feet and pigeon droppings to the place where this nameless friend of a friend of a friend is calling me. There he is at a Tinseltown swimming pool, in the shadow of a palm tree, wearing bug-eyed sunglasses from Yves St Laurent and running down the names of other writers for hire in his little black book.

"I'm very interested."

"Our mutual friend said you were the best."

"I try. Girl, be careful what you pray for."

"Would you be available now?"

"That depends…"

"Here's the deal. Get me a treatment I like by the end of this week and you laugh all the way to the bank."

"Artistic freedom?"

"Of course. That's why I'm calling you."

"What's the catch?"

"My name under the title."

"Oh…. My other line is ringing."

I count to ten, slowly. So, it's another ghost story. The Demon is back, rapping and tapping at my phone line. I write it. He gets the credit. Yours truly stays invisible. A trickle of sweat dripping in my eyes, I forget to stir the pot. The smell of onions scorching. Back on the phone, I ask his name. 'J P.' Of course. A guy like that couldn't have a name like Joe or Frank, certainly not Frank. "This is perfect for you," he says. I hear someone belly-flop into his pool in Hollywood— Smoke alarm screeching in my kitchen. My mother waiting on the other line, fuming about the long-distance charges. Suddenly, my radio goes on automatically, the way I programmed it to do. The lead story is about three dozen women blockading a cargo train carrying toxic waste. Now it's three dozen and the train is in Texas. One of the women says, "As long as there's breath in my body, they're not unloading this train in Texas." What's perfect for me? I've been wondering a long, long time. The ghostly faces stuck to my refrigerator door look back at me in silence.

J P is screeching into his phone.

"You still there?"

"I'm listening."

"If we buy this treatment from you, you get to sign your name on the next one, in big letters."

"Lots of if's."

"And you get fifty percent artistic control over the next script."

"How come?"

"A reward for working fast. We need this treatment by Friday."

"It's Monday today."

"Hey, I heard you could work fast. Maybe you can't."

"What's the deal?"

"Think Desert Storm."

"You want me to write treatment about the Persian Gulf War?"

"No way. Leave that to our rivals, at that other network."

"What then?"

"The flip side of the same thing from a woman's point of view, with plenty of action and lots of laughs."

"You want a sit-com?"

"You betcha."

"A sit-com based on Desert Storm?"

"A night-time show for women thirty-five to fifty-five, the prime market."

"Like a nineties 'MASH' set in the desert, with women soldiers"?

"Exactly."

"What's funny about women soldiers?"

"You're not thinking. They're hilarious. Besides, you don't have to worry about women soldiers. That's the other network. You come up with a new twist of your own."

"Women warriors?'"

"Now we're jamming. I love it."

"I don't know "

"Just use your imagination. Think sell."

"I see Joan of Arc leading her army to victory and I tell him, 'Yes.'"

"It all boils down to the same thing—sex."

"I see Elizabeth defeating the Spanish Armada, the arm of the Inquisition, and I tell him, 'YES.' 'Sex. And don't forget to make it funny.'"

Hey, this isn't as bad as it sounds. I get my name on the next one, guaranteed. You got to start somewhere in this business. I'm sure he said "guaranteed." Friday—only four days from now, not counting express mail.

Driving to my first contact with the world of women warriors, with a borrowed kid in the buddy seat. Ned, age eight, has agreed to wear his cub scout uniform in exchange for money. The plan is to use him as a foil to get into the naval base. The ensign at the gate waves him through for a nice swim at the base pool with the other future recruits. We pass an ocean-going war ship and a seaplane. There's got to be dozens of hilarious situations here. While Ned swims, I slip into the weight room, I can't imagine what I'm going to ask these warriors. Four women are working out. I try to chat with the brunette doing stretches. The conversation dies. I try the blonde on the weights. She spots my tape recorder—hidden in my leg warmers—and three furies pin me to the rug. The blonde asks the questions.

"What the hell do you think you're doing?"

"Nothing really, just visiting—"

"Just visiting with a concealed weapon." "It's just my Walkman."

"Call the M Ps."

"Wait. The truth is I'm doing research."

"For who? The C I A?"

"No...for...this television station."

"About us?"

"That's a strong possibility."

"A documentary?"

"No."

"A drama?"

"No."

"Get out of here before I call the M Ps."

"What did I say?"

"It's what you thought."

"Since when is thinking a crime."

"What do we do with intruders who think our job is funny? You want a laugh riot, go to the public health service."

Driving back home with Ned, who is crying because I made him get out of the pool before he was ready, we discuss talking to strangers. Ned says I need an attitude check.

"No one is ever going to tell you anything secret."

"What about something personal?"

"What's the difference?"

"And do you know why? Because you never smile and you look at the floor when you talk."

On the car radio, I hear the same story about the toxic train but this time I can hear every word the woman says. She is afraid the governor is going to agree to letting other states dump their radioactive wastes in east Texas. He claims the state needs the money to make up for the oil recession; he promises to reinvest half the money in Texas schools. Nuclear dumps make children sick, the woman says. I go to sleep that night counting the women chained to the cars on the train.

I get back home from driving the carpool at 7:50. I have until nine o'clock to work on my newspaper pile and listen to the radio before I go to the public health service facility. I'm not exactly sure what they do but it sounds like they wage wars against disease. And, since I think they wear uniforms, J P might go for it. I am reading a story about San Suu Kyi, the Burmese winner of the Nobel peace prize, when J P's messenger arrives with the contract. He doesn't want any coffee. He has to catch a plane back to LA in twenty-five minutes. "Why doesn't he just send it express mail?" —"You don't know how J P does business. Someone will be here Friday to pick up your treatment." The envelope looks like purple alligator skin. There's a handwritten note from J P:"We cast the lead. A great kid from Iowa. Her dad and I went to cub scout camp together in the Poconos. You'll love her." Scratch Joan of Arc and Elizabeth but keep the sex.

He already cast the lead and I'm still looking for an angle. What do I know about women warriors, cutting onions in my kitchen, driving the little league carpools. What if I don't sign the contract. The boys will never forgive me. They already told all their buddies I'm writing a blood and guts flick with lots of psychopaths. This morning, in the car, two kids asked me to autograph baseball mitts. Nine o'clock, going out the door, I pass the mailman, Mr Silence. Somehow, he knows too. Maybe the messenger squealed. "How's the script coming?," Mr Silence asks. "If there's anything you need, just let me know." He winks. It's hard getting used to so much attention.

I take Zoe, my golden retriever, with me to the public health service; I think she'll be a better foil than Ned. The building looks like any government building: bland. I'm going to have to talk up interior conflict to interest J P in this one. Zoe blinks at me as I go up to an old woman protesting animal testing in medical research. Her shoes are taped with silver duct tape. She is carrying a sign showing a rabbit in torment. Three other women are singing a rap song about condoms. I can't tell if they're in favor or against. It gets harder and harder to have an opinion nowadays.

The rappers throw handfuls of condom packages at the patrol car cruising by. A lady cop gets out of the squad car to have a look-see. On her badge it says her name is Winona, What a great name for the star of my new sit-com. I notice Winona is wearing seashell pink lipstick and iridescent eyeglass frames. She asks the three rappers if they have a permit to perform street music. While they sing an angry song about women in chains, Winona asks me if I have a vending license to distribute condoms. "I'm just out walking my dog," I say. Zoe wags her tail. Good girl. Meanwhile, the three rappers hurl more aluminum foil packets—directly at the lady cop. One must have a rock in it. Her forehead is bleeding. Suddenly, cops are swarming all over the stairs, arresting everyone but me, including the public relations officer for the public health service. I figure I'd better get out of there, quick.

Wednesday morning...already...and I don't have a plan yet. I wonder if I should call J P, just to check in. Better not. I call the public radio station instead and ask the program director if there's any more news on the toxic train. "You'd have to call our national office." I tell a young woman in D C I am worried about the women chained to the toxic train. She takes down my inquiry; promises me someone will process it...soon. I give her my phone number. Think I'll see about the old woman with the tape on her shoes. Her feet seemed the same size as mine. I find a battered pair of shoes in my closet; I pack them in a bag and check the batteries in my tape recorder. Tape Foot is making another rabbit sign in her jail cell. She wants to tell me about medical research but I knew that wasn't going to be funny. I half-way listen anyway, hoping Winona might show up at the jail for Tape Foot's arraignment, scheduled right now. Tape Foot tells about research dogs and monkeys, like beads on a rosary. Winona and the warden arrive. They let the old lady go free. She doesn't want the shoes I've brought. Tells me to save them for a rainy day. I tap Winona on the shoulder,"Can we talk?" Even though she is wearing the same shade of seashell pink lipstick, she looks very different under the jail lights, I don't know what to say to her.

The last time I was this close to a woman cop was at a Valentine panty sale. I had gone from size five to size seven panties wrestling with the Ghostwriting Demon. I started digging through huge bins of clearance underwear, looking for my new, big size. Other women join me. We help each other find the right size and style. A buff woman in pink works by herself at another bin, piling up mountains of lacy nylon. Two lady cops wearing guns and nightsticks show up. We figure the woman in pink is a shoplifter. But the cops don't even look at her. They dig deep into my bin. One of the cops asks if I had seen any leopardskin prints. The other wants boa bikinis. I am a pillar of salt. So are the other shoppers. Everyone in the department is a pillar of salt. The lady cops leave the money for their new panties on the counter, including the tax. Winona works half-days at a battered woman's center. She wears plain clothes. The center looks just like an old, wooden three-story house. No one is supposed to know that women hide from their batterers there. She likes the idea of doing a T V show about this part of her job, as long as I protect the identity of the women."Violence in the home. It's a terrible problem." This is definitely not funny, even though Winona is a woman warrior.

It's Wednesday afternoon. After two bum leads, I think I will do a little research. Sarah, the reference librarian, helps me sift through newspapers and magazines looking for real-life heroines in arms. "Patriotism with a twist of vodka," she says, laughing just in her eyes not to disturb the other readers. She started working in this library thirty-eight years ago, carding books and putting them back on the shelves. Her skin is pale and paper thin; it crinkles when she bends or smiles. Sarah suspects I'm homeless.

"We're about to close."
"Oh, I didn't notice it was that late."
"You could check some of those materials out." "It's raining. I'm afraid they'll get wet. I'll come back tomorrow."
"You'll catch your death. My friend works at the Y...I could call."
"I'll be fine."

At the doorway, Sarah hands me a book called *Memoirs of a Woman Warrior*. "It's my personal copy," she tells me. On the cover there is a picture of a mountain of books in flames and a woman with a hose trying to extinguish

the fire. The subtitle of the book, is *Fighting Words* by Lydia Semple.
"Lydia," Sarah says, "is a local writer." See if you like her book. If you do,
perhaps you'd like to meet her. She lives not far from here."
"Remember I have to write a treatment for a sit-com."
"What's funny is often just the other side tragedy."
"But the ACLU." "You can't imagine what they get into nowadays. Read."

I take *Memoirs of a Woman Warrior* home to read while I bake double-fudge
brownies, with walnuts, from scratch, for inspiration. There are only two
days left now before I default on my contract. I prop Sarah's book on the
recipe stand for later. A photograph flutters to the floor. Sarah and another
women who looks like Lydia are handing out bags of food to women
barracading a cargo train. The women look like prisoners of war. I'll make
a double batch of brownies, half for Sarah, the rest for the boys, watching a
replay of a Mariners' game on T V. Ken Griffey, Jr hits a ground ball out to
the rim of the world. Cheers as he rounds third base and heads to home
plate. I turn the volume way up on my radio, hoping to hear news about the
women chained to the toxic train. "Coming up, next, the strange story of a
cargo train carrying a deadly load of ecojunk." Three shrill whistles blare
through the radio speaker. The boys suddenly realize I am in the kitchen.
"Get back to work on the script, Mom."
"What if she doesn't write it?"
"No one will ever give her a job again."
They dream of movie stars sleeping in our house. "You could write a story
about a lady conductor."
"She's supposed to write about a woman warrior, stupid."

The reporter says, "Fifty cars long and no destination." I hear the screech
of metal against metal as the long cargo train slows down for another
interview. No matter what, everybody stops for an interview, even bank
robbers and brain surgeons. The reporter talks to the engineer. "Legend
has it you've been driving this train around the country for two years."
"Yup. Two years and five months. Been in every state except Hawaii
and Alaska."
"Where you headed to now?"
"I'm not at liberty to say."
"Why is the train camouflaged?"
"'Fraid I can't share that with you."
"Mom, when can we go to a Mariners' game?"
"Shhhhh. She's going to nail that engineer."
"She never takes us anywhere anymore."
The mike is up against his lips when the reporter asks, "What's really in
those cars?"
"Land fill."
"Just land fill?"

The phone rings. "No matter who it is, say I'm not home."
"That's a lie, Mom."
"Yeah, you told us not to lie."

The phone rings again. "Let the answering machine get it. I want to hear the rest of the train story." The boys lunge for the phone slipping, inevitably, on the dog dish. "It's mine." Thwack. Cain slugs Abel. "Mine!" Abel delivers a roundhouse. The boys are moaning. Dick grabs the phone. "It's Grandma. Should I say you're not here?" On the radio, the reporter is talking to an environmental activist over the melody for "Home, Home on the Range." The last words I hear broadcast are 'toxic' and 'ghost.' My mother almost never calls me, even on my birthday. So I figure this is bad news. She's laughing when I get on the line. Freak out.

"You'll never guess who I just spoke to," she says.
"Doris Stein? Who bought me a girdle for my thirteenth birthday? Mr Medvene? Who sold us family cemetery plots? Mrs Yuni, who taught me how to make clay snakes?"
"'No. It was that nice boy you saw in college. The one who took such good care of his mother."
"I saw a lot of mama's boys in college."
"This boy was a prince."
I'm still trying to hear the train story. "Who?"
"Steve."
I turn up the T V. The boys shouldn't hear this conversation. "Which Steve?"
"Wait. I'll think of his last name. He saw you on T V. Why didn't you tell me to watch you?"
"I wasn't on T V."
"Next time, tell your own mother first." "That's all?" "He asked if you're happy."
"What did you tell him?"
"I gave him your phone number. In the meantime, I have a wonderful idea for your T V project. You'll never guess. "
"I can't write about Marie Curie. She's too old fashioned, Mom. Too noble. Women in my generation won't go for her."
"Just think about it. That's all I ask."
"Bye, Mom."
I turn off the T V and stare into the screen.

Marie, Marie, Madame Curie.
Pierre's widow,
Mother of radiation,
I nearly forgot you.

Marie, Marie, Madame Curie
Sobs in the night

By the eerie light
Of pure radium.

"Watch the brownies, boys. I'm going to take a walk with Zoe."

When she wants something, she lays her muzzle on your lap and looks you straight in the eye until your will to say no goes out of you. It's a trick worth learning. Neighbors leave bones for her. All the kids know her name.

Star light, star bright, first star I see tonight.... Who are you kidding? From way up there, I'm invisible. Those stars don't know who I am any more than the folks on this street, all wrapped up in their coccoons by nine o'clock at night. Walking home from the library, a kid is stabbed in the leg. A football game on T V. No one hears her cry out for help. With Zoe, I can trespass. I peek into windows and see faces illuminated by the eerie light of television tubes. A sinewy girl swings from corner to corner of the screen, dangling from a fabricated vine. She holds a knife between her teeth and growls at the camera. Next door, in black and white, a chubby lady cop screams in terror as a rat runs past her booted feet. Hollywood warriorettes on little glass screens. Does anyone remember their names?

"Zoe, heel. Wait. Ouch." She yanks me down the alley to her friend's yard and scratches on the back door. Mrs Two Dogs opens it and we fall into her livingroom, panting. "Bad girl!" I try to drag her outside. "Come in, come in. I have a soup bone for you." She knows Zoe's name and mine. I don't know hers or her two dogs'. Three tails thud against my legs. A gilt-framed picture falls off a shelf. I see my neighbor, forty years younger in a military uniform I don't recognize and surrounded by dogs. "To Olga. with eternal gratitude." It's signed with a pawprint. "My pupils. Eyes for the blind, ears for the deaf, and fangs where need be." We sit at the kitchen table drinking licorice tea in a glass with jelly on the bottom, because Olga is Polish. She joined the resistance when Poland fell, training dogs for the army. In her frayed, red satin robe, she looks like an ancient porcelain doll. "After the war, I joined Barnum and Bailey Circus. My dogs wore their heroes' medals. Our act was a hit."

"Marie Curie was Polish, too," I say.
"I wanted to be just like her when I grew up."
"Even if it meant dying of radium poisoning?"
"None of us live forever, Marie is a star. More tea?"
"No, thank, you. I have some brownies baking."
"Come again soon and bring Zoe."
"Good night, then."

On my way back home, the stars seem closer. Some of my neighbors have turned off their T Vs. I wave as I pass their houses, hoping to catch a glimpse of a picture on the mantle or a shining medal, displayed in a velvet box. Warriors in my own back yard. Imagine a T V series about

my neighborhood. Olga is very photogenic. She could play herself. J P
would never buy it. Not enough laughs.

It's Thursday morning. I look in the mirror and ask mvself, "What's a
woman warrior, here and now, in the U S of A? Winona? Olga? Sarah?
The Tape Shoe lady, the rappers, the sailors? Now there's Lydia Semple.
I stayed up reading her book until three in the morning. She's been in jail
dozens of times, just for speaking out on behalf of banned books. Mary
Poppins and Huck Finn. A Lydia, a lawyer sitting in a jail cell with nothing
to read. At breakfast, the boys give me a present. It's a huge spread sheet
done on the computer, charting television highlights of the year. The
prime-time, gynocentric sit-coms are in bold print. The boys read from
it aloud:

"My turn! Undercover narc kills gang leaders. Isn't that a great idea?"
"Mine's better. Soldiers of fortune in petticoats."
"That's dumb. This one's the best: women hunters and their prey."

They watch me sip the coffee they made intently. It's very strong. I flip
through their spread-sheets. "What's this one? Environmental activists
tie themselves to a train?"
"Don't write about that one."
"Why not?"
"They didn't get killed."
"Write about the narc."
"Why are you crying, Mommy?"
I hug them both and we lie in the bed together.
"Are you going to start writing today?"
"Forgive me, boys," I say without a sound.

I go back to the library to ask about Lydia and the photograph of the
women barracading the train. Sarah is glad to see me. She asks if I've solved
the mystery of the sit-com woman warrior. I nod, "No." "Inspiration is
elusive," she says, "don't get discouraged." Sarah asks me what I did before
I started coming to the library. Most days, I chop onions and drive up and
down the interstate in a car with no doors. "Well, it's nice having you here.
You come anytime you want." I watch her go back to reference, stopping to
help a kid sharpen his stub of a pencil. The books on her desk took like old
friends. The girl at the check-out desk tells me Sarah is retiring at the end
of the month. I can't imagine her in the sunlight.
"What will you do, Sarah?"
"Same thing."
"Another library?"
"The place doesn't matter to me. Just being able to do my work is what
counts."
She takes off her glasses. I see her eyes are violet with yellow flecks like gold
in a mountain stream.

"I teach folks to read. *Crime and Punishment* or "See Jane run"... The way an old man or child says the words when the letters make sense ... it's always a miracle to me."

As I leave, Sarah gives me a yellow slicker with a hood. When I put it on, it keeps the shape of its former owner. Haunted. In the pocket there is a receipt from the Salvation Army, dated yesterday. I put Lydia's address and phone number in the same pocket. Walking down the stairs to the street, it feels like I am moving further and further away from my deadline.

If J P had half a grain of sense, he'd welcome a T V treatment about Sarah. Why does he have to have a sit-com. Sarah could be the inspiration for a modern-day Hypatia, the beautious librarian of ancient Alexandria who spurned all offers of marriage to pursue her love of science and literature. Maybe that's why Archbishop Cyril marked her for death in 415 in a hail of abalone shells. Then he burned her library and with it all the knowledge of the world.

Some kids skipping rope wave to me. I'm losing my touch, becoming visible. It's terrifying. A girl wearing saddle shoes sees my tape recorder.
"Are you a television reporter?"
"No." Her friends have stopped jumping and are listening.
"Then why do you have a tape recorder?"
"I'm writing a kind of play about women warriors..."
Her friends go back to jumping rope.
"Then write about me."
I see she has ringlets, like Scarlett O'Hara. "What makes you so interesting?"
"When I grow up, I'm going to climb up to the ozone layer and fix it. And you can make a television show about me."

That's it. I've been looking behind me all the time while a possible tomorrow beckons. Even the little girl thinks I'm a curator, an embarrassing artifact of the sixties in a nineties world.

The ravenous Cyclops eats maidens for dessert, nibbling their fingers and toes before he swallows them alive. He's invincible, except for his one bleary eye. Woe to the mothers and sisters of this land. Cunning Penelope weaves a new tapestry and history is rewritten. She tiptoes across warf and woof to the monster's climatically controlled geodesic dome, a sharpened pen in her hand. The beast hears her breathing. "Who's there?" "No man." Inside, the terrified panting of a girl marinating in amaretto sauce for the evening meal. Clever Penelope taps lightly on the door. "Who comes?" Again: "No man." Licking his lips, the monster peers out the door, visions of sugar plum lasses exciting his taste buds. In a flash, Clever Penelope is on him, inking out his one eye again and again, until all is blackness and silence.

No Man slew the Eater of Women. What were their names? No one? Nada? Nihil? Nihil, nihilo, nihil est. Nothing begets nothing. Come out, come out, wherever you are, to be named, to be known in the first hours of a possible tomorrow.

Back home in the kitchen, Thursday night. Cutting salad greens for inspiration. I bought five kinds of lettuce. Let's see if the boys like endive. On the radio, I hear a very short bit about the train. "A cargo train presumably carrying toxic waste is due to arrive in Seattle, Washington, at noon tomorrow. Some two-hundred women are chained to the train...." Someone, answer the phone for God's sake! And say I'm not home.

In my mind's eye, I see the train clearly now. It's five-hundred cars long and barreling north at two-hundred-fifty miles an hour. All along the track, there are women trying to stop the train. They grab hold of the caboose, fluttering in the wind like wash on the line, until they drop off in the gathering storm. Their features are very clear to me now. They're singing...
"Home, home on the range,
Where the deer and the antelope play..."
"Mom! The man says he has to talk to you. It's urgent."
"Who is it?"
"He says it's Steve. Steve the Prince."
"Coming...."
He says, "Hello," just like anyone and asks if it's me. "I got your number from your mother. We had it on file somewhere in the office. But this was just as easy. And I always did like your mother."

I'm backpeddling across the continent through all my Steve's to find a face to go with his voice. Washington, D C, famous for cherry blossoms and motorcades. My first Steve comes to my house in a crinkly white coat to tame my fever and betrays me. "How old are you?" I hold up three fingers and the knuckle of another. "This won't hurt," he says, icicle fingers on my burning thigh, a needle piercing my skin. My second Steve builds me a palace out of sand, with a kitchen that looks out on the sea. We drink tea in seashells and kiss each other in the air, with smacking vows of eternal love. Three days later, I have chickenpox real bad. Steve builds Maureen a sandcastle just as fine as mine. Always a Steve: in the park and at school, some tall, some skinny, and all of them better than me in math. I go to the prom with the captain of the football team and crush my corsage slow-dancing with Steve, I'm twenty-one and in love again with a new Steve. He joins the Marines and never comes back from Viet Nam. I'm twenty-five. Steve sends me his mother's engagement ring. I slip it on my finger once. No. No. His curses ring in my ears. I marry another man. My children drink tea in seashells. I don't remember this Steve, calling me long-distance, in a room full of office machines.

"So," he says as casual as a regular poker buddy, "How's it going?"
"Pretty good," my queen to his jack. "What about you?"
"Can't complain." I think I hear a paper shredder on the line. Yes, I'm
certain it's a paper shredder.
"You must be wondering why I called you after all these years."
Something about his voice. My heart misses a beat. "It's always nice
to hear from you. Are you planning to come out to the west coast?"
"You never know."
"It'd be nice to see you again."
"You too. Who could forget your hair. Chestnut brown waves down to your
waist."
I clench my teeth and hold my breath to explode twenty blurry years. Still
no image of Steve the Prince. "So are you still living in Washington, D C"
"I guess you could say it's home base. I'm on the move a lot."
"So am I—carpools."
"Funny thing about coincidence, I requisitioned a new desk and what do
you think I found in the top drawer?"
Once on a muggy summer day in D C, I left my bra on top of the filing
cabinet in the Labor Department —just a plain white underwire. What job
was that? What office building?
"I can't imagine. Tell me."
"A file with all kinds of pictures of you. Here's my favorite: you're in pink
bellbottoms, a tie-dye top..."
"No bra?" "Hard to say. But in this picture, you've got lots of chestnut
brown hair. Here's another one: you're on the mall with all those marchers.
The strap on one of your platform shoes is broken."
"And I'm smoking a joint?"
"That's nothing. It's the company you're keeping."
"Got any baby pictures?" He's got the whole C I A story of my life.
"Let's just see. Your file is so thick..."
"That was eons ago. Who cares anymore?"
"Do you know why you've never been arrested for some of those little
escapades?"
"Why would anyone arrest me? I'm a writer.... A ghostwriter. I don't have
anything to do with the national security."
"The national security is a very complex and far-reaching concept including
almost every aspect of everyday life...as needs be. For example, taxes,
licenses, health certificates..."
"What do you want?"
"You've never had a tax audit. Your husband has a license to practice
medicine. You drive a car across state lines."
"What do you want?" I said.
"The reason you have such a favorable score in our national security index
is because I do the rating."

Now I know who he is: Steve of the rates, of the protests and the all-night planning meetings, always taking pictures, our archivist and double-crossing, double-agent. Steve, who stood in the shadows wanting to caress my hair, taking pictures of me ruining my national security rating twenty years later.
"And today, I'm going to do you a favor, in return for another little favor."
Tit for tat. That's Steve the Prince
"Keep away from the train tomorrow." "What train?" "You know what train. You've been tracking it across the country since Monday."
"And how do you know that?"
"It's my business to know these things. Just be a good girl tomorrow and I'll obliterate all those old, funky photos."
"You want to put me in the paper shredder?"
"That's the idea." "I don't know."
"Maybe you want to talk to the boys about it… before they apply to college."

Everyone figures they're being watched, every now and then. Like when you can resist eating a grape at the grocery store. Hey, did you know you can get arrested for that? I knew a woman once who got sentenced to ninety days and a thousand bucks for eating gummy worms at the Safeway. Would you believe? With all this rain and the worms that wash up on your sneakers, I would never have snatched the gummy worms. The gummy bears are the best. Chewy like the jujubees I used to buy in the movies to share with Steve.

"Mom. I just found out there's a school for T V talk show guests. They teach you how to tell your life story on air so the whole country sends money to your foundation."
"That's dumb. Mom doesn't want to write about weepy ladies who can't stop marrying horrible men. What about a spy, like Mata Hari? Only she's really loyal to America?"
"Funny you should mention that," I say.
"I told you so. She likes it, she likes it! Here's all my stuff about spies."

My littler boy hands me a battered notebook, stuffed with newspaper clippings, photos, and crumpled pages. A chip off the old block. I open it at random and find an ad for the Clandestine Service, the C I A.
"We're looking for a few good spies,"it says in bold print. At the bottom of the page, there is a phone number for more information. I wonder if I can reach Steve at that exchange.
"Why are you crying Mom?"
"She's always crying now, ever since she stopped being a ghost."
"A ghostwriter."
"Visibility hurts," I want to say.

Tomorrow, first thing, I'm going to call that Steve and tell him not to shred my file. It's my life, the only one I've got. Friday morning, default day. I get up before the sun. A mailman I've never seen before taps at the back door. "Something from Washington, D C, overnight air. Must be pretty urgent." He winks. My stomach flip-flops. Mom, I sigh with relief. It's half of a newspaper clipping. I see a couple of tail-end cars of a camouflaged train and half the words of a story about three women who tied themselves to the caboose. The toxic train looking for a place to unload. On the other side, a story about nuclear energy. Mom's circled a paragraph about Marie Curie. Scrawled in the margin, a rebuke— "You think your mother is so old-fashioned. Read this."

Marie, Marie, Madame Curie
Mother of radiation.
What would you do
In my hiking shoes?

I call my mother.
"Steve, the Prince, you don't happen to remember his last name, do you."
"Wait, I'll think of it. You know how my memory is."
Give her enough time and she remembers everything.
"Did you get my letter?" "Yes."
"Something's wrong. I can hear it in your voice."
"It's only the morning you hear. It's still very early here."
"No. I hear a gathering storm in your voice. Don't write about Marie Curie. It won't hurt my feelings."
"Mother! His name…"
"I'm an old woman, used to being forgotten."
"His name!"
She whispers, "I'll think of it…later. Maybe after I have a nap. You know how my memory is."
"I wasn't always a ghost."
"Nor I. Visibility runs in your blood. Ask me someday." She hangs up, without saying goodbye.

On a hunch, I dial the phone number at the bottom of the want ad for spies. A woman with a mechanical voice answers the phone. I can hear the paper shredder in the background. "Can I speak to Steve?"
"One moment please."
"Recruitment."
It's Steve, the Prince.
"Listen here. About my security file "
"Don't worry. It's done. Now you can make a new beginning. By the way, I'll be out on the west coast next month. We could have a couple of drinks together. Talk about old times."
"I know someone you'd like much better. I'll give him your number. I'm sure you two can do business. He's crazy about mug shots and funny photos."

I dial the area code for Tinseltown.

"Hello, J P. I have just the person to write that televison treatment for you, the expert on past and present women warriors in the U S of A. I'm sure you can share a lot of laughs. His name is Steve, the Prince. Here's his number...."

"We're going for a walk." I put on my yellow rainslicker and check the pocket for Lydia's address. Zoe leads, following an inevitable trail. ...Hey there, you, Winona." I wave to a policewoman cruising the block; I leave two marrow bones on Olga's backstep. There's Lydia's house. I must have passed it a thousand times, walking Zoe. Her livingroom is dark. What if I'm too late. Then, from inside, I hear her composing a poem for the rally at the train station at noon.... What day is it today?
Is the ground poisoned?
What do the experts say?
That's no good.
What day is it today...?

I open the door, without knocking, knowing it will be all right, "'My name is Lena. Can I help? I'm a writer too."

P.S. I'm getting used to being visible. The boys promise to come to the next Save the Ancient Forests rally. I'm contributing a new poem, "Home, Home on the Range", dedicated to my mother, who taught me to sing my own song.

BLACKOUT

HAITI (A DREAM)

Karen Sunde

HAITI (A DREAM)
© copyright 1990 by Karen Sunde

Karen Sunde is an actor turned playwright. Off-Broadway she performed
sixty-some roles at C S C Repertory. Her works for theater—twelve plays,
four Kabuki plays, and a musical—have been performed in five languages
in eight countries. THE RUNNING OF THE DEER and BALLOON were
performed Off-Broadway. BALLOON, which is published by Broadway
Play Publishing Inc, won three *Villager* awards, was nominated Best Play by
the Outer Critics Circle, and performed on Radio France. DARK LADY was
produced at Aalborg State Theater in Denmark, the Abbey Theater in
Ireland, and P C P A in California. ANTON, HIMSELF, produced by Actors
Theater of Louisville, also played in Yalta and at the Moscow Art Theater.
Her Kabuki play ACHILLES, produced by The People's Light and Theater
Company, toured Cyprus, Hungary, and Japan before playing Philadelphia
and Malvern. IN A KINGDOM BY THE SEA and HOW HIS BRIDE CAME
TO ABRAHAM were produced by Playwright's Theater of New Jersey.
LA PUCELLE was produced by Cheltenham Center of the Arts in
Philadelphia.

HAITI (A DREAM) was first produced at Seven Stages in Atlanta, opening on 24 May 1990. The producer was Del Hamilton. The cast and creative contributors were:

SIRI . . . . Donna Biscoe
RUBIN . . . . Tony Vaughn
SAILOR . . . . Felix Knox
OLD WOMAN . . . . .Kuumba Alisa Foster

Director . . . . Robert Earl Price
Choreographer/dancer . . . . Ife Hendricks
Sound design . . . . .Klimchak
Light design . . . . .Eric Jennings
Costume coordination . . . . Felix Knox
Drummer . . . . Mossi

Radio version commissioned and produced by W N Y C, 1991, Marjorie Van Halteren, producer. Aired by W N Y C, W H Y Y, and N P R stations nationwide, 1992.

CHARACTERS

SIRI: *A young woman*
RUBIN: *Her husband*
SAILOR
OLD WOMAN

The setting is the dark hold of an overcrowded sailboat as it journeys from Haiti toward Florida. To stage it you need: a ladder, a post, and lights.

DEDICATION

For those who drown

Scene One

(Dark. Silence. Sounds of tropical night, at first distant, then fading in more distinctly as we adjust to dark. A slice of space is lit as a hatch is opened, above, and figures climb down into the hold. First down is a woman, SIRI, with a baby.)

SIRI: *(Hushed)* Wait. I can't see.

(A man, RUBIN, has stopped at top of ladder. SIRI feels her surroundings: dim shapes, mounds, bundles. At one spot, about center, a support post reaches from floor into the black above.)

SIRI: All right. But I don't think there's room.

(RUBIN pulls large trunk over edge of hold, supports it down the ladder. SIRI works her way forward.)

SIRI: Let's go back up. Must be a hundred down here already. No room. Too many people.

RUBIN: Over here. *(He sets trunk down, takes baby from her, sits.)* Here.

SIRI: We can't even lie down. Rubin, let's go back up. I'll feel better...breathing the air.

RUBIN: It'll be best down here. Come the rocking, come the storm. Come the day-long sun.

SIRI: I know, but for now...

RUBIN: Best take the place we can get. You see they're filling up.

SIRI: Where'd they all come from?

(She flops down, holds the sides of her head in her hands.)

SIRI: How'd they all hide? Scuttling out in the star night like lizards from under a rock.

RUBIN: *(Patting the baby on his shoulder)* Too many people in a rotten shallow boat. Here—lay him down.

(SIRI settles the baby.)

RUBIN: He'll sleep quiet here, sway softly here.

SIRI: Just let us onto the water, past the mosquito clouds. The tickets? Let me see the tickets to America.

RUBIN: Minute. A minute.

SIRI: You got three?

RUBIN: Here we are. One...two...three.

SIRI: *(Smiling, clutching tickets)* God, god. I couldn't believe the boat was here. A big sail floating, like a ghost dream.

RUBIN: You didn't believe? You pushed me all the way! I was the one wouldn't pay till we climbed on.

SIRI: That was bad, Rubin; they almost wouldn't have you. They got no need of our money.

RUBIN: Look, Siri. These are movie tickets!

SIRI: Long as they tickets out of here, doesn't matter.

(Dark shapes, lumps of baggage, continue to make their way down the ladder into the hold.)

SIRI: People crazy! Still pushing on. We're filled to bust already.

RUBIN: They'll have to cut loose soon to keep under dark. Soon, or sunlight'll catch the sails before we're past the line of ocean sky.

SIRI: Woe man, it smells already. Baby'll wake with the heat.

RUBIN: Be glad it's tight. Out on the water, we don't need leaking. *(Pause)* We don't have to go, Siri. Siri?

(She looks at him oddly, distracted by a memory.)

SIRI: The boat came ghostly. Sitting low, meshed in seaweed. A dark blot against the star map. My heart jumped feeling the breeze on my face, warm water lapping my thighs.

(Just as suddenly, she is back.)

SIRI: I don't like this, Rubin. There's too many here.

RUBIN: *(Holding her former mood)* Shhh, listen... Listen, the quiet. Night birds on warm wind. Listen. We won't hear it again.

SIRI: We'll hear it, Rubin.

RUBIN: Listen.

(Silence. Land-based night sounds.)

SIRI: Why don't they start. We were near last on. Why don't they start?

RUBIN: Shhhh.

SIRI: They aren't taking us! They take the money and leave us sit. We'll be found here in the morning. Nothing to stop it.

RUBIN: That would be bad business. If they leave us, others will hear. They'll get no money tomorrow.

SIRI: I know.

RUBIN: You found Fanon, you made sure it was him?

SIRI: Yes yes. Fanon's old and ugly, but he goes and he comes, many times, on the sea. Good business.

RUBIN: Yes.

SIRI: Why don't we go!

RUBIN: Quiet, now. We paid. *(Pause)* Listen…the frogs booming. They don't know we're going, won't hear them tomorrow.

(The hatch bangs open. A sailor calls down in a hushed voice.)

SAILOR: Up fast. We're overloaded. Can't move like this. Get off now and go tomorrow. Same tickets. Sea's better tomorrow, better boat. Up fast!

(The SAILOR descends, begins pommeling the shapes. There is murmuring among the bundles all around, some shuffling, movement up the ladder.)

RUBIN: Let's get off, Siri, yes? It's too crowded now. Not safe. Be better tomorrow.

SIRI: There's nothing tomorrow. Is he going to give the money back? Oh no. You try to find a boat tomorrow, you find only mist. Oh no. We're packed in, or not in at all. That's the choice.

RUBIN: Siri….

SIRI: And I made mine.

(There are muffled splashes above. The SAILOR moves through the bundles towards them.)

SAILOR: Up fast. That's it. People are getting off. Come on with the kid.

RUBIN: Siri, let's get off. You fussed—"The baby, the air." This isn't good.

SIRI: Is it worse than what we're leaving?

SAILOR: *(Counting off those that ascend)* That's nineteen up, that's twenty…

SIRI: Let those up top get off! It's easy to push them off, an easy slide.

(SAILOR laughs harshly.)

RUBIN: Siri, an overloaded boat, it's not lucky. Come.

(He reaches to help her up.)

SIRI: *(Refusing to budge)* Not lucky? We were born in an overloaded boat. And I stay.

(RUBIN *stands looking at* SIRI. *The* SAILOR *ascends.*)

SIRI: Better hope they don't ask tomorrow.

(*More splashes, moaning above and below. They sit, listening in the darkness. Silence. Then, finally, a creaking movement. The support post tilts.*)

RUBIN: There.

SIRI: What.

RUBIN: We're moving. That's it.

SIRI: We're moving.

(*Silence. Creaking of old wood. Then a sudden cry. It is coming from a bundle behind the man. It is piercing, mournful.*)

SIRI: What's that!

RUBIN: Hold the baby. My god.

(*On his feet, the man sees that the bundle behind is an* OLD WOMAN.)

RUBIN: Woman, hush. What has you. What is it?

SIRI: She must be crazy.

(*The* OLD WOMAN *is winding up to howl again, like an animal.*)

RUBIN: Don't! They can still hear us on land. It's dangerous.

(*The* OLD WOMAN *howls. The hatch swings open.*)

SAILOR: (*Hushed*) Shut it up! Somebody trying to get us all shot?

OLD WOMAN: (*A long wail*) My son!

(*The* SAILOR *descends, fast.*)

SAILOR: You think the patrol's asleep? Shut it up *now* or I put my knife through it.

OLD WOMAN: Where is my son?

(*As the* OLD WOMAN *begins another howl,* RUBIN *leaps, gagging her with his arm. The* SAILOR *looms over them.*)

SAILOR: She yours?

RUBIN: (*Holding her*) No. But I'll keep her quiet. She's calling her son. Is there someone on deck who...?

SAILOR: (*Turning abruptly away*) Her son got off to lighten the boat. He'll come on the next one. (*As he moves off*) Keep her still.

(*Ominous silence until the sailor has gone. Then the man carefully releases the* OLD WOMAN.)

RUBIN: Quiet, now, and I'll let go. Quiet... You heard? Your son got off. He comes next. Tomorrow.

(The OLD WOMAN *sinks, passive, as though dead.)*

RUBIN: *(To* OLD WOMAN*)* You heard?

OLD WOMAN: *(Pause, then low)* Lie. He lie.

RUBIN: No, it's true. They asked people to get off. We almost...

OLD WOMAN: Lie. My son don't get off. Not leave me.

RUBIN: But if they...

OLD WOMAN: He has paper. My medicine. He takes me for medicine. Won't leave me. What did they do to him?

(She begins to make another howl. RUBIN *stifles her, tries to comfort her. The baby begins to fuss.* SIRI *rocks it, hums.)*

RUBIN: Quiet, shhhh... Nothing to do now. Maybe he's up there, happy you're safe.

SIRI: *(Low, to* RUBIN*)* Or they just pushed him off. I've heard those things, Rubin.

*(*OLD WOMAN *tries to howl.)*

RUBIN: Shhh, shhh, bear it. *(Rocks her, humlike)* We're slipping now, quiet as a cat, quiet through night water, out away, away...

*(*SIRI *is humming to baby.)*

RUBIN: Up on deck we could see, see our home become an island behind us. First we'd see only dark, then a rough shape, dim edge against the sky, crumpled edge of our mountain humps up the black sky. Then mountain growing smaller, island moving away. A thousand glittering waves stretch the way between.

(Someone's transistor scratches on, then plays low, island music.)

RUBIN: Hear the island?

OLD WOMAN: I don't want to go to America. My son wants. He says I need medicine.

RUBIN: Listen...

OLD WOMAN: I don't want to go.

RUBIN: The island's moving away, but someone caught it in the air. Hear it?

OLD WOMAN: New medicine. Auuuw...son's don't believe in the old medicine. Faith's too weak.

RUBIN: Listen...the music.

OLD WOMAN: *(Fading into trance)* Faith weak...and gone.

(She sinks back into a dead stare.)

SIRI: What's she say, Rubin?

RUBIN: Nothing.

SIRI: She didn't want to come?

RUBIN: Yes. Just nothing.

SIRI: It will come right, Rubin.

RUBIN: Of course. Yes.

SIRI: We should feel a breeze.

RUBIN: Not down here.

SIRI: Yes. *(Pause)* Is she asleep?

RUBIN: No. Staring into nothing. Or asleep with eyes open.

SIRI: Maybe her sickness.

RUBIN: Her grip is like iron.

SIRI: What do you think happened to her son?

RUBIN: I don't know. Maybe she doesn't have one.

SIRI: That's not what you think. *(Pause)* Old woman. Grandmother, can I help you?

OLD WOMAN: *(Pause)* No one helps. The Power is going. Woods getting thin.

RUBIN: What's she saying?

SIRI: Nothing.

OLD WOMAN: Mango shrivels. Powers don't come.

SIRI: Is there something you need?

(OLD WOMAN looks at her, stares a moment, gives an odd laugh.)

OLD WOMAN: Need.

SIRI: Yes. Can I do something for you?

OLD WOMAN: Need. *(Pause)* You have food?

SIRI: *(Alarm)* Shhhh...why? You haven't any?

(The OLD WOMAN makes no answer.)

SIRI: Ooooooh...your son.

OLD WOMAN: My son carries food.

SIRI: Yes, of course. Of course we have food.

OLD WOMAN: Shhhh… be still with it. Many don't. They sold all they had to get money for their ticket. They think the sea is small, think one night is the whole journey, think they'll be soon fed, soon on land.

SIRI: We brought plenty.

OLD WOMAN: *(Laugh)* They don't know, don't know sailing whole weeks, whole month.

SIRI: Our trunk has everything.

(She stretches to unlock and open the trunk.)

SIRI: Food and linen. Law papers, treasures of family. My wedding dress. Are you…hungry?

OLD WOMAN: Are you not? Who comes to the night-boat not hungry? But don't give to me. Save it. Worse will come. Many will die, many starve. On the boats, worse comes.

SIRI: Quiet. We can give you something. We have figs and yams. Rice too.

RUBIN: Wait. She'll tell us when she needs it. In the morning. Spare it. It may have to stretch.

(He looks around the dark warily.)

RUBIN: Like fishes and loaves.

SIRI: My god, Rubin.

RUBIN: And don't be telling midnight stories, Gramma.

OLD WOMAN: You don't hear stories? Go you down to market, when traders are coming in, you'll hear. Stories for weeping in the bright noon.

SIRI: There are accidents, but most get through.

OLD WOMAN: Who say, who say they get through?

SIRI: We have letters. A friend sends money. The strong get through.

OLD WOMAN: For every one sends money, hundreds float head down, scraping their faces on the far shore.

SIRI: *(Puts her hands on the OLD WOMAN)* Don't talk like that, Gramma!

OLD WOMAN: *(Resists, pulling into herself)* Nobody know what's good for them! Spoiled niggers! On slave ships it was good. It was good on those boats. Slaves are worth plenty. Going where there's work to do. What are *you* worth? Who pays to have you come to America? Nobody. You pays. To leave where you got nothing, can do nothing, going to where you be worth nothing again. And already you paid the man. What's he got to gain by taking you there?

(There are thumps above, and splashes.)

SIRI: *(Alarmed)* What is it!

RUBIN: Something…sliding in.

SIRI: Rubin!

(The OLD WOMAN *is humming herself into a trance, while the noises continue.)*

RUBIN: *(Pause)* We should have left the child.

SIRI: I know that's what you think. But we couldn't.

RUBIN: We could. Your sister would have…

SIRI: My sister, no. The child is my reason for coming.

RUBIN: Siri, that's nonsense.

SIRI: *You* should have stayed. I could have sooner left you.

RUBIN: Siri, stop.

SIRI: I told you. Soon as I knew there'd be a child, I told you. "Go with me or not; no gaping mouth of mine will add to the street-mob. I won't have a child that cries for food."

RUBIN: We could have managed. We aren't stupid. You know there are ways.

SIRI: You begged me, "Wait." "Wait till the child comes. A child breathing, adjusts, comes along, needs little, only the breast. But mother breathing for both, she's delicate, too delicate."

RUBIN: I was right. You think you're a bull. Strong like a bull because your will is so fierce.

(The OLD WOMAN *nods, and her head snaps awake.)*

OLD WOMAN: Bull…? The snake…

SIRI: Yes, I'm fierce. I will get what there is to have. I know there's a life not hungry. And I will have it.

RUBIN: My woman is the poet of her life.

(The center post rocks. There are more splashes, creaking.)

SIRI: Something's going overboard.

RUBIN: You hear her, Gramma? A mighty poet.

OLD WOMAN: And you hear. We are overload.

SIRI: I'm no poet, I'm practical. He blames me that we came.

RUBIN: Leaving is a fool's chance. At home there's work to be done.

OLD WOMAN: You have job, you gave up *job*?

RUBIN: No. Work for the people, only for them.

SIRI: You see who's the fool? Aach, it's him. We had to come because of him. He should remember if he blames me. You know the election?

OLD WOMAN: Election? Yes, I know election. Celebration!

SIRI: Big party, yes. Did you go?

OLD WOMAN: Election. Big bus, riding. Painted, colors many, music, food, great lot of food. Everyone coming.

SIRI: You went to vote?

OLD WOMAN: I voted, yes. Everyone voted yes. I rode the bus, voted yes with everyone. Very happy. Stop bus, vote yes. Ride again bus, vote again yes. All around the island voting yes. Eight places I stopped, voted yes eight times. Happy party, singing for president. You voted too? How many?

SIRI: Once. One was all. *(Beat)* Maybe you won't understand. I voted yes, of course, like everyone. Three government men watched me. I turned to go, and I heard this man here. He came behind me, he had my baby. And I heard them ask him what he wanted to vote, and I heard him say "No". He voted "No". Now, all the people were surprised because all day since morning people were voting, and this was the first time someone voted no. So they asked him: No what? What does no mean. He said "No president for life. No for this president." Three times they asked him. Three times he answered the same. I waited. Like the mountain since the volcano stopped, I stood dead. Didn't scream. Didn't grab my child. I only stood dead, waiting to hear him shot.

(Tense pause)

RUBIN: And then they laughed. All three government men.

SIRI: They were sure you were crazy. Because everyone knows to vote yes!

RUBIN: That's why I voted no. So everyone sees it can be done!

SIRI: You hide nine years in mountains. Then show your face to say, "No"? What sense is that?!

RUBIN: My father's gone. That's the sense.

SIRI: They poisoned him, Rubin. Your lawyer daddy was poisoned.

RUBIN: It's our country. Free near two hundred years. Free country.

SIRI: Free for what? You get us killed, one way or the other.

RUBIN: Are we safe now?!

(They stare at each other for a beat. Suddenly, a thump, large splashes, creaking of wood. Involuntarily they cling to each other, looking up. There is alarm among the bundles. Baby cries.)

SIRI: Rubin!

RUBIN: Hold on! What can it be?

OLD WOMAN: *(Hisses)* The boat breaks now. The sea god is angry.

SIRI: Be still!

RUBIN: Maybe it's the Coast Guard. Americans. Maybe we're out that far.

OLD WOMAN: If they catch us, they'll throw us home again. *(Joyful, she begins a chant.)* Come catch us, come catch us, throw us home!

(It is a kind of prayer. There are murmurs of others joining her. Abruptly, the hatch opens, SAILOR descends, talking full voice for the first time.)

SAILOR: The noise up there, we call 'lightening the boat'. Going to make us run fast. We're slogging along like a leaky bathtub. Can't skim past the Coast Guard. So then, all bags goes up, up and over. Up fast!

(The murmurs turn to cries, shouts. The sailor begins heaving bundles and cases up out of the hold.)

SIRI: What will we do, what can we do!

RUBIN: Hold the baby. Here, against the trunk. Sit on it. Maybe they'll think it's theirs. Can the old woman sit on it? God, Siri, I don't know, I don't know!

(The SAILOR is rampaging along. Cries all around, screams of protest.)

SAILOR: Give a hand then, boy. Think you're on a luxury jet?

(He grabs the trunk with a rough laugh. RUBIN grabs the other side, pulls.)

SIRI: Noooo!

SAILOR: You planning to not cooperate?

(SAILOR kicks at RUBIN to get him loose.)

RUBIN: *(Struggling to hold on)* What are you doing! Why not kill us all now, throw the weight overboard!

SIRI: Hold on!

SAILOR: You something special? You got a ticket for this load?

RUBIN: Who leaves home with nothing...?

SAILOR: Who asked you aboard?!

RUBIN: ...Savage!

SAILOR: Who asked you to get off, go another day, make it easy. Get a moonlight cruise with extras.

RUBIN: You can't treat us like…

SAILOR: Niggers? Like niggers?

RUBIN: Your mother tell you you're not black as me?

(The SAILOR *drops the trunk, sweeps to grab* RUBIN *in his fists, raise him in the air, slam him to the deck.* RUBIN *sprawls, hurt, breathing hard.)*

SAILOR: Listen me good, stuck-up bastard. You do this once. Take your chance. Me, everyday. My neck, my ship, my sweet balls on the spike. For what? A little little money. I'd be happy to sleep on shore. So don't ask! Don't come sweeping off the island like rats, squealing and retching, and swamping my ship. *(Beat)* Now this goes!

(He lifts the trunk in one sweep. The woman grabs him.)

SIRI: You can't, you can't…

RUBIN: *(Hand on her)* Siri…

(The SAILOR *is swinging himself, trying to shake her off.)*

SAILOR: She's next. Over the side. She and the brat together!

(The woman bites him. With a yell, he drops the trunk and draws his knife. The man jumps between them.)

RUBIN: Let him take it!

SAILOR: *(Reaching for* SIRI*)* I'll snap this hen's head right off!

(Sudden loud sound from the OLD WOMAN. *She seems huge, raises her left arm with an odd gesture.)*

(Startled, the SAILOR *yells, dropping the knife as though it burned him, then his whole body relaxes into immobility. The others are stunned as well.)*

RUBIN: My god…what did she do?

(The SAILOR *grunts, reaching again for the trunk.)*

SIRI: *(Intense whisper)* The food. Rubin, the food…

RUBIN: Let us keep our food. Unless you plan that we starve as well.

(The SAILOR *eyes him, grunts again.)*

SAILOR: Show me.

(He lets the trunk slide. The man opens it, takes out a bundle from the top.)

RUBIN: Weighs less every day. We'll share.

(Short laugh, as the SAILOR *shoulders the trunk, and leaves. The* OLD WOMAN *has sunk back into a crouch, staring.)*

RUBIN: Grandmother?

SIRI: I save her.

RUBIN: What was that she did?

SIRI: What?

RUBIN: She stopped him. She raised her arm, and he stopped. He was frightened.

SIRI: I didn't see.

RUBIN: You did. You were frightened too. *(Pause)* You were.

SIRI: *(Pause)* The path on water.

RUBIN: What?

SIRI: Maybe...she found the water path.

(Blackout)

(In the dark, the sound of wind. The OLD WOMAN *sing-speaks as though from far away.)*

OLD WOMAN:
Day flows into weeks
on the open sea
a moment equals
eternity

Only man troubles
with time
his little time

Only man troubles
with time

Scene Two

(Light filters below, very bright light through open hatch. Dead stillness. All sleeping. Silence.)

(RUBIN sits up abruptly, wild-eyed. He stares intently, then darts his focus to another part of the hold and rivets, motionless, like a wary animal. Then, satisfied there is no sound, he finds and clutches his empty food bag, searches it in every corner that might hold something to eat. Finds nothing. Begins again, methodically,

obsessively. It is this sense of purpose with which he is trying to keep hold of his sanity.)

(Sudden sound. RUBIN curls instantly, feigning sleep. The SAILOR comes through the hatch and on down the ladder. He seems drunk, but it is exhaustion.)

SAILOR: *(Swagger)* Any still alive?

(He rummages among sleeping bundles, checking life signs. He slaps one, gets no response, rolls the body over.)

SAILOR: *(Distaste)* Ugh.

(He drags it to the ladder, hoists it on his shoulder, climbs through the hatch.)

(RUBIN's hand shoots into the air, and then moves carefully out, reaching for something he's spotted from where he lies. When his hand is directly above it he pounces, with a squeal.)

RUBIN: Iiiiiiah!

SIRI: *(Stirring weakly where she lies)* What?

RUBIN: A bean. A black bean. I found one. There's one left.

(The woman doesn't respond to the bean. Looks dully around. Her movements are very slow.)

SIRI: Are we moving?

RUBIN: No no no, of course not. Look at it, Siri. I give it to you.

SIRI: *(Checking the baby, cradled in her arm)* No. You found it.

RUBIN: But I love you, my darling one. I'll give it to you. I was dreaming... you, holding your skirt, thighs parting the water, sleek gliding, gliding....

SIRI: You dreamed? I too. Oh god! *(Covers her eyes)*

RUBIN: What, darling, my mermaid...what troubles? What did you dream.

SIRI: *(Sharply, checking the baby)* Is he breathing?

RUBIN: He sleeps, darling, don't be afraid, only sleeps.

SIRI: It was better when he cried. Even all night long. He was strong enough to cry.

RUBIN: He'll be strong again. Here. That's why you eat the bean. So you'll be strong to feed him. Don't cry...you've been so good, don't start. You need your tears for milk. Don't drop them. There, that's right.

SIRI: It's no good, it's over. Yesterday, the day before. He'd yank, angry. Then refuse and cry. Then pull again, nub nipple sucked into the curl of his dry tongue. Oh god! To be aching full again, to be dripping sticky milk in my sleep again, aching for his greedy tongue.

RUBIN: Love, my love.

SIRI: So I must still not cry. Save this teaspoon of tears...for what? It's over.

(The man holds her, sings.)

RUBIN:
No greater sorrow, Papa God, no greater woe
No greater sorrow come down on me
No greater sorrow, Papa God, no greater woe
Than the Mama got who can't feed her child.
(Speaks) Tell me your dream.

SIRI: I hope I'm forgetting. Dream pictures go away if you... No.
He's still there.

RUBIN: Who is?

SIRI: The old white.

RUBIN: What old white?

SIRI: I don't know. Are we moving?

RUBIN: No.

SIRI: I felt it. We slid to the side.

(Muffled splash)

SIRI: What's that?

RUBIN: Another who didn't wake. The sailor found three more. He slides
them silent into glassy sea, it won't shatter. What did you dream?

SIRI: Three gone? That's more room.

RUBIN: An old white. A man?

SIRI: Yes, a man.

RUBIN: What happened?

SIRI: I was swimming...

RUBIN: I saw you walking. In my dream.

SIRI: No, swimming. For miles. Miles and miles, the day, the night. My limbs
are heavy, slow, like stumps soon sinking. My lungs hurt. I gasp to stay
afloat, but the sea is warm... Then a piece of land. I can see it. I can reach it.
I can smell the ripe earth. Fruits hang over the water. Wet pine, wild
strawberry. But the water is still deep, even at the edge. I grab a flat rock,
stretch my arm across to lift me. But I slide, the rock is slippery. I reach
again, hear a laugh. An old white comes hobbling out onto the rock.
He laughs and, putting his foot on my head, pushes it under. Not far under,

just enough. He laughs another laugh. Being very careful that his shiny shoe stays dry.

(Silence)

(Note: Above could have birds, laugh, water sound as fantasy.)

RUBIN: I'll save the bean. Just till he's awake. Then I'll chew it soft, and give it to him.

SIRI: When the sailor took the three, the three who didn't wake, what did he say about the wind?

RUBIN: Nothing. I asked how is the sky. But the sailor said nothing. He did not look well himself.

SIRI: It can't be far. We must be close. I could smell the ripe earth.

RUBIN: Every day is a day, my mermaid, but...

SIRI: But...Saturday is not Sunday?

(The OLD WOMAN *stirs. The man is abruptly alert, like a squirrel, to watch her.)*

RUBIN: She's waking...ahah, ahah. Listen. She'll start mumbling.

SIRI: Never mind. Let her be.

(The OLD WOMAN *murmurs, inarticulate.)*

RUBIN: But how does she do it, what's she living on?

SIRI: Not our business.

RUBIN: She never took a bite from us. Not even a fistful of rice, not even at first.

SIRI: I don't know. It's her business.

RUBIN: But did you watch? She hasn't eaten. I swear. But I'm sure, I'm sure unless I'm crazy...she's getting stronger. First day she was a broken bird, almost dead. And now, after weeks, she breathes as full and sure as deep rolling surf.

SIRI: Where did you put the bean?

RUBIN: *(Cheerfully)* One bean, Gramma. That's all that's left.

OLD WOMAN: Did any go during the night?

(The man's delirious cheer is failing, sinking into panic.)

RUBIN: Three we know of. Three from down here.

OLD WOMAN: Not so many then.

RUBIN: You're looking well.

OLD WOMAN: Yes yes.

RUBIN: The cruise agrees with you.

OLD WOMAN: *(Chuckle)* Hmnmh. We ride low, ride stream of life.

RUBIN: *(Spits it out)* We riding nothing now. Still no wind.

OLD WOMAN: Don't be troubled. Water is path for spirit. The baby?

SIRI: *(Listless)* Drowned.

RUBIN: No, he sleeps. The crying stopped.

OLD WOMAN: Good. Sleeping good.

RUBIN: *(Pause)* Yes. *(Pause. Then, anger rising:)* It's a good joke on us, Gramma, think— this, us on this boat, we did ourselves, we *fought* for our place here. The last time our people were in a place like this, they were dragged on and chained to the hull.

OLD WOMAN: Chained, yes. But after weeks, they got food, plenty food, fatten the stock, the man-cattle, cattle are worth much. *(Emphatically)* The slave boats were better!

(Then, satisfied with her pronouncement, the OLD WOMAN *rises easily, moves to the support post, and begins circling it slowly.)*

RUBIN: *(Exploding irritably)* We're not lost, Siri, it's not possible, not now. There's radar. They can find anything. Bits of metal in space, electrons in vapor, anything! They've tracked us from the beginning. They know exactly where we are. We can't be lost!

OLD WOMAN: *(Hum-muttering)* Dadumm, dum dadadada dum...

SIRI: *(Dully)* No one said we're lost. There's just no wind.

RUBIN: There are helicoptors. There's radar. They know we're here...

SIRI: Rubin...

RUBIN: *(Rising)* They've decided. They're waiting until we all die.

SIRI: Rubin, don't. Don't. It's no one's fault. Don't use your strength like that. Don't. Come my darling. Sit.

(She is pleading, comforting. The OLD WOMAN *still moves around the support post, stooped, rhythmic, muttering.* SIRI *finally notices, and gasps, terrified.)*

SIRI: What's she doing? Stop her! Don't do that!

RUBIN: What?

SIRI: *(Pulls herself up to grab the* OLD WOMAN *'s arm)* Stop. Stop that. Stop.

RUBIN: Siri...

OLD WOMAN: Tend your own trouble, girl.

SIRI: You can't do that here.

RUBIN: What do you mean, Siri?

SIRI: She's opening the door. She can't.

OLD WOMAN: What I do, girl?

SIRI: You know, old woman.

OLD WOMAN: And you also know?

SIRI: *(Beat)* I won't let you.

RUBIN: What's this about, Siri?

OLD WOMAN: Be still. All be still. Look after your child, girl.

(SIRI sinks, sits, silent.)

RUBIN: Siri, what is it? Siri?

(Pause. SIRI does not respond.)

OLD WOMAN: Food all gone now?

RUBIN: *(He sighs, all tension gone.)* Yes.

OLD WOMAN: You got nothing left?

RUBIN: Something. *(His hand goes into his pocket.)* These. *(He pulls out a handkerchief, carefully unwraps it, shows the old woman some coins. He is weak, moves slowly.)*

OLD WOMAN: *(Picks up a coin, chuckles)* Your woman right. You crazy. These worth nothing. Too old.

RUBIN: Yes, they're old. From the mountain. I dug...many places. You can't buy a pig with these. But in America...you can buy more than a pig.

OLD WOMAN: America so stupid?

RUBIN: They're old. They're treasure.

(He is spreading the coins out on the cloth, one by one, like a picnic.)

OLD WOMAN: They from slave times?

(He is relaxed, seems discouraged, weak, limp.)

RUBIN: No. From the time the black man took his freedom. Revolution time. Only second time in the world, man took freedom. And that man was black.

OLD WOMAN: *(Examining a coin)* This man here?

RUBIN: That's King Henry. Henry Christophe. He built a great castle, to fight Napoleon. You know that castle, on the mountain top?

OLD WOMAN: *(She settles back, smiling.)* Proud old time.

RUBIN: *(Weak, breathing hard)* Still proud, still. And good, sweet people. People need to learn something, Gramma.

OLD WOMAN: *(Shakes her head, clucking)* Too much evil, evil world, honey-tongue boy.

RUBIN: They need to learn the world.

OLD WOMAN: *(Looks at him sharply)* Your woman is from the country, yes?

(RUBIN turns his head slowly, painfully, to gaze at SIRI.)

RUBIN: Yes.

OLD WOMAN: But not you. You speak together French. You teach her?

RUBIN: *(Ignoring the question)* What do you do at the post, Gramma?

OLD WOMAN: Post, aah. Post is crossing place.

RUBIN: Crossing place?

OLD WOMAN: Crossing—world of us, world of spirits. Spirit travels through the post. *(Glances at woman)* Your woman's afraid. Hunh. She believes.

SIRI: *(Turning away)* No, I don't.

RUBIN: Believes what?

OLD WOMAN: A child knows in its blood. Why don't you know?

(The man looks at her, first silent, then:)

RUBIN: Voodoo? My father...my family didn't allow....

OLD WOMAN: *(Interrupting, fixed on the woman)* She's stubborn, your woman, but she's afraid. She made you come on the boat?

RUBIN: No. It was my fault, because of the voting. I was angry. Angry I didn't fight. In hiding, I'm worthless to my people. I'm a coward, but must do something. So I voted no. Once, I dare. One time I wasn't a coward. Now...we're here.

OLD WOMAN: No coward. Here, we're close to water. Only a little skin between. Spirits speak, easy. Easy come through water from creation.

(Suddenly, the SAILOR blots the sun, moves through the hatch and down the ladder. He is sodden, stooped, blank.)

SAILOR: Any still alive down here?

OLD WOMAN: *(Eager)* Ah. The carrier death. You sure that man is dead?

(The SAILOR stares at her, then bends to hoist another bundled body. But she scuttles right up to him.)

OLD WOMAN: How far have we come?

(He ignores her, and she grabs him roughly. RUBIN and SIRI are alarmed at her daring.)

RUBIN: Gramma, come back!

OLD WOMAN: How far?

SAILOR: Let go!

(The SAILOR pulls away, climbs, with the body.)

OLD WOMAN: *(Taunting)* Skim fast now, uh? No weight left.

RUBIN: Gramma, still yourself!

(The OLD WOMAN crows after the SAILOR as he climbs through the hatch.)

OLD WOMAN: Less than thirty mile, you said yesterday. We're close now, less than thirty!

RUBIN: The boat can't move without wind. The sea is a dead pond. We sit rotting in the sun.

OLD WOMAN: No wind? We need wind.

RUBIN: *(Pause)* Are you a believer?

SIRI: No...

OLD WOMAN: Yes, believe now. You help. Take coins in cloth.

SIRI: Don't, Rubin.

RUBIN: Yes, I want to. *(Throwing coins into cloth, one by one)* Remember when my father died?

SIRI: Poisoned. He was poisoned.

RUBIN: He spoke to me alone.

SIRI: They chased him.

RUBIN: He had something to tell me...

SIRI: All your family hate voodoo, Rubin. It keeps us in jungle. We're going to a new world, Rubin. Where miracles come from men.

RUBIN: Maybe we won't get there, Siri. What I do with coins, Gramma?

(The OLD WOMAN is circling the post again, chanting. Drumming begins, against the wood of the boat.)

OLD WOMAN: Put them in cloth, loose. Shake it, make rattle.

(RUBIN does as she says. The OLD WOMAN begins dancing, chanting a song. The drumming swells, gets faster. SIRI grabs RUBIN.)

SIRI: Rubin, don't do this. You don't believe...

(RUBIN *pushes* SIRI *away from him. The tempo swells, the* OLD WOMAN *dances in frenzy, then falters, starts to fall.* SIRI *cries out, leaps up to catch her, holds her upright. The* OLD WOMAN *goes into a seizure.* SIRI *tends her, expertly. The drumming, faster, now changes rhythm. It is syncopated. Suddenly, the* OLD WOMAN *rises erect, huge, unlike herself. She thrusts her arm out in a commanding gesture.)*

OLD WOMAN: *(Deep voice)* Quiet!

(The others are frozen, stunned.)

RUBIN: What is it. What's happening?

SIRI: Nothing. Don't look.

OLD WOMAN: *(As Christophe)* Silence!

RUBIN: *(Grabbing* SIRI*)* Tell me.

OLD WOMAN: *(Christophe)* Little man! Get me my telescope.

RUBIN: *(Cowed)* Telescope?

(He looks around helplessly, speaks again to SIRI.*)*

RUBIN: Tell me!

(The OLD WOMAN *is striding about like a strong young man.* SIRI *listlessly picks up the stick the old woman had used for walking.)*

SIRI: It's not one of the gods. Telescope... It's Christophe. King Henry. Give him this stick.

RUBIN: *Him?*

OLD WOMAN: *(Christophe)* Give me my telescope! Clean the lens first.

RUBIN: *(Taking the stick from* SIRI*)* Of course.

SIRI: Bow!

(Confused, RUBIN *bows his head, and extends the stick toward the* OLD WOMAN. *She immediately raises the stick as a telescope, and boldly surveys the area.)*

OLD WOMAN: *(Christophe)* No clouds. No wind. A bad spot. Yes, children?

(The man rises uncertainly to face the OLD WOMAN.*)*

RUBIN: You are...King Henry?

OLD WOMAN: *(Christophe)* And you are...a slave?

RUBIN: I... *(Beat)* There are no slaves in King Henry's kingdom.

OLD WOMAN: *(Christophe. Hearty laugh, then:)* Some think there are.

RUBIN: Because...you are severe, King Henry. You work your people hard, you drive them.

OLD WOMAN: *(Christophe)* I drive them to their own honor, Monsieur. They think freedom means nothing but ease. I did not drive out the white man to rule a degenerate kingdom.

RUBIN: Yes, Monsieur, but...

OLD WOMAN: *(Christophe)* I will work them and drive them to greatness. Only then can they glare level-eyed at the white. The world is watching, little man. To see what the black man will do.

RUBIN: He will try to be white. He will murder his own. Scrape them to dust.

OLD WOMAN: *(Christophe)* No! That must end. Be wise, little man. The murders must end. Do not despair. Lead wisely. You know how.

(The OLD WOMAN swiftly lifts her left arm, and collapses in a faint. The boat begins to move. Support post lurches, then sways.)

RUBIN: *(Caught, suspended)* Wha...?

SIRI: We're moving!

RUBIN: Is she all right?

SIRI: He's gone. Christophe left. *(Beat)* We're moving.

RUBIN: *(Relaxing)* I had to do it, Siri. My father...

SIRI: He hated voodoo, Rubin.

RUBIN: Before he died, he frightened me.

SIRI: *(Realizing)* We're moving. There must be wind!

RUBIN: My father told me, I must serve the spirits. As he did, in secret. He, alone, protected my whole family. And now it's me. I have to...

SIRI: No! He hated voodoo, he said...

RUBIN: When he died, he told me: Love, love deep, to serve is good.

(The OLD WOMAN stares at him as though unable to comprehend, speaks faintly.)

SIRI: The boat sways...we're moving.

OLD WOMAN: *(Weakly)* It goes?

RUBIN: She's back.

SIRI: It goes. We're moving.

(A transistor plays island music softly.)

RUBIN: What did it mean, Gramma? What did you do.

SIRI: She doesn't know.

RUBIN: Doesn't know?

SIRI: No. She won't remember.

RUBIN: But she did it.

SIRI: The spirit took her body. Leave it now.

RUBIN: You said it wasn't a god.

SIRI: No! It was one of the dead. Leave me alone!

OLD WOMAN: Who came?

RUBIN: Henry Christophe. What did it mean, Gramma?

OLD WOMAN: *(Amused)* You must think. Speak with your heart.
Then you know.

RUBIN: But tell me…

OLD WOMAN: I know nothing. He came for you.

RUBIN: *(Collapses on his knees, hands to his head)* My father…he was so alone.

OLD WOMAN: With secret, yes. He hurt with secret. But not alone. The
lonely are those cut off. Your father served. He was connected to all life, all
death, all good in the world…above, beneath. He knew the way, the way to
seeing, to knowing, to peace.

RUBIN: The way to peace.

OLD WOMAN: Before, I was afraid. I was sick to death. My power weak,
people poor, no young to take my place. But now, on the water… On water
I feel spirits flow. I'm closer to creation. *(Pause)* What did Christophe say?

RUBIN: He said I know how to lead.

OLD WOMAN: Ahh.

RUBIN: Our people always know how to lead, have the idea to lead,
many leaders, many strong.

SIRI: *(Bitterly)* Idea to lead, yes. And the idea to not be led. Together, they
make blood, always blood. He leads. Then what? A strong man comes.
Then, the best way is exile. If not exile, then for sure, you get more blood.

OLD WOMAN: They tie you back to back. Sail you out. Out on water.
Bayonet your belly. Push you in. Sharks quick. Water warm.

RUBIN: Christophe gave the answer: no murder, no more.

SIRI: Christophe was a blood-soaked tyrant.

*(The wind is stronger. Island music swells, then crackle of static, then new music.
It is acid rock. It is a Miami station.)*

OLD WOMAN: Too much wind. Danger.

SIRI: Listen!

OLD WOMAN: Too strong.

SIRI: Hear it? Listen! That's America coming. I know that's America. We're close now, for sure. Listen!

OLD WOMAN: Wind too strong.

SIRI: We're going to get there, baby child. It's America, Rubin.

RUBIN: It could be.

SIRI: It is, it is. I know it. It's paradise.

RUBIN: Our island was paradise.

SIRI: No more. Our paradise was seventeen pieces of tin in places, cardboard and rag, the rest. The ditch between huts carries water, carries everything. The baby could die just breathing that sewer.

RUBIN: Siri, don't...

SIRI: I'll tell you paradise. We're on the way. We'll get there, you'll see.

RUBIN: It's cold there, in winter.

(SIRI *pulls herself to her feet, slowly building her volume into a rousing hymn.*)

SIRI: Some places, yes. It's big as the world. But different. In America no one is poor. They all have houses, rooms and rooms. Rooms warm when it's cold, cool when it's hot. And rooms have windows. Windows and windows. So cities glitter, diamonds in sunlight. And they're all soooo rich. They have cars and clothes and whatever they want. Just to be happy. And they all have jobs. Aaaand there is so much food. Piles and piles. So much...when their president hears of one hungry, just one...he won't sit to eat, will not take a bite, until that hungry person is fed.

(*Violent jerk*)

RUBIN: What's that?

SIRI: What.

RUBIN: Something happened.

(*Another jerk. Same crashing. Rocking of the boat increases.*)

SIRI: What is it?

(*The* OLD WOMAN *is muttering.*)

SIRI: Nothing can happen now. It can't.

RUBIN: I'm going up to see.

SIRI: I want to come.

RUBIN: No. Stay here.

SIRI: Then look with my eyes.

(RUBIN *creeps toward the ladder, unsteadily, and ascends.*)

SIRI: It's coming, my baby. We're almost there.

(*She holds the baby, looking up anxiously. Long pause, Only wind growing strong.*)

OLD WOMAN: *(Barely audible)* What do they speak there?

SIRI: What?

OLD WOMAN: What are they speaking there? The French?

SIRI: In America? The English.

OLD WOMAN: English. *(Pause)* You speak that?

SIRI: No. Why do we rock again?

OLD WOMAN: Then how can you talk? What job can you do?

SIRI: I can learn. I learn anything. Rubin says my mind is faster than lizards up the wall.

OLD WOMAN: So fast...and so still?

SIRI: Yes. Still like lizard. But waiting. He knows. He's lawyer, Rubin. His daddy made the President angry. He hid in mountains, nine years. Rubin came to hide too. He taught sometimes at my village, my school. He saw my mind. Rubin, he knows the English. He taught me his favorite English. It sings paradise. *(She speaks words strange to her.)* "Be not afeard; the isle is full of noises..."

OLD WOMAN: You sing clear. The power is in you.

SIRI: No.

OLD WOMAN: Power isn't dead because you deny it.

SIRI: Go away from me.

OLD WOMAN: Why be afraid?

SIRI: I'm not afraid.

OLD WOMAN: You know much.

SIRI: I thank you for this, old woman. I thank you for bringing King Henry to my Rubin. You helped him see his strength.

OLD WOMAN: But where is your strength? You're clouded, girl.

SIRI: I am at peace.

OLD WOMAN: Maybe you served, you were chosen?

SIRI: No!

OLD WOMAN: What good is a lie? Your spirit will be angry.

SIRI: No!!

OLD WOMAN: *(Commanding)* Your spirit's name. Your spir-iit...

(The OLD WOMAN draws out the word on a tone. SIRI is pulled to her feet, and finally cries out.)

SIRI: Siiiri, Siri, Sirene!

OLD WOMAN: *(Quietly)* Sirene...the mermaid.

SIRI: Don't speak it. Yes, I'm chosen. I...*(A whisper)* I have sight.

OLD WOMAN: Sight.

SIRI: Sometimes.

OLD WOMAN: You special child. Holy.

SIRI: No. I refuse. I don't want it. Don't want to see pain. Like Rubin. He sees in the streets pain; I, in the mind. People ask me the future. I see pain for them. No. No more.

(RUBIN crawls back down the ladder and moves toward them.)

SIRI: What could you see? Did you see America? I want to look.

RUBIN: Night is coming too early. The sky's strange.

SIRI: Did you see it?!

RUBIN: *(Beat)* The sailor's coming. The sails are down.

SIRI: Down!

(The SAILOR comes fast down the ladder, in bad shape, breathing hard.)

SAILOR: We've struck sail. Coast Guard is out with flood lights. Can't risk the sail being seen.

SIRI: We're close! We've got to keep sailing.

SAILOR: If we caught, you'll wish we were back in the middle of the sea.

SIRI: Why? What will they do?

SAILOR: Lock you in a chain-mail cage, fast as your eye blinks.

SIRI: A cage? A cage? For what? What reason?

SAILOR: Because you try to come in their country.

SIRI: Their foot... Are they white?

SAILOR: Not all.

SIRI: Shiny shoe.

SAILOR: No noise. Keep low. *(He turns to go.)*

RUBIN: What about the storm. Don't we have to ride with the sails up?

SAILOR: Sail is my business. You got storm, and you got Coast Guard. One you count on, the other not. If I've got to choose, I choose the storm, 'cause I don't know yet what he do to me. Coast Guard, I know what he do to me. With him I lose everything.

(Silence as the SAILOR ascends. They look at one another. SIRI wraps the baby tightly, rocks.)

OLD WOMAN: No sails.

SIRI: *(Pause)* You said sky looked strange. How?

RUBIN: Red.

SIRI: Red. Like sunset.

RUBIN: No, all red.

SIRI: *(Moved, but barely whispers)* Red.

OLD WOMAN: You see something.

SIRI: *(Sharply)* No! *(She remains, frozen.)*

RUBIN: *(Settling beside baby)* Little Siri. She wants to see everything. The whole world disappears into her eyes. World above, world below. She's the one who dives to find tiny scarlet darting, brilliant blue and silver, languid golden green, crab under the bottom sand. She dives, then shoots up laughing.

OLD WOMAN: She swim, your Siri?

SIRI: "Be not afeard. The isle is full of noises..." Rubin...tell me the paradise.

RUBIN: The English?

SIRI: Yes, again please.

RUBIN: You tell it. Lazy Siri.

SIRI: "The clouds methought would open and show riches...ready to drop upon me..."

RUBIN: *(Gently)* "...that when I waked..."

SIRI: "...I cried to dream again." To dream again. Hold me, Rubin.

(As RUBIN reaches for her, lightning strikes. Splashes. Violent storm now. The SAILOR comes down, clinging to the ladder.)

SAILOR: Men overboard! All men up to secure the mast. Up, up fast!!

(The SAILOR *pulls himself up through the hatch. The man begins to stand. A ghostly chanting begins.)*

SIRI: *(Frightened)* Rubin, no!

RUBIN: Be good, Siri. Siri isn't afraid.

SIRI: Rubin, I see!

RUBIN: You see a storm, dark night, close to America. You see a man not hiding.

SIRI: Please, Rubin. I see them all being swept into the water!

RUBIN: I have to go up, Siri. You know that…if you have sight.

(She falls silent, her eyes wide.)

RUBIN: Tell me you know.

SIRI: I know.

RUBIN: *(Taking the cloth with coins from his pocket)* Be wise. Remember, you are strong. You have the swift running mind.

(He tries to give her the coins, but she resists.)

RUBIN: Gramma. Take care of this one if I don't see you. You call me honey tongue, but she is the poet. Of plain tongue, and of the French. Soon English too. She will make our island proud.

SIRI: Rubin…

(A long cry from above)

RUBIN: *(Pressing the coins into her hand)* And though she is sweet as a soft fig, her will is fierce.

SIRI: Rubin, I will follow you.

RUBIN: You will obey me. And stay. Unless I call you. Now. Take your child.

SIRI: Rubin!

(She picks up the baby, while he moves to the ladder. Chanting grows higher. He climbs and disappears.)

SIRI: Mambo! I fear now.

OLD WOMAN: Nothing more to fear. We know all the fears. No darkness that has not taken us. No scream in the fire. No squeal of bodies torn, pieces ripped, eyes, bowels, sex torn away from still living souls. We know it all, we have it all on the tongue, in the brain, all still live, still alive.

SIRI: I denied you, my Sirene.

OLD WOMAN: She has no anger. All love.

SIRI: I brought him here. He could have led. He goes by my hand.

OLD WOMAN: What do you see in the red sky?

SIRI: Here. The child...

(She puts the baby gently on the old woman's lap and hands her the coins.)

OLD WOMAN: Why give me this?

SIRI: In America...baptize him, pass him over the fire. Call him Agwe, for the god of the sea.

OLD WOMAN: Girl, I am old. It's for you to replace me.

SIRI: You have strength now. You have as much milk as me.

OLD WOMAN: What do you see, girl?

SIRI: Call her, call! Sirene of the water. She takes me now.

(SIRI turns, intent, and places both hands on the support post. The OLD WOMAN wraps the baby closely in her arms and focuses on SIRI. The chant becomes drumming, with the sounds of the storm.)

OLD WOMAN: Dance, child. Dance. Sirene is your loa. Sirene of the water. She will attend. Does the man dwell with water?

SIRI: *(A cry)* I see...!

(She arches up and back, begins to sway slowly.)

SIRI: He dwells in water...turquoise clear water...singing cool in the sun

(Her movement grows in passion and carries her around the post.)

SIRI: He slices through water...turquoise clear water...embraces me laughing...tumbling as one

(Her dance approaches frenzy.)

SIRI: Our limbs twine in water, world under turquoise, bubbles veer lightward... from the bed we have won

(With a triumphant sound, she rises suddenly, huge, and moves to the ladder.)

SIRI: Aaaaaaaaaah.

(She climbs easily, swiftly, as though drawn upward.)

(The OLD WOMAN is lifted to her feet, crying out in terror, as SIRI disappears.)

(The chanting grows, becoming a deep chord of music that resolves up and up, as lights warm to a soft glow.)

OLD WOMAN: *(Cradling the baby)*
Dance your dance freely, child.
Enter the stream

Waken tomorrow
From your dark dream.

BLACKOUT

HALFWAY

Roma Greth

HALFWAY

For a bio of Roma Greth please see page 104.

HALFWAY was originally produced by the West Coast Ensemble in Los Angeles in 1986.

CHARACTERS

EDIE: *A woman in her forties*
DENNY: *A woman in her late twenties*

(*The scene is the "living room" of a halfway house established for people who have recently been confined to mental institutions. The building was once a Victorian mansion, although one of smaller proportions; ornate woodwork and chandeliers remain. Now the furniture looks second or third hand and very well-used. The T V set is maple wood and does not match the sofa. Nothing really matches; even the plastic flowers in a therapy-constructed vase are out of season in any season. There is an odd lamp with two sides that light. There is a small desk., nondescript, with a locked filing cabinet behind it. At the desk sits* DENNY, *short for Denise, short for a lot of things—like shelves, which she can never quite reach. At first glance she looks very young, perhaps ninteen or twenty, but a closer look reveals that she is a good ten years beyond that—a cherub face but lining. She is working on some papers and drinking a cola. She wears pants and a top, conforming as little as possible to what is probably a dress code for this place.*)*

(EDIE *comes down the stairs, fussing with her belt, straightening a cotton dress which looks as if it was bought for her, not by her. She is in her forties, with eyes which move restlessly. Her hair is neat but has not had good care for some years.* DENNY *looks up with what she thinks is a professional smile.*)

DENNY: Well! Here we are.

EDIE: I don't like that room.

DENNY: That's nice…oh. What's wrong with it?

EDIE: Reminds me. Of another room.

DENNY: I'm sure we're just a little upset…

EDIE: The two windows. Closet—

DENNY: Now you know one's first day outside for awhile is quite an adjustment and…

EDIE: I can't sleep in that room!

DENNY: This isn't a motel!

EDIE: I'll exchange with somebody. Anybody. If I explain…

DENNY: You can't go around asking these…people…to do things like that.

EDIE: Why not?

DENNY: They've got problems. That's why they're here.

EDIE: May I sleep on the sofa?

DENNY: No! Now drop it. If there's one thing I don't need this weekend, it's a big hassle just because you don't like the color of your woodwork.

EDIE: No, you don't understand. The bed... You see, it's in exactly the same position my bed was in. Right near those windows. And he...was always in it. Like part of the bed. Lying there, dirtying up the sheets. Don't you see? I'll go up there and I'll think I'm going to find him again.

DENNY: But you won't. Because you know that even if it looks the same, it isn' t. There won't be a man in your room. You should live so long around here. The only man we've got is John. They sent him here because...he feels more at home with women.

EDIE: Well....

DENNY: Look. Try it. For two nights. Okay? Then if it really bothers you, we'll see what we can do.

EDIE: Two nights?

DENNY: Hang in there.

EDIE: All right.

DENNY: Good girl!

EDIE: After all, he finally left, didn't he? So even if it is the same room, he won't be there.

DENNY: It isn't the same room! You've never been in this house before.

EDIE: *(Walking among the furniture)* Then why do you have my television set?

DENNY: Huh?

EDIE: That's the maple T V I bought when I got married.

DENNY: No. You see, it just looks like your T V set—

EDIE: And that chair. You know when I bought this? When we put the down payment on that house in the suburbs.

DENNY: There are a million old chairs like that one

EDIE: Oh! No!

DENNY: What's wrong now?

EDIE: The sofa.

DENNY: It's our sofa! It came from Goodwill Industries. We paid twenty dollars for it!

EDIE: No. It came from the home I lived in when I was a girl.

DENNY: You stop this right now!

EDIE: All the debris of my life has washed up in this house....

DENNY: Oh, wow! They really sent me a live one this time.

EDIE: The lamp.

DENNY: You are giving me the creeps!

EDIE: This lamp came from my first apartment. One side never worked.

(She turns on the lamp; both sides light.)

DENNY: See? See? It's not the same lamp!

EDIE: Somebody fixed it. That's right—I forgot. He fixed it.

DENNY: Do you want me to call the doctor?

EDIE: Why? Are you sick?

DENNY: Do you know what I can do to you with just one little phone call?

EDIE: Oh, you mean—

DENNY: Right!

EDIE: —to threaten me.

DENNY: I'm not threatening you. I'm just suggesting that you— Well, you'd better take one of your pills and calm down.

EDIE: I am calm.

DENNY: You are not calm!

EDIE: Would you like one of my pills?

DENNY: No! I've got my own pills! What I mean is—well, you'd better be good. Or else.

EDIE: I'm sorry. I didn't mean to upset you. It's just—this is a strange home.

DENNY: It's a halfway house, not a home. You'll get used to it.

EDIE: I thought there'd be more people here.

DENNY: There are.

EDIE: Where?

DENNY: Well, they have jobs. And some visit their families on weekends.

EDIE: Getting ready to join the world again.

DENNY: Right!

EDIE: Does everybody work?

DENNY: Not right away. One's taking a nap. And John's on the screened-in porch trying out his watercolors.

EDIE: He's an artist?

DENNY: Ha!

EDIE: Oh.

DENNY: We try everything here.

EDIE: Of course.

(She tries the lamp again.)

DENNY: Will you quit with the lamp?

EDIE: *(Leaves the lamp reluctantly; goes to a window)* The garden looks nice. Shady.

DENNY: That's a no-no.

EDIE: What?

DENNY: We don't go outside...alone. Not yet.

EDIE: You could come out with me.

DENNY: No-no. Weren't you given orientation about what to expect here?

EDIE: Yes.

DENNY: You don't seem to remember very well.

EDIE: It's just—seeing all my things again. *(She has been rooting down among the sofa cushions.)* Dad was always losing money in this sofa.

DENNY: *(Ignoring the coin EDIE holds up and becames very matter-of-fact)* In the kitchen is a list of who does what.

EDIE: To whom?

DENNY: Don't give me a hard time, will you? Like in—getting meals, cleaning...

EDIE: Oh, that's right. We have to....

DENNY: You're not in a hospital any more. You don't get waited on.

EDIE: I haven't touched a cookpot in two years.

DENNY: So at first you'll just wash dishes.

EDIE: I have forgotten your name.

DENNY: Denny. Short for Denise.

EDIE: I'm Edie. Edith Richards.

DENNY: I know. I have your file.

EDIE: Maybe I shouldn't be here. Not yet.

DENNY: Oh come on. The first day's always rough. Why don't you sit down and read a nice magazine? We've got *Better Homes and Gardens, Woman's Day, Christian Herald*—

EDIE: Dr Kort said I was ready. To try it.

DENNY: He should know, so relax. Your first night—you're our guest.

EDIE: What do you mean?

DENNY: You don't help with dinner.

EDIE: Oh, no! If I'm supposed to help, I want to.

DENNY: You're not supposed to. You start with breakfast tomorrow morning.

EDIE: I want to help!

DENNY: Not tonight!

EDIE: Tonight! I'm going to cooperate with you!

DENNY: Well, you're doing a piss-poor job of it! I have my charts all made out. See? *(Showing her)* All done. You're not on my chart until tomorrow morning. And I'm not about to redo tonight's chart. You think this is an easy job?

EDIE: Yes.

DENNY: Well, I got news for you.

EDIE: *(Looking over charts)* I could redo this chart in two minutes.

DENNY: *(Grabbing papers)* Butt out!

EDIE: How long have you worked here?

DENNY: Why?

EDIE: Dr Lort says...we must think about other people. Be interested.

DENNY: Long enough to know my job.

EDIE: Oh, I'm sure. *(She sits and stares at her.* DENNY *tries to work on a card file, but finally can't stand it anymore.)*

DENNY: What're you staring it?

EDIE: I'm interested in you.

DENNY: Get interested in T V instead!

EDIE: A month.

DENNY: What?

EDIE: I bet you haven't been here more than a month.

DENNY: I've been here every weekend for two months!

EDIE: Oh, you're just —

DENNY: You better believe I'm just. I couldn't take this shit five days a week.

EDIE: I think I'd like a job like this.

DENNY: Yeah, but we all know where you've been for the past couple years.... Oh, god. (*She is distressed that she has lost control to that extent.*) Can't you go read the *T V Guide*? Please!

EDIE: Maybe this isn't the same furniture.

DENNY: No shit?

EDIE: Maybe it's just that there's been so much furniture. In so many different rooms. I was the furniture keeper, you know.

DENNY: Umm.

EDIE: Cleaned it. Polished it. And finally...threw it away.

DENNY: Want a cola?

EDIE: All right.

DENNY: You'll be good? Remember...outside's a no-no.

(DENNY *exits.* EDIE *watches her go, then quietly moves to the lamp and turns it on. This time only half of it lights. She observes this for an instant, then turns it off. She goes to a table, runs a finger across it, and finds the table dusty. She frowns, then gets down on her knees and looks under the sofa. She reaches under and gets a handful of dust woolies.* DENNY *reenters with another bottle of cola and a slice of pie.*)

DENNY: Look what was left over from lunch! —Edie! Where are you? (*Spotting her on the floor*) What're you doing down there?

EDIE: Look at all this dust.

DENNY: So some of the women aren't too swift at cleaning.

EDIE: It chokes me!

DENNY: Sue us.

EDIE: It solidifies out of the air! My lungs are like the underside of a sofa. From all the years of dust. When I cough, I feel the rolls of dust inside me.

DENNY: Drink some cola.

EDIE: Do you know what's so terrible about being a woman?

DENNY: There's nothing terrible about it—

EDIE: We attract dust.

DENNY: Come again?

EDIE: Men don't attract dust. You look at men, you never think of dust. But women, you see, it follows us around.

DENNY: Why didn't I study bookkeeping when I had the chance?

EDIE: Listen to me! There are armies of women out there buying dust pans and dust mops! Fighting the never-ending battles of dust. The endless cleaning of all the endless rooms. Vacuum cleaner bags full of solidified dust. That's why cleaners weigh so much! We breathe it, die of it, and turn to dust. Men don't turn to dust. They just get hard.

DENNY: Now wait a minute—

EDIE: —They turn into fossils of porous dustrock. Pillars of dust that we see when we look over our shoulders. You know—there'll be dust rolling around under my coffin for some woman to clean up. You don't have to cremate women. Some of them turned to dust years ago. Like me....

DENNY: I thought you said it choked you.

EDIE: Well, it did. But I guess I finally got used to it. Now I buy little boxes of it at the store and put it on my face with a powderpuff. It's great for keeping the sun off your skin at the beach. Dust Guard under my arms. I also use a dust douche.

DENNY: Cut it out, Edie!

EDIE: Do you know what I have?

DENNY: Whatever it is, I hope it's not catching.

EDIE: Dust farts.

DENNY: What?

EDIE: Ever since my stomach went bad—after I got my ulcer—dust farts.

DENNY: Jesus. Your ulcer's healed. It says so on your chart. Have a piece of pie.

EDIE: No.

DENNY: It's homemade. Dust free. Non-institutional.

EDIE: Non-institutional...

DENNY: Your first slice of non-institutional pie in two years. Here. (EDIE *takes the pie but does not eat it.*) Laura baked it. She's the one easy to get along with. Mentally retarded.

EDIE: You're my first non-institutional person in two years.... That's more important, I guess, than being my first non-institutional pie.

DENNY: Thank you.

EDIE: *(Putting down pie)* Non-institutional person, may I tell you something?

DENNY: Of course. That is what we're here for.

EDIE: When I lit the lamp while you were in the kitchen, only half of it lit up.

DENNY: Here's your soda.

EDIE: I'll show you.

DENNY: Don't you go near that lamp! *(Going to lamp herself but not lighting it)* Look, if I can prove that it isn't your lamp, will you stop about the lamp?

EDIE: You can't prove it.

DENNY: It is my lamp. I donated it to Halfway House. I had it in my apartment—the dumb thing never did fit in. So I brought it over here. I thought it'd go great with the rest of this junk. *(EDIE stares at her.)* Sorry it's such a shock.

EDIE: You have an apartment—

DENNY: I've got to live somewhere.

EDIE: You've been married.

DENNY: How'd you know that?

EDIE: It didn't work out. Sex every morning—

DENNY: Much you know!

EDIE: You have trouble holding jobs. That's how you ended up here on weekends.

DENNY: No! That's not —

EDIE: I'm looking in a mirror!

DENNY: The mirror's in the hall —

EDIE: I'm seeing myself fifteen years ago!

DENNY: What you're seeing is the doctor! *(Going to the phone)* They told me I don't have to put up with you flakes if you get too unstrung.

EDIE: *(Coming quickly to put her finger on the phone, cutting the connection)* No.

DENNY: Don't you try anything funny! I have buttons to press—I can get help in two seconds

EDIE: I'm not violent. Please. I just got out.

DENNY: What I'd like to know is—how?

EDIE: I could have gotten out any time I wanted in the past two years. You just start putting on lipstick again. Ask to go to a hairdresser. Show an interest in clothes. And those jackass male doctors rush to sign the release.

DENNY: No—

EDIE: Ask any woman up there.

DENNY: Well, maybe—

EDIE: *(Looking closely at her)* You are me.

DENNY: Now don't start that again!

EDIE: Have you got psoriasis?

DENNY: I didn't when I came in here today.

EDIE: But I broke out with it when I reached thirty.

DENNY: See? I'm somebody else.

EDIE: You'll get it. Any day now.

DENNY: Guess what you're going to get?

EDIE: What?

DENNY: A bad mark on the report card that goes to Dr Kort.

EDIE: It won't matter. I can fool them any time I want.

DENNY: Yeah, but you're not fooling me. You don't belong here.

EDIE: You do?

DENNY: It's my job!

EDIE: You're halfway, Denny.

DENNY: What?

EDIE: Halfway to that hospital up country. You can't hold a job.
Your marriage was a mess. How many friends do you have?
Anybody who misses you weekends? And you can't handle this place.
Even those simple charts have you up the wall.

DENNY: Stop it!

EDIE: You're the attendant. I'm the inmate. Make me stop.

DENNY: Eat your pie!

EDIE: No.

DENNY: Sit down!

EDIE: *(At the lamp; turning it off and on; both sides light now)* No.

DENNY: Don't do that!

EDIE: It's fun. They wouldn't let me do this up country.

DENNY: I'm calling them! So help me—even if you get down on your knees and beg.

EDIE: *(As* DENNY *goes to telephone)* How many times have you had to call for help, Denny? Won't they soon get tired of your inability to deal with things?

*(*DENNY *stops, then turns, grabs* EDIE, *and pushes her into a chair.)*

EDIE: I bet you're not supposed to lay a finger on us. When I report this you'll be in big trouble.

DENNY: What are you trying to do to me?

EDIE: What have I done to myself?

DENNY: I told them I could handle you people!

EDIE: You'll do well up country. You have to be able to lie up there.

DENNY: Damn you! *(She goes to the desk and sits, puts her head in her arms on the desk, and remains motionless.)*

EDIE: What're you doing? …Oh; I know. Escape. Into the circles of your own arms. And everything you don't want goes away. Only I won't go away because I'm part of you.

DENNY: I'm Denise Rourke! I've got a birth certificate to prove it. And you're a nut and I've got your file to prove that.

EDIE: I'm not a nut. Don't you call me a nut.

DENNY: Nut! Nut! *(*EDIE *picks up the slice of pie and calmly smears it over* DENNY's *face.)* Oh, my god—I—if Mrs Winslow comes in now, she'll— Why didn't they keep you up there in the nut house? What do you want out of me?

EDIE: You're a mess. You have pie smeared all over your face.

DENNY: I'd like to.

EDIE: Of course you would, but that isn't the answer. You'd only be hurting yourself.

DENNY: Ohhhh —

EDIE: Maybe you'd better go wash before Mrs Whoever comes. I'd hate to see me lose this job.

DENNY: Listen to me. Is your name Denise?

EDIE: No.

DENNY: Good! You're doing well. Now. If we're the same person, how come I have a different name?

EDIE: It's my nickname?

DENNY: Did anybody ever call you Denise?

EDIE: No—guess not.

DENNY: Then that proves we're not the same person.

EDIE: All it proves is that somewhere along the line I changed my name. Women change their names when they get married.

DENNY: Not their first names!

EDIE: Uh huh! In my generation! Mrs Charles Burdock. Ffft. No name of your own!

DENNY: Was your husband's name Edith?

EDIE: Now that you mention it, I think it was.

DENNY: Edith is a woman's name!

EDIE: My first name was Denise and then I got married and became Mrs Edith Richards.

DENNY: *(Wiping her face with tissues)* I don't believe this is happening to me.

EDIE: You know we're the same person. You were even saying "we"—including yourself with me when I came downstairs.

DENNY: I was, wasn't I?— I always do that!

EDIE: Why?

DENNY: It seems more— Never mind. I don't care what happens to me, I'm going to get hold of Dr Kort. They're going to come and get you.

EDIE: I'll just come back again.

DENNY: Yeah, but maybe I won't be here by that time.

EDIE: Going to lose this job too, Denny?

DENNY: After this—probably.

EDIE: I wish I could help.

DENNY: Oh, you've been a big help.

EDIE: *(As DENNY goes to phone)* Oh, come on—let's bring the two halves of our split personality together and see if we can't figure out something.

DENNY: *(Allowing herself to be pulled from phone)* I must be nuts. Otherwise, I'd call. That's the sane thing to do.

EDIE: You have to help yourself, Denny. Nobody else is going to help you.

DENNY: That's what psychiatrists are for!

EDIE: Then how come you haven't gone to one?

DENNY: Well. I...

EDIE: Ah ha. We know.

DENNY: We know....

EDIE: It's starting to make sense to you, isn't it?

DENNY: I don't want to be you fifteen years from now!

EDIE: But you will be.

DENNY: I'm— No!

EDIE: Yes.

DENNY: Maybe.

EDIE: Isn't it logical?

DENNY: Kind of, but —

EDIE: But you'd like to change it, right?

DENNY: Yes.

EDIE: How?

DENNY: I— Look for another job?

EDIE: You've done that before.

DENNY: Yes—well—

EDIE: Get married again.

DENNY: Now I know you're crazy!

EDIE: Ninety-five percent of the people still do it.

DENNY: But it didn't work out for us! No, no. I didn't mean that. I have a whole history of my own!

EDIE: So do I. A dozen of them. Which would you like to hear? I have a simply marvelous "I was born in a ghetto" history that'll—

DENNY: I only have one!

EDIE: Well, it takes time. The others'll come to you.

DENNY: They will, won't they?

EDIE: Uh huh.

DENNY: What in God's name am I going to do?

EDIE: Accept. Compromise. Fit the pattern. That's what they tell you.

DENNY: Who?

EDIE: Them. Quick, Denny! Do it. Before people notice and turn away. And oh how they turn away when you're sick. All your friends. Suddenly you don't have any.

DENNY: I can't fit the patterns!

EDIE: We could kill ourself.

DENNY: That hurts too much.

EDIE: Doesn't it hurt now?

DENNY: You're not going to talk me into that trip! No way. Because there's one thing you're forgetting, Edith Richards, I've got hope.

EDIE: Really? Why?

DENNY: Just because. That's why.

EDIE: I don't think that's very logical.

DENNY: Hope. H-O-P-E!

EDIE: Define it.

DENNY: Well—every job I get might be the one I'll keep. That's hope.

EDIE: Strikes me as being impractical in view of past performances.

DENNY: So's prayer impractical.

EDIE: Prayer?

DENNY: Maybe it wouldn't hurt you to try a little prayer.

EDIE: To what?

DENNY: How do I know to what? To whomever the New Age believes in. The vegetarian god of the Seventh Day Adventists. Get saved.

EDIE: Wouldn't work.

DENNY: You ever tried it?

EDIE: Did you?

DENNY: I will! Someday.

EDIE: I forgot how silly I was at that age.

DENNY: I'm going to keep on trying. That's hope. *(She turns on the lamp; both sides light.)* It's brighter in here already.

EDIE: Only because you turned on my lamp.

DENNY: No, because I have hope.

EDIE: I think you'd better try one of my pills. I'll bet yours are just the kind they advertise on television.

DENNY: I feel fine now. I don't need a pill.

EDIE: Come! Join the tranquilized society. *(She tries to give* DENNY *a pill;* DENNY *knocks the pills out of her hand, scattering them.)* Hey! I can't live without those pills!

DENNY: Have you tried lately?

EDIE: *(Turns off the lamp)* Shit on your hope! Help me pick up my pills! *(Instead,* DENNY *steps on the pills, smashing them.* EDIE *shoves* DENNY *aside and starts scrambling after the pills.)* You always have to spoil everything! Like my lamp! Why'd you take off that glass knob on the top? It was the prettiest thing about my lamp.

DENNY: There was no glass knob on top of this lamp.

EDIE: There was! I remember—

DENNY: Not on this lamp!

EDIE: *(Pausing)* Not on that lamp?

DENNY: No!

EDIE: But my lamp had a glass knob on top.

DENNY: Then I guess this isn't your lamp. *(EDIE sits as if worn out.)* It is my lamp— Wow. You really had me going there for a while. I've got to get a different job. I'm just no good at this. Hey. Are you all right?

EDIE: Yes.

DENNY: The doctor will give you more tranquilizers.

EDIE: Sure.

DENNY: I won't say anything about this—afternoon. *(EDIE nods listlessly.)* Edie—you got this far. That's halfway.

EDIE: *(Rising)* I think I'll go to my room for awhile.

DENNY: I won't say anything about this—afternoon.

(EDIE nods listlessly.)

DENNY: Edie, you got this far. That's halfway.

EDIE: *(Rising)* I think I'll go to my room for a while.

DENNY: I thought you didn't like that room.

EDIE: I'll get used to it.

DENNY: All right. I have phone calls to make anyway.

(EDIE watches uneasily as DENNY *slowly goes up the stairs a few steps.* DENNY *turns away.* EDIE *pauses. Instead of going to the phone,* DENNY *moves to the lamp.*

She can hardly bring herself to touch it, but does so, turning it on. Now only half of it lights up. DENNY *turns away, staring at the light. Finally she forces herself to run to the phone and dial.)*

DENNY: Mrs Winslow?... Yes, it's Denny. I know I shouldn't call you so often, but— Well, I really need to get out of here. Right now... It's hard to explain, but— You see, there *are* other things I can do. There are! Places I haven't gone. People I haven't— There's even this guy I met. Well, he seems nice, and he did kind of mention moving in together.

EDIE: *(Who has been watching and listening)* Oh, Denny. No. Not another meaningless relationship.

*(*DENNY *jerks around as if she has been physically touched, dropping the phone, which makes squawking sounds.)*

DENNY: It might work out this time! It could! It could...it could.

(As DENNY *stares at* EDIE, EDIE *comes down the stairs again. Their eyes meet.* EDIE *moves forward with her hand outstretched.* DENNY *also moves, her own hand outstretched toward* EDIE. *But before they come together, they stop, frozen in their forward movement.)*

BLACKOUT

HELEN MELON AT THE SIDESHOW

Katy Dierlam

HELEN MELON AT THE SIDESHOW
© copyright 1995 by Katy Dierlam

For all rights please contact Broadway Play Publishing Inc.

Katy Dierlam is an actress who has worked extensively with The Ridiculous Theatrical Company in New York City where she has appeared in plays including HOW TO WRITE A PLAY, SALAMMBO, MEDEA, and TURDS IN HELL. She has been on the Joan Rivers, Jerry Springer, and Maury Povich television shows, and she can be seen in Woody Allen's SHADOWS AND FOG, Alan Parker's ANGEL HEART, and Peter Medak's ROMEO IS BLEEDING. She developed HELEN MELON AT THE SIDESHOW May through September 1992 during a stint working as the Fat Lady at Coney Island's "Sideshows by the Seashore" in Brooklyn.

CHARACTERS

BALLYER
HELEN MELON

DEDICATION

For Ned

(The setting is a carnival sideshow. Banners lure patrons to the Tattooed Man, Sword Swallower, Rubber Man, and other exhibits that utilize the human body as entertainment. Projections of sideshows and circuses might flash across the stage. The BALLYER *is a male voice-over. He is never seen. During the* BALLYER's *introduction,* HELEN *is seated upstage center with her back to the audience. As is traditional for sideshow Fat Ladies, she wears a baby doll costume with big bows and a flowered straw hat.)*

BALLYER: *(Male voice)* Step right up ladies, gentlemen, and small wonders. Don't be shy. I am here to introduce you to the last Ten-in-One Sideshow left in America. Ten-in-One. Lucky for you, that means ten astonishing acts for one low, low price. You can't see anything from way back there. Come closer. That's right. Short ones in front. You can hear me better up here. And you can see what's for sale. Right here, yes, right on this very spot you will see the India Rubber Man, the Snake Lady who slithers and twines herself around her rare nine-foot albino python. Or is it he who winds himself around her luscious…? You decide. You'll see the man who walks on glass and eats it, too! And the Illustrated Man, with every pore of his colorful body covered with elaborate tattoos! You'll gasp as the Sword Swallower bites the big one. Flinch as a gorgeous gal steps into the blade box to be pieced with a dozen razor-sharp steel knives. But best of all, the prize attraction of our show—the woman you'll never see anywhere but here—Helen Melon, the fattest Fat Lady of them all! It takes four men to hug her and a box car to lug her! She is SO fat she was born on the first, second, AND third of August! We have her birth certificate to prove it! *(Sounds of a cane tapping rapidly against a table)* It's show time! Get your tickets and come right in. Hurry! We haven't fed Helen for an hour and she's starting to shrink! Come right in. It's show time! Hurry!

HELEN: *(Rising and walking toward audience)* Hi, there. I'm Helen Melon, and I am fat. Take a good, long look. This is all here just for you, just for today. Five hundred pounds of soft, round, delicious female. All Fat Ladies are different you know. Some fat ladies are big up here *(Grabs her breasts and shakes them)*, some are big down here *(Runs her hands over her low-slung belly and hips)*, and some of us are boffo in the back *(Turns and shakes her rear at the audience)*. I'm big everywhere!

Oh, I know what you are thinking. I've heard it all ten thousand times before so let's get it over with right now. "Oh, my god, look at her!" "Yo, there's your girlfriend, Leroy!" *(Into the mike, miming mockery of herself*

walking past:) "Baboom, baaboom, baboom, baaboom." "Thar she blows!"
They yell it out from passing cars and trucks. Women come up to me like I
was public property and say, "You should be ashamed of yourself." But my
favorite, my absolute favorite, is my mother-in-law's: "I just worry about
your health, dear."

People ask me, they say, "Helen?" They call me Helen. "How did it happen?
How did you get to be so..uh...so, uh...heavyset?" FAT! Pu-leeze! The word
is FAT! F-A-T. Fat. A perfectly good English word. It means what it says
and nothing more.

I weighed five pounds six ounces at birth. And it's not glandular, either.
It seldom is. I'll tell you a secret. One of my earliest memories—I must have
been around four—is of waiting for the ice cream truck to ding-a-ling onto
my block, my tiny hands clutching pennies I had stolen from my mother's
purse. Oh, Mama! She taught me right from wrong, just like your Mama
did, I'm sure. *(Seeking audience response, teasingly:)* Didn't she? Sure she did!
But I just went my own way. And I'm not sorry.

That's right. I'm an appetite outlaw with wild, wild ways and a baaaad
attitude. I love fruits and vegetables...apples with sugar and butter,
strawberry dacquoise, mushrooms in rivers of cream—I adore the basic
food groups. These things are my passion—or one of them, anyway.
(Laughs) As a matter of fact, you all look so good out there I could eat you
with a big soup spoon. Hi there, little pumpkin. *(Picks a child in the audience)*
You look awfully sweet. Could I have you for dinner tonight? Watch out!
(A mock lunge) The fat lady will get you. *(Diabolical laugh; pause)* No, you're
too sweet, even for me. Even for dessert.

Joking aside, folks, there's history here.... That's why you've come, isn't it?
(Laughs)

There have been Fat Ladies in sideshows since the beginning of ballydom.
Baby Ruth Pontico who worked for Ringling Brothers weighed eight
hundred-fifteen pounds at her top weight. *(Awed)* She was the fattest Fat
Lady I've heard of. *(Pause)* I wish I could have known her.... But the most
famous Fat Lady was Dolly Dimples. See, back in Dolly's time, in the
thirties and forties, there was no television. *(Shudder)* No *Roseanne* or *Melrose
Place* or even *Eyewitness News*. People went to the circus and the carnivals
for entertainment and to find out what was new in the world. Dolly was
famous from coast to coast for being fat. Sad to say Dolly retired from
the sideshow in 1950. She gave it all up, went on a diet, and wound up
weighing one-hundred-twenty-two pounds more or less for the rest of her
life. Wouldn't you know, she wrote a book called *The World's Greatest Diet*.

My husband read Dolly's book when he was ten years old and—get
this—he fell in love with her "before" pictures! He spent a lot of his young
life looking for a lady as fat, as smart, and as pretty as Dolly. There are a lot

of us out there, but lucky for me I'm the one he found. Of course, I was suspicious at first. See, there are these chubby-chasers and I didn't and don't want to be anyone's fetish. "What do you want a fat lady like me for?" I demanded. Well, I'm not going to tell you what he said because this is a family show. *(Grins)* We have standards.

I will tell you one thing, though. It is a lot harder to be a Fat Lady now than it was in Dolly's day. *(Pause)* Everyone is out to reform you. *(Sigh)* The mail comes with flyers for health clubs and aerobics classes. The supermarkets are filled with ultra fat-free slim-you-down bleechs. *(Indignant)* There were low-calorie potato chips in the snack section and skim-milk egg nog in the dairy container yesterday. Can you believe it!? I have to be on constant guard against dwindling. *(Outraged)* There's a dietary virus running rampant in our grocery stores and no one even cares!

Oh, well…. You know it's not over till the Fat Lady sings, so I'm going to sing my husband's favorite song. *(She sings "Ain't No Sweet Man Worth the Salt of My Tears," or "Kitchen Man", or similar blues song traditional in sideshows of the thirties.)*

That's all for now, folks. But there are nine more mouth-watering acts to come, so stay seated. And when you leave, walk around the fair and help yourself to the spun sugar candy, giant hot dogs with mustard and sauerkraut, honey-coated roasted peanuts, chocolate fudge ice cream, and an extra-large helping of those crispy deep-fried potatoes. Enjoy your lives. *(Mae Westish:)* But save a morsel for me.

BLACKOUT

IN THE BEGINNING

Rebecca Ritchie

Rebecca Ritchie graduated Goucher College and the Law School of the University of Pennsylvania. She is assistant general counsel for Health Care Plan, a health maintenance organization headquartered in Buffalo, New York. She is a member of the Dramatists Guild, the Western New York Playwrights Workshop under the direction of Emanuel Fried, and Polaris North in New York City. For the past twenty years she has written extensively for national and international publications, among them *The Washington Post, The Buffalo News, Arts and Antiques Weekly, Childbirth Educator,* and *Contemporary Senior Health.* Her plays include THE SHIVA QUEEN, AMATEURS, EXIT EDEN, THE WEDDING CONTRACT, AN UNORTHODOX ARRANGEMENT, THE GRATZ DELUSION, and A PERSONAL EXCHANGE.

IN THE BEGINNING had a workshop production by Polaris North at the 29th Street Theater, New York City on 18 November 1991. George Rondo was the director. The premier production was at The Alleyway Theatre, One Curtain Up Alley, Buffalo, New York on 11 June 1992 as part of the 1992 Buffalo Festival of Short Works, Neal Radice, Artistic Director.

LILITH . . . . Jeanmarie Lally
EVE . . . . Edna Pelonero
RACHEL . . . . Patricia Hartman

Director . . . . .Joyce Stilson

CHARACTERS

RACHEL: *A documentary film maker*

EVE ADAMOVICH: *The oldest living pioneer and widow of Adam*

LILITH CLAY: *The first woman*

(Scene: A hill overlooking the Tigris-Euphrates Valley with a view of the Persian Gulf. Time: The present.)

(At rise: EVE supports herself with a cane; she carries a large canvas bag. RACHEL, in safari outfit and pith helmet with lenses draped around her neck, accompanies her to the crest of the hill. LILITH sits on a park bench, unnoticed by the others.)

RACHEL: There you are. A nice seat in the shade for our star.

EVE: Star! Ha.

RACHEL: When I finish with you, you'll be a star!

EVE: A star with a bad hip.

RACHEL: Maybe you'd better sit down.

EVE: I'm okay. Been sitting all day.

RACHEL: You're sure you can't remember where that tree stood? It would add a lot if we could film you on the exact spot.

EVE: Got no idea. Could have been anywhere.

RACHEL: Maybe if we drove around…

EVE: It's all changed. Hills used to be covered with forests. I couldn't recognize one tree.

LILITH: We hung a hammock from it. Between that one and the willow.

RACHEL: A friend of yours?

EVE: Her? I thought she was one of your people.

RACHEL: Never seen her before.

LILITH: Scrawny tree. Not much to look at.

RACHEL: *(Aside)* Let's find another place.

LILITH: She don't bother me.

RACHEL: As long as you're happy…. Now don't move, Eve, OK?…
I've got to supervise the camera set-up. But I'll be back in a few minutes.
But until then, stay in the shade. We don't want you keeling over.

EVE: Heat's fine. It's the cold I can't stand.

RACHEL: *(Fanning herself)* Brutal today.

EVE: You should have seen it before air conditioning.

RACHEL: There's lemonade in the Thermos. Keep your fluids up.

EVE: I'll be fine. Enjoy yourself.

(RACHEL *off*)

EVE: *(To* LILITH, *indicating the bench)* It's all right by you?

LILITH: It's a free country.

(EVE *sits on the park bench next to* LILITH, *takes a ball of wool from the canvas bag, and begins to crochet.)* Lilies of the valley and Rose of Sharon.

EVE: Excuse me?

LILITH: The delta. Used to be covered with them.

EVE: I'd forgotten that.

LILITH: And the lilac. It bloomed all year, not like now. The scent so heavy, it woke you in the morning.

EVE: I remember that.

LILITH: *(Indicating the crochet work)* A baby blanket?

EVE: A sweater. For my granddaughter... The young ones walk around half-naked these days.

LILITH: They've got the legs for it.

EVE: Cover up, I tell her. Men like a little mystery.

LILITH: What is that color?

EVE: Fig green.

LILITH: Look nice with a tan... The girl you were with, she's making a film?

EVE: Sure, she's making a film. She's a director.

LILITH: A director?

EVE: Documentaries. Writes the script. Produces. Everything.

LILITH: Jewish?

EVE: Yeah, she's Jewish.

LILITH: Nu, what's the film about, she's making?

EVE: My husband.

LILITH: Your husband? Important man, your husband?

EVE: First man in the delta. They're building a monument to him.

LILITH: You don't say? Just for being first?

EVE: Sure.

LILITH: What else did he do?

EVE: When?

LILITH: After he was first.... What did he do, they should make a film about him?

EVE: He lived. He worked. Provided for the family.

LILITH: You did nothing in all this?

EVE: Sure. I helped.

LILITH: So the film...it's about you, too?

EVE: It's about my husband. He's not alive, olov hasholem. *[Pronounced av-rah-SHAL-um]* In the film, they interview me about my husband.

LILITH: His story.

EVE: You got a problem with that?

LILITH: I got no problem.

EVE: You seem to have a problem.

LILITH: *(Shrugs)* Very nice, a film about your husband.... You probably got plenty to say.

EVE: I'll tell what I remember.... We did some of this already, at my apartment. They take lots of film, save what they want.... Cut and paste, you got a movie.

LILITH: He was a good man, your husband?

EVE: Why wouldn't he be a good man?

LILITH: I wondered, that's all.... I knew him.

EVE: You knew my husband?

LILITH: In the old days.

EVE: When in the old days?

LILITH: In the beginning.

EVE: There was nobody else there in the beginning.

LILITH: So I didn't know him.

EVE: There's nobody left from the beginning. They put ads in the papers. Nobody answered.

LILITH: I'm here, aren't I?

EVE: How come I don't know you?

LILITH: You weren't around.

EVE: I've always been around.

LILITH: Before you.

EVE: What are you talking about? There wasn't anybody before me.

LILITH: So I'm wrong.

EVE: What's your name?

LILITH: I'm wrong. You don't need to know my name.

EVE: We're having a conversation. I'm asking your name.... I'm Eve.

LILITH: Delighted.

EVE: And you...?

LILITH: Lil.

EVE: Adam never mentioned a Lil. I got a very good memory. A Lilian from the old days, he never mentioned.

LILITH: My name's Lilith.

EVE: Lilith?

LILITH: That's right.

EVE: Oi.

LILITH: So. You married that shmendrik. *[Pronounced SHMEN-drick and means a fool]*

EVE: You didn't like him, fine. Just don't call him a fool in front of me.

LILITH: No offense meant, but to me, he wasn't much.

EVE:Excuse me if I disagree. He was my husband, and I was happy with him.

LILITH: Congratulations.

EVE: A respected man.

LILITH: Who's saying no?

EVE: You wouldn't believe all the articles they wrote about him. An obituary took half a page. *(Beat)* You stay with him long?

LILITH: He didn't tell you?

EVE: He mentioned there was somebody else. Your name slipped out.

LILITH: I'm surprised he remembered it.

EVE: He thought about you, too, sometimes. I knew, because he would spit on the ground three times.

LILITH: Lovely habits that man had.

EVE: When the children were born, he tied red ribbons all around the crib. He didn't say anything, but I knew.... You don't like red?

LILITH: Not my color.

EVE: So exactly how long were you together, you and my husband?

LILITH: Not long. It was annulled.

EVE: Glad to hear it. Left you bitter, though. I can tell.

LILITH: I got no beef.

EVE: Something's up. This is no coincidence, you sitting here, just when we're doing the filming.

LILITH: I'm enjoying the view. Two rivers coming together makes a nice view.

EVE: Why'd you leave him?

LILITH: We had differences.

EVE: What kind?

LILITH: Man and woman differences.

EVE: Ha! We never had that trouble.

LILITH: It's not what you think.

EVE: Pardon me. You left my husband, I thought maybe you had a problem.

LILITH: I had no problem...but you...maybe.

EVE: What's that supposed to mean?

LILITH: What you going to tell the director about Adam? The truth or some bubbe meiseh [pronounced BUH-beh-MY-seh, and means old wives' tale] she wants to hear?

EVE: The truth. I always tell the truth.

LILITH: Just wondered.

EVE: I got no secrets. I had a long and happy marriage.... Not like some people.

LILITH: Who's saying different?

EVE: My husband was a tower of strength.

LILITH: To you, I'm sure he was.

EVE: He built this nation single-handed, out of nothing.

LILITH: Now this I find hard to believe.

EVE: He could do anything. He was very handy.

LILITH: Handy! He couldn't turn over a rock!

EVE: Excuse me! He could do anything he set his mind to.

LILITH: Like what?

EVE: Well....

LILITH: Herd sheep?

EVE: I usually did that.

LILITH: Weed the garden?

EVE: My job.

LILITH: Build the irrigation system?

EVE: Oh, that was Adam's idea.

LILITH: How big an idea is it to bring water to plants?

EVE: He thought of it first.

LILITH: And he built it?

EVE: I did most of the digging. I always had a better sense of direction.

LILITH: So what else could he do?

EVE: Well...he named the animals. He was good at that.

LILITH: He thought up names by himself?

EVE: Most of them. I did the rest.

LILITH: And he could remember these names?

EVE: He had a little trouble sometimes. Dyslexia, they call it.

LILITH: He gave an animal a name and couldn't remember it?

EVE: He needed a little refreshing sometimes. Like, he'd say, "What was that thing with the four legs? The one with the marks and the long neck?" Giraffe, I'd say. "And the fat one that floats, the biggest one." Whale, I'd say.... That's all he needed. A little push. Then he remembered.

LILITH: A genius you married.

EVE: A zoologist.

LILITH: You gonna tell this to Rachel, the director?

EVE: About naming the names? Sure.

LILITH: That he couldn't remember them? Had one job all his life and couldn't do it right?

EVE: Look, he was my husband. I lived with him. I don't need you to go around tearing him down.

LILITH: Pardon me. You said you were going to tell the true story. I'm just surprised at what you think is the truth.

EVE: You've come back to ruin this film. That's what you're doing. You read about it in the paper, and you want to ruin it for me.

LILITH: Why would I ruin it for you? You seem like a nice lady.

EVE: This film is important. The director goes to film festivals, wins big prizes. She wants to make a film about me, I'm not going to stand in her way.

LILITH: I thought this film was about your husband.

EVE: It is about Adam. But I'm his widow. It's an honor for both of us. Not everybody gets to be in a film.

LILITH: For this honor you'll stretch the truth?

EVE: I'm not stretching anything.

LILITH: Just put a nice light on it. Make him seem better than he was.

EVE: He was a good man. He deserves a film.

LILITH: You're a good woman. Let them make the film about you.

EVE: What's there in my life to make a film about?

LILITH: Got to be something.

EVE: I lived a life. Had my children, joined my organizations. When my legs gave out, I retired.... That's not a movie.

LILITH: You worked.

EVE: I worked all the time. How's that make me different from anybody else?

LILITH: You did things in the beginning they don't do anymore.

EVE: Flicking chickens, women don't do much anymore. And I had my children on straw.

LILITH: See, you got a story.... At least it would be the truth.

EVE: They want action for a film.

LILITH: From what I heard, you had plenty of action.

EVE: What'd you hear?

LILITH: About the eviction.

EVE: Oh, that.

LILITH: That was something. You stood up for your rights.

EVE: What? I never made a stand.

LILITH: It wasn't a matter of principle?

EVE: It was all a misunderstanding.

LILITH: Some misunderstanding. One rule: Don't eat from the fruit of the Boss's tree. Simple rule. How'd you come to break it?

EVE: The Boss never told me the rule.

LILITH: Never told you? But the man knew the rule.

EVE: We're the same person, suddenly? The rule was for Adam. Not to eat from the tree. An old rule, from before I came along.

LILITH: Still, only one rule.

EVE: One rule, she says. One rule. The tree was in my backyard. Don't eat from the tree that's right by your door, eat from the one aleh drairden [pronounced alah-DRARE-den and means far away] at the other side of the world. That's all right. Make the woman work. Tell her she can't eat from her own tree.

LILITH: So you didn't make a stand.

EVE: It was not a political statement.

LILITH: You discuss it with the Boss?

EVE: Are you kidding? Talk to me?

LILITH: Guess not.

EVE: As far as He was concerned, I was an afterthought. You make a man, give him animals to play with, trees to prune, he's not happy. Kvetches all day that he needs company. So you make him a woman out of scrap. Birds, the Boss thought through. Cows, He gave a lot of thought. Woman...I'm lucky anything works.

LILITH: You gonna say this on the film?

EVE: The film don't have to know this.

LILITH: It couldn't hurt.

EVE: They like cheerful, so people will watch.

LILITH: If it's true, they'll watch, even without cheerful.... Go on, tell the director the story of your life. She'd be interested.

EVE: There's no story. They want drama in a film.

LILITH: Drama? Okay. You could tell them about the snake.

EVE: The snake?

LILITH: He started your trouble.

EVE: He had nothing to do with it.

LILITH: No? People blame the snake.

EVE: An innocent party.

LILITH: You knew him well?

EVE: We were neighbors. Didn't you know him?

LILITH: Never had the pleasure.

EVE: Very pleasant. We talked a lot.

LILITH: You talked with an animal?

EVE: For the record, cobras are reptiles. Very romantic creatures. It's their three-chambered hearts.

LILITH: What did he talk, the snake?

EVE: A lot of nonsense.

LILITH: In Yiddish?

EVE: Aramaic— He was a goy.

LILITH: You discuss anything special?

EVE: "Good morning. How's your digestion?" What else do people talk about?

LILITH: I don't know.... Nice story for a film, a talking snake.

RACHEL: (Enters) Eve! How you doing? You all right?

EVE: Sure. We're fine.

RACHEL: We're only running half an hour late. Not too bad.... You make a friend?

EVE: (Introduces them) This is Lil... Rachel, the director.

LILITH: Pleased to meet you.

RACHEL: You from around here?

LILITH: I used to live in this neighborhood.

RACHEL: Did you know Eve's husband? Adam Adamovich? An inventor and agronomist.

EVE: She didn't know him.

RACHEL: Major figure in the Middle East. Rugged individualist, politically astute.

EVE: He had stubby fingers. Wore a pinky ring.

LILITH: An Adam Adamovich with a pinky ring I don't remember.

RACHEL: We're looking for recollections from the old days. *(To* EVE*)* Sit tight. Got to check on the sound equipment. *(She exits.)*

LILITH: She always in a hurry?

EVE: Time is money.... How come you didn't tell her you knew my husband?

LILITH: You wouldn't let me.

EVE: You could have said.

LILITH: It's your film. You want me in it, you tell her.

EVE: Rachel wants people who knew him.

LILITH: I'm not people who knew him. I'm people who married him.... She asks me a question about that man, I'll tell her the truth. This you don't seem to want in your film.*(She opens a brown paper bag and exhibits the contents.)* Banana?

EVE: I got gall bladder.

LILITH: Better health than sickness.... I got a little halavah and some tea. That would agree with you.

EVE: I'll pass.

LILITH: An apple, maybe?

EVE: Jokes I don't need.

LILITH: Green and red. Yellow, you can't find this time of year.

EVE: Maybe a slice. If it's not too much trouble.

LILITH: No trouble. *(She cuts* EVE *a slice of apple.)* Your apple, what was it like?

EVE: Like an apple.

LILITH: Ida Red? Red Delicious? Granny Smith?

EVE: What do I know from apples? It was green.

LILITH: Firm and green is a nice apple.... The snake eat some too?

EVE: Oh, sure. A gourmande. Very cultured.... And a sense of humor like you wouldn't believe. You ever hear the joke about the Frenchman and the bicycle? That was his.

LILITH: A comic.

EVE: We laughed all the time back then. Played canasta. If I was going somewhere, he did my hair.

LILITH: You don't say?

EVE: Artistic in a lot of ways. Music, dance… And could he cook! My best recipes, I got from him. An apple strudel so light, it floated. Apple crisp, he made…I'm drooling just thinking about it. Baked apple with a little cinnamon and walnuts.

LILITH: No wonder you got gall bladder.

EVE: We cooked and talked. You know how it is, leaning over a stove: You say things you wouldn't tell anybody…. And he was such a good listener…with his hoods flared out on either side, his whole body swaying back and forth, listening.

LILITH: Hard to find a friend like that.

EVE: And honest! Completely frank…. He told you a dress was a rag, you might as well just throw it out.

LILITH: Hard to shop alone.

EVE: Interested in everything, the snake. All your complaints. How your bones ached at the end of the day. The loneliness and fear out there…with the woods and the space and the man.

LILITH: The world was bigger then.

EVE: And quieter…. The snake filled the air with sound…laughter and music and song. (Shyly) He wrote rhymes in the dust with his tail.

LILITH: Did he?

EVE: One for me he wrote I still remember:
"As an apple tree among the trees of the woods,
so is my lover among men.
I delight to rest in his shadow,
and his fruit is sweet to my mouth."

LILITH: He wrote that for you?

EVE: He was always writing things.

LILITH: A poet, too…. He still alive?

EVE: God knows…. Never saw him again after all the trouble. My husband put his foot down.

LILITH: You let him interfere with your friendships?

EVE: I had enough trouble in those days. I didn't need to argue over little things.

LILITH: It wasn't so little.

EVE: No, it wasn't…. I never made a friend like that again.

LILITH: Put his poem in the film. To remember him.

EVE: A love poem? They don't want to hear that from an old person.

LILITH: It would add something. Besides, you're not so old.

EVE: I don't feel old. It's crazy, but I can remember the day I was born like it was yesterday.

LILITH: Me, too. How was yours?

EVE: Birth? Like a falafel. *(Pronounced fah-LAH-f'l and means a Middle Eastern dish)*

LILITH: Really?

EVE: The Boss, He started with the rib and fleshed it out.

LILITH: From a rib, He made you?

EVE: Sure, Adam's rib. Isn't that how He made you?

LILITH: Clay. Red clay. Same as Adam.

EVE: I never knew that.

LILITH: Sure. He had lots of ways of making things. People, animals. Take kangaroos. The hopping ones.

EVE: I know kangaroos. I picked that name.

LILITH: The Boss wants to make a kangaroo, He walks along, sings a little song. Where the notes fall on the ground, up hops a kangaroo.

EVE: You don't say!

LILITH: Me, He made from clay. By the river bank, there was always plenty of clay.

EVE: I never heard this story!

LILITH: Sure. He molded it…made little hands, a little face, two bodies just the same…well, almost the same.… Then a quick kiss on the lips. That's it.

EVE: He didn't use ribs?

LILITH: Not a single one in my whole body.… Which accounts for this nice waist I still got.

EVE: I can't believe this. My husband drove me crazy with that rib.
The four pints of blood he needed, the six hours on the operating table.
He was that close to dying, from the rib transplant.

LILITH: Made you feel grateful, didn't it?

EVE: Grateful?

LILITH: You make a woman from clay, same as a man, she's not indebted. Doesn't have to pick up the man's laundry, clip his toenails. Can do what she wants.

EVE: The man always did what he wanted.

LILITH: Not with me, he didn't. What he wanted was a woman within calling distance. What he wanted was to give all the orders, make all the decisions, good, bad, or indifferent. He was obsessed with it.

EVE: I can believe it.

LILITH: He started by just mentioning it, now and then, how it would be nice for him to be in charge. How he was real leadership material. Could bring a new direction to the organization.... Finally, the Boss says to me...

EVE: The Boss talked to you?

LILITH: Sure. I'm supposed to read His mind?

EVE: He never said anything to me. Not so much as one word.

LILITH: We talked plenty.... Still do, when we get the chance.

EVE: *(With awe)* You have discussions with the Boss?

LILITH: If you call talking in circles a discussion.... But this time with Adam, the Boss finally had enough. He says, "The man's driving me crazy. Says he wants to call the shots." I say, "Forget it. You made us equal. Told us to look after the fish, the birds, the cattle. A two-person job. Why should Adam be in charge?"

EVE: You got a point.

LILITH: But Adam wouldn't leave it alone. Starts talking productivity and quality improvement and who knows what mishegas. *(Pronounced mish-eh-GAHS and means craziness)* Day after day, week after week until the Boss's head is spinning. I don't need to tell you how it ended. The Boss says, "From now on, Adam's the team leader. You take notes and do the typing. Take it or leave it."

EVE: What'd you do?

LILITH: *(Sarcastic)* Typing?

EVE: So you just walked out of Eden?

LILITH: Best career choice I ever made.

EVE: What did the Boss do?

LILITH: What could He do? He made me an honest offer. Couldn't very well complain when I went. But He says to me, "I won't make that mistake again. This is the last time I ever ask a woman to speak her mind."

EVE: I think I got a heart palpitation.

LILITH: You okay?

EVE: Give me a minute. I get upset, my mitral valve acts up. *(She takes deep breaths and massages her neck.)*

LILITH: Want to lie down?

EVE: Lie down? I'd like to kill somebody! You sure about all this?

LILITH: I'm old; I'm not senile.

EVE: He didn't have to make me from the man's rib?

LILITH: He had plenty of stuff he could have used. Rusty wire, an old broomstick.

EVE: Did Adam risk anything when he gave up that rib?

LILITH: What risk? Look who did the surgery!

(EVE moans.)

LILITH: You okay? You got a headache?

EVE: I got a hole in the head, that's what I got! I spent half my life apologizing to that man. Every time the faucet leaked, or the gribbenes *[Pronounced grib-en-iz and means chicken skin fried in chicken fat]* gave somebody heartburn, it was my fault! And now you tell me if I'd been made from clay, everything would have been different?

LILITH: I didn't say that.

EVE: Oh, yes, you did.

LILITH: It was different for me, that's all I said. Maybe it was the rib, maybe it wasn't.

EVE: Without that rib, we would have been equals. Partners. I would have had a vote.

LILITH: If you'd wanted it.

EVE: I wanted it.

LILITH: Maybe. If you took a stand.

EVE: I would have!

LILITH: Then do it now. Tell the director how it really was. Put the record straight.

EVE: It's too late. She started filming. She's got footage.

LILITH: So she'll do it over.

EVE: She can't do it over. This is the movie business. It costs too much.

LILITH: The truth always costs.

EVE: Don't you understand? They won't make this movie if I tell them the truth. You think they'd make him a hero if they knew about the rib? You think they'd put up a monument to him, make a film about him, if they knew how he treated me?

LILITH: So they don't make a film, they don't put up a monument. You really care?

EVE: Sure, I care. It's a film. About me.

LILITH: About him.

EVE: Close enough.

LILITH: You let Rachel make this film, people will believe he did it all, your husband. You had no part in it.

EVE: I had a part.

LILITH: Then tell her.

EVE: She won't change anything now. She's over budget.

LILITH: Then what was all that talk about the snake? Your honest friend you miss so much. You know why you never made a friend like him again? You're afraid of the truth. You lost the knack of it.

EVE: I have a role in this film. It's the role they want me to play.

LILITH: You'll leave it at that?

EVE: What can I do now?

LILITH: Tell the director how it was. You won't get a chance like this again. What you say now, that's what people will remember. They'll say, "Look at her. That woman knows what she's talking about."

EVE: I can't. I'm not used to thinking about my husband like that. I'm confused. I need a chance to think.

LILITH: What's to think? Just tell your life on the film: This is what happened.

EVE: You still hate him.

LILITH: I don't hate him. I don't feel anything for him. I just lived my life different.

LILITH: *(Sarcastic)* Different.

EVE: I think fair is fair and give credit where it's due. Look: You had a part—he made you think you didn't. I had a part... nobody will ever know that. Unless you tell them. You got the chance. Nobody else.

EVE: I'm too old to take chances.

LILITH: *(She packs her bag and prepares to leave.)* Fine. Good. You're content: You'll be remembered for all of history as a woman who did absolutely nothing in her life...except eat one apple too many.

RACHEL: *(She enters carrying a microphone.)* We're finally ready! How are you two? Feeling fine? Great! Now, Eve, we're just going to have you talk a little to see how the sound's working. *(She clips the microphone to EVE's blouse.)* Look over there at the camera. Right there, see? The cameraman's on that crane on the bluff. Not nervous, are you? No, you're a trouper.

LILITH: You can still tell her.

RACHEL: Just talk. Say anything. A little history, a little nostalgia.

EVE: *(To LILITH)* To say it in public...I can't.

RACHEL: Sure you can. Talk about your husband.

LILITH: Tell her about your husband. The tower of strength.

RACHEL: How he organized the housing, set up communication lines.

EVE: To say this in front of people...

LILITH: Or talk about the snake.

RACHEL: The snake?

EVE: An old friend...

RACHEL: Mrs Adamovich. Eve. I know the heat's bad up here. But let's just get focussed. Let's concentrate. Think about your husband. The patriarchal government. The foundation of monotheism.

EVE: *(To LILITH)* To be a movie star, at my age. Is that so much to ask?

LILITH: You want applause, you got applause. You want the truth, you got to take a stand.

RACHEL: Eve?

EVE: What do I do?

RACHEL: What you do is start speaking. Now! I've got a crew standing around, and the clock is running. We've got to move!

LILITH: *(She pulls a green apple from her bag.)* I still got an apple left, if anyone wants a bite of it.

EVE: *(Long pause as EVE stares at the apple)* Rachel...Miss Director. It's like this. In the beginning, there was the heaven and the earth. And the earth was unformed and void and darkness lay upon the face of the deep. We all know this. This isn't new.... It's just....

(RACHEL *turns* EVE *toward the camera.*)

EVE: What I told you on the film, the part you shot before, it isn't the whole story. You see…after the beginning, in the garden…things got a little complicated….

(*Lights fade as* EVE *bites into apple.*)

BLACKOUT

JIM'S COMMUTER AIRLINES

Lavonne Mueller

Lavonne Mueller is director of playwriting at the University of Iowa. Her plays include KILLINGS ON THE LAST LINE, LITTLE VICTORIES, THE ONLY WOMAN GENERAL, COLETTE IN LOVE, CRIMES AND DREAMS, BREAKING THE PRAIRIE WOLF CODE, THE ASSASSINATION OF FEDERICO GARCIA LORCA, LETTERS TO A DAUGHTER FROM PRISON, WAR 7 THINGS, VIOLENT PEACE, and FIVE IN THE KILLING ZONE. Her plays have been produced at many theaters, including The American Place Theatre, Theatre Four, Apple Corps Theatre, Samuel Beckett Theatre, Horace Mann Theater, and the Nat Horne Theater, all in New York City; and in many regional theaters including The Round House Theater in Washington, D C, and Trinity Theatre in Chicago. Her work also has been produced in India and at the Edinburgh Festival in Scotland. FIVE IN THE KILLING ZONE was selected for the Sundance Festival. Her play VIOLENT PEACE was Critic's Choice in *Time Out* magazine in London.

Her textbook on creative writing is published by Doubleday and The National Textbook Company. Two of her screenplays have been optioned for the movies. She has received grants from the National Endowment for the Arts, New York Foundation for the Arts, N E H, Illinois Arts Council, John Simon Guggenheim Foundation, and the Rockefeller Foundation. She is currently a Woodrow Wilson Visiting Scholar.

(The office of Jim's Commuter Airlines. A large picture of JIM's *gray-haired mother hangs on the wall. At rise,* JIM *is looking out the window as* DORIS, *a young woman pilot, comes into the office carrying a fry pan and eggs.)*

JIM: *(He is happy as he looks out the window.)* We're going to pitch like a circus tent in a windstorm.

DORIS: If the weather holds up. *(She turns on a hot plate on top of a file cabinet, slaps fry pan on it.)*

JIM: It'll hold up. *(Beat)* You cooking in my office again?

DORIS: Scrambled. With diced onions.

JIM: You're going to stink up my office.

DORIS: You want eggs. I can't cook on the tarmac. *(A beat, as she begins to cook. She looks up from her cooking to the window.)* Might be clearing…to the east.

JIM: There you go again, always the pessimist. *(Beat)* I got up this morning happy. I said to myself, Jim, you're going to take a two-hundred-mile-an-hour sled down a slope of black snow. Now…look at that! A slant of light!

DORIS: Eat your eggs. It's not going to clear up.

JIM: Finally get me a good stormy day.

DORIS: Believe me, it'll stay stormy.

JIM: You know what the passengers are like when it's clear?

DORIS: You only let me fly once a month. But yah. I know what they're like.

(He takes pan of eggs from DORIS *and begins eating.)*

JIM: They want you to call out when you're going over Sears and Penney's like a bus driver. *(Beat. Still looking out the window:)* It's getting darker. Ah, nice wall of festering clouds to the west. Fog ridges. Stalactites of muck. Froth. Sludge. I'm going to be able to hot-dog it all over the sky. Yah. Nice clouds of cast iron.

DORIS: I worry about you, Jim. You're losing your cool these days.

JIM: Don't preach to me, Doris. You only have to go up once a month.

DORIS: I'm waiting for more fly-time, Jim. You keep promising.

JIM: You're never happy. I'm taking a risk here. Big time. My men could quit on me 'cause of you. The guys are already yelling.

DORIS: I'm supposed to get down on my hands and knees and thank you for one lousy day a month?

JIM: *(Looking out window)* Ah…remember that time last week? When I landed on the expressway? Weather was about like it is now. I could hear the passengers scream on that one. It was like music to me. I just coasted her with the flaps down. Lowered the gear. Slowed the descent. Hit the expressway with my wheels tearing off. Belly of the plane breaking apart sweet like tinfoil around a Thanksgiving turkey. Now that's friction, Doris. Digging up the asphalt like a giant plow. I even flattened a Cutlass Supreme. Slid its bucket seats down the pavement at a hundred miles an hour.

DORIS: I heard. We all heard.

JIM: F A A don't even slap my hand.

DORIS: We heard.

JIM: The expressway!

DORIS: We heard. A hundred times.

JIM: So when did you ever land on a highway?

DORIS: I do all right.

JIM: I can't tell you the number of times I've seen you lumber down a runway. *(Beat)* Ever see me fly around wind shear? Did you? *(Beat)* Over Paw Paw, Illinois. Coralville, Iowa. Did I come in during that tornado last June? Not me. I dived to nine G's. My passengers felt the force of gravity to nine G's. Kids had nose bleeds. Old men had strokes. A woman delivered a baby three months early. I was written up in the *National Enquirer*. *(Beat)* You don't learn that kind of thing on a simulator.

DORIS: Yah, I learned on a simulator. And I'm proud of it.

JIM: You learned on a dummy computer, Doris.

DORIS: It's where you learn theory. You could use a little theory, Jim.

JIM: Don't tell me about theory. Jim's Airlines has got more passengers than any commuter airlines in the U S of A. Not because of theory.

DORIS: Because of your old man. You inherited all this. *(Beat)* Your dad never let you eat all these eggs.

JIM: I fly in the face of cholesterol. Like the weather. *(Beat)* Where's the butter?

DORIS: You're flying in the face of your monthly weigh-in. *(A beat as she takes out a piece of paper from her pocket.)* Oh, by the way, I took this message for you. From your mother. She called just before you got in.

JIM: *(Looks at picture of his mother)* Why didn't you tell me right away!

DORIS: You always want eggs right away.

JIM: So help me, if there's anything wrong with Mom and you....

DORIS: Nothing's wrong.

JIM: Don't scare me like that, Doris.

DORIS: It's nice news.

JIM: I can always use nice news.

DORIS: Your mama is flying Jim's Commuter Airlines some time today. To visit family.

(Silence)

DORIS: Jim?

JIM: What flight?

DORIS: She wouldn't say. She doesn't want to make you or any of your five pilots feel beholden to her.

(Silence)

DORIS: She just wants you to know that for once she isn't taking the train. That's how much she believes in you.

(Silence)

DORIS: Jim?

JIM: Doris, don't stand there and tell me my mother is flying our airlines today.

(Silence)

JIM: Doris!

DORIS: Under a false name.

(JIM abruptly throws the pan of eggs into the trash can.)

DORIS: Why'd you do that?

JIM: Those are eggs, Doris!

DORIS: Just like you have every morning.

JIM: I'm not going to die up there from clogged arteries. Not now. Not when Mom could be on my plane.

DORIS: She won't be on your plane.

JIM: I got to be alert. You want me clobbering another crate? Mom's going to be up there in my sky.

DORIS: Do you have any idea where she might be going?

JIM: I got a brother in California. A sister in Florida. A cousin in Detroit. Aunts in Texas. Cousins in Alaska. I got more relatives than thunderheads out there. She could be taking us to any connecting flight in the country.

DORIS: Calm down.

JIM: *(Looks out window)* Some of them cloud tops are probably up to fifty-three-thousand feet. And every one of my pilots—except you— is going up today.

DORIS: Yah. There's Tully—he'll be doing his usual banking in the headwinds…bending the old plane like a bronco buster. And Roy. He'll be up to his near-misses on Loons, Piper Cubs, low-cruising pigeons….

JIM: I don't want to hear all that.

DORIS: This morning—it's hand-to-hand combat with the elements, Jim….

JIM: You go on being negative like that, Doris, and you'll find yourself cleaning up a large oil spill with a very small rag.

(A beat)

JIM: Today, everybody's going to fly right.

(DORIS *laughs.*)

JIM: Doris, you're not hearing me. Today, every pilot on Jim's Commuter Airlines is going by the book.

DORIS: *(Laughing)* The book.

JIM: Yah. The book.

DORIS: O K. O K. Joke's over, Jim.

JIM: This is no joke.

DORIS: Jim, you're losing it.

JIM: Don't tell me I'm losing it.

DORIS: Your old lady decides to go up—and you're losing it.

JIM: That old lady's my mother.

JIM: *(He turns from* DORIS. *Pensively:)* Doris, get two flashlights ready.

DORIS: Why?

JIM: Why do you think why?

DORIS: We're not...we're not....

JIM: That's right. You and me. We're getting flashlights and we're dropping to our knees. To check the undercarriage on all the planes.

DORIS: It won't work.

JIM: Don't tell me it won't work.

DORIS: You can't fly chicken.

JIM: I'll fly chicken!

DORIS: You can't fly chicken. You don't know how. You don't have the experience.

JIM: I'll fly chicken today. And so will every pilot in Jim's Commuter Airlines.

DORIS: You're risking your whole career. Just for one day.

JIM: I tell you, I can do it.

DORIS: It's impossible. Hear me? You don't have the background. You don't have the stomach for it. You book this airline...you go straight...you chicken this flight, and you and all your passengers won't make it. *(A beat)* When's the last time you ever read a pressure gauge on your tires? When's the last time you checked to see if anybody pulled the locking pins outta your wheels so you could retract after take-off? *(A beat)* You gotta fly like you always fly. The way the rest of your men fly. Like lunatics. Lunatics never get cancer. Look it up, Jim. Lunatics and crazies never get cancer.

JIM: *(Calmly)* Give me the Squawk-box. I'm going to brief the men.

(DORIS just stares at JIM.)

JIM: I said, give me the Squawk-box.

(DORIS hands JIM the box microphone. JIM flips some switches to talk to his fellow pilots who are in the hangar. As JIM is talking, DORIS sits in a tilted-back chair and makes faces and rolls her eyes in disgust and reacts as all the men must be reacting during this speech.)

JIM: *(Talking into the Squawk-box)* Men, this is Captain Jim. With the morning briefing. *(A beat)* I want to tell you all I'm real proud of last week's on-time-arrivals. We're way ahead of any other commuter airline. And that's what flying's all about—look-ahead capabilities—I don't care how many alternative airports you landed at or what holding pattern you cannonballed through. *(A beat)* Now today, men, I'm asking you all to fly S O P. Standard Operational Procedure. I know a lot of you find the flight manual tedious. Grant you, boredom brings on fatigue. And fatigue can cause accidents. So do what you have do to stay alert. I'm turning my head today when it comes to a little blackjack and poker in the cockpit. I'm turning my head today to a little off-track betting at the controls. But men—today, you're going by the book. That's an order. And don't question why. (*A beat*) Now, I know a lot of you are going to test me. I'm telling you now—don't. You'll want to shut down an engine over Iowa City, maybe. Advance the three throttles with your feet. Land in a cow pasture for some homemade yogurt. Do it tomorrow. Next week. 'Cause you're not going to do it today. (*A beat*) We got us a captainess as you all know. Doris. We let her go up once a month. She's sitting right here next to me. When she flies for us, she flies by the manual. All the time. Women are mandated to. That just shows how easy it is. (*A beat*) This company is democratic. Seniority is the basis for promotion. That's why I'm here. And that's why you are there. (*A beat*) I don't have to tell you I grew up at the airplane fence. I've been flying since I was nine. My first solo was like my first kiss. Took me out across pea patches and corn fields in a rig I built myself out of orange crates and my sister's roller skates. Used to get airsick so I flew with a bucket between my legs. In high school, I asked for the old man's plane the way other kids asked to use the car. (*A beat*) Now I know that what I'm asking you to do today is not cool. I'm not advocating the old days. I'm as modern as anybody. I like to use the log-book now and then to swat junk on the windshield. I like to fly "homing pigeon" just like the rest of you—no radar, no visibility, no ground flares, diving at the runway, landing in a mall to check out the cute college girls. Look, I understand how you feel. But today, it's dress code all the way. That means—no surf pants, no Grateful Dead tank-tops, no shoulder chains or boat cloaks. (*A beat*) When you're nose to rear burning fuel on the taxiway waiting to depart today, you remember that sometimes we gotta grit our teeth when the Company asks us to. That means no flying on the edge of a stall. No square loops, double snap rolls during takeoff. I like to hear the passengers squeal as much as the rest of you. I like a good tail slide...put the plane backwards for a while before nosing over. A few hammerheads and vertical climbs by Moline's McDonald's. Who doesn't? I'm the one who took the first Jim's Commuter in a loop-marathon. Sixty-four consecutive spins carrying fifteen tourists over Sandwich, Illinois. So don't tell me what I'm giving up. O K? (*A beat*) I'm not asking you to do something I'm not doing. I got my manual right here. And I'll see you in the troposphere. Have a good flight.

(JIM *switches off the Squawk-box.*)

JIM: Get the flashlights.

(DORIS *just stares at* JIM.)

JIM: The flashlights!

(DORIS *gets two flashlights from a file cabinet. She hands one to* JIM *and keeps one for herself.* DORIS *turns off the office lights. They both turn on their flashlights and exit through the door. They slam the door roughly, causing the picture of Mom to fall to the floor as the lights go down.)*

BLACKOUT

LIFE GAP

Y York

LIFE GAP
© copyright 1995 by Y YORK

Y York's other plays include: ACCIDENTAL FRIENDS; AFTERNOON OF THE ELVES; THE BOTTOM OF THE NINTH; THE SNOWFLAKE AVALANCHE; GERALD'S GOOD IDEA; RAIN. SOME FISH. NO ELEPHANTS. (published by Broadway Play Publishing Inc); AMERICAN 60s IN THREE AX; MELINA'S FISH; MOM GOES TO THE PARTY; THE PORTRAIT, THE WIND, AND THE CHAIR; THE LAST PAVING STONE; and most recently, THE SECRET WIFE. Y lives with Mark Lutwak, to whom most things are dedicated.

CHARACTERS

RUDY: *Seven or eight years old*
RANDALL: *Fourteen or fifteen years old;* RUDY's *brother*
JEANNIE: *Their mother*
OLMA: *Her mother*
WILNA: *A wealthy outsider*

SETTING

The combination living room-kitchen of JEANNIE's tenement apartment. The bedrooms and bathroom are offstage. The boys and OLMA also live there. This is the home of a very poor family. Some things are very neat (RUDY's) and some are very messy (RANDALL's). It is the disarray that arises when too many people live too close together.

A note on performing LIFE GAP: There is no sentiment in this play. The characters are neither monsters nor victims; they just try to do the best they can. Only RUDY is aware of the change in the big picture.

Scene One

(The sound of a T V is heard offstage. RUDY is on stage, engaged in a serious search. He is holding a pencil. At one point, RANDALL comes out of the bedroom and watches RUDY search, loses interest, and goes back into the bedroom. RUDY finally finds a relatively clean piece of lined white paper and starts to write. RANDALL reenters.)

RNDALL: What's that?

RUDY: Letter.

RANDALL: Who you writing to?

RUDY: Santa Claus.

RANDALL: What for?

RUDY: Socks.

RANDALL: Don't ask for socks.

RUDY: Why not?

RANDALL: You won't get them.

RUDY: How do you know?

RANDALL: You just won't. Ask for something bigger.

RUDY: Why?

RANDALL: If you aren't gonna get it, it oughta be bigger.

RUDY: I want socks.

RANDALL: You won't get them.

RUDY: Why?

RANDALL: *(Pause)* You got a stamp?

RUDY: What stamp?

RANDALL: You gotta have a stamp. You gotta buy a stamp.

RUDY: Where can I?

RANDALL: That's right! Where?!

RUDY: I'll get a stamp.

OLMA: *(Enters from another room)* Out of my way. Out of my way! I'm going to the bathroom. Get out of my way!

RUDY: Olma, you got a stamp?

OLMA: A stamp! Get out of my way, child. Out of my way.

RANDALL: It's stopped up.

OLMA:No!

RANDALL: Yeah, it is. For sure.

OLMA: I don't care, get out of my way.

RANDALL: Go next door.

OLMA: Get out of my way!

RANDALL: Go next door.

OLMA: I don't like them.

RANDALL: We have to go next door. You have to, too.

(OLMA starts toward her room.)

RUDY: Where you going, Olma?

OLMA: My room.

RUDY: But you have to go. You said.

OLMA: I don't like those people.

(OLMA exits to her room.)

RANDALL: She'll shit in her room.

RUDY: She won't.

RANDALL: She will. I know her. Where you going?

RUDY: Buy a stamp.

RANDALL: I have a stamp.

RUDY: You do?

RANDALL: Well, I know where one is.

RUDY: Can I have it?

RANDALL: You can have it if you ask for something bigger.

(RUDY writes something on the letter.)

RANDALL: What are you writing? What are you askin' for?

RUDY: *(Writing)* Something bigger. Can I have a stamp, now?

RANDALL: In Ma's good hat. In the band.

(RUDY *looks in the hat band.)*

RUDY: How did you know this was here?

RANDALL: I saw her hide it there.

RUDY: Maybe she has a plan for it.

RANDALL: She doesn't. She just keeping it for herself.

RUDY: You got an envelope?

RANDALL: You don't need one. Just fold it.

RUDY: How?

RANDALL: So that the writing is inside. Then put the stamp on the outside.

(RUDY *folds the letter.)*

RUDY: Okay?

RANDALL: You gotta write "Santa Claus" on it. And the address.

RUDY: I don't know the address.

RANDALL: It doesn't matter, you're not going to get anything.

RUDY: I might.

RANDALL: No. Where you going?

RUDY: Mailbox.

Scene Two

(OLMA *is sitting alone on stage, rubbing her feet, seemingly talking to herself.)*

OLMA: When you're young, and strutting down the street, and your mind's on who's looking and who's not looking, and why's he not looking? You don't figure that someday you're gonna judge a good day from a bad day by whether or not you can pass wind.

(RUDY *enters, carrying a plunger.)*

OLMA: When you young and buying shoes because they make your ankles look slim, you don't figure that someday you gonna wish you'd never smoked all them cigarettes, because it hurts so when you breathe. You don't think of now then, because then you was only thinking of...then.

RUDY: Toilet's fixed, Olma.

OLMA: Praise the lord.

(OLMA *exits to the bathroom.* RUDY *stares at the plunger.*)

Scene Three

(OLMA *is cooking at the stove.* JEANNIE *is sewing blue jeans at the table.*)

OLMA: Who told you to have boys?

JEANNIE: It's not a thing you get to choose.

OLMA: You think boys let their mother come to live with them when she gets old?

JEANNIE: Rudy would.

OLMA: With his head in the clouds? He'll be some help for you when you're old. Take real good care of you.

JEANNIE: He will. Randall, he won't.

OLMA: Randall be gone in a year or two. You'll never see him.

JEANNIE: You hush.

OLMA: Don't you tell me to hush. You hush.

JEANNIE: No. Be quiet. There's somebody at the door.

(OLMA *and* JEANNIE *listen.*)

Scene Four

(OLMA *and* JEANNIE *as before, except both are standing. The front door is open and* WILNA *stands in the doorway, neither quite in nor quite out.* WILNA *carries many boxes decorated with Christmas paper.*)

WILNA: There's this…program. Uh. The post office. You can go and get letters. You know, the ones the kids write to Santa Claus? You can just go and get a letter and answer it. And I did. I got this one. And…here's the stuff.

Scene Five

(RUDY *and* RANDALL. RUDY *has boxes and boxes of socks.*)

RUDY: I told you. I told you I'd get them. See. Look at all these!

RANDALL: I told you to ask for something better.

RUDY: No you didn't.

RANDALL: I did. I said ask for something better.

RUDY: You never did.

RANDALL: I said! Ask for something BETTER!

RUDY: You said ask for something bigger.

(RUDY *holds up bigger socks.*)

RUDY: Here some for you. And there's some for Olma and for Ma. Bigger.

RANDALL: You shoulda asked for something better.

Scene Six

(JEANNIE *and* OLMA. WILNA *stands in the doorway. During her speech she walks into the room and sits down at the table.*)

JEANNIE: What is it that you want?

WILNA: I'm not sure. I probably shouldn't have come. It's just…I mean. Socks. He asked for socks. I mean I practically broke down and cried. I mean I used to write letters to Santa Claus when I was a kid, and I remember what I used to ask for. Total recall. It's a curse. What somebody was wearing at a certain holiday party? Just ask me. I can tell you down to the last dinner ring. I remember what I used to ask for, and believe me, it wasn't socks. A pony. One year I asked for a pony. Got one. But it wasn't the one I wanted. I wanted a palomino. This one was brown. Just brown! Things like that hurt a kid. Being a kid is lousy. I mean, shit. But socks. Well. Socks! God, socks. Shit.

Scene Seven

(OLMA, RUDY, *and a cheese.*)

OLMA: What is it?

RUDY: Cheese.

OLMA: This isn't cheese.

RUDY: She said it was cheese. It's cheese.

OLMA: It's white.

RUDY: I can see it.

OLMA: Let me have some. It bites back. Mmmm.

RUDY: I like it.

OLMA: I like it.

(RANDALL *enters, wearing a new coat.*)

RANDALL: Check me out! Check me out!

RUDY: Where'd you get that?

RANDALL: Where! She bought it.

RUDY: You gonna keep it.

RANDALL: I told you to ask for something bigger.

(RANDALL *exits to bedroom.*)

Scene Eight

(WILNA *and* RUDY. WILNA *has a bag, out of which come many things.*)

WILNA: If you can't read, you're trapped. Stuck. Immobilized. Frozen in time.

RUDY: I can read. Randall, he can't read.

WILNA: If you can't read, your sources of information become extremely limited. You're limited to—God help you—the television news. Adages you hear on the street. Or the slogans of nationalistic demagogues. You're a prisoner. Oh, you're walking around, all right, but you're in prison, nonetheless. Freedom comes from exposure. Exposure to different ideas and points of view. It's not until you have all the information that you can make an informed choice. And you don't get all the points of view by watching television. You only get the really different points of view by reading *The New York Times.*

RUDY: Tell Randall.

(RUDY *throws down a book and runs out of the tenement.*)

Scene Nine

(JEANNIE *alone on stage. She is looking at a torn page from a magazine.* RUDY, *enters wearing a pair of* RANDALL's *trousers.*)

RUDY: What's that, Ma?

JEANNIE: It's a pattern. See? Here's the sweater and here's how you make it.

RUDY: You going to make it?

JEANNIE: I'd like to. Sometime. Let's see about those pants.

(RUDY *stands on a chair.*)

JEANNIE: Randall ought to take better care of his stuff.

RUDY: They're okay.

JEANNIE: Nothing of his lasts, and you're always growing.

RUDY: I'm sorry.

JEANNIE: *(Laughs)* Yeah? You sorry you're growing?

RUDY: No, I want to grow.

JEANNIE: *(Playfully)* Why do you want to grow?

RUDY: So you don't have to shorten my pants.

Scene Ten

(WILNA *and* JEANNIE. WILNA *is wearing an outfit that* JEANNIE *tailors with pins.*)

JEANNIE: I adored him. Worshipped him. Loved that man. I could feel my face change when I looked at him. Could feel what had been an expression, a normal expression, turn into a bowl of gooey mashed potatoes. Wide-eyed adoration. I'd seen the same expression on the faces of other women. They looked stupid. I had no reason to think I looked any smarter. I felt embarrassed. Ashamed that I loved him so much. You never see that expression...dumb love...on men's faces. Sometimes I'd see it on his face when we were alone. But never when we were outside. When we were outside, he'd sort of suck in his cheeks and look down his nose at me, all-knowing like. Cocksure. So. I started to work against having it on my face. When I'd feel all this love well-up, I'd think something bad...like, he don't really love me, or, he has secret girlfriends...like that.

(RUDY *comes in; he is unseen.*)

And the good feeling would go away and I could suck in my cheeks and cock my head, and look suspicious at him. I could do that when we were alone, and I could do that when we were in public. Pretty soon, it became my normal reaction. Whenever he said anything nice, or touched me, I'd just feel suspicious and look down my nose at him. Got so bad, that by the time he went away, I didn't even care.

WILNA: Men are jerks.

JEANNIE: Yeah.

Scene Eleven

(RUDY, RANDALL *with new clothes*)

RUDY: You got to give it back.

RANDALL: What?

RUDY: You got to give it all back.

RANDALL: No way, Jose.

RUDY: You look like a pimp. Those are pimp shoes. That's a pimp hat.

RANDALL: Hey, Mom!

RUDY: Leave Ma alone. She's trying to sew.

(JEANNIE *enters.*)

JEANNIE: What, Randall? My, that's quite an outfit.

RANDALL: What about you?

JEANNIE: This old thing?

RANDALL: Old from yesterday.

RUDY: What?

RANDALL: Yesterday was Ma's turn. You just chill out, Rudy. She'll get around to you.

RUDY: I don't want nothing.

JEANNIE: Givers gotta have somebody to give to, or else everybody's a taker.

RUDY: You shouldn't take the stuff.

RANDALL: Why not?

RUDY: I don't know! I just don't know.

(RUDY *holds his head.*)

Scene Twelve

(RUDY *and* RANDALL. *The room is cluttered with used sports equipment.* RANDALL *is looking at a tennis racquet.* RUDY *enters from outside.*)

RUDY: What's all this stuff?

RANDALL: It's from her.

RUDY: What's it for?

RANDALL: It's for us.

RUDY: *(Picking up skis)* What are we gonna do with skis?

RANDALL: I don't know.

RUDY: She musta cleaned out her place and brought us all the junk.

RANDALL: This isn't junk.

RUDY: It's junk. It's junk to her.

RANDALL: It isn't junk to me.

RUDY: What are you gonna do with that?

RANDALL: Learn how to play. Tennis ace.

RUDY: Watch it! You're gonna break something.

RANDALL: Then I just get her to buy me a new one.

RUDY: You're a jerk. Where's Olma?

RANDALL: She's gone to lunch.

RUDY: She's what?!

RANDALL: Lunch, man. Ma took her to lunch.

RUDY: Gramma don't go to lunch. Gramma sits in her bedroom and watches T V and eats pretzels. What are you doing?

RANDALL: Take this stuff down the street. See what I can get for it.

(RANDALL exits. RUDY, alone on stage, picks up the tennis racquet and smashes it into the floor.)

RUDY: Tennis ace.

Scene Thirteen

(JEANNIE is giving WILNA a manicure.)

WILNA: I pass a guy sleeping on a bench and I think, "I've got a home and you don't." Going down Fifth Avenue in my taxi looking at people standing up in crowded buses, and I think, "I get to sit and you don't." I have this secret feeling of glee because I have options. I can sit on a bench, but I don't have to stay there. I can stay as long as I want, and then I can go home. I could take a bus if I wanted to. But I don't have to. You know what I'm saying?

JEANNIE: I'm always real glad when I get a seat.

WILNA: But see, once you've got the seat, you've got the option.
You don't have to keep the seat. You can give it up.

JEANNIE: What do I want to do that for?

WILNA: It's not that you want to, it's that you can. But see, if you don't have the seat, no option. No choice. You gotta stand. It's only the people with seats that have the options.

JEANNIE: People with a seat aren't gonna stand.

WILNA: But they can! See, this is mine. *(A ring)* I own this. I can wear it. I can keep it in my drawer. I can throw it away.

JEANNIE: Don't do that!

WILNA: I won't, but I can.

JEANNIE: But you're not gonna throw it away, so what difference does it make if you can throw it away?

WILNA: It's all the difference. It's the whole difference in the world. It's everything. I've got a choice. I can give this to you.

JEANNIE: You can?

WILNA: Of course I can!

JEANNIE: You can, just like that?

WILNA: Yes!

JEANNIE: So now, it's mine?

WILNA: Oh. Sure. Sure. Now it's yours.

Scene Fourteen

(OLMA *and* WILNA. *There is a fur coat on the table.* OLMA *touches it once in a while.*)

OLMA: Randall, he first called me it. I started looking after him so Jeannie could work. He called me "Ma." I said, I'm not your Ma, I'm your old Ma. He laughed and started to shout, "Olma, Olma." I liked it. *(Pause. She touches the coat.)* I'd feel silly in this.

WILNA: Old, young. Everybody needs a treat once in a while.

OLMA: Jeannie, she needs a pretty thing now and then. And the boys, too. But I don't. You don't once you're old. I need to be warm, that's all. If I'm warm I'm happy. I remember listening to my gramma when I was a girl. Child, she'd say, put something away for a rainy day, because nothing's worse than being in the rain. I didn't listen. Wish I had. And now the boys don't listen to me when I tell them.

WILNA: It's a perfect universe. Balance.

OLMA: But I'm fine since the landlord fixed the furnace. We got plenty of heat. How'd you get him to do that? We been trying to have him fix the heat for years.

WILNA: A city inspector came. The landlord got a summons.

OLMA: We tried the city. Nobody ever came before.

WILNA: Huh.

OLMA: Well, it's sure warm now. I don't need another thing.

WILNA: I think you ought to take this, Olma. *(Puts the fur coat around* OLMA's *shoulders)* Nothing around is going to keep you warmer than this.

OLMA: Oh my. Oh my.

Scene Fifteen

*(*RUDY *is frantically rolling yarn into a ball.* JEANNIE *enters.)*

JEANNIE: What have you got there, Rudy?

RUDY: Look at it, Ma. It's wool.

JEANNIE: Where'd you get that?

RUDY: *(Lying)* It was on the street. It was just lying there. In a trash can. On the lid of the trash can. Somebody must have put it there. So it didn't go to waste.

JEANNIE: What do you want with wool?

RUDY: It's for you, Ma. The sweater. So you can make the sweater.

JEANNIE: Oh.

RUDY:Don't you like it?

JEANNIE: She bought me a sweater, Rudy. You put that wool back. On that trash can lid. Or wherever it came from. Let somebody else find it.

Scene Sixteen

*(*RANDALL *and* OLMA. RANDALL *has on* OLMA's *fur coat.)*

OLMA: Randall, take that off.

RANDALL: No way, Jose.

OLMA: That's mine Randall. She give that to me.

RANDALL: You never go out. I want it.

OLMA: You look silly. It's for a woman.

RANDALL: What? You never seen boxers wearing their furs? It's as much for a man as it is for a woman. And I'll use it. You'd just snuggle up to it in your bedroom.

OLMA: I can do what I want with it. It's mine. Give it to me.

RANDALL: You want it so bad, take it away.

OLMA: What?

RANDALL: You want it so bad, take it away from me!

OLMA: You're bad, Randall. You're bad through and through.

Scene Seventeen

(The family after dinner)

RUDY: What do they have you do, Mama?

JEANNIE: I just cook. That's all I do is cook.

RANDALL: You can't cook, Ma. Who'd pay you to cook? You burn beans and your greens are always mush.

JEANNIE: The cook that's leaving shows me. She's not American. I can hardly understand her. And she smells. And I don't know why she's leaving. Maybe they fired her, but nobody says.

OLMA: How come you go in so late?

JEANNIE: I don't have to be there until three. They give me ten dollars for a taxi to come home. And that's extra from the three-hundred-and-fifty dollars. So if I take the bus, that's an extra forty-five dollars.

RANDALL: Three-fifty. That's not so much.

JEANNIE: A week, Randall! Not three-fifty a month. It's three-fifty a week.

(Silence)

RUDY: But you like to sew, Ma. You don't like to cook.

JEANNIE: You know how many hems I have to measure to earn three hundred and fifty dollars? I'll learn to like to cook.

RUDY: Are they nice?

JEANNIE: I haven't seen anybody except the cook.

OLMA: And I bet you can sometimes bring home extra food.

RUDY: Stop it. Stop it. Just, stop it. *(Holds his head)*

Scene Eighteen

(RUDY writes a letter, and RANDALL)

RANDALL: What are you doing?

RUDY: *(Writing a letter)* Never mind what I'm doing.

RANDALL: Who you writing to?

RUDY: Never mind, just never mind.

RANDALL: So who cares! *(Exits the apartment)*

RUDY: *(To letter)* He's gotta take her back.

Scene Nineteen

(RUDY and OLMA. RUDY is going through mail.)

OLMA: What are you doing?

RUDY: Looking for something.

OLMA: Get out of them bills. What're you looking for?

RUDY: A letter.

OLMA: Who's writing to you?

RUDY: Santa Claus.

OLMA: What?

RUDY: I wrote and asked him to take her back.

OLMA: Child, she's not from Santa Claus. That lady, she's from a program.

RUDY: Then how can I make her stop?

OLMA: You can't make her stop. There's no way you can stop a program.

Scene Twenty

(WILNA, *then* RUDY)

RUDY: *(Entering)* What are you doing here?

WILNA: Just waiting.

RUDY: You got a key now, or what?

WILNA: Sure. Jeannie gave me a key.

RUDY: Why don't you just move in? Take over mine and Randall's room, or put Olma on the couch. You might as well. You're always here.

WILNA: I hear you're trying to send me back to Santa.

RUDY: Oh shit.

WILNA: All the nice things I've done for your family.

RUDY: You don't know how to stop.

WILNA: That's true, I don't.

RUDY: Mama hates her job.

WILNA: She doesn't.

RUDY: She does, she just doesn't say. I hear her talk about those folks. Ma's gotta call her Mrs Stevens, and she calls Ma Jeannie, and she's not even as old as Ma. Teaching Ma the right way to stir. You stir, that's how you stir. You don't have to teach it.

WILNA: She makes a lot of money.

RUDY: That doesn't make a thing okay.

WILNA: Well, Rudy. You're wrong, it does.

RUDY: No, it don't.

WILNA: Yes, Rudy, it does.

RUDY: It don't. You don't know. You don't know everything. What's this? What are we supposed to do with this? *(An object of some size)* Ma just has to dust it, we can't use it. We can't sell it, Randall tried. And what are we supposed to do with a tennis racquet? *(Picks it up)*

WILNA: *(Picks up the racquet)* Tennis is good for you. It's fun. It helps you meet people.

RUDY: Don't you have some other place you can go? Don't you have a job, or some horse club you can go to?

WILNA: All those and more. I just like it here.

RUDY: I don't like you here. I don't want you to come back.

WILNA: The rest of the family might miss me.

RUDY: Maybe for a second, then they'd remember how nice it was before you came.

WILNA: You're just a rude little shit!

RUDY: Don't call me names, you....(*Swings at her with tennis racquet*)

WILNA: Stop it! Put that down! Stop it!

RUDY: You just get out of here. I'll break your kneecaps. Then you won't be able to get up our steps. *(Hits her with tennis racquet)*

WILNA: You cut me!

RUDY: You better get out or I'll cut you some more.

WILNA: You little piece of shit! You little turd. Here, you piece of dogshit, how do you like it? *(Begins to hit RUDY with her tennis racquet)*

RUDY: Ow.

WILNA: Right, ow! On the face, maybe. On the ass for good luck. *(Continues to hit him)*

RUDY: You...cunt.

WILNA: That does it. Yeah, that's the prize winner.

(Blackout)

Scene Twenty-one

(OLMA, JEANNIE, RANDALL, WILNA. JEANNIE *is washing* WILNA's *hands.* OLMA *is scrubbing the floor.*)

OLMA: Always with his head in the clouds. Not like any other child I even knew.

RANDALL: A jerk.

WILNA: He hated me. I never knew.

RANDALL: Go home, Wilna.

WILNA: I'm going.

JEANNIE: Go. Go now.

OLMA: Go home. Drink some whiskey.

RANDALL: Hey, Wilna?

WILNA: Yes?

RANDALL: We'll see you tomorrow.

OLMA: Yeah, you come by tomorrow, Wilna.

JEANNIE: *(In horror)* Tomorrow?

WILNA: Yes. I'll see you tomorrow. *(Exit)*

BLACKOUT

METAMORPHOSES
A Triptych
June Siegel

METAMORPHOSES

June Siegel is a member of B M I, Dramatists Guild, and M A C, and is co-treasurer of the League of Professional Theater Women. A graduate of Wellesley College, she received a doctorate in French literature from Columbia University, where she taught for half a decade before mutating into a lyricist and sketch writer. Her work has appeared in musicals and revues Off and Off-Off-Broadway—among them, A...MY NAME IS ALICE and its 1992 successor, A...MY NAME IS STILL ALICE; PETS (Judith Anderson Theater); THAT'S LIFE! (Jewish Repertory Theater); SKIRTING THE ISSUE (cabaret benefit for The Women's Project); and WHEN THE COOKIE CRUMBLES... (Theaterworks/USA). Her soap opera SUDS AND LOVERS (SAVONE CON CARNE) was seen in The Ten-Minute Musicals Project in San Francisco. The cast album of her first revue, THE HOUSEWIVES' CANTATA, is now out on C D. She has received nine music festival awards and has participated in the B M I, ASCAP, and Dramatists Guild workshops, from which a work-in-progress, THE CARE AND FEEDING OF THE YOUNG, emerged as an O'Neill finalist. Her lyrics have been aired on Brian Lehrer's "On the Line" (W N Y C) and anthologized in Sheila Davis' THE SONG-WRITERS IDEA BOOK. Her verse and articles have appeared in *The Dramatists Guild Quarterly* and other publications. Right now she's resuscitating her theater piece LIFE FORMS, first presented at the Theater for the New City.

I: GARRETT—THE PYGMALION THING
PHYLLIS: *Woman in her early thirties*
II: HENRY
EVELYN: *Woman in her sixties*
III: ARLIN
MARIE: *Woman in her late thirties, with a slight Southern accent*

Note: GARRETT may be done with or without music, PHYLLIS's *versified lines can be treated like lyrics (if there's a composer on premises), or they can just be spoken conversationally. The back-up trio, however should be musically activated.*

I: GARRETT—THE PYGMALION THING

PHYLLIS: *(On phone)* That's all I am to you, Allen? A lawyer with a great bod who makes terrific lasagna?... *(Furious)*
—You think I'm upset? Well you're right—.
And I have my needs— So goodbye, Allen... What?...
No, it is not still on for tonight!

(Slams down receiver)

I've just broken up with Allen
Swear I'll never try to cope with another
Unsupportive self-involved bachelor boy
Who's looking for a mother.
It's Friday, 'round six, in the office
Nothing much to do
Weekend looms ahead
Like a lifetime of déjà vu
I'm at the new Panasoma computer
Latest miracle from Japan
Riffling through the menu
Trying not to think about a man....

"S-S-P/E-X/M-A-T/E-R/Control/Control"—never saw that code before.
(Hesitates, shrugs) Why not?...All at once, I'm inside a new feature: "3-D Transmorphic Model." Graphics! Haven't done that since high school.

(Back-up trio of female VOICES *materializes—electronic, enticing, mysterious.* PHYLLIS *is unaware of them.)*

VOICES: S-S-P/E-X/M-A-T/E-R
CONTROL/CONTROL
3-D TRANSMORPHIC MODEL

PHYLLIS: My fingers start flying across the keys
An image begins to emerge
A human being...a male...
And suddenly all of my pent-up desires
And longings seem to converge
On that image...
The image grows clearer and more complete

I cut and I paste and I scan
And I've got it! At last! On the screen. In color.
A model of the perfect man.
The man every woman dreams of. In three dimensions.

VOICES: *(Exultant)* S-S-P/E-X/M-A-T/E-R
CONTROL/CONTROL
3-D TRANSMORPHIC MODEL

PHYLLIS: I can't resist. I press "Print." Name of file?
(Thinks a moment)
"Garrett." Enter—
The printer lets fly with a burst of sparks
It looks like it's blowing its brain
Then up comes this cloud of blue smoke— Oh my God!
That's twelve-thousand bucks down the drain!
Quel disaster!
But the smoke slowly clears... (VOICES *under, in angelic choir:*
"AHH...AHH...AHH...")
....and there he is. Astride the printer. Tall and beautiful. And perfect.

VOICES: *(Ecstatic)* S-S-P/E-X/M-A-T/E-R
CONTROL/CONTROL
3-D TRANSMORPHIC MODEL...

PHYLLIS: He detaches himself from the paper track
He smiles—and the room seems to shine
He glides to the floor...comes toward me—this can't be happening!
Then—I'm in the arms of the perfect man
Gentle and strong—and all mine!
Garrett!

VOICES: *(Echoing)* GARRETT...GARRETT...GARRETT...

PHYLLIS: Three incredible months go by. I take a leave from the firm.
Garrett and I are inseparable. We watch the sunrise together. Take long
walks. Play Parchesi.
I'm relieved that my friends have stopped calling me up
The world is just perfect for two
I rediscover everything I thought I'd lost forever
I'm born again each day—fresh, creative, new....
No cares have I
'Cause for once in my life
I am loved for myself
I'm adored and admired
There's no effort required
I curl up in his arms
Feeling safe and secure

I am showered with love,
Affirmation—

VOICES: -FIRMATION

PHYLLIS: Affection—

VOICES: AFFECTION

PHYLLIS: Approval—

VOICES: APPROVAL

PHYLLIS: Attention—

VOICES: ATTENTION

PHYLLIS: And cocoa and Twinkies—

VOICES: AND COCOA AND TWINKIES

PHYLLIS: Cocoa and Twinkies?!?...A terrible thought crosses my mind.
I run to the mirror. A fat little girl with a bow in her hair and a Twinkie
in her hand stares back at me. Oh, no! I stagger back.

The truth at last confronts me
And I realize, somehow or other,
It isn't a perfect man I want—
It's a perfect mother!

VOICES: 3-D TRANSMORPHIC MOTHER

PHYLLIS: I know what I have to do. I dash to the office, sit down at the
Panasoma. My hands are trembling, but I'm in control...

VOICES:(*Agitated*) S-S-P/E-X/M-A-T/E-R
CONTROL/CONTROL...

PHYLLIS: Name of file: Garrett. Command: Erase.

VOICES: (*Fading*) 3-D TRANSMORPHIC MODEL...MODEL...MODEL...
MODEL...

(*Back-up trio disappears.*)

PHYLLIS: It's Friday, 'round six, in the office
Nothing much to do
The weekend looms ahead
Like a lifetime of déjà vu...
The phone rings. (*Phone rings. She picks up.*)
Oh—hello, Allen. (*To audience*) It's Allen.
(*Into phone*)
Yes, of course I've been doing all right...
You're what?.... Lasagna?... You're making lasagna?
(*Smiles*) No, I guess I'm not busy tonight.... (*Blackout*)

II: HENRY

EVELYN: Retirement? No big deal. When the time came, I said goodbye to the bookkeeping field, picked up my pension, and went. Pretty soon I was busier than ever. Yoga class, art tours, my great books group, my matinee ladies, and candy-striping at the hospital once a week. But Henry… *(Shakes her head.)* The firm threw him a big party at Le Bernardin, and the next day he started his life as a vegetable. He was never the great communicator—with his clients, yes, but not with me. I thought maybe being thrown together now, we'd make up for lost time. But instead, he practically stopped verbalizing altogether. Just sat in front of T V, eating carrot sticks and salt-free pretzels, and mourning his lost kingdom. This went on for months. Gradually I began to notice a change in his appearance. Nothing specific. But he seemed softer, rounder, more…cushiony. I told him he should get some exercise.…*(She shrugs.)*

One evening, he emerged from the bathroom with a towel around his middle. It was unmistakable: Henry had breasts! I didn't say anything. Why upset him? But during the next few weeks I observed him closely as, to my—what?—horror?…astonishment?…delight?—he slowly changed into a…woman. And I must tell you, it's made a tremendous difference. Henry is a new person. He's learning macramé, tap dancing and Mandarin Chinese cooking at the Y; he's taken up the accordion again, which he hadn't touched since high school. And talk! We can't seem to find enough time for everything we have to say to each other. The world has opened up for both of us. I admit I miss the sex a little. But in every other way, Henry and I are much happier.

BLACKOUT

III: ARLIN

MARIE: It wasn't easy to explain. I mean, you take home this cute little frog, kiss it on the nose, and wake up—tada!—with a prince in your bed. A tall, dark, handsome prince—every inch a man. And naked as a jaybird. Dad and Mom were pretty skeptical, although they knew I stood firmly by my upbringing. Fortunately, Arlin was a charmer, and very sincere, and when they saw we were serious, they gave us their blessing. We had a lovely June wedding. Despite the differences in our backgrounds, our home life was idyllic. I avoided frog jokes, and Arlin, who was decidedly left of center, never discussed politics. But eventually, I guess, the conflict was inevitable.

The trouble started when I joined Crusade for the Unborn. I've never seen Arlin so angry. He was hopping mad. He began ranting at me...right in front of the children. "Do you realize what you're doing, Marie?" he shouted. I told him it was unnatural and ungodly to take the life of a poor little...."Unnatural!" he yelled. "What do you humans know about natural?" —You humans... That's the first time he ever said "you humans"— "You think you have the right to overrun this planet like some kind of insatiable parasite. You think every one of your fertilized eggs is a mystical achievement, a religious experience, an exception to the laws of nature. What if frogs got fanatical like that about every egg they laid? You'd have thirty billion extra Kermits every year, at each others' throats like people." He saw the look on my face. "Marie," he said, "I love you and the children. But all children need a place in the sun, a peaceful pond, a lily pad of their own...."

He turned and left the room. Happiness-ever-after was over. We went our separate ways. I picketed the local clinics. He became a keynote speaker for the National Organization for Women. We saw so little of each other, I wasn't aware of how he'd changed till one evening, shortly after the Clarence Thomas confirmation, I turned on the "MacNeil-Lehrer News Hour". There was Arlin on a panel with a legislator from Louisiana and a congressman from Utah. He looked tired, sallow, and his hair was thinning. I admit my heart went out to him. His eyes still bulged with liberal humanist zeal, but there were tears in them. He gave a passionate harangue about the plight of women and children, the fate of all mankind. When he'd finished, the congressman leaned over, real sympathetic like, put his hand on Arlin's shoulder, and said, "Face it, son. Choice is dead." It was like

Arlin suddenly deflated. He shook his head slowly and sadly. All he said was... "Not for me." At that moment the "News Hour" theme music came up. MacNeil said, "Sorry, gentlemen, we're out of time" and thanked them for their participation.

I don't know if he noticed the handsome green frog that hopped across his desk and disappeared under the closing credits....

BLACKOUT

THE NIP AND THE BITE

Judy GeBauer

Judy GeBauer started writing and acting as a child in her hometown, Berkeley, California. She appeared locally with children's theater and later with such professional companies as Berkeley Repertory Theatre, the California Shakespeare Festival, and the National Shakespeare Company.

In 1980 she was invited to the National Playwrights Conference at the Eugene O'Neill Theatre Center to develop her play SECONDS. She coauthored the Off-Off Broadway musical salute to old-time movies, THE WORLD OF BLACK AND WHITE. Her drama THE PONY RING opened the 1986 season at Houston's Chocolate Bayou Theatre and was nominated for a P I P Award. The same summer GeBauer presented a one-act, BEER MONEY, at the Bay Area Playwrights Festival. Two of her dramas, A DISCOURAGING WORD and A CEREMONY WITHOUT CRYSTAL, have been presented at the Firehouse Readers Theatre in Portland, Oregon. In 1987 she returned to the O'Neill with RECLAIMED, which was a finalist for the Susan Smith Blackburn Award for women playwrights, and which was subsequently produced at the Long Wharf Theatre Second Stage in New Haven. In 1991 the play was performed in Philadelphia for the Women's Theatre Festival. It has been read at La Mama La Galleria and The Women's Project. Two plays, MAGICIAN REVERSED and THE TRANSLATOR, were produced in the Iowa Playwrights Festival. The latter was given a staged reading in fall 1991 at La MaMa La Galleria. In 1990 GeBauer received a Christina Crawford Playwriting Award for her one-act, GIRLS RULES. Her docudrama about the Irish hunger strikes, BOBBY, CAN YOU HEAR ME?, was presented at the O'Neill in 1990 and was granted the H B O Writers Award and the Dennis McIntyre Memorial Playwriting Award. The play premiered at the Philadelphia Festival Theatre for New Plays and at New York's Irish Arts Center in 1992 retitled BOBBY SANDS, M P. A new play, THE HIDDEN ONES, awarded a W Alton Jones Foundation grant, premiered at Philadelphia Festival Theatre in 1994. Currently, she is working on a new script commissioned by Irish Arts.

A recipient of the Norman Felton Playwriting Award and the Barry Kemp Playwriting Scholarship, GeBauer received her B A in Theatre Arts from San

Francisco State University and her M F A from the University of Iowa Playwrights Workshop. She has been a guest lecturer in Irish Studies at Iowa and dramaturg for the Centennial Play at the University of Colorado at Boulder. She lives in Colorado with her husband, dancer Gene GeBauer, and their daughter, Amber. Away from the theater GeBauer is a passionate Dodger fan.

CHARACTERS

ESTEBAN *is Mexican, about thirty-five years old. He is a proud, educated man with a passion for his family and a driving need to give them the life in keeping with their status and his adoration of them. He is deeply religious. He has a gentle and even humorous side, but it is rarely seen. He is selective about whom he opens himself to. There is about him a refinement, an intensity, and certainly a sense of danger, for he is a master of his craft.*

THE AMERICAN *is in his mid-thirties, a bright, streetwise man who has garnered an education, is a crack legal counsel for people who are decisive, unscrupulous, and powerful. At heart he is still the happy street kid from Bayside, Queens whose greatest pleasure is stickball; but he has taken on the hardness of his employers, and made power his idol. This struggle has made him erratic, unpredictable, and volatile.*

THE TOURIST *is an American in his early thirties. He is easy and affable, and these are genuine traits even in the face of stressful and dangerous circumstances. He is world-weary, and lives as he must. He loves the myths of America. He is at heart a simple, uncomplicated soul who has lost hope. He has a steady, methodical personality and likes to work out details rather than ad lib his moments. In losing hope he also has lost all trust.*

MIGUEL *is a Mexican youngster of between ten and twelve. He has a keen intelligence, which is both playful and canny. He is not the needy child of the streets that he likes to pretend; his sense of adventure drives him into this sort of role playing. He is a devoted and loving child, deeply aware of a fierce private crisis in his home.*

FLORA *is a Mexican woman of about twenty-seven. A well-bred woman, she has found a man to love and has lost him to forces of power and expediency. She is the one character in the play who is prepared to take any measure, and risk everything, to bring things into balance. She is sensitive and brave, but can also be imperious and demanding.*

ROCHELLE *is an American woman in her early thirties, the ex-wife of* THE TOURIST. *She has a very earnest and sincere desire to meet her own potential and be everything she can be. She is still hobbled by early conditioning which tells her she can't be whole or stable without a man who will take care of her. She has a genuine warmth and little acrimony about the past.*

TIME

The early 1990s

SETTING

A border town in Mexico and a small town in the midwestern U S.

DEDICATION

For Gene and Amber, my parents, and my brother

I

(A basement. ROCHELLE is holding a bunch of flowers. She stands amidst paint buckets and a drop cloth. She has a cold. THE TOURIST is sitting, practicing guitar scales. He belches now and then and appears uncomfortable.)

ROCHELLE: You know what he was guarding? Used sanitary napkins. And his name, believe this or not, his name was Maupassant.

(Guitar scales)

ROCHELLE: What's it mean?

(Guitar scales)

ROCHELLE: That's the third dream I've had like that in a week. Three in one week.

(Guitar chord)

ROCHELLE: You didn't even hear me.

THE TOURIST: Third dream about used Kotex this week.

ROCHELLE: About dogs. DOGS!

THE TOURIST: Guarding Kotex.

ROCHELLE: What about Maupassant? *(She sneezes.)*

THE TOURIST: About what?

ROCHELLE: Maupassant. Maupassant.

THE TOURIST: I don't know what that is.

ROCHELLE: This used to drive me crazy when we were married.

THE TOURIST: I heard every word. I don't know that word. Say it again.

ROCHELLE: You hear but you don't acknowledge. You know how maddening that is?

THE TOURIST: What should I do?

ROCHELLE: Grunt. Make a sound. Let me know you're following a conversation. Maupassant. The Frenchman.

(THE TOURIST belches.)

ROCHELLE: You can't just belch now and then.

(THE TOURIST *plays a chord.*)

ROCHELLE: You could play in a band.

THE TOURIST: I don't think so. I'm not the type.

ROCHELLE: How did you hurt your finger there?

THE TOURIST: Painting a second floor apartment.

ROCHELLE: Seems odd you'd hurt your finger.

THE TOURIST: Manual labor. There's a slight risk, you climb a ladder with a bucket. *(He riffs on guitar.)* Can you do me a favor this weekend?

ROCHELLE: How'd you really cut your finger? You're so secretive.

(THE TOURIST *takes up a chisel.*)

THE TOURIST: You used to like that.

ROCHELLE: You don't even know what I'm talking about.

THE TOURIST: It's when you get into dog dreams, that kinda stuff, I don't know what you're talking about.

ROCHELLE: Don't do that. Don't flip a chisel around like that. No wonder you cut yourself.

THE TOURIST: Can you take Fudge for the weekend?

ROCHELLE: If you're going to Reno—

THE TOURIST: I'm not going to Reno—

ROCHELLE: —someplace like that, blowing money—

THE TOURIST: I'll just be away for the weekend.

ROCHELLE: Where are you sneaking off to this time?

THE TOURIST: What sneaking?

ROCHELLE: Then tell me.

THE TOURIST: Surprise.

ROCHELLE: Why can't you take the kids?

THE TOURIST: I'll bring them souvenirs.

ROCHELLE: You never liked travelling when we were together. I couldn't get you to budge.

THE TOURIST: My stomach's upset.

ROCHELLE: Probably an ulcer, the way you live.

THE TOURIST: I got bromo back there in the cabinet.

ROCHELLE: Which cabinet?

(He prowls around, massaging his stomach.)

THE TOURIST: I ate too many donuts. That's what it is.

ROCHELLE: Where's some water?

THE TOURIST: The tap's there.

ROCHELLE: You can't drink out of the tap. You'll get sick, this city water.

THE TOURIST: I ate five donuts.

ROCHELLE: You've got very delicate insides. Remember that Christmas.

THE TOURIST: No.

ROCHELLE: I hate you drinking out of the tap.

(THE TOURIST drinks the bromo.)

ROCHELLE: You got out your old football pictures.

THE TOURIST: Guys quit smoking, they do that, eat a couple gallons of ice cream, three, four pizzas a day. I can't stop putting stuff in my mouth.

ROCHELLE: The old scrapbook. You used to keep this on the coffee table. All those clippings of your favorite pros.

THE TOURIST: Haven't smoked one for three months.

ROCHELLE: I'm glad you're sticking to your promise. Gee, look at these. These are great.

THE TOURIST: It's hard.

ROCHELLE: I hear it's like heroin withdrawal. It scares me, you ate five donuts.

THE TOURIST: It's the swallowing I like.

ROCHELLE: Why did you ever start smoking in the first place?

THE TOURIST: So I wouldn't eat.

ROCHELLE: You're bottled up, you won't expel your pain. So you get into these weird excesses.

THE TOURIST: I'm studying music, for Chrissake.

ROCHELLE: So is it nostalgia made you take out those clippings?

THE TOURIST: How long does it take this stuff to work?

ROCHELLE: It's not a miracle drug. Five donuts stuck inside there. *(She holds up the flowers.)* You picked these for me, didn't you. You didn't buy them. That's sweet of you to pick them.

(THE TOURIST *grunts.)*

ROCHELLE: You don't have to do anything for my birthday.

(THE TOURIST *grunts.)*

ROCHELLE: But thanks anyway. By the way and for your information, I might be getting married.

(Silence)

THE TOURIST: Then you won't need my check every month.

ROCHELLE: For the kids' sake.

THE TOURIST: Is it this latest guy?

ROCHELLE: Excuse me? Latest guy? You know how that makes me sound?

THE TOURIST: The guy with the dope?

ROCHELLE: He's an anaesthesiologist. Guy with the dope!

THE TOURIST: The kids hate this guy.

ROCHELLE: The kids call him the guy with the dope?

THE TOURIST: I'll keep my eye open for someone you'd like.

ROCHELLE: You should be looking around for yourself.

THE TOURIST: Women want kids.

ROCHELLE: That is a gross generality, and offensive.

THE TOURIST: I got kids.

ROCHELLE: Why don't you take your kids on trips?

THE TOURIST: I take them camping.

ROCHELLE: Last place you took them was a football game.

THE TOURIST: I take them all over the place.

ROCHELLE: They should cross some borders, see some other cultures.

THE TOURIST: I took them to try sushi.

ROCHELLE: You go some dirty place, catch some God-awful disease, then where will you be?

THE TOURIST: That's not your worry anymore. Who says I'm going some dirty place? You don't know where I'm going. O K for Friday? Me bringing Fudge over?

ROCHELLE: His kidneys have failed. Come on. He's got pain all the time.

THE TOURIST: I won't put him asleep. Don't you do it either.

ROCHELLE: I wouldn't do it behind your back.

THE TOURIST: I'm gone just a couple of days. Some good stuff's happening.

ROCHELLE: Why do you keep a secret?

THE TOURIST: What secret?

ROCHELLE: You know what.

THE TOURIST: Secret what?

ROCHELLE: I don't know. It's a secret, isn't it.

THE TOURIST: Rochelle, man, you are so...twelve years I did the best I could. I loved you the best I could.

ROCHELLE: That was never the problem. That part was perfect.

THE TOURIST: I WANT TO SMOKE! JESUS CHRIST, I WANT A SMOKE!

(She starts to go.)

THE TOURIST: The kids don't like the guy you're dating!

ROCHELLE: Because he's not you!

(He holds her; they kiss.)

ROCHELLE: We better not. No, no, come on, we can't.

(He releases her but holds her hand.)

THE TOURIST: Funny. Get so attached to a smelly old bone-bag like that.

ROCHELLE: OK. I'll take care of it.

THE TOURIST: I didn't ask you. Did I ask you?

ROCHELLE: I know your signals. I'll do it.

THE TOURIST: Am I chicken shit or what?

ROCHELLE: You're chicken shit.

THE TOURIST: I don't want the kids to go to the vet. Just you take Fudge by yourself.

(She kisses him.)

ROCHELLE: Count on me.

THE TOURIST: Is that for sure, Shelley?

ROCHELLE: And no smoking.

THE TOURIST: You know the filling station. Well, it's about the filling station I'm making this trip. I don't want to say anymore.

ROCHELLE: Tourist.

THE TOURIST: You're all up-to-date. You know all about my trip, you know all about me.

ROCHELLE: One of these days you're going to stop talking about that filling station and buy it and become a man of substance. Then you're going to have to change.

II

(A street in a Mexican border town. It is late afternoon. A TOURIST, American, is walking. Enter a Mexican boy, MIGUEL.)

MIGUEL: Hey. Hey...Gringo. You know Clint Eastwood? Who you know? You know big star? Rambo? Who you know?

(THE TOURIST ignores him.)

MIGUEL: You want see town? I show you. Good bars.

THE TOURIST: Hey, go home, quit following me.

MIGUEL: You got car? I show you town, we ride in car.

THE TOURIST: Here. Here's a peso. Happy now? Go on home.

MIGUEL: Hey. Gringo. You want girl? I show you.

THE TOURIST: On my own. Understand?

MIGUEL: You want buy souvenir? I know shop.

THE TOURIST: Yeah, shops stay open all night long in this town.

MIGUEL: You like this? I sell this to you good price. *(He produces a postcard.)* I shine your shoes good price.

THE TOURIST: Now come on, don't talk to strangers. Nobody ever teach you that? You should never ever talk to strangers.

MIGUEL: I got six brothers, six sisters. My grandmother, she sick. You got money, maybe you like this. I sell cheap to you. *(He takes out a pocket knife.)*

(THE TOURIST examines the knife.)

MIGUEL: No steal. You like? ¿Sí?

THE TOURIST: It's a very nice one. You keep.

MIGUEL: No good this knife?

THE TOURIST: Yeah. It's fine. Swiss Army. The best. I got a couple of my own.

MIGUEL: You like knife? I got many.

THE TOURIST: Is that so.

MIGUEL: Like Rambo.

THE TOURIST: Like some sort of collection?

MIGUEL: The kind with blade snap out. Push a button. I know good one.

THE TOURIST: Run along.

MIGUEL: No. Señor. Sir. You pay money, I take you.

THE TOURIST: Take me where?

MIGUEL: Where the knife is. What kind you like?

THE TOURIST: I don't go anyplace with strangers. Not when they're talking about knives.

MIGUEL: This one lie in a deep place. No one know it there now. Very special.

THE TOURIST: This a rip-off?

MIGUEL: ¿Qué?

THE TOURIST: Take me special place me get robbed?

MIGUEL: Señor. I am guide. No thief. The switch knife. American all love.

THE TOURIST: Far?

MIGUEL: Little far. We take your car?

THE TOURIST: We walk. No car. No taxi rides.

MIGUEL: How much you pay?

THE TOURIST: I can get one in a shop. Thanks anyway.

MIGUEL: Not like this one. You do me great personal service you buy from me, señor. I save for a journey.

THE TOURIST: I'm waiting for a phone call. See? I've got to stick around my hotel for a while.

MIGUEL: I stick around with you.

THE TOURIST: Why don't you stick around an ice cream cone. Then you go on home. When's your bed time?

MIGUEL: I am open all hours for business.

THE TOURIST: Nine o'clock too late?

MIGUEL: I meet you there. On corner.

III

(Another street in the town. It is evening. THE AMERICAN *and* ESTEBAN *enter.* THE AMERICAN *carries a small heavy sack.)*

(He pulls out a pinch of cocaine and snorts it, then bays at the night sky like a wolf.)

ESTEBAN: You keep your voice low.

THE AMERICAN: You're an artist, amigo, a Michelangelo. I wish I could call you by name.

ESTEBAN: No names, Señor.

THE AMERICAN: I am not believing what I saw you do back there.

ESTEBAN: This was a disgraceful thing.

THE AMERICAN: I am in awe.

ESTEBAN: You have made a bad mistake.

THE AMERICAN: I don't even want to think about it.

ESTEBAN: This is your doing.

THE AMERICAN: I assume full responsibility.

ESTEBAN: Give the bag to me.

THE AMERICAN: Hey, hey, hey, hey, this is the trophy, this is the grand prize. I don't part from this. This is my Open Sesame back home. This buys me life in the shade, my man, this buys me senators and congressmen salaaming me on the steps of the Capitol. Don't you look so worried. You're going to share in this.

ESTEBAN: You give to me, you trust me, I bury.

THE AMERICAN: I keep this. ¿Comprende? I hang on to this baby. One down, one to go.

ESTEBAN: I will not do the other man now.

THE AMERICAN: Now just a minute. Whoa. Wait just a minute here. That is unethical. Bad business practice.

ESTEBAN: What is unethical is you and this...this obscene.... *(He drops the machete.)*

THE AMERICAN: I was out of line. I got excited. It was an impulse.

ESTEBAN: It was stupid.

THE AMERICAN: I got rambunctious. It seemed appropriate to me.

ESTEBAN: I do not associate with stupid men.

THE AMERICAN: Now look, don't let's fall out over a little thing like this. Hey, where do you think you're going?

ESTEBAN: Señor, you are a great fool.

THE AMERICAN: Don't be rude, I am paying your extremely hefty stipend. And your job's still only half done. We stick together here.

ESTEBAN: You are a fool.

THE AMERICAN: This bastard, this guy here.... I'll tell you who's a fool... *(He speaks to the sack and to* ESTEBAN.*)* ...this guy in here...you know what this guy used to make me do? This guy made me do shameful things. Let me tell you. Shameful things. I'm an attorney. Hey, OK, no names, don't get antsy. I'm a member of the legal profession. I'm ashamed of what he made me do. *(He sings:)* "I'm losing my head over you." How's that one go? "You go to my head like champagne."

*(*ESTEBAN *throws away machete.)*

THE AMERICAN: I gotta tell you this, you are pure samurai. ¿Comprende samurai? Capisce Toshiro Mifune?

ESTEBAN: Dogs, they smell the blood, they come.

THE AMERICAN: Poor guy in here, starts out a sack of crap, ends up a sack of crap. Justice is sweet.

ESTEBAN: You will be quiet, Señor.

THE AMERICAN: Hey, I'm sorry. Are we not getting along anymore? Is it my fault?

ESTEBAN: The bag.

*(*THE AMERICAN *hands* ESTEBAN *the bag.* ESTEBAN *exits.* THE AMERICAN *follows.)*

THE AMERICAN: Can I get it back? Do I get to have it back?

IV

(A small room. MIGUEL *and* THE TOURIST *sit and wait.)*

MIGUEL: You drink much tequila?

THE TOURIST: Just the water. I'm OK.

MIGUEL: You look sick. You sick?

THE TOURIST: Where'd you learn English?

MIGUEL: Rambo. You like my English?

THE TOURIST: Better than I speak Spanish.

MIGUEL: You want learn Spanish, I teach.

THE TOURIST: You're what we call back home a real entrepreneur, aren't you.

MIGUEL: I am a Spaniard. My father has Spanish blood.

THE TOURIST: How much for Spanish lessons does a real Spaniard charge?

MIGUEL: You take me cross the border.

THE TOURIST: Cagey. So whose place is this?

MIGUEL: She come pretty soon.

THE TOURIST: A woman has this kind of knife to sell? What else she sell?

MIGUEL: She no like that!

THE TOURIST: Too bad for me. I could sure use it.

MIGUEL: SHE NO LIKE THAT!

THE TOURIST: Sorry. Really. Don't shout. OK? I didn't mean to insult you. You said...before, earlier today, you said about wanting a girl. It's the way you said it, I thought you meant this one.

MIGUEL: This one no for sale.

THE TOURIST: I see. No hard feelings?

MIGUEL: This good woman. She one time live with other girl. Other girl, she that kind. I take you later. Don't be nervous, Señor.

THE TOURIST: I told you, it's just the water.

(They wait in brownout as lights up in:)

(A dingy chapel. A few candles burning. ESTEBAN *is praying. He lights a candle, genuflects. On another wall is a picture of the martyrdom of St Sebastian.* THE AMERICAN *sits waiting, the sack on the floor at his feet. He is looking at the Sebastian portrait.)*

THE AMERICAN: He still looks pretty fierce, doesn't he.

ESTEBAN: Arrows don't frighten the saint.

THE AMERICAN: Bet they hurt him like hell. Let's get out of here.

ESTEBAN: We wait here.

THE AMERICAN: For what?

ESTEBAN: We wait.

THE AMERICAN: You still believe. That's wonderful. I do it maybe once a year, Christmas Eve Mass. Most times I'm caught up in the ratrace. I should get back to this. This is right, this is good. I feel at peace here.

ESTEBAN: I tell Holy Mother I have no anger for this man.

THE AMERICAN: Don't worry, amigo, I had enough anger for both of us.

ESTEBAN: Is that why you come with machete? Is that why you interfere?

THE AMERICAN: The machete was just a souvenir I bought. I wanted to see you do it. I wanted to see you shoot the bastard down. OK, I wrecked everything, I admit it, I'm sorry. I'll see that you get double wages. When you take care of the other guy.

ESTEBAN: We wait, we decide.

THE AMERICAN: What are we waiting for?

ESTEBAN: We wait.

THE AMERICAN: OK. We wait. Say now, amigo, you wouldn't go around confessing something like what happened tonight.... I mean to Holy Mother here it's OK, but to someone real.

ESTEBAN: I am in business.

THE AMERICAN: So's the priest. You come in with a story like what you did tonight, the priest might find it very hard to let you off with a couple of Hail Marys....

ESTEBAN: Be cautious how you speak to me.

THE AMERICAN: You know who this guy was? This guy was a VIP in certain quarters.

ESTEBAN: You offend me, Señor.

THE AMERICAN: This guy's passing could touch off an international incident. This guy made some friends, played pretty good golf with the right people, had the kind of face you want to vote for, solid businessman, set up a few little businesses not so nice, places like Central America. This guy'd lived, you know what he might've done? Got to be president. Secretary of state. Think about that. Tonight you did a service to mankind.

ESTEBAN: And you are the man he trusted.

THE AMERICAN: That's his misfortune. I trusted him. How about that? I trusted this man. I'd have voted for him, hey, I'd have laid down my life for this man. Just let's set the record straight. The world is a cleaner place because this man has been exterminated. This man was a vampire sucking blood out of people like you, me, ordinary, hard-working, genuflecting people.

ESTEBAN: Your nose run all the time. Your mouth, too.

THE AMERICAN: Now the other guy. He's crazy. An athlete, you know. Fast. Strong. And a pill-popper. This guy comes back, finds that body—

ESTEBAN: He will not find the body—

THE AMERICAN:—and that body has no head on its shoulders!—

ESTEBAN: I destroy the body—

THE AMERICAN:—he's going to be seriously disturbed. I don't know if I make myself clear.

ESTEBAN: I know my job.

THE AMERICAN: A good idea might be something along the lines of Saint Sebastian here.

ESTEBAN: What you did to this man you hate, what you did was cruel, it was not human.

THE AMERICAN: Well, I'm sorry, I told you that. What did I do exactly?

ESTEBAN: With the machete. It was not natural.

THE AMERICAN: I lost control. But you...you took it right off with one swipe...that was artistry.

ESTEBAN: And now we all have trouble. The other man run away. He has seen my face. He has seen your face.

THE AMERICAN: I keep telling you, he's another bowl of borscht. He's crazy, he takes pills. So let's be sure you get out there and sanction this jock before he catches up with me.

ESTEBAN: You take your ticket. Go to the airport. Talk to no one. Take a plane. Anywhere.

THE AMERICAN: When do I hear from you?

ESTEBAN: You will hear from me.

THE AMERICAN: How you gonna do it?

ESTEBAN: He see his friend cut to pieces tonight. He see it is you. He come for you is his right. I take his life is my job. My own way, my own time. I meet this man alone. With this man I am merciful and swift.

THE AMERICAN: Let's get something totally straight here. I and some very important colleagues are paying you a helluva lot of money, my man. Just bear that fact in mind. I want to know how you finish him off. I want full details. I want pictures drawn, graphics, whatever it takes. I want this guy off my back.

ESTEBAN: Then wait.

THE AMERICAN: How long?

ESTEBAN: Until I say.

(Blackout chapel)

(In the room)

(Enter FLORA.)

FLORA: ¿Miguel? ¿Tu padre?

MIGUEL: You do business.

THE TOURIST: Hi. I'm looking to buy a knife. A certain kind of knife. She understand me?

FLORA: Trouble.

THE TOURIST: No maam. Souvenir. No trouble. You got a knife to sell?

MIGUEL: Sure. She got one. The switch knife. Tell him. He can maybe be the one.

(FLORA speaks to MIGUEL:)

FLORA: Tú no tenias permiso paras irto de la casa. Estaba preocupada por ti. Ahora tu vienes a casa, y traes un extraño contigo. *[You had no permission to leave the house. I was worried about you. Now you come home, you bring a stranger with you.]*

MIGUEL: El tiene dinero. El nos puede ayudar. *[He has money. He can help us.]*

FLORA: ¿Y si tu padre regresara? ¿Cómo explico este hombre? *[What if your father should come? How do I explain this man?]*

MIGUEL: ¿No le puedes decir que queremos ir a Estados Unidos? ¡El nos puede ayudar! *[Can't you at least tell him we want to go to America? Can't he help us?]*

FLORA: ¿Es un buen hombre? ¿Cómo lo puede saber un niño? *[Is he a good man? How can a child know?]*

MIGUEL: Lo hice por ti. Parece un buen hombre. Preguntale. No hace daño preguntar. *[I did it for you. He looks like a good man. Just ask him. It doesn't hurt to ask.]*

(In English, to TOURIST:)

FLORA: No knife here.

MIGUEL: She have. She tell lies to you.

(FLORA slaps MIGUEL.)

FLORA: No me hables de esa manera enfrente de la visita. *[You do not speak to me that way before a visitor.]*

MIGUEL: Disculpame, pero— *[Forgive me, but—]*

FLORA: No knife here.

MIGUEL: She say she sell knife, buy new life. ¡Preguntale!

FLORA: How much you pay?

THE TOURIST: How much does a new life cost?

FLORA: The boy, he like make up adventure.

THE TOURIST: Can I see the knife? If it's what I want I'll pay you well.

FLORA: You are rich? Big car?

THE TOURIST: Came down on the bus.

MIGUEL: ¡Preguntale!

FLORA: You know Los Angeles?

THE TOURIST: Heard of it.

MIGUEL: Is nice place?

THE TOURIST: I don't guess I'd want to start a new life there, but I hear it's a nice enough place.

FLORA: The boy knows where knife is. Vamos, Miguel.

(MIGUEL *runs out.*)

FLORA: Excuse me that I hit him. He is naughty always.

THE TOURIST: They can be that way.

FLORA: Where do you live?

THE TOURIST: Midwest.

FLORA: Is in Texas?

THE TOURIST: Not quite.

FLORA: What business you have?

THE TOURIST: I'm in oil. Joke. I part own a gas station.

FLORA: You have a wife?

THE TOURIST: What is this, the police department? *(He notices an object on a chain around her neck.)* Is that a bullet? That's quite a trinket to wear around your neck. Why don't you wear a cross like most girls in this country?

FLORA: It remind me always that we are only...mortal. Is that a word?

THE TOURIST: Yeah...it's a word....

FLORA: If you don't want to suffer, you can always stop.

THE TOURIST: Interesting philosophy.

FLORA: Bullet is smooth, always cool.

THE TOURIST: Not always maybe. But you don't suffer. You're a good-looking girl. You must have plenty of guys coming around.

FLORA: That is not to suffer?

THE TOURIST: I'm sorry. I don't mean anything. The only Mexican women I know about are...you know....

FLORA: No.

THE TOURIST:...nice to the gentlemen.

FLORA: You do not know Mexican woman at all. That is sad for you. I can give you something to drink?

THE TOURIST: Can I see that again? You speak good English.

(He comes close to her and examines the bullet. FLORA draws away.)

FLORA: The convent.

THE TOURIST: The boy. Your little brother?

FLORA: My son.

THE TOURIST: You don't look old enough to have a son.

FLORA: What is old enough to have a son in U S?

THE TOURIST: The boy says you used to live with another girl.

FLORA: Magdalena. He tell you about her? My cousin. A long time ago. She say let us live in the town where there is men. I come with her. I am young. I meet man. He ask me to marry. Magdalena want man so bad. Man come for me.

THE TOURIST: Life's never fair.

FLORA: This knife no legal in U S.

THE TOURIST: No.

FLORA: Why you want this knife?

THE TOURIST: Souvenir. A good deal.

FLORA: Good deal always mean risk.

THE TOURIST: What's taking him so long?

FLORA: He must go to a special room. Move things with care. Take the knife. Put back the things so disturb nothing.

THE TOURIST: Is he stealing it?

FLORA: Yes.

THE TOURIST: He said it was his.

FLORA: He play a joke.

THE TOURIST: I guess I don't see it. I don't feel very good. Tonight...I saw.... I had a bad shock....

FLORA: I have rum.

THE TOURIST: No thanks. *(He trips on a large jagged piece of glass.)* Somebody could get hurt with this.

FLORA: Somebody did.

(He picks up the glass.)

THE TOURIST: What should I do with it?

FLORA: Drop it on the floor. Is not mine. Belong to Esteban.

(He does. She glances past him out a window.)

THE TOURIST: You mean your kid?

FLORA: His father.

THE TOURIST: The man who took you away from the carefree life with Magdalena?

FLORA: He is a brave man. A clever man. Could maybe be a great man.

THE TOURIST: Is he a good man?

FLORA: Our son name is Esteban, like him. But I call the boy Miguel, his second name, so maybe he not become like his father. I want very much my son to go where he do not meet his father.

THE TOURIST: Isn't he a good man?

FLORA: One time a very good man. One time...do not laugh at me, I say he is like sunrise to me, this man.

THE TOURIST: No woman ever thought I was the sunrise.

FLORA: Our son is born, he beg my pardon for this pain. He would bear it for me if he could. He bring small flower to me sometime. He say poetry sometime. He is funny, make us laugh, make joke, be like movie character or so. Now I sit. Sometime this room I sit by window, I watch, wait for the father of my son, like I do now. Fear what place he come from.

THE TOURIST: Is he bad to you?

FLORA: Is too good to us. For this good heart he has lost his soul.

THE TOURIST: He doesn't, you know, shove you around. Beat you up. Nothing like that.

FLORA: No. Nothing like that. But it would be good for Miguel to go away. What are you?

THE TOURIST: What do you mean, what am I? I own a gas station is what I am. American is what I am.

FLORA: Are you a good man?

THE TOURIST: Does it matter?

FLORA: Of course.

THE TOURIST: Sometimes.

FLORA: You are an honest man.

THE TOURIST: Sometimes.

FLORA: You like weapon. The father of Miguel is very fine with weapon. Broken glass. Weapons of the streets.

THE TOURIST: This was a mistake.

FLORA: You could help us, no? You could take my son with you maybe.

THE TOURIST: Your husband would love that.

FLORA: If Miguel go away, then Esteban and me alone for a time, together for a time, maybe Esteban be good man like before.

THE TOURIST: Then it's his knife you're stealing.

FLORA: I play a joke.

THE TOURIST: Don't get me wrong about this, but he walks in, no son, no knife, the joke's on you. Sunrise or no sunrise.

FLORA: He will not harm me. Will you take the boy? I can give you name, address, people in Los Angeles he can live with.

(Enter MIGUEL. *He holds out the knife.)*

FLORA: Try it, Señor. Make sure of it.

*(*THE TOURIST *works the knife.)*

FLORA: Is fine enough?

THE TOURIST: I can't take it. Not like this.

MIGUEL: You won't pay me?

THE TOURIST: I can't take this knife. It's dangerous for you.

FLORA: You will take my son with you?

THE TOURIST: I can't.

FLORA: I ask nothing for the knife. You take the knife. You take my son away from this place.

THE TOURIST: It's just not possible.

FLORA: I do not know you. But you are kind to my son. You have a good face. I ask nothing but that you take him back across the border. Buy a ticket and send him to Los Angeles. I only ask that much. I will pay you for the ticket. I promise I will. I can give you some now.

THE TOURIST: I can't explain.

FLORA: So you will pay him for his knife? With money I can find a way to send him.

(THE TOURIST *counts out a wad of bills, hands them to* MIGUEL.)

THE TOURIST: Here's a hundred bucks. That's one hundred dollars American. It'll get you to L A.

FLORA: Give me your name, your address. I will pay you back.

THE TOURIST: I get the knife.

FLORA: Not worth one hundred dollars.

THE TOURIST: Give me something to write on.

FLORA: Miguel.

(MIGUEL *runs out.*)

THE TOURIST: I'm sorry I can't help you. I hope it works out for you. I go alone. That's how it is.

(MIGUEL *returns with a school pad and a pen.*)

THE TOURIST: I don't want you showing this around. If anything goes wrong....

FLORA: I will send you the money.

MIGUEL: I keep this safe. (*He tucks the paper in his pocket.*)

THE TOURIST: Well. So long.

FLORA: Why? I thank you for this help. But why?

THE TOURIST: Tonight I saw.... I want to make something good.

FLORA: Adiós.

THE TOURIST: Miguel, pleasure doing business with you.

MIGUEL: I can show you town, show you best restaurant. Take you visit mama's cousin.

FLORA: Miguel, vamos.

MIGUEL: Por favor, Mama...

THE TOURIST: Mind your mother. It's past your bedtime. Remember this. You never met me. You forgot there ever was a knife.

FLORA: He do not harm us. We are his life.

MIGUEL: Hey, Gringo, you maybe take Mama cross the border. Say she your daughter. She called Flora.

FLORA: Shhh, Miguel. You can find your way? You need Miguel to show you?

THE TOURIST: He should stay here with you. I'll be O K.

FLORA: Good luck to you.

THE TOURIST: You, too. If I'm ever in L A.... *(He goes out.)*

V

(A bar. Table, chairs. THE AMERICAN *with his sack.)*

THE AMERICAN: There's a kind of suffering that you can't cure, it's a suffering of the deepest recesses of the soul. You wouldn't know anything about the soul, would you. You can't take an aspirin for it, you can't put it to sleep or cut it out with a scalpel. But it gets sick. It's a withering of the spirit. I'd just like to go on record with that. I'd just like you to hear it because I tried to explain it to you one time and you were deaf. Using your putter there on the carpet. You didn't want to hear.

(Enter THE TOURIST, *looking for someone. He sees* THE AMERICAN *and starts to leave.)*

THE AMERICAN: Hey. Nearest cat house is couple blocks that way. You lost?

THE TOURIST: Fellow American?

THE AMERICAN: Do I hear Yankee Doodle striking up? Get over here and sit down.

THE TOURIST: What part?

THE AMERICAN: Queens. New York. Bayside, Queens. You?

THE TOURIST: Always scared to go see New York. You hear about all the crime.

THE AMERICAN: Take a chair. Here's a bottle of tequila. Get loaded.

THE TOURIST: Here on business?

THE AMERICAN: Know how you beat sleep? Little secret. Get hold of some dust. Know what I mean? Jacks you up, keeps you alert as hell. Business? You would not believe the business I am conducting.

THE TOURIST: Your package is leaking there.

THE AMERICAN: Oh. Thanks. Hey, I mean it. Get plastered here. It's on me. Keep an old compatriot company. Man, I am expecting amazing things to occur here, I could use a friend. I'm not even supposed to be in this country. How about that?

THE TOURIST: I gotta hit the john a minute. Thought they boiled the water in these places.

(He retreats.)

(THE AMERICAN *takes out tissue and wipes the stains on the table around the sack.)*

(THE TOURIST *returns.* THE AMERICAN *doesn't notice him. He finishes wiping, sits up, starts violently finding the other man right there.)*

THE AMERICAN: Jesus. You fuckin' freaked me right out. *(He puts down the tissue on the table. It is bloody.)* Hey. Drinks are called for here. Sit.

THE TOURIST: Bloody nose?

THE AMERICAN: Hell no. Just runs all the time. This damned stuff fucks up your sinuses. But, man, what's a mere sinus, that's my motto. *(He notices the bloody tissue.)* Oh. Yeah. That. It did bleed a little.

(THE TOURIST *sits down.)*

THE TOURIST: Get down to this part of the world often?

THE AMERICAN: Often as I can. This is God's country.

THE TOURIST: Thought that was Australia.

THE AMERICAN: Australia's chamber of commerce would like you to believe that. Far as I'm concerned, this is the land God made for his personal vacation spot.

THE TOURIST: My first time.

THE AMERICAN: They got it all, man. You can sin from Friday night to Monday morning nonstop. The place never shuts down. Know what I mean? I can show you a place, I'll take you down a street or two that will turn your life around. New York'll look like Disney World.

THE TOURIST: What do you do? I mean, usually. For a living.

THE AMERICAN: I'm in you might say the investment field. I am legal counsel on some very delicate investment/venture capital kind of deals. With political implications. Need I say more. You?

THE TOURIST: Got a gas station. Me and the brother-in-law.

THE AMERICAN: Keep you hopping.

THE TOURIST: With oil prices hiking the way they are, the Gulf situation—

THE AMERICAN:—the guy's a lunatic, a madman, the Gulf guy—

THE TOURIST:—we're going to need bodyguards pretty soon.

THE AMERICAN: Body guards.

THE TOURIST: You know, guys who keep you from getting your head knocked off.

THE AMERICAN: I guess I don't get you.

THE TOURIST: You know what scares me about coke? Not the brain cell part. It's the talking too much part.

THE AMERICAN: Hey, look, set me straight here—

THE TOURIST: You snort some, drink a few shots, snort some more, pretty soon you're telling your life story. Before long you're opening packages, showing strangers what you have in them, one thing leads to another.

THE AMERICAN: Got some kind of holy hang-up about dope? Are we having the same discussion here or what?

THE TOURIST: I think we are. Roughly.

THE AMERICAN: I gotta apologize. I've got the shakes pretty bad. You won't believe what I saw tonight. Gruesomest sight I ever saw. A picture of Saint Sebastian stuck full of arrows. I mean arrows, man, capital-A arrows. It was fuckin' ballistic. And get this. This is in a church, where people go for comfort. I mean, I want the Chamber of Horrors I take in Madame Toussaud's. I don't drop into St Mary's. I'm in there with a friend who always prays and lights a candle before he eats dinner with his wife. How about that for devotion? These people, man, these people are pure, these people are so basically pure, they terrify me. I'm grubby, man. I have a grubby soul. This man, he prays before he sits down to dinner with his family, he cleans his soul like he cleans his hands. These are clean people, don't ever let anybody say they're not. These are the cleanest people on earth.

THE TOURIST: We must scare the hell outa them.

THE AMERICAN: Hey, listen, these people. Don't let them kid you. These are shrewd savvy people. ¿Comprende? You think we scare them? They scare the crap outa me. They see you, they take one look, some gringo rube from the north, they got your wallet all sized up, they know how to work you. Those brown eyes, Hey Gringo I got a dying sister, they can melt you like butter in a second. Hey, I can say this. I come down here, I live like they live,

I admire these people. Look what they put up with. I admire them. Don't get me wrong. But keep your wallet where you can see it. I am Charlie to my friends, and you are...?

(He reaches out his hand. THE TOURIST *does not take it.)*

THE AMERICAN: Hey, drink my liquor, shake my hand.

THE TOURIST: Wash 'em first.

(There is blood on his hand.)

THE AMERICAN: You're uptight, man. I don't know if it's my fault. Am I dominating the rap?

THE TOURIST: You're gonna be Saint Sebastian himself if you don't put your tongue back in your face.

THE AMERICAN: It was you. You were there. You saw it happen. You were there tonight.

THE TOURIST: Listen. I come down for the weekend. Pick up a case of Montezuma's Revenge, chase a little tail, write a few postcards, home on Monday bright and early to work. I got part ownership in a filling station. Put in fourteen hours a day. Alimony, child support once a month. Second-hand car payments. Take the kids bowling on their birthdays.

THE AMERICAN: Hey, if you don't want me to know you're here, I've already forgotten about you.

THE TOURIST: Me, I'm like an elephant. I never forget.

THE AMERICAN: Who do you work for?

THE TOURIST: I got ears like twenty-twenty vision. Some guy starts yakking, says he met me someplace, I find out about it. I got these two good ears. You, my man, let me be real clear here, you only got one tongue.

THE AMERICAN: There was another guy. It was you. You were driving. You were the one we were waiting for at the church.

THE TOURIST: You split. Right now. Take that door. Take this key. My room.

THE AMERICAN: Who do you work for?

THE TOURIST: No talking. Go. Let me take out the trash. Leave that here.

THE AMERICAN: Hey, that belongs to me.

THE TOURIST: You'll never get it through customs.

*(*THE AMERICAN *hesitates, then leaves the sack and hurries out.)*

(Through the next scene THE TOURIST *remains seated at the cafe table in brown-out.)*

VI

(ESTEBAN *is searching through a trunk.* FLORA *comes. She is gripping the broken glass. He does not turn to her.*)

FLORA: Tu devoción te ha convertido en un demonio. Tu eres así. Como este pedazo de vidrio. Un fragmento. Te gastas las rodillas rogando a la Madre Santa. Pero tu esperitu ya hiso su jornada. Porque estás en el Infierno. Tu nos has condenado, a quien tú amas, tu esposa, tu hijo, por la misma jornada. Nunca se termina. El camino al Infierno es el infierno mismo. Desearia tener el valor de acabar contigo. Desearia tener el amor para acabar contigo ahora. *[Your devotion has made you a demon. You are like this piece of glass. A fragment. You wear out your knees beseeching Holy Mother. But your soul has already made its journey. Because you are in Hell, you have condemned us, whom you love, your wife, your son, to the same journey. It is never finished. The road to Hell is Hell itself. I wish I had the courage to finish you. I wish I had the love to finish you now.]* (*She drops the glass.*)

(ESTEBAN *rises, comes to her, caresses her. She wants to resist. He is gentle. She relaxes.*)

FLORA: Desearia tener el valor de amarte mejor, Esteban. *[I wish I had courage to love you better, Esteban.]*

(*He toys with the bullet at her throat.*)

(*Distant guitar music*)

VII

(*The music plays louder.*)

(*The chapel as before.* THE TOURIST *comes in, looks around for* ESTEBAN. *Seeing that he is alone, he finds a chair and sits. Clearly he is not at home in this environment.*)

(ESTEBAN *comes in. He genuflects and starts to say a decade of the rosary.* THE TOURIST *remains seated, watching him.*)

(*After a few moments,* ESTEBAN *breaks off.*)

(*Pause*)

THE TOURIST: The café. I waited. Like always.

ESTEBAN: I could not come this time.

THE TOURIST: The American was there.

ESTEBAN: That is unfortunate.

THE TOURIST: He's my worry. The football player is our worry. I figure this guy, you can't take him up close.

ESTEBAN: I love my son very much. Holy Mother have a son.

THE TOURIST: What weapon will you use?

ESTEBAN: Tonight I come to my home, my son ask me questions, I try to answer, questions about square roots—

THE TOURIST: Are you listening? We've got half the job left to do and it's going to be harder now. You must understand something. This guy, Madjanski, he was a god, once he could run like the wind.

ESTEBAN: You call him a god.

THE TOURIST: So how will you do it?

ESTEBAN: Why do you call him a god?

THE TOURIST: We called him Mercury. Everybody did. The whole country. Fleet of foot. I always wanted to play like him. I was pretty fast in those days, too. But I had small bones. I couldn't take the punishment.

ESTEBAN: My friend, tonight I collapse inside.

THE TOURIST: I know.

(ESTEBAN *crosses to* THE TOURIST.)

ESTEBAN: Tell me what we do is worthy.

THE TOURIST: I don't think about it that way.

ESTEBAN: Something inside me die tonight.

THE TOURIST: This is a rough one.

ESTEBAN: Tell me what we do is worthy!

THE TOURIST: Morality got junked way back. I don't even remember when.

ESTEBAN: You bring your crime to my country.

THE TOURIST: This is the discussion we promised we'd never get into.

ESTEBAN: You put your dirt on my streets.

THE TOURIST: I don't know, maybe you're a religious man, maybe you're not. I don't know you. Me, I'm not. But the way I look at it is there are men like Jesus. There are men like us. He was the holy man. We are the soldiers.

ESTEBAN: We kill many men.

THE TOURIST: He can't do our job, we can't do his job.

ESTEBAN: Do you have a son?

THE TOURIST: I won't let you use the machete on this man.

ESTEBAN: The machete is not my weapon.

THE TOURIST: We must be equipped and disciplined at every level of our work.

(ESTEBAN *takes out a pistol and handles it gently, aiming it in the general direction of* THE TOURIST.)

ESTEBAN: I am afraid.

THE TOURIST: This time isn't like the other times.

ESTEBAN: You, too, are afraid?

THE TOURIST: I don't know.

ESTEBAN: You have a wife? *(Silence)* You have a wife?

THE TOURIST: We stay strangers. That's how it's got to be.

ESTEBAN: Answer me!

(He continues to hold the gun as they continue talking.)

THE TOURIST: Did have.

ESTEBAN: My wife, she is my honor, she is my secret heart. All I do is for her good. She deserve only the finest life.

THE TOURIST: I can't know about you.

ESTEBAN: I give her everything good. She come, she go like she want. She will not be happy.

THE TOURIST: Don't tell me.

ESTEBAN: Her eyes are too clear, she see what I shut away from her. But never does she speak of it. Tonight she is different. Tonight she say something. I do a terrible thing to her.

THE TOURIST: I don't want to know this.

ESTEBAN: You must know this. Who better than you? You must know how close I come to kill this woman. So close. I love her more than my soul. Do you love a woman so much?

THE TOURIST: Yes.

ESTEBAN: This is not a time to lie.

THE TOURIST: Yes I do love a woman so much.

ESTEBAN: I cut her hand. Very bad. How can I do such a thing to her? How can I hurt her? But is not for the woman to judge. They do not do our work, they cannot judge our work.

THE TOURIST: Listen, just listen to me, just hear what I say. Then never again do we talk about this. We're mercenaries. That's it. Just accept that. I am a man with no skills. Little education. I can't make it in my country. No. It's so. You find that hard to believe. It's so. Take my word. You are a man with good blood, skills, a good education. Your country doesn't have a place for you, either. Life is hard. People depend on us. We do what we must. This is something I can do, you can do, we do it well so we get paid well. So our children can have it better. Many times, many, I've trusted my safety, my life, to you. Always, always my trust in you has been repaid. Because of you I come back. Every time. Because of you my kids are protected. That's all there is. It's a shitty job. We try to do it with some.... I don't know...do it well.

ESTEBAN: You go away. Back to U S. Back to your children. My family is here. We have no place to go, no place else to look.

THE TOURIST: You hear this, man, you get this. We've got to be strong for this work, we can't think about it, we can't talk about it. Or about ourselves or our kids, our wives, or...next time we meet, we can't do our job.

ESTEBAN: Do you go into your home with anger? Do you strike your children? Do you cut your wife's hand?

THE TOURIST: No.

ESTEBAN: The day will come.

THE TOURIST: No!

ESTEBAN: It will!

THE TOURIST: No!... It won't. I'll never let that happen.

ESTEBAN: You will not be able to stop it.

THE TOURIST: I don't live with them.

ESTEBAN: Because of what you are.

THE TOURIST: Because that's the way it's got to be.

ESTEBAN: Because it could happen—

THE TOURIST: Because, O K. It could. If I was there. Living with them. It could. Or I could say something. It's better if I'm not there.

ESTEBAN: And so you leave your family.

THE TOURIST: There are lots of reasons why a man leaves his family.

ESTEBAN: If you play football, if you run like a god, if your country find a place for you, then do you leave them?

THE TOURIST: Some guys do.

ESTEBAN: You? Do you?

THE TOURIST: It was the silence that got to her. Me never talking, never telling her anything. She knew I was keeping things from her.

ESTEBAN: She is a good woman?

(THE TOURIST *nods*.)

ESTEBAN: You miss her?

(THE TOURIST *nods*.)

ESTEBAN: We will not speak of this again, my friend.

THE TOURIST: The American.

ESTEBAN: I do it for you.

THE TOURIST: No.

ESTEBAN: You have no stomach for it.

THE TOURIST: Do Madjanski. I don't think, tonight, him standing right there, I don't think I was going to do it.

ESTEBAN: This pistol will be swift.

THE TOURIST: In my country he was like a king. Then one day he was nobody.

ESTEBAN: I don't need to know a man to kill him.

THE TOURIST: It's got to be quick, quiet, and from behind.

ESTEBAN: I do not destroy from behind.

THE TOURIST: Makes me sad.

ESTEBAN: Turn away your eyes.

(Darkness)

(Guitar music in blackout)

VIII

(Bright daylight)

(Guitar out)

(The hotel room of THE TOURIST. THE AMERICAN *sits with ice cubes on his eyes.* THE TOURIST *is shaving with a straight razor.)*

THE AMERICAN: I guess I caused a lot of trouble. *(Silence)* This guy cheated many people. Many Americans. This guy wanted the White House. You know that about him?

THE TOURIST: You gotta teach some guys where the line is. My rule of thumb: Guy takes a nip outa me, I take a bite outa him.

THE AMERICAN: I'll remember that. That's good. That's masterful prose. God, my eyes are like...I don't know, burning coals here.

THE TOURIST: Thanks for the use of the mirror.

THE AMERICAN: Hey, it's your room. Be my guest. What did become of the running back? Mercury Madjanski. Remember when they called him that?

THE TOURIST: I don't like to talk too much in the morning. Mind if I use the head?

THE AMERICAN: What head?

THE TOURIST: You know. The john. The toilet. Got a case of the runs you wouldn't believe.

THE AMERICAN: Stick to tequila and rum, my man. Down here you do not, repeat, Do Not!, drink the water.

(THE TOURIST *goes.*)

THE AMERICAN: I gotta tell you this, you guys have my admiration. You guys are the very best. I'll put your names in the right ears.

THE TOURIST: You don't know our names.

THE AMERICAN: You know what I mean.

THE TOURIST: Nobody even knows what we look like.

THE AMERICAN: You're exclusive.

THE TOURIST: You're the only one.

THE AMERICAN: Makes me exclusive.

THE TOURIST: You're a lawyer. You understand the concept of professional etiquette?

(THE TOURIST *pulls out the knife, snaps it open.*)

(*Silence*)

IX

(*The basement. Empty.* ROCHELLE *comes in. She is carrying a bundle of mail. She sets it down. Starts to go.* THE TOURIST *comes in with a bromo.*)

ROCHELLE: Didn't know you were back yet.

THE TOURIST: This morning.

ROCHELLE: You overdo it on your trip?

THE TOURIST: Here's some stuff I bought for the kids.

ROCHELLE: You don't look good.

THE TOURIST: You take care of Fudge and everything?

(She touches his face.)

THE TOURIST: Thank you.

ROCHELLE: Here. I brought in the mail.

THE TOURIST: Thanks.

ROCHELLE: You didn't start smoking again, did you.

THE TOURIST: Didn't even think about it.

ROCHELLE: You should see a doctor.

THE TOURIST: Maybe you're right.

ROCHELLE: The deal go O K?

THE TOURIST: ...what?...

ROCHELLE: The filling station.

THE TOURIST: Yeah. That looks good. I got the bank roll I needed.

ROCHELLE: Great. Can I know how?

THE TOURIST: I didn't rob anybody.

ROCHELLE: I wasn't accusing you. So.

THE TOURIST: Thanks. About Fudge.

ROCHELLE: He's better off.

THE TOURIST: Better off dead?

ROCHELLE: Well, look, the kids want to see you. They want to cheer you up.

THE TOURIST: I'll call.

ROCHELLE: The dog dreams stopped. Odd, isn't it. *(She starts to go.)* I nearly stole something out of a store. Really. I nearly did. You look at me like.... I picked up this pretty glass dish. Smoked glass. Very, very nice. Expensive. I'm handling it, holding it up to the light, then I just start walking away. Slow. Toward the street door. Nobody says anything. I reach the door. I have my hand on the door. What's wrong with me? Doing something like that? It's not me.

THE TOURIST: How much is the thing?

ROCHELLE: It's not my style. And they say it gets easier.

THE TOURIST: What gets easier?

ROCHELLE: Criminals say you do it once and after that it's not so bad, it gets easier.

THE TOURIST: You like the dish?

ROCHELLE: That's not the point. I put it back. But why did I want to steal it?

THE TOURIST: I'll get you the dish.

ROCHELLE: It's not the dish. The dish doesn't matter. Fuck the dish. Maybe you reach some point in your life. You think I'm at a point?

THE TOURIST: You just got an urge. You won't do it again. One time I got a little drunk, I clipped a pack of baseball cards out of the store. No big deal. I felt stupid, that's all. I never did it again.

ROCHELLE: When did you do this?

THE TOURIST: High school.

ROCHELLE: You were drunk! How old were you?

THE TOURIST: The cards probably have some value now. Wish I knew what I did with them.

ROCHELLE: Why didn't you ever tell me about this?

THE TOURIST: It was a prank. I never tell you things because you get so worked up.

ROCHELLE: You were about fifteen, sixteen, walking around drunk?

THE TOURIST: At a football rally. I drank a beer.

ROCHELLE: You couldn't handle one beer?

THE TOURIST: WILL YOU GET OFF MY BACK!

(She recoils.)

THE TOURIST: I'm telling you, it was a hundred years ago. Ripping off a store happens in a person's life. I promise, Rochelle, you won't do it again.

ROCHELLE: What's the matter with you?

THE TOURIST: It was a thirty-cent pack of cards.

ROCHELLE: This is a thing I should have known about.

THE TOURIST: You're starting in.

ROCHELLE: I'm not starting in.

THE TOURIST: I'll get you the dish. I want you to have it.

ROCHELLE: Forget about the dish. I brought it up because my actions scared me. I wanted your feedback.

THE TOURIST: I'm not the guy to ask about things like that.

ROCHELLE: Well. I respect your opinion. Sue me. Don't feel too bad about Fudge. It was time.

(He browses his mail as a way of avoiding her eyes. She hesitates, waiting for something from him.)

ROCHELLE: Your stomach better?

(He has found a letter and is tearing it open with something like alarm.)

ROCHELLE: You've got very sensitive insides.

(He lifts out a note and two fifty-dollar bills and a small object, a bullet. ROCHELLE does not notice this.)

ROCHELLE: Oh honey. I know. He was a sweet puppy. He was a beautiful puppy. I know how you feel.

(He is reading.)

(In the church:)

(ESTEBAN enters, genuflects, but does not kneel or pray. He studies the Sebastian statue.)

ESTEBAN: The hundred dollars is yours. The bullet you will recognize. You have the knife. You have taken what is mine. My son. You have come into my home. You have broken what we agreed. Watch for me now. I do not destroy from behind.

(The basement:)

(THE TOURIST drops the letter, fumbles with the money and the bullet. He seems about to fall.)

ROCHELLE: Bad news? The money fall through?

END

OCEAN DREAM

Nancy Rhodes

International opera and musical theatre director Nancy Rhodes is founder and artistic director of Encompass Music Theatre in New York City, where she directed ELIZABETH AND ESSEX starring Estelle Parsons; THE MOTHER OF US ALL by Gertrude Stein and Virgil Thompson; and REGINA by Marc Blitzstein and Lillian Hellman. She staged WEST SIDE STORY in Istanbul, KISS ME KATE in Ankara, CARMEN in Oslo, DEATH IN VENICE in Stockholm, HAPPY END in Finland, and ECCENTRICS, OUTCASTS, AND VISIONARIES for The Holland Festival in Amsterdam. She teaches musical theater workshops in Europe and Asia, and she is the vice-president and U S delegate to the International Theater Institute's Music Theater Committee. She is on the faculty of the Manhattan School of Music. She recently directed and cowrote the book of THE GLASS WOMAN, a new opera, and adapted and directed Molière's THE IMAGINARY INVALID for the Academy Theater in Atlanta.

OCEAN DREAM may be presented with or without the original music composed by Victor Kioulaphides.

DEDICATION

To Tina Howe
who loves the sea
as much as I do

CHARACTERS

CHILD
GIRL

(Late day. Brilliant sun colors the sky. Birds, water, waves. Breezes blowing. Isolation. A GIRL strolls languidly along the water's edge. She hums to herself, feeling the breezes through her hair, the sun against her skin, the water and sand on her feet. She prances and dances among the waves, running forward and back, laughing to herself, circling in the water, humming, circling until she makes herself dizzy and falls laughing into the water.)

VOICE: *(In the distance)* Help me, oh, please, please help me.

(The GIRL is lying flat on her back, rolling and playing in the water.)

VOICE: Someone please help me, please!

(The GIRL sits up. She looks around, but does not see anything.)

VOICE: Hurry, please hurry, someone please help me.

(The GIRL gets up on her knees, listening intently.)

VOICE: Here, I'm here, please help me, please!

(The GIRL gets up, frightened, looks up and down the beach. She runs. Music. A dark shadow falls across the sky.)

VOICE: Help me, please.

GIRL: I'm coming, where are you?

VOICE: Here, here, here.

(The GIRL sees something behind the tall grass. She goes toward it. It is a wooden cage. There is a CHILD inside. She is very young. The GIRL falls down on her knees, staring at the CHILD.)

CHILD: I thought you'd never come.

GIRL: I'm sorry, I didn't know where you were at first.

CHILD: Please, let me out, I want out.

(The GIRL tries to open the wooden cage, then thinks better of it.)

GIRL: Who are you?

CHILD: Roses are red,
Violets are blue,
Sugar is sweet,
And so are you.
Ha, ha, ha, ha, ha, ha.

GIRL: Where is your mother?

CHILD: You know the answer to that.

GIRL: No, I don't. I want to help you. Who are you?

CHILD: Mirror, mirror
On the wall,
Who's the fairest
One of all?

GIRL: Snow White?

CHILD: That's right. You know me now?

GIRL: No, I never saw you in my life.

CHILD: Oh, yes you have.
Ashes to ashes,
Dust to dust,
If it weren't for boys
Our lips would rust!

GIRL: You frighten me. *(She begins to back away.)*

CHILD: Wait, don't leave.
Come back, Mary,
Mary quite contrary,
How does your garden grow?
With silver bells and cockle
shells, and...
Wait, come back!

(The CHILD *rattles the cage loudly.)*
Mirror, mirror
On the wall,
Who's the fairest
One of all?

GIRL: *(Screams)* SNOW WHITE!

CHILD: That's right, Snow White,
That's right, Snow White,
That's right, Snow
White, White, White,
You know me,
You know me,
You know me,
Snow White, Snow so White,
Snow
Dripping, oozing, melting

Through your fingers,
Snow so white,
Until it turns red,
Blood-red, dripping,
Oozing, melting,
Through your fingers.
My heart in your hands,
Pulsing, pounding,
Crying out for you,
Crying out for you,
Snow White, in the night
Crying out for you.

GIRL: Please don't,
I'm choking,
I can't breathe,
Please, please.

CHILD: Let me out, let me out!
I waited for you,
Remember, remember?

GIRL: No, no, no I don't remember.

CHILD: Snow White, look at me,
In the mirror,
What do you see,
Tell me, what do you see?

GIRL: *(Hysterical)*
See, see? I see
Nothing in the mirror,
The mirror so silver
And shining like moonlight,
Glistening on the water.
I blow my breath upon the mirror,
And all I see is smoke,
Fog and smoke. It disappears,
I look, again, and I see nothing.

CHILD: *(Whispering)*
Snow White, Snow White,
Take this apple, this
Ruby red apple,
Take one bite, just one
Delicious bite.
It is good, so very good, and
If you take just one bite,

You will become the queen,
Just think...you the queen!

GIRL: I, I, I, I?

CHILD: Yes, you, you, Snow White.
Just one bite,
One tiny bite.

(The GIRL takes the apple and looks at it a long time.)

CHILD: Go on, go on,
You will like the taste.
It's crisp and tender,
Just like you, Snow White.

(The GIRL bites the apple. A storm.)

GIRL: Ah, ah I feel dizzy, I feel sick. My pulse is racing my head is.... Help me, oh please, please help me! *(It grows very dark.)* Someone please help me, please.

CHILD: Open this cage, Snow White,
Open this cage and let me out!

CHILD and GIRL: *(Sing together)* Hurry, please hurry, someone please help me.

(The GIRL is overcome from the apple, and is so weak, She has to crawl toward the cage. She opens the door. The CHILD climbs out and begins to dance.)

CHILD:	GIRL:
Free, I'm free	Please help me, please!
Free, I'm free	Please help me, please!
I am free, free,	Help me, help me,
Free!	Help me!

CHILD: Dance, Snow White, dance
See, see the light
Feel the air
Dance and twirl
Step and whirl
Dance, dance, dance!

(The CHILD grabs SNOW WHITE's hands and pulls her onto her feet. She begins to twirl the GIRL.)

GIRL: Oh my, oh my, oh my, oh, ah!

CHILD: *(Going faster and faster)*
Come on Snow White
Dance with me

See the light, through the night
Feel the air, dance and twirl
Taste desire, dance like fire
Step and whirl, dance and twirl,
Dance and prance, and dance and prance
And dance and dance and dance
Snow White!

GIRL: Ah, ah, ah!!!

CHILD:	GIRL:
Fly, Snow White	Fly away
Feel the air	See the light
Fly above, far away	Far away
Far beyond, fly beyond	Fly beyond
Far beyond, fly beyond	Fly beyond

CHILD and GIRL: (*Together*) Fly, fly, fly!

(SNOW WHITE *collapses to the floor, breathless and dizzy. The* CHILD *goes to* SNOW WHITE, *kneels, and begins to rock her as* SNOW WHITE *lays her head in* CHILD's *lap.*)

CHILD: Beautiful princess,
Now you are the queen,
You, only you, nobody else.
The kingdom is yours.

(CHILD *holds up a hand mirror; the* GIRL *takes it, mesmerized.*)

CHILD: Take this mirror,
Hold it tight.
Close your eyes
And see the night.
Stars and moon
Revolve and turn,
Make one wish and
You shall learn.

GIRL: One wish?

CHILD: One wish.

GIRL: Kiss me, rock me, never leave me.

(CHILD *leans over and kisses* SNOW WHITE. *She begins to revive.*)

CHILD: I knew you'd come back,
I waited for you.
See, I am just the same,

I have not changed.
It is only me you see.

GIRL: CHILD:
(Weeping)
Yes, yes, yes,
I lost you,   Lost you
Could not find you,   Find you
Could not hear your voice   Hear your voice
I longed for you,   Longed for you
Wondering where you were,   Wondering, wondering
And now, you are here,   And now, you are here
Here with me.   Here with me.

(Together)
At last, I found you,
Found you, found you.
How I searched and searched
For you, lonely in the night,
Crying out, in the night,
Longing for your voice to
Guide me through the dark
My heart racing, pulsing, crying,
Longing for your eyes to light
My path to you, to you
Longing, longing for you,
Here with me, here with me.

CHILD: Yes I am here,
Snow White, Snow White,
With you forever, and
Ever and ever.
Sleep, Snow White, sleep,
Tenderly dream,
Sleep through the night,
Beautiful Snow White.
And when you awake,
I will be gone,
Gone far away,
Far, far away,
Only a dream...
Only a dream...
Only a dream...

(The CHILD gets up, looks around, and runs off.)

(Ocean sounds, waves crashing, breezes blowing)

GIRL: *(Waking up)*
Where am I?
(Sees empty cage)
What has happened?
What time is it?
What day?

(She looks around.)
Oh. Oh, oh,
I, oh my, I… oh…
Where am I?
(Looks around again)
I feel different, lighter,
Something has changed.

(Sees a crown, which the CHILD *left)*
Oh, this is beautiful,
so, so beautiful
It glitters and sparkles
like sunlight on water,
sparkling and beautiful,
sparkling and beautiful,
Sunlight and water,
sunlight and water,
sun and light and light and sun
and sun and light and sun and light,
so beautiful, so so beautiful.
Light as air, light as air,
I feel, like air,
dancing in air,
floating in air,
floating and dancing, floating
in air,
water and air, water and air
water and light, sparkles of light
everywhere, everywhere,

I am everywhere,
floating and flying and flying and floating
away, away, away
Ah, ah, ah
my heart, my breath, my heart—flying.

Skies, ocean, sun and wind
floating with you,
breathing with you,

my heart flying with you,
with you, with you, with you.

(Brilliant sunlight)

BLACKOUT

ORIGAMI TEARS

D Lee Miller

ORIGAMI TEARS

D Lee Miller is the author of ENDANGERED SPECIES, ANIMATION IN
DUST, THE BEULAH BALLANTINE CONTEST, A FEAST OF RIDDLES,
and RED QUARTERS, among other plays. Honors include Critic's Choice at
the Double Image/Samuel French Short Play Festival, for ORIGAMI
TEARS; finalist at the Actors Theatre of Louisville, the Ensemble Studio
Theater, the George Kernodle, Dogwood, Playwrights' Forum, and
Playwrights Studio of Milwaukee competitions. Among others theaters, her
plays have been presented at the Ensemble Studio Theater, the Shenandoah
Valley Playwrights Retreat, and Alice's Fourth Floor.

ORIGAMI TEARS was originally produced by the Actor's Outlet Theater
as part of the Double Image/Samuel French Original Short Play Festival
in New York on 12 and 16 June 1991.

MAX . . . . Kilian Ganly
MARSHA . . . . .Lynne McCollough
Director . . . . Ken Lowstetter

CHARACTERS

MARSHA RIFKIN: *A tired, older woman; she is* MAX's *widow*
MAX RIFKIN: *A ghost of an older man; he progressively fades through the play*
MRS EFFRON: *(Voiceover) A friend of* MARSHA's

TIME

The present

(*The* RIFKIN *apartment in Brooklyn. Lighting is dim. The few furnishings are old. The kitchen and front room are joined by the dining room. The front room has a small couch with a throw. A monolith of raw marble stands with a small shawl draped over the top. The door is half-closed to this room. An eerie light hovers from an overhead fluorescent bulb in the kitchen. It is the only room fully lit. The eerie kitchen light comes from an overhead fluorescent bulb. There is an easy chair in the kitchen, a snack table, and a small T V on another snack table. The small kitchen table is in the otherwise empty dining room. Sitting on the couch in the front room, staring at the marble slab, is* MAX RIFKIN. *In his hands are sculpting tools.*)

(NOTE: *This play is composed of many memory episodes. One way to delineate memory from real time is by lighting cues. Suggested cues are included in the script.*)

(*Entering from the back bedroom is* MARSHA. *She is in a slip. She goes to the ironing board and starts her makeup while ironing the black dress. She makes a cup of tea; turns the T V on. Turns it off. Puts an ice cube in the tea, now it isn't good.* MAX *enters from the front room. He marches through the dining room.*)

MAX: Where's my beret?

MARSHA: How could you ask for your beret at a time like this?

MAX: Just like this: (*He silently mouths the words.*)

MARSHA: Aren't you late for induction or something?

MAX: That's all you have to say?

MARSHA: —I'm not ready for this. I've never done this before.

MAX: So don't go.

MARSHA: Don't you tell me what to do.

MAX: So go. But first tell me where my beret is.

MARSHA: I'm not going. I don't care how it looks.

MAX: It'll look funny.

MARSHA: I don't care! You die on me—at the worst possible time. It's a very cold climate now. —And look at you! You don't even have the common decency to wear the blue suit I brought you! (*Pause*) You closed your business, Max Rifkin! Without even talking to me! You closed it to wear a beret!

MAX: I did what I had to do.

MARSHA: Don't play Mr John Wayne with me. I have to hear, "Mr Seidman I will no longer be balancing your books, so if you would call Ronald Goldfinkle of Ocean Parkway, he will be happy to handle your business and personalized accounts."

MAX: Goldfinkle is happy to do it. His daughter moved back in and he needs the money. She got divorced, you know.

MARSHA: *(Mimicking the conversation)* "You're not well?" "Who in this world couldn't feel a little better?" You belong on Ed Sullivan. "You're moving to your children?" he has to ask. All those years he doesn't know you don't have children? It was like a knife in my heart. "It's been a pleasure." "Likewise." I'll give you "likewise." So we retired.

MAX: I retired. You never worked.

MARSHA: So I have to overhear?

MAX: It's better than from a stranger.... Isn't there anything you want to say to me?

MARSHA: Did you ever tell me anything? Even simple things people tell each other—that they need to hear?! They'll understand why I'm not there.

(Lighting change: Past)

MARSHA: You got the test results? *(Silence)* They're not good? *(Silence)* You showed him that shake you started?

MAX: I don't shake. Only when you yell.

MARSHA: If we're retiring I need to know.

MAX: Why do you need to know?

MARSHA: I clean that front room every day so your clients should feel clean when you do their taxes.

MAX: I never asked you to. In fact, leave it closed.

MARSHA: Now he wants to shut out the heat from the bedroom.

MAX: There's something I want to do with it.

MARSHA: Don't start with stories about girls. It's cute at the Concord, it's not cute here.

MAX: You know who was a great man? Michelangelo. He had genius.

MARSHA: So do you. Sit down and eat.

MAX: I will be using the front room. As a studio. I am going to be a sculptor.

MARSHA: A sculptor? And sculpt what?

MAX: I won't know until I see the marble. It is what is inside clawing to come out; that is the art. Freeing that.

MARSHA: *(To the air)* He's gone mad. Has he gone mad?

MAX: You're talking to your friends again, Marsha? Girls, tell her I've read more than just tax manuals in my life.

MARSHA: You're closing the business to make another David? There is a David. There was a Michelangelo. You're Max Rifkin. With a stain on his tie. Give me that.

MAX: I want no talk! And what Max Rifkin says goes!

MARSHA: And what Marsha Rifkin cooks stays in this kitchen! Now sit down and use a napkin. That's why God made them.... So Goldfinkle's daughter is getting a divorce?

(The buzzer rings. MARSHA is startled. She answers.)

(Lighting change: Present)

MARSHA: Who is it?

MRS EFFRON: *(Voiceover)* Guess who?

MAX: She couldn't be more original?

MARSHA: Shah... *(Into speaker:)* In two minutes. *(She continues dressing.)*

MAX: I thought you weren't going?

MARSHA: I'm not. But I have to tell her and then I'll take a nice walk— to the museum and back.

MAX: Always the museum!

MARSHA: You're making a mess. I just cleaned up!... It's your fault we were never anywhere on time. Never.

MAX: I'm not going without my beret.

MARSHA: Well, it isn't in the tablecloth drawer! Where did you leave it? —You're going to ruin this funeral. Everybody's already there and you're going dressed like a beatnik.

MAX: Your zipper's open.

MARSHA: Get away. I got it. Celia said I'll have dinner with her and Lily tonight. She won't take no. And any night this week, just to say the word.

MAX: Aren't you lucky I'm busy?

MARSHA: She's a liar but she doesn't have anyone.

MAX: Now she'll have someone with heartburn. The woman can't cook a sandwich.

MARSHA: I shouldn't have a nice dinner cooked for me for a change? Get out of my way. You stay and look to your heart's content but I don't want to make her late. There are people waiting—

MAX: They won't start without me. *(Pause)* Ah—I see. You already got someone? You always said you were waiting for this day. Now I know why. *(Staring at his marble)*

(Lighting change: Past)

MAX: I waited for the day when I would become a great artist but I became an accountant. Debits and credits. I've got to give it a try. They say there's not much time.

MARSHA: But to use our nest egg! I will never forgive you for that, never! You don't tell me. You just go and buy your marble and set it down in the front room. I can't bring company in there so I have to entertain only in the dining room which means constantly serving. And the air in there! You won't blow away if you open a window! It sits on your chest it's so compressed. You can cut that air with a knife. What? What is it?

MAX: *(He absentmindedly folds little pieces of paper.)* I can't think. I can't see what's in there.

MARSHA: That's because it's a block of stone! Do what you do. Count it. Weigh it. Sell it to someone who wants a stone doorstop quarried all the way from the seven hills of Italy. Everything we worked for has turned to stone. It's like a Grimm's fairy tale.

(Lighting change: Past)

MAX: You done with the crossword? Give me the paper.

MARSHA: It's on the table. Think of it as a field trip.

MAX: You want coffee?

MARSHA: Sure. Does it hurt today?

MAX: Sugar?

MARSHA: They say you've got to exercise, eat right, and keep up your strength. I've been reading. There's no law against reading.

MAX: Sugar?

MARSHA: Forty years and you don't know?

MAX: I thought you might like a change. *(Pause)* Sugar?

MARSHA: Did it make you feel sick today?

MAX: If I could only find out where it is to start on this stone. Art is a beautiful thing, Marsha. I know you go to the museum a couple of times a year—you have a real appreciation—but I forgot it's a wondrous thing. I can't be too hasty. I don't want to start it wrong. Make a mistake. You can't erase them. Stone is here long after you or I will be.

MARSHA: What is it you do in there all day? I don't hear anything. *(She exits.)*

MAX: So your ears are finally going. *(He sadly folds origami goldfish. Soon it seems there are hundreds of them. He hides them in shoe boxes, in bags, anywhere he can.)*

MARSHA: *(From another room)* Listen: I'm taking your tan and grey suits. It's for a good cause and you don't fit in them now you're back to army weight. Okay?

MAX: *(To himself)* I look at the Pietà. The Moses. It is a lost art, I think, but it isn't a lost desire. *(He kneels before the marble. He holds up one origami piece.)* God is all-knowing, isn't he? So he must know sadness.

MARSHA: *(She reenters and takes away the bags around him. He doesn't notice.)* I told your brother Joe about the beret. He says everyone said he was the lunatic but he always knew it was you. He said he plays his own music but you march without the drummer altogether. So, Joe was always a lunatic. It's getting worse, isn't it?

(Lighting change: Present)

(Phone rings)

MAX: You're not going to get it?

MARSHA: I can't talk to anybody. *(She picks up the receiver and puts it down.)*

MAX: You finally realized.

MARSHA: I don't know what to say!

MAX: *(Pause)* You have too much face on. You look like a clown.

MARSHA: It's your fault I had to cover the mirrors. I can't check. *(She evens out her rouge.)* Better? Did you notice I changed my hair?

MAX: Why? Did you ever notice mine?

MARSHA: You were losing your hair when I met you. I don't know why you're so upset about your hat. Hats don't make the man.

MAX: It's a beret!

MARSHA: I can't find my bag. Anyone sees me they'll think I'm falling apart— Where's my black bag?

MAX: I was never so embarrassed in all my life when you got that call. Why of all times did you throw out our whole life together?

MARSHA: Me?! We had bills to pay! I started with the crystal we got at our wedding. Then I sold the silver-plated sugar and creamer from our anniversary. Manny Weinblatt took care of it for me. You are selfish, selfish, selfish!

(Lighting change: Past)

MAX: Where are my goldfish? Where are the bags from in here, Marsha?

MARSHA: I told you they went to the charity auction. You had so much in here it's amazing you could find the marble at all.

MAX: You threw them out?

MARSHA: But the funniest thing is the call I got. They opened up our boxes and bags and found all these delicate pieces of origami. Didn't you show Joe's wife's kid, Alan, how to do that once? —Or did he show you? I forget. The thing is, the head of the charity drive says they look like these little tears—

MAX: They're goldfish. I only know how to make goldfish.

MARSHA: People are actually putting bids on them! They're doing better than those old beer trays—the Pabst Blue Ribbon ones? The Black Label ones? She says everyone's heart beats a little faster from them. They're so beautiful, people hold them like babies. The auction is tomorrow and they're going to go like hot cakes. Where are you going? Max? You can't go out at this hour!

MAX: But they're not for sale! No one can have those! They're mine! *(He tears out of the room.)*

MARSHA: *(Yells after him)* That's right! Leave! Forty-five minutes before a dinner party! Don't you miss a chance to embarrass me in front of company! I saved for weeks to make a nice meal to repay the kindnesses of your friends and you leave. You don't lift a finger in this house to help me but you have the strength to run out at all hours! The strength to raise your sculpting tools up and down. Up and down. For what? Every day I watch you waste away but the marble's just as healthy as ever, Michelangelo! Not a scratch! Fine. Don't be here to greet your guests. Let me think of some new excuse for you. For me.

(Lighting change: A short time later)

MAX: *(He reenters with the bags. He sets them in a trash can and burns them. He cries. MARSHA sees nothing.)* Just tell me you hate me. It isn't a surprise. Tell me!

MARSHA: What do I smell? What's burning? Please, not the roast! *(She runs into the kitchen.)*

MAX: *(To audience)* With the most brilliant of stone before me, I cannot create. There is nothing to leave. I don't know where to start. It's in my heart. Honestly. I don't want to die. Don't you know I don't want to die?! I don't want my account swept clean like I never was.

MARSHA: *(Running to* MAX) I knew there was something burning! What are you doing? What are you doing, you crazy man? You have to deny other people happiness?!! They love them. They love them, Maxmillian.

MAX: She loves Maxmillian Schell. My wife.

MARSHA: They said your goldfish were beautiful, Max.

(Lighting change: Fade to a dreamlike Present)

MAX: *(To himself)* How could I tell her they were my tears? They used to be goldfish. But you turn them upside down, they're my tears. They were once fresh newsprint with the letters filled in— *(Looks at his crossword puzzle)* sometimes wrong—but they've smudged and faded. They were once my first prize in arts and crafts and my dream of giving to the world, but now there are no first prizes and they are tears for the artist I am not.

MARSHA: "How many ninety-degree angles are in a goldfish"? You used to ask the neighborhood children when you helped them with their arithmetic. Now I remember. You made each of them a goldfish. *(Pause)* You didn't talk to me for weeks after you burned them. My heart ached but I'm not sure why.... (MARSHA *returns to the front room. He follows and returns her bag.)* ...Let's dance.

MAX: There's no record player. You got rid of it.

MARSHA: It became a chicken symphony. *(She pulls him out of the chair.)* Let's dance.

MAX: There's no music.

MARSHA: It's the music inside. Clawing to come out. *(They dance. His legs crumble beneath him. She catches him.)*

MAX: Did you ever love me?

MARSHA: What kind of a question— There's nothing left from our marriage. It was all sold. *(Silence)* They said our marriage would never last but I always told them I knew him when. They said he didn't talk. I said not to worry. He talks to me. But you didn't. They said he didn't smile. I said not to worry. He smiles for me. But you didn't. They never knew why I didn't leave you. *(The downstairs buzzer rings again.)*

(Lighting change: Present)

MARSHA: Who is it?

MRS EFFRON: *(Voiceover)* Guess who?

MAX: Miss Originality.

MARSHA: *(Into the speaker)* Coming! *(Pause)* The only thing you loved was that damn stone.

MAX: Do you think it's possible I wanted to carve the sculpture for you?

MARSHA: Oh, so now I'm to blame? I'm your excuse?

MAX: And where are you going that I'm your excuse for the thousandth time? The museum!

MARSHA: —Because like you said, I can appreciate—

MAX: What?

MARSHA: People who talk through art.

MAX: You can appreciate—?

MARSHA: *(Reaching)* —that you couldn't say the words—

MAX: "I love you"—

MARSHA: —and now you tell me you were trying to sculpt them...? *(A light dawns on her.)* —For me? Oh, Max. *(Pause)* There. You're late for your own funeral. Are you happy? Look at me in my bare feet...

MAX: *(Discovers)* I did. I did it for you. At least, I tried. I couldn't find where to start. But it's there. Do you see?

MARSHA: You threw away everything—

MAX: —for the chance of something better. Not everything is accountable. Love doesn't come with a manual.

MARSHA: *(She opens a nearby shoe box. Inside is an origami tear.)* They said you never showed an emotion. And I said not to worry. He does to me.

MAX: Did you love me because I was a failure?

MARSHA: You were a man who made magic goldfish. They're yours outright. Upside up they swim with beauty and upside down, they mourn. But they're not your tears. They're God's tears. That's why everyone had to have one. That's why I loved you.

(They stand together at the door.)

MAX: I should be going.

MARSHA: I have to go, too. There are people waiting for me. You didn't find your beret?

MAX: I'll live. After you.

MARSHA: No, after you.

MAX: So go already.

MARSHA: Don't you tell me what to do!

(He exits. She enters the front room and gets her shawl from the top of the marble slab. She finds the beret under the shawl.)

MARSHA: The stone, Max? It'll be made of Italian marble. *(She tears a corner of the shawl, puts it over her head, and exits.)*

BLACKOUT

PANICKED

Sally Ordway

Sally Ordway's plays have been performed in New York at Theatre Genesis, Town Hall, St Clements, Theater for the New City, Phoenix, Playwrights Horizons, Women's Interart Theater, and the American Place Theatre. Her work also has been produced at the Mark Taper Forum and the O'Neill Playwrights Conference. She is a past recipient of an A B C-T V Fellowship at Yale University; an N E A and a C A P S grant; and has been a fellow at the MacDowell Colony, Yaddo, and the Edward Albee Foundation. She was for several years a playwright at the Eugene O'Neill Theater Center. Her plays are published in *Scripts* magazine, *Yale/Theatre*, and *The Scene*. She is writer-in-residence for the Encompass Music Theater and has written the libretto for THE GLASS WOMAN, a new opera under grants from Opera America and the N E A, produced by Encompass and the Interart Theater in 1993. She is a member of P E N, The League of Professional Theater Women/N Y, N Y Women in Film, and the B M I Workshop.

CHARACTER

PETULLA

DEDICATION

To Will Montague and Dr Yan

(PETULLA, *a woman in her thirties, forties, or fifties, comes on a bare stage carrying a large globe of the world. She puts it on a stool and turns to the audience.*)

PETULLA: *(Smooth, friendly)* Hi, I'm Petulla and I'm your performance artist. My piece tonight is called "Panic Attack." And, yes, it is autobiographical and, yes, I named myself after Petulla Clark.

("Downtown" plays in the background.)

I wanted a name that would resonate. And now Panic Attack— A turn-of-the-century experience. *(She becomes slightly more agitated as she relates her tale.)* I woke up one morning in spring two years ago and felt like one of those stomach things from *Aliens* was inside my body just waiting to splat out, so I weighed myself. I still weighed ninety-five pounds, a size four, but my steps were heavy, my balance was off. I felt like I just got off a very woozy cruise ship. And my toe hurt. I thought back to that day, a week ago, when the cat climbed on top of the bookcase and knocked the complete set of Proust off onto my second toe. That was it—my toe was broken. I conferred with everyone I knew about broken toes. They said, Yes, it might give you those symptoms, but that it would heal in six weeks. So, O K I'll wait and everything will be O K in six weeks.

But Christ, I forgot, I've got to go to my [fifteenth, twentieth, twenty-fifth, thirtieth] reunion at Sweet Sweetbriar College in Virginia. I haven't seen some of those belles in [fifteen, twenty, twenty-five, thirty] years, when we all wore symbolic white gloves and wanted to be ladies. How can I explain to them that I didn't become Meryl Streep? How can I explain being a performance artist named Petulla, when they knew me as Patsy from Paducah? And they've never even heard of Lifetime Cable TV—the Women's Channel. Wait, I know. I'll show them my slide show about architectural phallic symbols in America.

So, I went and showed the slides. It seemed to make my collegemates' husbands deeply nervous that I kept measuring them. *(Pause)* The phallic symbols—obelisks and the like—their heights and circumferences.

I told them all about Dr Blatty and his monument in Rome, Georgia. Dr Blatty was a breakthrough nineteenth century gynecologist, first to perform clitoridectomies to calm down women who got hysterical from dealing with their husbands. After the slide show I had one confrontation with Anna Lou, now a buyer for a Richmond department store, who objected to my whole, what she called, "icky feminist stance". Anna Lou said she liked being called a girl. I said, "Anna Lou, we haven't been girls since we were eighteen, and don't you think it's time to take off the white gloves?" Well, of course, I was the hit of the reunion, but when I got back, I'd gained five pounds. The six weeks for the broken toe were finally up, but I still felt unbalanced and alien.

So I called Dr God, my generically uncommunicative internist, who told me to get tests from his expert doctor friends. I took a nine-hundred-dollar CAT scan from Dr Head, who said, "No, Miss, I don't see any evidence of a brain tumor." Next a five-hundred-dollar thyroid test from Dr Gland, who said, "No, you don't have what either the President or Mrs Bush had." I didn't have anything they could name. Anxiety mounted. I gained five more pounds. "Take a vacation," screamed the T V. So I went to Paris to celebrate their bicentennial. When I got there I looked for the miniature guillotines like they sold in the real revolution, but the French hadn't had the sense to make them again, so they missed a lot of tourist dollars, pounds, and yen. Two weeks in Parisian restaurants with bargain three-course meals—offers I couldn't refuse, I gained another five pounds. More anxiety. One day after my return to N Y C the streets started to scream at me, people loomed up like out-of-control puppets—Punch and Judy raging at each other. Restaurants seemed like three-ring circuses. One day my best friend, who watched me cower before a two-pound lobster in a seafood place, told me I was having a panic attack. She'd seen them before. Her sister had them. It was just a matter of taking a pill to make them go away. So I saw Dr Panic and took the pills, which made my mouth dry and gave me constipation for the first time since mother gave me Milk of Magnesia. About this time my lover, Larry, left me. He said I'd gotten fat and tense and constipated and it made me sexually unresponsive. I was very depressed. Dr Panic added another pill to my repertoire that pepped me up. But he said, "My dear, you know the pills aren't enough, you must join my group therapy session and find out the root of your anxiety." Dr Panic, who was deeply Freudian, gave me his published treatise on guilt. —So I was prodded into the group.

The group— One woman was in love with her womanizing alcoholic younger brother who her suicidal mother had neglected her for. Another woman was so angry at men, she couldn't decorate her apartment. Another hadn't taken off her sunglasses indoors for fifteen years and only liked her mother when she had been helpless from a stroke. Then the men. There was the compulsive candy bar eater whose sisters had taken away all his toys so he couldn't find friends as a grownup, and the other talked endlessly about the bleak outlook of his real estate business and how his ex-wife tried to eat his balls. For six months I listened to tales of their Grimm fairy-tale childhoods. I told them all about my father, my mother, my childhood, my love of horses, my fear of snakes, my sex life. I was very honest, but I disappointed Dr Panic because I couldn't uncover some deep hidden black hole in my life. When I told the group I wanted to leave group, they attacked me. "She's a play-actor. She's been lying. Her childhood's a lie. She's hiding the truth. ACTOR ACTOR ACTOR." I left anyway, because almost all of them had been coming to Dr Panic for ten to twenty years, and they still seemed frozen in their problems, and addicts of the good doctor.

Well, call me Actor, Actor, Actor, but I don't want that for a future. Now I wanted to stop taking all the pills, clean out my body, and be reborn. Finally I was off everything. I went on Fit For Life diet to lose that anxious weight. Fit For Life had lots of rules: Never eat a starch with a protein; never never. Dismiss all you were told about the four food groups and never eat all four at one meal. Eat lots of fruit, but only at the right times." Now I've never been an organized person, so I had to carry around a notebook of do's and don'ts. But I did lose a little, then I plateaued. So I picked up a new diet book. It asked, "Are you a carbohydrate addict? You are if you eat a carbohydrate and that leads to another and another and another and another until you're OUT OF CONTROL!!! So, addicts, the answer is to avoid those nasty carbs until your evening reward meal *(Getting excited)*, and then you can eat everything you want." BUT you have to eat it within a sixty-minute period. That's it: The sixty-minute meal. Well, this regime worked for a while, but then I began to get incredibly tense again. My neck felt frozen and there were pains in my arms and legs and feet and toes. Back to Dr God. "Well, my dear, you're just chronically anxious. Take the pills again. One hundred dollars, please." "Oh, thank you, Dr God." (Chronically—why not terminally?) "Oh, Doctor, will this give me a stroke?" "No, don't be silly. Now just try to relax." Relax, what is there out there to be relaxed about. I mean, you don't need a dysfunctional family or abused childhood to be anxious in this world. I mean, help!

(Spinning globe)

Look, we've broken the planet. We're breaking the cities. The government's breaking itself. Communism's gone, the Nazis are back. Europe's coming together, breaking apart. Mother Russia falls to pieces. BUT the war is over. They say, "We are Free. Free! Free to be tribes (Ourselves) again. And we hate them. We always have. Now we have taught our children to hate them too. We want them to disappear. We don't want them here, because this is our land. Our blood is here."

(Lights change. She spins globe again.)

Lands divide…fragment…disappear. And people die. Yes, the war is over. Let the war begin.

Please, please let me out of this world. There's a plague in this world and it can kill anyone and go anywhere.

(She takes out a cellular phone with a weird antenna.)

I'm calling my spaceship now. Where are you, gentle E T, and your smart, silver siblings? All you aliens out there: We need your help. We need you to tell us how to start again and get it right this time. Helloooo out there—

(Lights dim as she spins the globe.)

A PERMANENT SIGNAL

SIGNAL

Sherry Kramer

A PERMANENT SIGNAL

Sherry Kramer's plays have been produced in New York at The Second Stage Theater, Soho Rep, and The Ensemble Studio Theater; and regionally at Yale Repertory Theater, The Woolly Mammoth Theater in Washington D C, as well as other theaters here and abroad. She is the recipient of playwriting fellowships from the N E A and the New York Foundation for the Arts; received the Weissberger Playwriting Award, a New York Drama League Award, and the Marvin Taylor Award for WHAT A MAN WEIGHS (published by Broadway Play Publishing Inc); the L A Women in Theater Award for THE WALL OF WATER (also published by Broadway Play Publishing Inc); and the Jane Chambers Playwriting Award for DAVID'S REDHAIRED DEATH (published by T C G in their *Plays in Process* series). Other plays include NAPOLEON'S CHINA, THINGS THAT BREAK, WOMEN ARE WORK, PARTIAL OBJECTS, and a music/theater adaptation of Bulgakov's THE MASTER AND MARGARITA (O'Neill Music-Theater Conference). She is an alumnae of New Dramatists, and holds M F As in both fiction and playwriting from the Iowa Writers Workshops.

CHARACTERS

NOREEN *and* BETTY: *sirens. Literally. These are* BETTY *and* NOREEN, *the mythical siren sisters. Part bird, part female. They are hugeish, opulent, like opera singers crossed with Big Bird, dressed by Liberace, to look like insane angels.*

MARY: *Painfully ordinary in every way. Probably a mousy blonde. Wearing a white cotton nightgown that has seen better nights.*

SETTING

MARY's bathroom. It may have some Italian tile work of good quality as well as other Annunciation touches here and there.

(A tuning fork is struck.)

(It makes its clear, bell tone sound. Three gorgeous women's voices rise to meet the sound—imagine the music of the spheres...then imagine a composer creates the music when the spheres turn out to be too busy. The music is magical and glorious, as only song without the burden of words can be. The singing lasts as long as the ring of the tuning fork, and it fades with it, receding along the aural paths. Lights up.)

(NOREEN and BETTY are hovering in the air, in MARY's bathroom. They are reaching out to her, as the angels do in some Annunciation paintings. MARY, about to sit down on the toilet, is startled, shocked, amazed, and holds one hand up, in a protective, cowering gesture.)

NOREEN/BETTY: *(Sung like the Hallelujahs in Handel's* Messiah.*)* WEEEEEEEEEEE *(Arpeggio, please)* E E E E E E E E E ARE GOING TO S U U U U U U U U U U U U CK

BETTY: ALL THE—

NOREEN: ALL THE—

NOREEN/BETTY: ALL THE SWEETNESS SWEETNESS SWEETNESS

BETTY: SWEET, SWEET WE ARE GOING TO SUCK ALL THE

NOREEN: SWEET, SWEET WE ARE GOING TO SUCK ALL THE

NOREEN/BETTY: SWEETNESS OUUUUUUUUUUUT OF YOUUUUUUUUUUUUUUUUUU! *(Pause. BETTY and NOREEN bask for a moment in their own splendor.)*

MARY: Fuck you. *(She unfreezes, puts the toilet lid down, and sits.)*

(NOREEN and BETTY fall to the floor with a thud.)

BETTY: Oh, dear. *(Pause)* Fuck you is not exactly the reply we had in mind, is it? *(They pick themselves up off the floor, preen their feathers a bit.)* Well, maybe it was the element of surprise. Maybe we accidentally coded in a biological reflex response to this moment, that feels like surprise, and so, under the circumstances—

NOREEN: THE SINGLE SWEETEST INDIVIDUAL IN THE UNIVERSE DOES NOT SAY FUCK YOU UNDER ANY CIRCUMSTANCES! PARTICULARLY NOT THIS ONE!

BETTY: I'm sure she didn't really mean it—after all, it's just one of their little colloquial metaphors—

NOREEN: Metaphor! Metaphor! Don't get me started on metaphor!

BETTY: I think you're going to have to let go of your little metaphoric prejudices for the moment, Noreen—

NOREEN: Why? I am right about metaphor. It's vile. And unwholesome. It always has been and it always will. And now her filthy little metaphor has ruined the sweetest moment in the universe!

BETTY: Noreen, I know it's your nature to be pessimistic, but—

NOREEN: PESSIMISTIC! You're complaining about pessimistic when I could have dialed for suicidal this incarnation?

BETTY: Do we HAVE to talk about this now, Noreen? Do we?

NOREEN: You know I wanted to dial for suicidal this incarnation. I begged you, Betty, let me be suicidal this time, let me, for once in my lives, be suicidal, get it out of my system, next time I'll dial for Rebecca of Sunny Black Hole, but no, no, you just couldn't let me, could you, just hold out dear, you said, the age of sweetness is almost upon us, hold on. Well, a fat lot of good it did me.

MARY: Uh... Excuse me?

BETTY: What.

MARY: Is it okay if I say something? Ask a question?

BETTY: The tradition does allow you a brief catechism at this point, Mary, if you so desire.

MARY: Good. Because—well, correct me if I'm wrong, but it seems to me that the basic situation here—editing out the peripheral chit-chat—the basic situation here is that you—either separately or together—are going to suck all the sweetness out of me. Right?

BETTY: Yes. That was the general idea.

MARY: Okay. So far, so good. Well—I have to be very honest with you here. *(Pause)* It sounds sexual to me.

BETTY: What?

MARY: It sounds like a kind of sexual act. Which I am not adverse to, you understand—

NOREEN: She thinks this is a se—se—sexual act? I think I'm going to be sick...

MARY: Look, I'm just giving you my right-off-the-top-of-my-head first impression of the event—

NOREEN: It just goes from bad to worse, doesn't it? From bad to worse. Now she wants to give us something off the top of her head.

BETTY: Noreen—

NOREEN: The sweetness, as any biped knows, is always located near the pancreas, which is located—

BETTY: Noreen?

NOREEN: Don't treat me like an idiot, Betty, I helped plant the sweetness too, I know where it is, and it's nowhere near the top of her head.

BETTY: Noreen!

NOREEN: Well do you want something off the top of her head? It sounds corporeal and depressing.

BETTY: Noreen IT'S A METAPHOR. *(To* MARY*)* So—you were saying?

MARY: Well, to get back to the sexual aspect—

BETTY: Oh, we don't think of this as a se...sexual event, Mary. In fact, the s...sexual aspects are the last aspects we're thinking of.

MARY: Really? You're sure? (BETTY *nods.)* Look—I don't mean to pry, but—have you two ever—ah—done this kind of thing before?

BETTY: No.

MARY: You've never sucked the sweetness out of anybody?

BETTY: Well of course we wanted to—but it wasn't ripe until now.

MARY: Oh. Well, you know, the first time you do something—I find— that you really learn how to do it as you go along.

NOREEN: She's implying that we don't know what we're doing. She's implying that we don't know how it's done. For your information, WE have degrees in this. WE have matriculated through full undergraduate and graduate courses and have certificates attesting to postdoctoral work in Class A Sweetness Sucking to prove it.
   Can you say you've prepared for this moment the way we have? Can you say the same?

MARY: Well—in a way. I mean—I have been waiting thirty-three years for it.

BETTY: You have no idea how we've looked forward to it too. So it's understandable, with emotions running so high, that Noreen here is— *(Pause)* Thirty-three? How do you figure you're been waiting thirty-three years, dear?

MARY: I've been waiting for this since I was born, so it's been thirty-three years.

BETTY: You're sure you're thirty-three?

MARY: Well, people always say I don't look it.

BETTY: It's just you're supposed to be— (Consults a bit of music in the air) Twenty-nine.

MARY: I am?

NOREEN: I KNEW IT! I knew there was something wrong! We're four years off!

BETTY: They're tiny years, minuscule years—what's a measly four years' margin of error over a four-hundred-million-year project, Noreen?

MARY: .00000000003

BETTY: What?

MARY: Point 00000000000—

BETTY: You see—it's insignificant! Infinitesimal! Spit!

NOREEN: (Flinches at the word "spit") A metaphor marathon. That's what this is.

BETTY: Noreen—buck up! (To MARY) Noreen's just experiencing a bit of performance anxiety, Mary. I'm a little nervous myself. It's to be expected. After all—you're the first..

MARY: Well, I'm very...flattered.

BETTY: It's a great honor, you know.

MARY: I'm sure.

BETTY: As a matter of fact Mary, THIS—is the happiest day of your life. (Musical flourish—a short bell tone)

(MARY makes no response at all, other than smiling weakly.)

BETTY: I know, of course, that you cannot understand the true nature of this happiness, since the instant we suck all the sweetness out of you, it will occur to you that you have never had the slightest chance of ever truly understanding a single thing about what happiness truly is. Nevertheless, this...is...the happiest day of your life.

MARY: Thank you.

BETTY: Not at all. Just doing our job. (Pause) Well, now that that's out of the way—was there anything else the tradition demands at this point— (Counts off on her fingers)...made the announcement, told her how wonderful but impenetrable it was, engaged in a little conversation—well, it looks like that's about it, so if you're ready, Noreen, we'll just get started here.

(BETTY *takes out a tuning fork, strikes it so it sounds the key.* NOREEN *and* BETTY *take classic opera diva poses, they clear their throats, tap their chests—a very big deal here.*)

(*The sound of the tuning fork affects* MARY *profoundly. She is almost immediately transported to ecstasy.*)

(BETTY *and* NOREEN *begin to sing to the same music played during darkness at the top of the show.* MARY *forces herself to jam her fingers into her ears.*)

MARY: No—no—not yet—please—wait—wait a minute, please—

BETTY: (*They deflate a bit, from the interruption, but keep on singing.*) Keep on singing, Noreen—

MARY: YOU CAN'T DO IT LIKE THIS!!! (*They don't stop, so* MARY *makes a desperate grab for the tuning fork, closing her hand over it to silence it.* BETTY *and* NOREEN *stop singing the instant her hand touches the fork. For* MARY—*it's as if she's electrified by it—she can't let go, she's vibrating wildly, she's in trouble now, wailing away.*)

NOREEN: Now you've gone and done it. How could you let her touch it like that!

BETTY: Me? ME? I let her touch it? You were the one in change of making them afraid of tuning forks.

NOREEN: I thought you were taking care of it.

BETTY: You insisted on designing all the phobias!

NOREEN: But they weren't supposed to be phobic about tuning forks— they were supposed to have an instinctual, deep-seated fear!

BETTY: Tuning Forks, Phobia Of. (*Yanks up* MARY's *wildly thrashing head, points to a specific location*) Located at point 5439801. I remember it distinctly from the blueprints. (*Pause*) Oh, why. Why. Why do I have to do everything myself? (*Lets the writhing* MARY *go*) Mary?

MARY: (*She struggles to speak over the storm that rages inside her.*) Yyyyyyyyyyyyyes?

BETTY: You have in your hand one of the universe's great primes. You are grappling, quite literally, with a small, harmonically tuned piece of the great mystery. Unless you put it down you will be swallowed up. Engulfed. Consumed. Understand? (MARY *nods, yes.*) On the count of three, Mary— let go. (*Pause*) One.

NOREEN: Oh, she'll never be able to let go. Never.

BETTY: Two.

NOREEN: She won't let go, and we'll get caught holding a four-hundred-million-year-old bag.

BETTY: THREE!

(MARY *is unable to let go.*)

NOREEN: See? I told you so.

(MARY *lets go. She falls to the floor, gasping.*)

BETTY: Brava! Brava! *(She applauds.)* I didn't think you had it in you—it's an excellent sign! Most of your run-of-the-mill species, they get a hold of the great mystery, they turn to jelly. Pudding. (NOREEN *flinches.)* Putty. Right then and there. *(Pause)* Ready when you are, Noreen. *(She strikes the fork again. They begin singing.)*

MARY: *(Rousing herself from the floor heroically, gasping, etc.)* But you can't—can't do it—like this— *(They sing and sing.)* You can't do it like this because—because—because—

(She has jammed toilet paper into her ears to keep the music out, but it still affects her. She has to go for the tuning fork again. It has much the same effect on her as before, only less violent. BETTY and NOREEN stop singing.)

NOREEN: Here we go again.

BETTY: On the count of three. One. Two. Three.

(MARY *pulls herself away from the fork, and recovers quickly.)*

MARY: Because—because you just can't waltz in here, announce to a girl you're going to suck all the sweetness out of her, and then just do it, just like that.

BETTY: We can't?

MARY: No.

BETTY: Why not?

MARY: A girl likes—you know—dinner first. Dinner, and maybe a movie or a play or something that constitutes a date before a sexual act.

NOREEN: THIS IS NOT A DATE!! IT IS AN EVENT OF UNIVERSAL PROPORTIONS. AND I DO MEAN UNIVERSAL. Dinner and a movie or a play are quite out of the question.

MARY: How do you know? You just admitted you've never done this kind of thing before.

NOREEN: So? Betty made sure we followed the conventions—I mean, we are very conventional, in our way, not that it's anything to feel self-satisfied about—we dialed for conventional, so that's the way we are. *(Pause)* Betty—I'll take my cue from you.

(BETTY *again strikes the tuning fork; they begin singing.* MARY *grabs the fork, but this time she battles her reaction herself, and forces herself to let go of it without any help from* BETTY. *They regard her, as* MARY *lies gasping on the floor.*)

BETTY: She's getting good at this, isn't she?

NOREEN: Yes. If I weren't so depressed about it all, I'd be quite impressed.

BETTY: This dating impulse—this instinctual urge to be wined and dined— I never dreamed the desire for dinner and a movie could overcome an elemental force of nature—one of the singing singular primes. You have to admire her for that.

NOREEN: But it's getting on my nerves—it's going to affect my performance. My concentration.

BETTY: It'll all be over soon, dear. Here—let's start at the beginning again. *(She strikes the tuning fork again.)*

MARY: *(She touches the tuning fork; stopping it, it seems to have no effect on her at all—she just blows on her fingers, to cool them.)* Now I have a little list in the other room, of medium price range restaurants, and I've got today's paper, so we're all set on movie and theater listings.

NOREEN: And to think I was looking forward to this. I was. Do you know how hard it is for a pessimist to look forward to something? Do you?

MARY: Of course, I want you both to know that I myself am not actually interested in the dinner or the movie—not in themselves. It's what they represent—how they communicate, to me, your feelings. It's—

NOREEN: THAT'S IT! THAT'S THAT! I'VE HAD IT! NOT ANOTHER NANOSECOND!

BETTY: Noreen, please, just hang on —

NOREEN: The single sweetest thing in the universe would NEVER negotiate for dinner and a movie! Never! Not in a million years.

MARY: Why not? It seems like a reasonable request to me. If anything, I think I'm being quite modest in my expectations. What's dinner and a movie in the cosmic scheme of things? Nothing. Nothing at all.

NOREEN: And how would you know?

MARY: Well just because I'm sweet doesn't mean I'm stupid.

NOREEN: Sweet? You? You have not, in either word, deed, or aspect, manifested a shred of sweetness since we arrived here.

MARY: So? Maybe I'm hiding it.

NOREEN: Hiding it? HIDING IT!! Do you have any IDEA who you are dealing with young lady?

MARY: Yes.

NOREEN: Oh, you do, do you.

MARY: Yes. You're Noreen. And you're Betty. *(Exact music from top of the show is heard—a recording of it—from far away—with three women's voices, not just* BETTY *and* NOREEN. *They are unearthly women's voices.)* You are Betty and Noreen Siren. The Siren Sisters. I have been waiting my entire life for you to come to me. *(Almost as if she's in a trance)* And here you are.

BETTY: SHE KNOWS US NOREEN! SHE KNOWS US!

NOREEN: Now wait a minute, young lady—you know who we are? You knew, from the beginning, who we were?

MARY: *(No trance music for a moment)* Well of course. A girl doesn't wait her entire life for her fate to walk in the door, and then not recognize it. *(Trance music pops in again, then dies again.)* But aren't there supposed to be three of you—I'm sure there were three of you in those visions—yes, there was a third sister, and her name was—her name was—

BETTY: She even remembers Charlene! Oh, if only there really were Gods, I'd get down on my knees and thank them.

NOREEN: You were the one who vetoed the Gods, Betty. Charlene and I were all for them from the start.

BETTY: Just because I vetoed them, it doesn't mean I can't appreciate how convenient they are when it comes to making the big dramatic gestures.

NOREEN: Which is precisely why we wanted them in the first place!

BETTY: It is not! Drama had nothing to do with it! You only wanted them because religion was the most pessimistic thing you could think of.

NOREEN: That's patently untrue! I lobbied for the Gods purely on their esthetic merits! Charlene was the one who had this thing about organized false hope systems, not me!

BETTY: It was against the rules and I vetoed it! But did that stop you two? No. Every time my back was turned you and Charlene were out there loading god concepts into the DNA—etching superstitions and divine gullibilities into the racial memory—

NOREEN: But it gave the project a certain—profile, Betty. Our special signature.

BETTY: You think God is a special signature, Noreen? It is the most redundant design in the universe. It is the first and last word in cliché.

(The trance music has bubbled up during their argument. It swells full and hypnotic and sweet.)

MARY: Noreen, Charlene, and Betty Siren. Yes. The Siren Sisters.
(The trance and the trance music end.) So—what happened to Charlene?

BETTY: She got out of agriculture altogether. Couldn't take the length of most growing seasons—one-hundred-million years here, four-hundred-million years there—she just wasn't cut out for the time it takes the average sweetness crop to mature. Charlene hated the passage of time. Couldn't stand to think about it. It's nothing she dialed, we're fairly sure about that. In fact, it might be a dialing disorder—but she's getting the best of help. It was hard splitting up the act, but you grow up. You go on. *(Pause)* She does atmospheric special effects now, freelance, when her doctors feel she can take it on. They job her in, she takes care of aurora borealis, eclipses, that sort of thing. Gets the schedule up and rolling, and doesn't have to think about it again—doesn't have to spend an instant considering her work as it moves through time.

MARY: How nice for her.

BETTY: I'll be sure to tell her you asked about her. *(Pause)* She was really looking forward to being here tonight. At least for the first fifty-million years or so. Just alive with anticipation.

MARY: I know what you mean. I was that way, too, for a long, long time. Oh, you should have seen the way I used to imagine it was going to happen. Not at all the way it just did. I would be lying on top of my bed, on top of my beautiful white sheets, listening to the music—you know, that eternal, wise, gorgeous music...lying perfectly still. Perfectly ready. Perfectly attuned to a state of grace. *(Pause)* I really do think you could have waited for me to get back into bed instead of accosting me in the bathroom. No one can maintain a state of grace in the bathroom.

BETTY: Sorry.

MARY: When I was little—I never went to the bathroom at all during the night, no matter how badly I needed to go. No, I wanted it to be exactly right, when you came to me. I always kept a little burnt offering smoldering near the window—oh, it was nothing much, really, as burnt offerings go, most of the time it was just trash, or scraps from dinner, but it was important to me. To make sure everything was just exactly right. And you should have seen my nightgowns. I was nothing special to look at during the day, but the minute I slipped on my nightgown and got into bed, anybody could tell—I had something special inside me.*(Pause)* I have to tell you. At first—I liked being different from everybody else in the world. *(Pause)* At first—it was just fine. If you call spending every night of your life lying in a room that always reeks of smoldering trash, in a white nightgown that shows all the dirt, with a bladder that always feels like it's going to burst—if you can call that fine. Yes. Everything was just fine. And then I went away to college. Well, I knew your annunciation/visitation would never work with some poli-sci major from Idaho lying in the next bed yelling, Can't you keep that deeply mysterious and mystical experience DOWN! I have a test in the morning. I mean how could that ever work? So I got a single, but it was a fight. A struggle. And I'll be honest with you—I don't think that was right. I don't think that was fair. I got this reputation for being a bitch—which I've never quite been able to shake— here I was, the sweetest girl in the world—and I had turned into a bitch.

NOREEN: Damn it. Here we go with the metaphors again.

MARY: It is not a metaphor. It is the truth.

BETTY: No, dear, metaphor is never the truth. It feels like the truth, otherwise there would be no point in making it. But it is clearly not the truth.

MARY: How do you know? You drop off this seed of sweetness four hundred million years ago, like you were leaving a jacket at the cleaners—

NOREEN: She just won't stop, will she—

BETTY: That wasn't metaphor you know, Noreen. That was simile.

MARY: —and you expect it to be waiting for you, all clean and pressed and ready, for whenever you happen to decide to stop by and pick it up.

BETTY: Time is relative, Mary. We tried to stick to the schedule, but—

MARY: YOU'RE LATE!!! YOU'RE LATE, do you hear me. LATE!!

BETTY: Yes, well, maybe a little, but you knew we were coming sooner or later, and that's the important thing, you know.

MARY: AND YOU NEVER CALLED! YOU NEVER WROTE!!!

BETTY: We left signs for you everywhere! Everywhere you looked we left plenty of signs!

MARY: Bullshit.

BETTY: You must have noticed some of them.

MARY: Like what.

BETTY: Well, like rainbows, for instance. Just what do you think a rainbow is?

MARY: Well, it used to be God's promise that he would never destroy the world again with water. (BETTY *glares at* NOREEN; NOREEN *shrugs.*) Now, of course, it's a simple natural phenomenon.

NOREEN: Simple?

BETTY: Simple?

NOREEN: Oh, it's a good thing Charlene isn't here to hear you talk like that. Simple. HA! Her greatest achievement! Her masterwork!

(Pause)

MARY: And that's another thing—there were supposed to be three of you and I don't think it's fair that there are only two. We have this thing about threes, you know, the magic number three—

NOREEN: That was my idea, actually. Do you like it?

MARY: How would I know? I don't have any choice. It's a genetically engineered part of me—that's my point. You installed this rule of threes—and then you go and break it. You show up and there's only two of you. Well, I was promised three.

BETTY: I explained about Charlene.

MARY: So what! You get a picture in your head of the way it's supposed to be—a picture which, may I remind you, you planted inside me like a four-hundred-million year time-release cold capsule—I mean, whose fault is it if the picture's too strong? It's yours. Whose fault is it if the rule of threes prevails? Whose fault is it that it's too late!

BETTY: Ours?

MARY: You're damn straight.

BETTY: So—what you're really waiting for is not dinner—not a movie—but an apology.

MARY: Well, I'm not saying an apology wouldn't be nice. Even if it is too late, an apology is always nice.

NOREEN: This too late business is making me nervous. I hate being nervous and suicidal at the same time. What's the point?

MARY: The point is, it is too late.

BETTY: Too late for what? The movie you wanted to see—

MARY: To suck all the sweetness out of me.

BETTY: But we just got here.

MARY: Yes, but you're still too late.

BETTY: How late?

MARY: You were supposed to be here four years ago. That makes you .0000000003 percent too late.

NOREEN: I knew it! I knew it! I sensed it the instant we got here! But would you listen to me? Noooooo. You're just being pessimistic, Noreen. Pessimistic. HA.

MARY: If I had known for sure that you were coming, then maybe I could have held on, but—

BETTY: But what about the signs, Mary. The SIGNS!

MARY: You mean, like the rainbow? I'm supposed to look up in the sky, see the rainbow—a rainbow, which I remind you, EVERYBODY can see, every Tom, Dick, and Harry with an eye in his head can see just as easily as I can—I am supposed to look up at a rainbow and know that you are coming for me? Is that the message I was supposed to get when I looked at a rainbow, Betty? That no matter how hard it was to hold on to this thing inside me, that someday it was all going to be all right?

BETTY: Well, that was the general idea, Mary. The basic design concept.

MARY: It sucks.

NOREEN: IT DOES NOT SUCK!! A RAINBOW CANNOT SUCK!

MARY: Did it EVER occur to you to stop and think of how much of a problem this kind of specialness would be? How it would get in the way? No, it didn't cross your minds. Well what about me? What do I get out of it? What do I get, except a life where nothing is enough and nothing is good enough and nothing, nothing fills me because somewhere, in the hazy future, there's this moment I'm waiting for—this blindingly beautiful moment that will justify and illuminate and complete my life. *(Pause)* I spend my life dragging this specialness around inside me like a lead weight, and for what? Everybody can see the goddamn rainbow.

BETTY: But the music you heard—that eternal, wise, gorgeous music— that was just for you, Mary. No one else in the history of your world has ever heard that music. Just you.

MARY: You don't get out much, do you?

BETTY: What do you mean?

MARY: *(She grabs a book off the back of the toilet, opens it.)* The Odyssey. By Homer. Chapter 12. And I quote: "First you come to the Sirens, who enchant all men, whenever anyone comes upon them, with their clear-toned song."

NOREEN: Give me that. *(She grabs the book, looks at it.)*

BETTY: You can't blame us if this Homer person remembered our music in a racial memory flashback. It doesn't mean he's actually heard us singing.

MARY: It goes on. *(She takes the book back from NOREEN.)*
"Come near, much praised Odysseus, the Achaians' great glory.
Bring your ship in, so you may listen to our voice.
No one ever yet sped past this place in a black ship
Before he listened to the honey-toned voice from our mouths,
And then he went off delighted and knowing all things.
For we know all the many things about broad Troy.
We know all that comes to be on the much-nourishing earth."

You see? The music tells Odysseus exactly the same thing it told me. Leaving out the business about Troy, of course. *(Pause)* Now how could Homer have known EXACTLY what the music sounded like—if he hadn't heard it himself?

BETTY: I don't understand how it could have happened—I was so careful—

NOREEN: It was an accident, Betty. Charlene was getting so sloppy—of course, she dialed for sloppy, said it gave her work that extra added dimension of random chance—but even her sloppiness was sloppy—oh, I felt bad about it, Betty. I did. Even before I started dialing for pessimism.

BETTY: I don't know what to say, Mary—except—I'm sorry.

MARY: "So they said, sending their lovely voice out. My heart desired to listen." I remember what it was like, reading this for the first time. Reading this—and realizing I'd been cheated. Cheated! Lied to! Betrayed!

BETTY: Now Mary, you've gotten your apology—and you deserved it, Noreen and I both admit that—but there's no reason to take it so personally. So the odd Greek visionary happens to remember a memory of our singing—it can happen, at the initial seeding, you commit a little overkill to make sure the planting takes—

MARY: IT'S EITHER MINE OR IT ISN'T! It's either just for me or what's the point! *(Pause)* Oh, I tried to rationalize it, I tried to convince myself that the Odyssey itself was a message, a sign. I admit it—I was using literature, like so many people do, as an emotional crutch. But I was just kidding myself. I had been lied to, and I was lost. And that's when I lost it.

BETTY: Lost what?

MARY: LOST WHAT? LOST WHAT!! WHAT THE HELL HAVE WE BEEN TALKING ABOUT! THE SPECIAL PART! THE SWEETNESS! THAT'S WHAT!!!

NOREEN: Now that I come to think about it, I think dialing for suicidal would be too easy. Suicidal is better than I deserve. There are so many ways to kill yourself painlessly. Efficiently. Professionally.

BETTY: I think I'm beginning to see the situation a little more clearly.

MARY: You are?

BETTY: We're not too late—we're too early.

MARY: What are you talking about—

NOREEN: Maybe I'll dial a perpetual molt. An itchy. Endless. Embarrassing shedding.

BETTY: The projections were precise, but with Charlene along you can never be really sure. Sloppy or not, we have to face the music.

NOREEN: Maybe I'll dial a perpetual molt coupled with an unceasing desire for flight. Yes. Two absolute opposites. Pair bonded. Relentlessly chained. The molt necessary for flight—that never ends in it. Need and desire. Desire and need. So close—so far away. Exquisite. Perfect. I can hardly wait.

BETTY: Mary—you're not the one.

MARY: Of course I am—

BETTY: But you're not sweet at all, dear. What you are is pathetic.

MARY: But I was sweet—terribly, impossibly special. That was the problem, you see—there was something so wonderful inside me that it made everything around me empty by comparison—there was a truth—a knowledge inside me that made everything outside of me a lie—so I had to let go of it, you see—I had to let it go, so I could go on with my life.

BETTY: What do you mean, you let it go?

MARY: One day, I woke up—and it was gone.

BETTY: No, dear. I don't think so. The kind of specialness we're talking about—the kind of sweetness we plant, and harvest, and use as currency in the seven-thousand systems, give or take a nebula or two—it just doesn't wander out the door and take a walk. The kind of sweetness we're talking about stays.

MARY: But it did stay. It stayed, no matter how much bullshit happened to me because of me—I held on to it, I never gave up hope even though I never understood the signs, I held on to it through all the bullshit—for the longest time.

(Pause)

BETTY: We'll make our computations, come back in another three of four generations or so—it'll be sure to be ripe by then. Ripeness is all, isn't it Noreen? No metaphor intended.

MARY: But I was the one!

BETTY: Well, you live and you learn. Right, Noreen?

NOREEN: Yes. If you've dialed for it, that is.

BETTY: I won't make the same mistake twice. No small talk. Suck first. Ask questions later. (They start to elevate.) Let's not take this little debacle too much to heart. First harvest, and all. Got to expect a few mistakes. Especially with Charlene's handiwork popping up all over the place.

MARY: Hey—

NOREEN: I really did mean to tell you about the Homer thing—but with one thing and another—

MARY: Where are you going?

BETTY: Don't give *The Odyssey* another thought.

MARY: Hey—you guys—wait—

BETTY: That's no excuse for shoddy work like that. Yes, the book is heroic—but where's the sweep? Where's magic? Where's the—well, there's just no other word for it—some call it truth, some call it beauty, but the simple fact is—Homer's *Odyssey* needs sweetness. How it has managed to survive as a classic when it is almost completely sweet free is quite beyond me.

NOREEN: Well, you know what they say in literature—if you can't cut sweet—cut deep.

BETTY: Do they really say that, Noreen?

NOREEN: Constantly.

MARY: Wait a minute—wait a goddamn minute—you can't just leave like this—

NOREEN: Why not?

MARY: What about me?

BETTY: What about you?

MARY: I kept it for you—I held on to it—I—

BETTY: Yes, but where is it now?

NOREEN: We lent it to you, your species has had the use of it and all its attendant side effects and signs for four-hundred-million years, and now that we're here to harvest it—now that we have politely asked for it back—

BETTY: It's not that we're Indian givers, Mary. After all, it wasn't exactly a gift.

NOREEN: It was agriculture.

BETTY: It was business.

NOREEN: And our business now takes us elsewhere.

MARY: Please—at least sing for me before you go—

NOREEN: Absolutely out of the question. In the first place—it would drive you completely mad.

MARY: I don't care.

NOREEN: Driving you mad for no reason would be sloppy, Mary. And I never dial for sloppy. Even in my dreams.

MARY: But I've got to hear the music—I've got to hear it again—

BETTY: Please, stop begging, Mary. It's unbecoming. We can't sing except during the initial seeding or the harvest itself. I assumed you would intuit that.

MARY: But if I could just hear the music—I'd get the sweetness back—I know I would—if I could just—

NOREEN: She really is pathetic, isn't she?

MARY: I know I said I lost it, but it's still inside me—I know it is—it's just hiding, that's all, it's hiding from the—from the bullshit, you know, I admit I wasn't up to the bullshit, I admit that about the bullshit, I should have done better with the bullshit—but even so—it's still there.

BETTY: No, dear. You were right the first time. It's gone. You have spent your entire life waiting for a bright shining moment to waltz into your life and give it meaning. A moment that would burn through all the bullshit. That would redeem you. Rescue you. Make everything make sense. *(Pause)* The problem is, if we did burn through the bullshit, there'd be nothing left. *(Pause)* You have missed your chances in life, Mary. You've missed every chance up to and including this one. And now there's nothing but bullshit left. (MARY *begins to weep.*) Oh, now, Mary, don't cry. You have a perfectly lovely life ahead of you, I'm sure. You'll forget all about us, and all this nonsense about specialness, and sweetness, and a music so beautiful to hear a single note makes your heart ache with longing and your brain do the cyclone spin kick of madness, oh you'll forget about it all. You'll become more and more like other people everyday. *(Pause)* I know this is all a little anticlimatic for you—after all the years of waiting and preparation—but there's no getting around it. You're being tossed back into the common sea of life. Sink or swim, dear. And remember, it's easier if you don't try to fight the tide.

MARY: You couldn't sing—as a way of saying goodbye?

BETTY: Let's get something straight about the singing, Mary. *(Pause)* It's brutal, exhausting, back-breaking work. *(Pause)* You see, it's not the terraforming and the harrowing and the planting and the waiting that makes sweetness such a difficult cash crop to bring to market. If it were just a matter of that, the entire universe would be one big sweetness farm. No, Mary—it's the singing that's the hard part.

NOREEN: I believe it's because the act of singing is never a metaphor for anything. I have come to believe that singing is one of existence's few primes.

(They ascend higher.)

BETTY: Maybe so, Noreen. Maybe so.

MARY: So—this is—it?

BETTY: In a manner of speaking—yes.

MARY: I've been waiting all my life for this moment—and it ends like this?

BETTY: Well, not exactly, Mary. *(Pause)* To be absolutely accurate—it ends like this.

BLACKOUT

A PLACE WHERE LOVE IS

Sally Dixon Wiener

A PLACE WHERE LOVE IS
© copyright 1995 by Sally Dixon Wiener

For all rights please contact Broadway Play Publishing Inc.

Sally Dixon Wiener's produced plays include TOUCH ME,
TOUCH-ME-NOT; THE BIG PICTURE (Love Creek's Environmental
Festival cowinner); THROUGH A GLASS, DARKLY; SHOW ME A HERO
(Winner, Carmel Playwriting Award; semifinalist, Louisville and Stanley
Drama Awards); THE PIMIENTA PANCAKES; and A FISH IN A
CHIMNEY. Her work in musical theater has included TELEMACHUS,
FRIEND; MARJORIE DAW; THE BLUE MAGI; and FLYIN' TURTLES. She
is a member of the Dramatists Guild, The Writers Room, and the League of
Professional Theater Women/New York.

A PLACE WHERE LOVE IS premiered in September 1991 by Love Creek Productions at the Nat Horne Theater in New York and was the winner of Love Creek's Women's Perspectives Festival. The cast and creative contributors were:

PAPA ....Francis Callahan
CECIE .... Deborah Clifford
LOLLY .... Judith Maxfield

Director .... Cynthia Granville

CHARACTERS

PAPA: *Elderly, terminally ill*
CECIE: *(Pronounced CESS-EE) His older daughter, thirty-five and gaunt*
LOLLY: *His younger daughter, twenty-seven, attractive, cheap*

TIME

Late afternoon, fall of the present year

SETTING

A shabby rural parlor

DEDICATION

For my daughters, my role models

(A shabby rural parlor with a big round table, candlestick, and framed photo on the mantelpiece. A screen partially covers the doorway to an adjoining sickroom where CECIE's *father lies, terminally ill. There is a front door, and another door leading off to the kitchen. At the rise,* PAPA, *who speaks from the sickroom throughout the play, is calling for* CECIE, *who comes on from kitchen, wearing a coat over an old sweater and apron, carrying a laundry basket. She is thirty-five, but gaunt enough to pass for fifty, on the edge. It is late afternoon in the fall of the present year.)*

PAPA: Cecie! Cecie...?

CECIE: It's okay, Papa. I'm right here. Just went out back for the laundry. *(She folds down a towel.)* So worn out. Softer than my hands. *(She glances at photo.)* Your hands ever get this way, Mama? So rough and red. I don't remember they did. 'Course they wouldn't have been at the end, when you were so sick after Lolly was born.

PAPA: You talkin' about Lolly again? You keep sayin' she's comin', but I'm liable to go before she gets here.

CECIE: She's drivin' all the way from Springfield and you're talkin' about goin' before she gets here! No, Papa! Don't you dare!

PAPA: Break my heart not to see her again.

CECIE: *(Snapping a pillowcase)* Break hers, too, now wouldn't it? So I'm not comin' in there to let you hold my hand and just slip away. Too late for that. You gotta hang on till she gets here. Isn't that so?

PAPA: Reckon. But it's gettin' harder.

CECIE: You can do it. Do it for her, Papa... It's a fact, Mama, he is goin', and I'm so wrung out with it all, I feel like I'm goin' right along with him. I can't stand bein' so all alone here. Make Lolly come soon, Mama.

PAPA: You sure she's comin'? You're not just sayin' that to—

CECIE: I told you— She called from the café at the junction about an hour ago. Just got off the highway.

PAPA: Lolly looks so much like your mama did.

CECIE: Always has. From the day she was born.

PAPA: You remember?

CECIE: I was eight, Papa. I remember. She's always acted more like you, though.

PAPA: Hah! Well, a body can't help bein' what they're like, can they? People don't change.

CECIE: Love can change people. It changed me, and it woulda changed—

PAPA: Just 'cause Lolly's comin' you gotta chew yer cud on all that again? Love! Virgil Johnson was no-good white trash!

CECIE: That was your opinion. Not mine!

PAPA: Lolly, poor motherless little thing going off with that tramp!

CECIE: She was seventeen and I'd raised her the best I could, like I promised Mama. And damn little help from you! But if anybody was a tramp, it was her. My own sister! I loved him, Papa. She didn't!

PAPA: Prob'ly not. Just got her wild! Turned out okay for her anyway, what with it startin' her career, singin' and all, up there.

CECIE: If bein' a cocktail hostess is a career. Okay for you, too, huh, with you needin' somebody to take care of you. But what about for me?

PAPA: You've always had a roof over your head. Funny, though, Lolly always wantin' whatever you wanted.

CECIE: Only thing I ever wanted in my whole life was Virgil.

PAPA: Cecie, you turned him into some kind of picture book man with all your moonin' around. Why can't you ever just let it go, girl! I said good riddance back then, same as Lolly said afterwards, too.

CECIE: Virgil and me would have been long gone before all that if you hadn't been so hard on him, makin' us wait so long and all—And I would have had somethin' in my life to— He did love me, Papa.

PAPA: Not once your sister started rubbin' up on him.

CECIE: She never would have got interested in him if you hadn't painted him up such a bad character! And all on account of some old gossip down at the Elks!

PAPA: Where there's smoke there's fire.

CECIE: I was twenty-five. That was my business to worry about. Not yours!

PAPA: Seemed like it was my business to worry about you! But then there went Lolly, runnin' off with him. Been runnin' ever since, too.

CECIE: You did some in your time.

PAPA: Huh! So long ago I nearly forgot.

CECIE: Well, I didn't! And neither did Mama...

PAPA: Don't you go talkin' about your mama like that—

CECIE: I wasn't talkin' about her. I was talkin' about you, you and that—

PAPA: ...Charlene. May she rest in peace.

CECIE: And Mama, too.

PAPA: Look, it's gettin' real bad again. You got anymore of those pills?

CECIE: *(Looking at watch)* It isn't time yet. Just try and sleep a little, Papa, till—

PAPA: Wait for Lolly... Wait for the pill... Waitin' to die, that's what I'm really waitin' on....

CECIE: *(Goes to check on him. He's asleep. She touches his forhead, returns to parlour, sits.)* Is that what I'm waitin' on, too, Mama? I think maybe something inside of me is broken, too. Something that's never goin' to get better. Like Papa isn't.

(A light knock on the door. LOLLY *enters with wrapped bouquet of roses and a suitcase.* LOLLY *is twenty-seven, attractive, but cheap-looking.)*

LOLLY: *(Goes to* CECIE, *embraces her)* Oh, honey! Tell me I'm not too late! *(She takes out a handkerchief.)*

CECIE: You're always late. But you're too early if you brought these for the funeral and if what you came for was Mama's silver.

LOLLY: *(Laughing with relief)* Oh, you always were a mean one, Cecie!

CECIE: Had to be. Not that it did you any good.

LOLLY: Well, thank the Lord Papa's—

CECIE: *(Puts fingers to her lips)* He just dozed off.... But he's not doin' so—

LOLLY: Didn't expect he was.

CECIE: Or you wouldn't have come.

LOLLY: Now don't start in on me, Cec! *(Takes off her coat and hat)* God, it's so gloomy in here. Is it too disrespectful to turn on some lights!

CECIE: Didn't notice it was gettin' so dark.

LOLLY: Oh, Cecie, how can you stand it, honey? This smell and all?

CECIE: I'm sorry! I do the best I can. Electric bill's so high, oil bills, too. I can hardly keep the windows open this time of the year. Well, what did you expect, Lolly?... I'll get a vase for the roses. You were nice to bring them. I'm sorry about what I said before about— *(She goes off, returns with vase.)*

LOLLY: Papa's always loved roses.

CECIE: *(Smelling them as* LOLLY *unwraps the bouquet)* Maybe these will help.... Lolly, that smell—it's the smell of dying. The whole house is full of it.... *(She puts her apron to her face.)* I smell of it, too!

LOLLY: Oh, Cecie, no…

CECIE: It's like when Mama—

LOLLY: Well, you can't expect me to remember that—

CECIE: I wouldn't expect you to remember anything ever about what's gone on in this house, Lolly.

LOLLY: Cecie. I told you a long time ago I was sorry about all that.

CECIE: About Mama…

LOLLY: No! That wasn't my fault! You know what I mean—

CECIE: You mean about Virgil…

LOLLY: Well, yeah… You better believe I was sorry about it.

CECIE: You even took my suitcase.…

LOLLY: …We wore the same size—shoes, dresses, everything, and, well, there it was, all packed and—

CECIE: Of course it was all packed! I was goin' away with him! That very next morning!

LOLLY: But then things sort of began to get out of hand later that night, and—

CECIE: And what?

LOLLY: I mean, well— Oh, what could I possibly have said or done to make anything better? Tell me!

CECIE: You could at least have left me my own trousseau!

LOLLY: …Oh, Cec! I can't believe I did that. But there it was, your suitcase, right there by the door, like in some movie! Except the movie didn't turn out very good.

CECIE: No, it didn't.

LOLLY: I never told you, but we were only married for one week. He wasn't at all like what I thought he'd be, and I just took off and left him—

CECIE: I always thought he left you!

LOLLY: What's the difference!

CECIE: I thought he'd realized he'd made a mistake, and—

LOLLY: I don't get it. I was the one who made the mistake!

CECIE: You didn't really love him.

LOLLY: I guess I just thought it would be sort of exciting to—

CECIE: And you must have hurt him, you just leavin' him like that.…

LOLLY: Who? Virgil? I doubt it. He was no good, honey!

CECIE: I'd have liked to have found out for myself.

LOLLY: Well, you would have soon enough! Look, you oughta thank me for saving you the trouble!

CECIE: If it had been me instead of you, maybe he'd have been different....

LOLLY: Hey, a man's a man. They're all alike. Virgil included.

CECIE: I don't believe that! But I'll never know, will I? Stuck here all this time with Papa. And before that, stuck here with you.

LOLLY: Stuck here with me? What do you mean?

CECIE: I promised Mama I'd take care of you.

LOLLY: Did she ask you to? Look at me! I said did she ask you to?

CECIE: No, I guess not. I just promised her I would before she—

LOLLY: Well, then don't blame that on me! Okay?... Hey, if you want a man, I'll introduce you to plenty! And fix you up with a nice dress, too. Got all my glad rags right in here— *(Opens suitcase, takes out dress)* Still wear a ten?

CECIE: I don't know.

LOLLY: *(Holding dress up to* CECIE, *staring at her)* ...Oh, God, Cecie, what's happened to you? You look awful! When did you last have your hair done, for heaven's sakes? ...All that gray! You need a tint job and some styling— maybe frosting around the front here. Honey, I can't bear to see you looking this way. At least just put on a little lipstick— *(She rummages in her pocketbook.)* Everything's right here in this little kit. No, let me do it! With this brush. There! See? ...And some blusher. Now how about your eyes. Let's see... Already you're looking better!

CECIE: *(Looking in* LOLLY's *mirror)* I see what you mean. But what for?

LOLLY: For me, honey! For Papa. For yourself, dummy! *(She looks around, notices photo.)* For Mama! You still talk to her like you always used to when I was little? *(*CECIE *doesn't answer.)* I bet you do... *(*CECIE *turns away.)* Cecie, when was the last time you were out of this house?

CECIE: I...don't remember. Well, Bernard takes me over to the K-Mart once in a while, to stock up on things I need, for Papa.

LOLLY: You still go to choir practice, don't you?

CECIE: I had to quit a couple of years ago. I can't leave Papa that long, especially in the evening. He gets real restless and— Look, Lolly, you know, sometimes, since Papa's been sick, I guess I just forget who I was, or who I am. Not that it makes all that much difference.

LOLLY: Well, that's a damn fool attitude! And take off that apron!

CECIE: Just how do you think you'd make out here?

LOLLY: Oh, honey. I wouldn't have the first idea of how to even go about dealing with something like this!

CECIE: It doesn't take much to learn how to handle a bed pan and fix trays and deal out pills. That isn't the problem, it's—

LOLLY: Oh, I can just see myself now, bustling around in that ratty apron, and— Hey, Cecie, is it real bad, I mean seein' him the way he looks now?

CECIE: No worse than seein' me, I guess.

LOLLY: Hey, come on! You've just been lettin' yourself go. He's sick!

CECIE: Real sick, yeah. Oh, Lolly, he talks about you all the time. You know how he's always been so crazy about you.

LOLLY: Well, I couldn't help that! And I couldn't help looking like Mama, either—so I hope he doesn't bring that up again! Every time I walk in here he—

CECIE: Which has been three times in the last five years! What is so wonderful about bein' a cocktail hostess that you can't come home to your own house more often?

LOLLY: Because—it's what I do! And there are some compensations. This is gonna be your house, anyway. That's what you told me the last time I was here. So I've got my own little security problems to work out, don't I?

CECIE: It doesn't seem fair, somehow. This was your home as much as mine.

LOLLY: Oh, forget it. You've earned it. Lock, stock, and barrel. I'll make out okay. Now let me put some lipstick on, myself…. Listen, I hope Papa wakes up pretty soon… Want to see him as much as I can, but, I've got to get on the road again early tomorrow.

CECIE: I thought this time you'd be stayin' a while! Well, I mean, you brought that big suitcase, and—

LOLLY: Oh, that's 'cause I don't like leavin' my stuff around there. But I could only get the one night off. Hey, you know, a funny thing—the last time I had a night off, couple of weeks ago, somebody said Virgil showed up at the lounge, speakin' of the devil! Back in town and fatter and sassier than ever, I hear tell.

CECIE: You didn't see him?

LOLLY: I told you! It was my night off!

CECIE: Do you think he'll come back there, to that place?

LOLLY: Well, I suppose so, if he's living in Springfield again.

CECIE: But what would you say to him, if he comes in there and—

LOLLY: What I'd say to any other guy that came in! Hey! How's it goin'? You're lookin' great!

CECIE: That's all?

LOLLY: Honey, what the hell else is there to say? Then I'd just give'm a wink and move on— He's not gonna cramp my style, that's for sure. I got my little act right down cold.

CECIE: Your act?

LOLLY: Oh, it's no big deal. It's easy, working a room like that, once you get the hang of it. *(She's still putting makeup on.)* You want to know the secret of it?

CECIE: Well, I suppose you first of all put on all the makeup and perfume and nail polish, and you're dressed up like—

LOLLY: A lot of sequins doesn't hurt, either. Then, all you've got to do is keep sayin' to yourself, "I love my face. I love the way my body moves in my beautiful dress. I am love. And I will make this whole room and everybody in it into a place where love is."

CECIE: "Where love is..."

LOLLY: *(Getting up, taking candlestick from the mantelpiece)* That's right. And then, when I get my chance to fill in for the singer, when she's taking her break or something, I go out and come back in, and I stand there, still as water, and I light this candle, and I go real slow over to the piano player, feeling all that love working its way up there with me, and I just sing one of those old standards, real slow.

CECIE: Like "Deep Purple" or something? *(LOLLY nods.)* Suppose you forget some of the words?

LOLLY: You don't ever let on , you just shut your eyes and hum, and let everybody else in there do it for you. They all know the words anyway, you know. And they love you! It just comes all pouring out at you, all that love. Okay, it isn't for real, but that's how I try to make it real for them.

(LOLLY starts singing "Deep Purple"; CECIE joins in, and PAPA wakes up.)

LOLLY: "When the deep purple falls
Over sleepy garden walls
And the stars begin to flicker in the sky
Through the mist of a memory
You wander back to me
Breathing my name with a sigh..."

PAPA: Lolly! That you, baby?

LOLLY: That's right, Papa! I'm home!

PAPA: Oh, honey! I'm goin', I know, but I just had to hang on till you got here!

LOLLY: I'm comin', Papa....

CECIE: Lolly. He's scared....

LOLLY: So am I....

CECIE: You can do it.

LOLLY: *(Picks up the roses and goes into* PAPA's *room)* Hey! How's it goin'? You're lookin' great!

CECIE: ...And I can do it, too! I can do it! I can do it, can't I, Mama? Listen to me, Mama! "I love my face. I love the way my body moves in my, my beautiful dress. I am love." And I will light the candle and stand there, still as water, like Lolly says, and I will feel all that love, all around me, coming to me. Only I will do it real, not like Lolly. And Virgil will be there, Mama. Yes, he'll be there! And he will know that I am doing it real. That I truly am love.

(During the preceding speech CECIE *puts dress back into* LOLLY's *suitcase. She has put the makeup kit into her own handbag, folded her apron over a chair, put her coat over her arm, and picked up* LOLLY's *car keys. As the play ends, she blows out the candle, takes* LOLLY's *suitcase, and quietly lets herself out the front door.)*

CURTAIN

POOF!

Lynn Nottage

POOF!

The live stage production rights to this play are represented by Broadway Play Publishing Inc. For all other rights please contact Helen Merrill Ltd, 435 W 23rd St, N Y N Y 10011.

Lynn Nottage is a playwright from Brooklyn. Her other plays include LAS MENINAS, (commissioned by Actors Theater of Louisville, Voice and Vision Retreat, Mabou/Mines Suite, N Y S F New Works Project); EULOGY FOR A MISSING PLAYER (Talking Drum Theater Company); BROOKLYN AFTER THE GLOW (winner White Bird Playwriting Contest); and PARENTHETICAL GLANCE AT THE DIALECTICAL NATURE OF THE AFRICAN AMERICAN'S QUEST FOR AUTONOMY (The Black Theater Festival at the University of New Haven, Rites and Reasons). POOF! was also produced at City Ensemble Stage and The Action Theater in Singapore, and received the Heideman Award. In addition, her work has been featured in New York at The Knitting Factory and B A C A Downtown. Lynn was a contributor to A...MY NAME IS STILL ALICE, produced by Second Stage and regional theaters throughout the country. She is currently working on WELCOMING GERTE, commissioned by Second Stage and scheduled for development at the Sundance Playwrights Laboratory; and THE POR'KNOCKERS, commissioned by Dance Theater Workshop, where it will premiere as part of the "Out of the Shadows" series. She recently completed TABLE STAKES, a screenplay for Joan Micklin Silver. She is a member of the Playwrights Horizons African American Writers Unit, The Next Step, and was a resident artist at Mabou Mines (1992-93). Ms Nottage is the recipient of the 1993-95 Playwriting Fellowship at New Dramatists, and the 1994 Artists' Fellowship from the New York Foundation for the Arts. She is a graduate of Brown University and the Yale School of Drama.

POOF! premiered at Actors Theater of Louisville on 20 March 1993 as part of the Humana Festival of New American Plays.

LOUREEN .... Elain Graham
FLORENCE .... Yvette Hawkins

Director .... Seret Scott

CHARACTERS

SAMUEL
LOUREEN
FLORENCE

(Darkness)

SAMUEL: WHEN I COUNT TO TEN I DON' WANT TO SEE YA! I DON' WANT TO HEAR YA! ONE, TWO, THREE, FOUR—

LOUREEN: DAMN YOU TO HELL, SAMUEL!

(A bright flash. Lights rise. A huge pile of smoking ashes rests in the middle of the kitchen. LOUREEN, a demure housewife in her early thirties stares down at the ashes incredulously. She bends and lifts a pair of spectacles from the remains. She ever so slowly backs away.)

LOUREEN: Samuel? Uh! *(She places the spectacles on the kitchen table.)* Uh!… Samuel? *(Looks around the stage)* Don't fool with me now. I'm not in the mood. *(Whispered)* Samuel? I didn't mean it really. I'll be good if you come back…. Come on now, dinner's waiting. *(She chuckles, then stops abruptly.)* Now stop your foolishness… And let's sit down. *(She examines the spectacles.)* Uh! *(Softly)* Don't be cross with me. Sure I forgot to pick up your shirt for tomorrow. I can wash another, I'll do it right now. Right now! Sam?… *(Cautiously)* You hear me! *(Awaits a response)* Maybe I didn't ever intend to wash your shirt. *(Pulls back as though about to receive a blow; a moment)* Uh! *(She sits down and dials the telephone.)* Florence, honey, could you come on down for a moment. There's been a…little…accident…. Quickly please… Uh!

(She gets a broom and a dust pan. She hesitantly approaches the pile of ashes. She gets down on her hands and knees and takes a closer look. A fatuous grin spreads across her face. She is startled by a sudden knock on the door. She slowly walks across the room like a possessed child and lets in FLORENCE, who wears a floral housecoat and a pair of over-sized slippers. Without acknowledgment LOUREEN proceeds to saunter back across the room.)

FLORENCE: HEY!

LOUREEN: *(Pointing at the ashes)* Uh!… *(She struggles to formulate words, which press at the inside of her mouth not quite realized.)* Uh!…

FLORENCE: You all right? What happened? *(She sniffs the air.)* Smells like you burned something? *(Stares at the huge pile of ashes)* What the devil is that?

LOUREEN: *(Hushed)* Samuel… It's Samuel, I think.

FLORENCE: What's he done now?

LOUREEN: It's him. It's him. *(She nods her head repeatedly.)*

FLORENCE: Chile, what's wrong with you? Did he finally drive you out your mind? I knew something was going to happen sooner or later.

LOUREEN: Dial 911, Florence!

FLORENCE: Why? You're scaring me!

LOUREEN: Dial 911!

(FLORENCE *picks up the telephone and quickly dials.*)

LOUREEN: I think I killed him.

(FLORENCE *hangs up the telephone.*)

FLORENCE: What?

LOUREEN: *(Whimpers)* I killed him! I killed Samuel!

FLORENCE: Come again?… He's dead, dead?

(LOUREEN *rings her hands and nods her head twice mouthing "dead, dead."* FLORENCE *backs away.*)

FLORENCE: No, stop it, I don't have time for this. I'm going back upstairs. You know how Samuel hates to find me here when he gets home. You're not going to get me this time. *(Louder)* Y'all can have your little joke, I'm not part of it! *(A moment. She takes a hard look into* LOUREEN's *eyes. She squints.)* Did you really do it this time?

LOUREEN: *(Hushed)* I don't know how or why it happened, it just did.

FLORENCE: Why are you whispering?

LOUREEN: I don't want to talk too loud—something else is liable to disappear.

FLORENCE: Where's his body?

LOUREEN: *(Points to the pile of ashes)* There!…

FLORENCE: You burned him?

LOUREEN: I DON'T KNOW! *(She covers her mouth as if to muffle her words. Hushed:)* I think so.

FLORENCE: Either you did or you didn't, what you mean you don't know? We're talking murder, Loureen, not oven settings.

LOUREEN: You think I'm playing.

FLORENCE: How many times I have heard you talk about being rid of him. How many times have we sat at this very table and laughed about the many ways we could do it and how many times have you done it? None.

LOUREEN: *(Lifting the spectacles)* A pair of cheap spectacles, that's all that's left. And you know how much I hate these. You ever seen him without them, no!... He counted to four and disappeared. I swear to God!

FLORENCE: Don't bring the Lord into this just yet! Sit down now...
What you got to sip on?

LOUREEN: I don't know whether to have a stiff shot of scotch or a glass of champagne.

(FLORENCE takes a bottle of sherry out of the cupboard and pours them each a glass. LOUREEN downs the glass of sherry, then holds out her glass for more.)

LOUREEN: He was....

FLORENCE: Take your time.

LOUREEN: Standing there.

FLORENCE: And?

LOUREEN: He exploded.

FLORENCE: Did that muthafucka hit you again?

LOUREEN: No...he exploded. Boom! Right in front of me. He was shouting like he does, being all colored, then he raised up that big crusty hand to hit me, and poof, he was gone.... I barely got words out and I'm looking down at a pile of ash.

(FLORENCE belts back her sherry. She wipes her forehead and pours them both another.)

FLORENCE: Chile, I'll give you this, in terms of color you've matched my husband Edgar, the story king. He came in at six Sunday morning, talking about he'd hit someone with his car, and had spent all night trying to out run the police. I felt sorry for him. It turns out he was playing poker with his paycheck no less. You don't want know how I found out.... But I did.

LOUREEN: You think I'm lying?

FLORENCE: I certainly hope so, Loureen. For your sake and my heart's.

LOUREEN: Samuel always said if I raised my voice something horrible would happen. And it did. I'm a witch...the devil spawn!

FLORENCE: You've been watching too much television.

LOUREEN: Never seen anything like this on television. Wish I had, then I'd know what to do.... There's no question, I'm a witch. *(She looks at her hands with disgust.)*

FLORENCE: Chile, don't tell me you've been messing with them mojo women again? What did I tell ya.

(LOUREEN stands and sits back down.)

LOUREEN: He's not coming back. Oh no, how could he. It would be a miracle. Two in one day…I could be canonized, worse yet he could be.… All that needs to happen now is for my palms to bleed and I'll be eternally remembered as St Loureen, the patron of battered wives. Women from across the country will make pilgrimages to me, laying pies and pot roast at my feet and asking the good saint to make their husbands turn to dust. How often does a man like Samuel get damned to hell and go.

(LOUREEN breaks down as though crying. As FLORENCE consoles her friend, she realizes that she is actually laughing hysterically.)

FLORENCE: You smoking crack?

LOUREEN: Do I look like I am?

FLORENCE: Chute, I've seen old biddies creeping out of crack houses, talking about they were doing church work.

LOUREEN: Florence, please be helpful, I'm very close to the edge!… I don't know what to do next! Do I sweep him up? Do I call the police? Do I.…

(The phone rings.)

LOUREEN: Oh God.

FLORENCE: You gonna let it ring?

(LOUREEN reaches for the telephone slowly.)

LOUREEN: NO! *(She holds the receiver without picking it up, paralyzed.)* What if it's his mother?… She knows!

(The phone continues to ring. They sit until it stops. They both breathe a sigh of relief.)

LOUREEN: I should be mourning, I should be praying, I should be thinking of the burial, but all that keeps popping into my mind is what will I wear on television when I share my horrible and wonderful story with a studio audience.… *(Whimpers)* He's made me a killer, Florence, and you remember what a gentle child I was. *(Whispers)* I'm a killer, I'm killer, I'm a killer.

FLORENCE: I wouldn't throw that word about too lightly even in jest. Talk like that gets around.

LOUREEN: You think they'll lock me up? A few misplaced words and I'll probably get the death penalty, isn't that what they do with women like me, murderesses?

FLORENCE: Folks have done time for less.

LOUREEN: Thank you, just what I needed to hear!

FLORENCE: What did you expect, that I was going to throw up my arms and congratulate you. Why'd you have to go and lose your mind at this time of day, while I got a pot of rice on the stove and Edgar's about to walk in the door and wonder where his Goddamn food is. *(Losing her cool)* And he's going to start in on me about all the nothing I've been doing during the day and why I can't work and then he'll mention how clean you keep your home. And I don't know how I'm going to look him in the eye without…

LOUREEN: I'm sorry Florence. Really. It's out of my hands now.

(She takes FLORENCE's hand and squeezes it.)

FLORENCE: *(Regaining her composure)* You swear on your right tit?

LOUREEN: *(Clutching both breasts)* I swear on both of them!

FLORENCE: Both your breasts, Loureen!. You know what will happen if you're lying. (LOUREEN *nods. Hushed:)* Both your breasts Loureen?

LOUREEN: Yeah!

FLORENCE: *(Examines the pile of ashes, then shakes her head)* Oh sweet, sweet Jesus. He must have done something truly terrible.

LOUREEN: No more than usual. I just couldn't take being hit one more time.

FLORENCE: You've taken a thousand blows from that man, couldn't you've turned the cheek and waited. I'd have helped you pack. Like we talked about.

(A moment)

LOUREEN: Uh!… I could blow on him and he'd disappear across the linoleum. *(Snaps her fingers)* Just like that. Should I be feeling remorse or regret or some other "r" word? I'm strangely jubilant, like on prom night when Samuel and I first made love. That's the feeling! *(The women lock eyes.)* Uh!

FLORENCE: Is it…

LOUREEN: Like a ton of bricks been lifted from my shoulders, yeah.

FLORENCE: Really?

LOUREEN: Yeah!

(FLORENCE walks to the other side of the room.)

FLORENCE: You bitch!

LOUREEN: What?

FLORENCE: We made a pact.

LOUREEN: I know.

FLORENCE: You've broken it... We agreed that when things got real bad for both of us we'd...you know...together.... Do I have to go back upstairs to that.... What next?

LOUREEN: I thought you'd tell me!... I don't know!

FLORENCE: I don't know!

LOUREEN: I don't know!

(FLORENCE *begins to walk around the room, nervously touching objects.* LOUREEN *sits, wringing her hands and mumbling softly to herself.*)

FLORENCE: Now you got me, Loureen, I'm truly at a loss for words.

LOUREEN: Everybody always told me, "Keep your place Loureen." My place, the silent spot on the couch with a wine cooler in my hand and a pleasant smile that warmed the heart. All this time I didn't know why he was so afraid for me to say anything, to speak up. Poof!... I've never been by myself, except for them two weeks when he won the office pool and went to Reno with his cousin Mitchell. He wouldn't tell me where he was going until I got that postcard with the cowboy smoking a hundred cigarettes.... Didn't Sonny Larkin look good last week at Caroline's? He looked good, didn't he....

(FLORENCE *nods. She nervously picks up* SAMUEL's *jacket, which is hanging on the back of the chair. She clutches it unconsciously.*)

LOUREEN: NO! No! Don't wrinkle that, that's his favorite jacket. He'll kill me. Put it back!

(FLORENCE *returns the jacket to its perch.* LOUREEN *begins to quiver.*)

LOUREEN: I'm sorry. (*She grabs the jacket and wrinkles it up.*) There! (*She then digs into the coat pockets and pulls out his wallet and a movie stub.*) Look at that, he said he didn't go to the movies last night. Working late. (*She frantically thumbs through his wallet.*) Picture of his motorcycle, Social Security card, driver's license, and look at that from our wedding. (*Smiling*) I looked good, didn't I? (*She puts the pictures back in the wallet and holds the jacket up to her face.*) There were some good things. (*She then sweeps her hand over the jacket to remove the wrinkles, and folds it ever so carefully, and finally throws it in the garbage.*) And out of my mouth those words made him disappear. All these years and just words, Florence. That's all they were.

FLORENCE: I'm afraid I won't ever get those words out. I'll start resenting you, honey. I'm afraid won't anything change for me.

LOUREEN: I been to that place.

FLORENCE: Yeah? But now I wish I could relax these old lines (*Touches her forehead*) for a minute maybe. Edgar has never done me the way Samuel did you, but he sure did take the better part of my life.

LOUREEN: Not yet Florence.

FLORENCE: *(She nods.)* I have the children to think of. Right?

LOUREEN: You can think up a hundred things before...

FLORENCE: Then come upstairs with me... We'll wait together for Edgar and then you can spit out your words and...

LOUREEN: I can't do that.

FLORENCE: Yes you can. Come on now.

(LOUREEN shakes her head: No.)

FLORENCE: Well I guess my mornings are not going to be any different.

LOUREEN: If you can say for certain then I guess they won't be. I couldn't say that.

FLORENCE: But you got a broom and a dust pan, you don't need anything more than that.... He was a bastard and nobody will care that he's gone.

LOUREEN: Phone's gonna start ringing soon, people are gonna start asking soon, and they'll care.

FLORENCE: What's your crime? Speaking your mind.

LOUREEN: Maybe I should mail him to his mother. I owe her that. I feel bad for her, she didn't understand how it was. I can't just throw him away and pretend like it didn't happen. Can I?

FLORENCE: I didn't see anything but a pile of ash. As far as I know you got a little careless and burned a chicken.

LOUREEN: He was always threatening not to come back.

FLORENCE: I heard him.

LOUREEN: It would've been me eventually.

FLORENCE: Yes.

LOUREEN: I should call the police, or someone.

FLORENCE: Why? What are you gonna tell them? About all those times they refused to help, about all those nights you slept in my bed 'cause you were afraid to stay down here? About the time he nearly took out your eye 'cause you flipped the television channel?

LOUREEN: No.

FLORENCE: You've got it, girl!

LOUREEN: Goodbye to the fatty meats and the salty food. Goodbye to the bourbon and the bologna sandwiches. Goodbye to the smell of his feet, his breath, and his bowel movements... *(A moment. She closes her eyes. As though reliving a horrible memory, she shudders.)* Goodbye. *(She walks over to the pile of ashes.)* Samuel?… Just checking.

FLORENCE: Goodbye Samuel. *(They both smile.)*

LOUREEN: I'll let the police know that he's missing tomorrow….

FLORENCE: Why not the next day?

LOUREEN: Chicken's warming in the oven, you're welcome to stay.

FLORENCE: Chile, I got a pot of rice on the stove. Kids are probably acting out…. And Edgar, well… Listen, I'll stop in tomorrow.

LOUREEN: For dinner?

FLORENCE: Edgar wouldn't stand for that. Cards maybe.

LOUREEN: Cards.

(The women hug for a long moment. FLORENCE exits. LOUREEN stands over the ashes for a few moments contemplating what to do. She finally decides to sweep them under the carpet, and then proceeds to set the table and sit down to eat her dinner.)

CURTAIN

REPAIRS

Susan Miller

REPAIRS

The live stage production rights to this play are represented by Broadway Play Publishing Inc. For all other rights please contact the Joyce Ketay Agency, 1501 Broadway, #1910, N Y N Y 10036, 212 354-6825.

Susan Miller is an Obie Award-winning playwright whose most recent play, MY LEFT BREAST, was produced in the 1994 Humana Festival of new plays by the Actors Theater of Louisville. Her play, IT'S OUR TOWN, TOO was included in *Best Short Plays of 93/94*. Her plays NASTY RUMORS AND FINAL REMARKS, FOR DEAR LIFE, and FLUX were produced by Joseph Papp and the New York Shakespeare Festival. FLUX also was produced by The Second Stage in New York. In Los Angeles, CROSS COUNTRY and CONFESSIONS OF A FEMALE DISORDER were produced at the Mark Taper Forum. An O'Neill playwright, Miller has received N E As, a Rockefeller Grant, and twice has been a finalist for the Susan Smith Blackburn Prize in playwriting. She is also a Yaddo Fellow. Her television work includes THIRTYSOMETHING, L A LAW, and TRIALS OF ROSIE O'NEILL, among others. She is on the part-time faculty of N Y U's Dramatic Writing Program.

REPAIRS was originally produced by HOME for Contemporary Theater and Art in New York in February 1989.

CHARACTERS

BARBARA: *A woman in her late thirties*
CAROL: *A writer;* BARBARA's *best friend*
JERRY: BARBARA's *husband*

(Lights up on a half-finished basement)

(BARBARA is painting or applying spackle to a wall. She's wearing a bandana and other appropriate-to-the-task clothes—which make her even more attractive in a disheveled way. Hanging around a stepladder, pouring herself coffee, is BARBARA's best friend, CAROL.)

CAROL: So then he says—listen to this—"No one takes their dreams seriously anymore." I'm in the middle of a real crisis. I have lost my address book and he is kvetching about the unconscious. He takes a cigarette from my pack—this is a man who has been off of it for five years—and says, "What's therapy been to you? You don't write down your dreams. You won't take the unconscious seriously...." Smoking and scolding me, this stupid Jungian. "I dream of digits, I tell him. Numbers in the wrong sequence. Dr Jones, I have no way to get in touch with my friends. I call information twenty times a day. Life as I have known it is over. I'm in great distress!" By the end of the hour, I'm hoarse, and Barb, I look over at Jones and there are tears running down his face. And he's hinting around that he might leave the profession. He tells me to call before I show up for our next session. Just in case. *(Beat)* You'd think a psychologist would have a field day with the loss of such an item as I have lost. I'm sure a Freudian would take the ball and run with it. My God, the implications! *(Beat)* I've been with Jones a long time. He can't do this to me. I just can't tell my story to one more person!

(BARB holds up a tile.)

BARB: What do you think?

CAROL: *(Distracted)* What?

BARB: The tile. What do you think?

CAROL: I don't know. It's so adult.

BARB: It's imported.

CAROL: Do you think we're going to age well?

BARB: From Italy.

CAROL: It's, you know, parenty.

BARB: I'm parenty. *(Beat)* Can you reach that box?

CAROL: *(She gets the box.)* Albums!

BARB: I like turning a dark place into something else.

CAROL: *(Rifling through)* God.

BARB: You know how there are these places. Which sort of hold time.
I mean, they contain the past and the future. That's almost their whole
purpose.

CAROL: *(Looking at a picture)* Who's this?

BARB: Me.

CAROL: Where was I?

BARB: *(Looking at photo, distractedly)* I was fat.

CAROL: Where was I?

BARB: I want this to be a successful room.

CAROL: *(Still looking at photograph)* I love how you look here. Your mouth
kind of hanging open. It's the way kids concentrate, you know. How they'll
be watching TV or something. It breaks my heart.

BARB: *(Deep in thought)* I don't know what comes next.

*(Lights fade on women. Lights come up on stairs leading to basement. JERRY,
BARB's husband, sits and talks to the audience.)*

JERRY: So, she wakes me up in the middle of the night and says, "I'm
scared." And I think, who isn't, but I try and you know, be a grownup.
So I hold her and say, "Scared of what, honey?" And she says, "Nuclear
Winter." Well, I figure now's not the time to tell her about the toxic cloud
over New Jersey or the killer cheese and the salmonella outbreak. So I tell
her Carl Sagan's a know-it-all. And I sing her the score of *My Fair Lady*.
(Beat) Well, she's out like a baby. But now I'm wide awake and completely
terrified.

(Lights on women)

BARB: You know, when Mary Tyler Moore's son killed himself, he was
saying—reported to be saying— "She loves me. She loves me not. She loves
me, she loves me not." Carol, the thing is, that's right out of Chekhov. I was
reading "The Seagull" again—Jess had to do a paper on it for English class,
so I read it again. And the boy, the son—Konstantin—says the very same
thing. And his mother is also a famous actress. Arkadina. Remember?
The boy puts on a play for her which she doesn't think much of and later,
when he's a successful writer, she never even reads his stories. She loves
me, she loves me not. He says it at the beginning of the play. And at the end,
he shoots himself. *(Beat)* I don't know. What do you make of that, Carol?
Do you think Mary Tyler Moore's son was reading "The Seagull" or what?

CAROL: She looked sensational on the cover of *Rolling Stone*.

BARB: It's just that she made me so happy for a lot of years. Mary and Lou and Ted and Rhoda and everyone. Murray. I liked the way she always called him, 'Mur'.

CAROL: It's all right, Barb. She's all right. Mary's all right.

(Lights off, as CAROL moves into the dark.)

(JERRY, wearing a baseball cap, holding a notepad, enters the space, but he is now an interviewer.)

(Lights up)

JERRY: Okay, let me just get this right. You're finishing your basement.

BARB: Uh huh. Yeah.

JERRY: All right. Let's get a little historical perspective before I ask you the tough ones. *(Beat)* Is this your first?

BARB: Well, I've *used* other people's finished basements. But no, this is—yes.

JERRY: I'm interested in how you can reconcile this in light of everything else.

BARB: You mean—

JERRY: How can you justify finishing a basement in this day and age?

BARB: You mean—what, the money?

JERRY: In 1993. With all that's happened. With the threat of extinction. Poverty. How do you reconcile panelled walls, a new floor....

BARB: I was thinking of a bar.

JERRY: A bar. Right. Well, you'd have to have a bar.... That's true. *(Catching himself)* But coming back to my question—

BARB: It's a thing to do. It's labor.

JERRY: Some people might call it self-involved. A neurotic retreat.

BARB: It's hope. *(Beat)* See, if I do this thing. Well, people can come down here and dance. They can have a good time. My son can bring his friends here. And they won't be out in the world. They won't be riding down some country road where someone drunk could mow them down. Or on the highway where a truck could spill its chemicals and overcome them. They can kiss here. And live.

(Lights fade as JERRY goes back to the steps and CAROL walks back into the room.)

CAROL: Lately, I can't stop thinking about cancer. *(Beat)* Just when I have this really well constructed, possibly truthful paragraph going, it comes over me.

(BARB buttons a button on CAROL's sweater or arranges her scarf.)

BARB: You're not worried about cancer. You're worried about your deadline.

CAROL: I don't want to get it.

BARB: Carol, honey, it's my feeling that you're going to be with us an inconsiderately long time. Old enough even to take up with cats.

CAROL: I don't want anyone I love to get it.

BARB: Now you're pushing.

CAROL: I just don't like the word.

BARB: That happened to me once with 'cemeteries'.

CAROL: Really?

BARB: I had to go great distances out of my way in order not to pass one. My parents were very worried, not to mention greatly inconvenienced.

CAROL: But you got over it.

BARB: Let's just say the existence of such a place does not occupy my thoughts. But I wouldn't say I'm thrilled by the idea.

CAROL: It's the word, though.

BARB: Uh huh. CANCER. CEMETERY. Uh huh. I know.

CAROL: It's always being mentioned. Someone's always saying how this or that causes it. Jesus, these are toxic times.

BARB: Maybe if we broke it down to see how many other words we could get out of it. *(She reaches into a carton for some paper and a pencil.)*

CAROL: Do we get points? I really do better when you get points.

BARB: Okay... *(She writes a word, then says it out loud:)* CAR

CAROL: *(Writes)* CAN

BARB: RACE

CAROL: NEAR

BARB: Uh...CARE

CAROL: Good one. Umm...ACE

BARB: ARE

CAROL: Uh...CRANE

BARB: Now let's rhyme. Dancer, prancer—

CAROL: Answer.

BARB: This woman in my exercise class—she has only one breast. She wears a leotard with a silicone form in it. You'd never guess with her clothes on. In the sauna, though, it's just—there's only one breast and a scar on the other side. She's in public relations.

CAROL: She doesn't mind everyone seeing her naked? She's not embarrassed?

BARB: She's got a tattoo.

CAROL: What do you mean? On her...where it used to be?

BARB: Shaped like a vine. It's blue and green and winds around the scar. She seems to go about her life.

CAROL: One out of eight women, they say.

BARB: Let's hammer some nails.

CAROL: What?

BARB: You know. Pound.

CAROL: Pound.

BARB: Men do this. And they're much happier. Hand me a tool.

(Lights fade on women. Lights up on stairs. JERRY begins to sing "Chances Are". BARB and CAROL join in from their area of the basement, as if they were singing this song, themselves, a recollection of pajama parties past.)

JERRY: (Singing) Chances are, though I wear a silly grin, the moment you come into view, Chances are you think that I'm in love with you—

CAROL and BARB: Do be doo. Doo be doo. Do bee doo.

JERRY: (To audience) It's a terrible thing. The day it finally dawns on you. That you're never going to play the clarinet. Or go to medical school. I mean, Jesus.

(Lights up on women as BARB is pouring herself more coffee.)

CAROL: When I see someone holding a cup of coffee, I know everything's going to be all right. In a movie when people sit down at the kitchen table with their mugs, it saves me. You know what I mean? There's a problem or a crisis, right, and someone brews up a pot of strong coffee and you've got a good solid pause in the events. It's a comfort, because you know they're going to stop for a little while and have a conversation. All the time, holding the cup—steam rising. Someone taking a nice, long swallow, then moving to the stove for a refill. Pouring someone another cup. Pouring, matter of factly, serious matters at hand. Someone thinking: This is good.

(They take a long swallow at the same time.)

BARB: This is good. You want another cup?

(CAROL *and* BARB *smile at each other, as lights dim.* CAROL *exits.* BARB *turns on the portable cassette player, which is permanently placed near her paint cans.* "Theme from a Summer Place" *comes on.* BARB *walks to the stairs, sits on a step slightly below* JERRY.)

BARB: Hello, you.

JERRY: Imagine how cramped and lonely a grown man can get sitting on a damp stairway. In the underbelly of his house. In the dark.

BARB: It's beyond imagining. (*Beat*) Carol was here. Avoiding.

JERRY: What did you two talk about?

BARB: Supply side economics. You know.

JERRY: Let's run away.

BARB: From home?

JERRY: From it all.

BARB: To where?

JERRY: A different place.

BARB: Maybe this new room.

JERRY: Somewhere out of this world.

BARB: I like this world. It's what I know. I mean, how would the other one smell? And suppose there were no one-hundred percent cotton sheets. Or Peanut butter and jelly sandwiches?

JERRY: That would be hard. That would be a loss.

BARB: (*The strains of* "Summer Place" *in the background*) Remember this song?

JERRY: We made out to it in Richie Brenner's basement. Every Saturday night. It just played over and over. No one could ever get up and turn it off.

BARB: Your mouth.

JERRY: Your skin.

BARB: See, good things happen. (*Beat*) Why won't you come down here?

JERRY: What happens when it's all done?

BARB: We get to enjoy it.

(*Music stops.*)

JERRY: Yeah, but once it's finished—

BARB: We're not, though. We're still here.

JERRY: Remember when Jess was five. He used to say "One Home Run Cleaners." There'd be a sign—CLEANERS. And underneath it would say,

ONE HR And every time we'd pass, Jess would yell out, "There's One Home Run Cleaners!" *(Pause, sadly)* The thing is, he knows what it means now.

BARB: Oh, Jerry. *(She touches his hand, then starts to sing:)*
I have often walked
Down this street before
But the pavement always stayed beneath my feet before...
(Beat)
The rain in Spain
Stays mainly on the plain.
I think she's got it.
By George, she's got it.
(Beat)
I'm getting married in the morning.
Ding dong the bells are going to chime.
(As JERRY *joins in)*
Bring out the...something...
Something something something—
(Lights fade as we hear the rest of this in black.)
But get me to the church on time!

END OF PLAY

THE SLEEP SEEKER

Staci Swedeen

THE SLEEP SEEKER
© copyright 1995 by Staci Swedeen

A playwright, actress, and director, Staci Swedeen is the coauthor of CALL
ME WHEN YOU'RE IN SOMETHING: A NEW YORK ACTORS' GUIDE
TO PRODUCING SHOWCASES (Broadway Press, 1987). A recipient of a
1991 Tennessee Williams Playwriting Scholarship to the Swanee Writers
Conference, her one-act plays have been produced at the Nat Horne
Theater, Terry Schreiber Studio, Synchronicity Space, and Hunter College
Theater. She has written commissioned children's plays for Sundance
Publications and has hosted a Westchester cable-T V series, "Interviews
with Authors." She served as the first executive director for the Hudson
Valley Writers' Center. She is a member of the Dramatists Guild.

THE SLEEP SEEKER won first place in the Love Creek Annual Short Play
Festival in 1992 and was staged at the Nat Horne Theater in New York City.

DORCAS . . . . Rebecca Hoodwin
NURSE HANSON . . . . Sherri Rose
MR BERTONI . . . . Richard Kent Green
NORMA . . . . Dawn Jamieson
JAN MALONE . . . . Debra Major
SHIRLEY GIBSON . . . . Irma St Paule

Director . . . . Cynthia Granville

It also was produced in 1992 at the Terry Schreiber Studio in New York
City, directed by Carol Millican, as part of GRAVE TRANSFORMATIONS,
an evening of one-acts by Staci Swedeen.

The version of "Happy Birthday" used in this play is based on a Mahler
Waltz. It is in the public domain.

CHARACTERS

DORCAS GIBSON: *An attractive, heavyset woman in her late fifties*
NURSE HANSON: *A woman in her mid-thirties*
JAN MALONE: *A social services agency caseworker, in her mid-twenties*
MR BERTONI: *A man in his forties; DORCAS's employer*
NORMA: DORCAS's *friend, a woman in her fifties*
SHIRLEY GIBSON: DORCAS's *mother, a woman in her seventies*

DEDICATION

To Ralph Pape

(Changes in time should be represented either by music or light cues, or both, and kept very short. The set represents a small, carefully kept studio apartment. There are a few fine pieces of china, a small table, bed with a phone nearby, and a hot plate. A window faces out into the audience. As the house lights dim, there is the sound of a distressed infant crying and crying. Finally a light is snapped on in the apartment by DORCAS GIBSON. *She is wearing a blue floor-length gown. She gets up rapidly, puts on her robe, and goes to the wall stage left.)*

DORCAS: For God's sake! It's six-thirty in the morning! Please! If you don't shut that child up I'll call the cops! See if I don't—you can't just keep letting that kid cry all night.... *(The crying has stopped. She pauses, then to herself:)* Well, great. *(With a yawn, she turns the radio on low, puts a cup of tea on the hot plate, looks out the window. The crying starts again.)* Oh my God. I can't take this any longer. Day in and day out, and they just let that baby keep— *(Going to wall)* Stop it! I—I—I'm going to call! Do you hear me? I'm going to call someone! I mean it! I'm going to do it this time! *(To herself)* They don't care, they— *(Going for phone book, she puts it on the table; reading from book:)* Law enforcement agencies, mental health—women—children's services; ah! child abuse—okay. *(Goes to phone and dials. The crying has stopped.)* It's too late! I'm dialing! It doesn't matter now. I'm already dialing.... *(Completes dialing, into phone)* Hello? I—I'd like to report a baby crying. No, I mean *really* crying. I can't get any sleep, and—yes. Yes, I think there's something wrong, I—why? Why do you need MY address —yes, next door. You don't tell them who called, do you? I wouldn't want—it's Dorcas Gibson. *(Spelling it)* D-O-R-C-A-S. It's a biblical name, it means—oh never mind. No, *Miss* Gibson. 161 Tanglewood Drive, apartment 3B. That's correct, right around the corner from the old church on Maple. *(Hanging up, the crying starts again.)* Didn't you hear me? For God's sake! Stop it! Stop it! Stop it!

(Music/light cue. NURSE HANSON *is standing,* DORCAS *is seated at the table; a hospital form is before her.* NURSE HANSON *smokes.)*

NURSE HANSON: It's important we know what your wishes are. *(Pause)* Whether you want extraordinary means used.

DORCAS: Extraordinary means?

NURSE HANSON: Artificial respiration, C P R, artificial nutrition and hydration—

DORCAS: Her—her birthday's this week. We've been planning the party. I've already bought the decorations.

NURSE HANSON: No one can predict—your mother's just suffered a series of small strokes, but after all, she is in her seventies.

DORCAS: She promised me she'd make it to ninety!

NURSE HANSON: Going over her forms this morning, Dr Robertson...he...we...felt that this was important.

DORCAS: I've signed so many forms, I can't remember what I've signed. *(Holding her head)* Oh, God.

NURSE HANSON: Excuse me, but do you have an ashtray?

(Music/light cue. MR BERTONI appears in DORCAS's apartment. NURSE HANSON is oblivious to him.)

MR BERTONI: I've never stopped by an employee's apartment before, but I think this is important, Dorcas.

DORCAS: If it's about being late, Mr Bertoni, I can explain that. Really. I've... the last couple mornings, well—

NURSE HANSON: Miss Gibson?

MR BERTONI: No, no, it's not just about the being late.

(Music/light cue. BERTONI is gone.)

NURSE HANSON: *(Holding out cigarette)* An ashtray?

DORCAS: Oh, God. I'm sorry. *(Getting ashtray)* I was just thinking about work. Usually I'd be there by now but—my allergies. My mother used to—this sounds silly—but she used to rub under my toes when I got sinus headaches. Right underneath the toes.

NURSE HANSON: Yeah? I was thinking about taking one of those courses—what is it—foot reflexology? A couple of the other girls at work—

DORCAS: Do you have a mother, Nurse Hanson?

NURSE HANSON: *(Taken aback)* Why—yes. Yes, of course I do.

DORCAS: Brothers and sisters?

NURSE HANSON: An older brother.

DORCAS: So your mother is—I mean, you're not the only one who has to deal with—

NURSE HANSON: Well, no, I—

DORCAS: See, my mother—it's a great thing, isn't it, to be the center of someone's life?

NURSE HANSON: I wouldn't know.

DORCAS: Oh it is! I'm fifty-six years old and—

NURSE HANSON: About these forms—

DORCAS: *(Small laugh)* I mean, I didn't even get married because of— that's pretty strange, isn't it?

NURSE HANSON: No, I mean I don't know, I—

DORCAS: Pretty strange. So. *(Signing the paper with determination)* There. I want everything done, all right?

(There is a quick knock at the front door, which then opens. NORMA walks in, carrying a grocery bag.)

NORMA: Oh, I'm sorry. I didn't realize you had anyone here.

DORCAS: Norma, this is Nurse Hanson. She works down at Cedar Crest.

NORMA: Your mom?

DORCAS: Is fine. Just some paperwork. Everything's fine.

NORMA: Should I come back?

NURSE HANSON: No, no, I'm all done. I'm just leaving. *(Picking up signed form, to DORCAS:)* I'm—I know this is difficult.

DORCAS: No, it's just that I didn't get very much sleep and—well, I appreciate your coming by.

NURSE HANSON: Just part of the job. *(Exiting, to NORMA)* Nice meeting you. *(To DORCAS)* We'll keep you appraised of any changes in her condition. Bye.

NORMA: *(Taking items out of bag)* Here, I picked you up some orange juice, Kleenex, some Contact, aspirin, Sinutab, and this looked good, TheraFlu, just in case…Dorcas?

(DORCAS has not been listening to her. She is very still, listening intently for sounds from the neighboring wall.)

NORMA: Dorcas?

DORCAS: *(Absorbed, listening. In a minute she brings her attention back to NORMA.)* I'm sorry, Norma. What were you saying?

NORMA: That I picked up those things you asked for from the store. *(Short pause—DORCAS listening at wall)* Well, I better get going —

DORCAS: Norma—you know those neighbors I've told you about? The ones that live on the other side of this wall?

NORMA: I don't remember.

DORCAS: I just hope—just tell me I've done the right thing.

NORMA: Why? What'd you do?

DORCAS: I called a child abuse agency.

NORMA: What?!!

DORCAS: I hear them night after night, and—

NORMA: Oh, Dorcas.

DORCAS What? You don't live right next to them!

NORMA: You hear them beating a child? You actually hear—

DORCAS: No, but I hear—I hear this baby crying and crying.

NORMA: Then you don't know if that's what's happening, do you?

DORCAS: Why else would a child cry like that? It doesn't make any—

NORMA: If you'd ever had any children—there are a thousand reasons why they cry. Colic. Ear infections. Gas. Fear of the dark. Stubbornness. When I first had Brian, he cried—he cried for the first year and a half. I wore ear plugs just so I could hang on to my sanity. It's not that unusual.

DORCAS: Yes, but—

NORMA: But what? Don't get involved, Dorcas. Don't.

DORCAS: But—

NORMA: Plus, what are you going to say to the parents when you pass them in the hall? "Nice day for baby beating, isn't it?" You don't want to be this kind of neighbor.

DORCAS: I never see them, and—I don't know why you're acting like I did something wrong. The agency said that they'd protect my identity, wouldn't tell them who called.

NORMA: Oh, sure. Don't you watch T V? They always find out, track you down—it doesn't matter if you have plastic surgery or—

DORCAS: All right! I didn't tell you this to get a big lecture. Anyway, no one from the agency showed up.

NORMA: Thank God. I mean it, Dorcas, you don't want to get involved with something like this. When I lived in California, the man next door to me was shot. For dealing drugs. I moved the very next day.

DORCAS: I've missed work so many mornings because—

(Light/music cue. NORMA is gone and MR BERTONI has taken her place. He is holding a very large computer manual in his arms.)

DORCAS: If it's about being late, Mr Bertoni, I can explain that. Really. I've… the last couple mornings, well—

MR BERTONI: No, no, it's not just about—

DORCAS: You see, my mother's—and then these neighbors —

MR BERTONI: It's about the computer training class, Dorcas. I have a report here that says you left at the end of the first day and didn't go back.

DORCAS: Oh.

MR BERTONI: We spent a lot of money—we're spending a lot of money to update this facility and part of that money went to pay for computer training for you.

DORCAS: Mr Bertoni, I'm a fast typist. I've been here for—it'll be sixteen years next March, and no one here types faster than I do. No one in the whole plant.

MR BERTONI: Dorcas, we're going to be taking that typewriter off your desk and putting a computer there and you won't know how to run it.

DORCAS: Oh. *(Pause)* You're going to take it away?

MR BERTONI: Everyone is going to have a computer. We're all going to be hooked up to the same system. We can't have you off in your own little typewriter world. *(Handing her the heavy manual)* Here. This is your computer manual—you left it on top of your desk. I thought maybe you could study this and—

DORCAS: *(Taking manual)* Oh.

MR BERTONI: I've never stopped by an employee's apartment before, but I think this is important. You've been a good worker for many, many years. I want to know what the problem is.

DORCAS: Excuse me?

MR BERTONI: What's your problem with the class? Was the instructor all right? Was the information presented clearly?

DORCAS: No, the instructor was—all right. It's just that—he kept talking about these little disks and random memory and saving your work— how you could create something but that if you didn't save it, it was gone— plus that little blinking light kept flashing at me, and then whenever I would type something my fingers would jam up. I've typed my whole life and that's never happened to me! Never!

MR BERTONI: Well, sometimes it takes a while to learn a new—

DORCAS: And when I looked up the teacher's lips were moving but no sound was coming out— So I thought maybe he's not saying anything to me. Like those dog whistles, my ears just didn't have his frequency. What was the point of staying?

MR BERTONI: *(Short pause)* Dorcas...I don't know how to put this to you. We're—the company is having one last class next week —

DORCAS: I do remember one thing he said before the frequency changed. Something about the save and exit key being the same. He said if you didn't watch what you were doing you could think you were saving something but really you'd lost it. Does that make sense to you?

MR BERTONI: Please, listen to me. You have a choice of either taking that class or—

DORCAS: I just want someone to explain that to me. How you could think you were saving something but really you'd lost it. Is the reverse true, too? Like, maybe you think you'd lost something, but really you'd saved it? And here's the real question—where do you go to look for it?

MR BERTONI: Dorcas. Miss Gibson. Did you hear what I was saying?

DORCAS: Oh. Yes. You're going to take my typewriter away.

MR BERTONI: No, more than that, you need to—

DORCAS: Mr Bertoni, do you mind if I go take an aspirin? I've got the worst headache.

MR BERTONI: Well—

DORCAS: I'll come right back.

MR BERTONI: No, that's all right. You go on. Go ahead.

DORCAS: Thank you. *(Exiting)* Oh, and Mr Bertoni—about my being late. It won't happen again, I promise.

(Light/music cue. BERTONI exits. DORCAS is off. There is a loud knocking at the front door.)

JAN: *(From off)* Hello! Hello! Anyone home? Excuse me, is anyone home? *(More knocking)* Hello!

DORCAS: *(Entering from off with a towel around her head)* Hold on, hold on, I'm coming. Just a minute. *(Opening door)* Yes? May I help you?

JAN: Is this 161 Tanglewood, 3B?

DORCAS: Yes.

JAN: *(Stepping through the door. She is holding a small brown paper bag that holds a cup of coffee and a bagel. A purse is over her shoulder.)* Hi, I'm from the Child Protection Service, my name is— *(Referring to paper bag, which is wet on the bottom)* Oh, geez—don't you hate this? You ask them to be sure and put the lid on tight and then the bag —

DORCAS: Listen, I called yesterday morning, not—someone was supposed to be here yesterday.

JAN: *(Struggling with bag)* I'm sorry, do you have a napkin or—?

DORCAS: *(Getting napkin)* I have to get ready for work—

JAN: This'll only take a minute. *(Looking around)* This is a nice apartment. *(She has pulled a bagel out of the bag.)*

DORCAS: Nice and small. I've lived here a long time.

JAN: Yeah, but you got this big window here—and to look out and see something like that tree. Nice. You want half a bagel?

DORCAS: Oh, no, thank you.

JAN: You don't mind if I—?

DORCAS: No, no, go ahead.

JAN: Thanks. My caseload is so heavy it seems I never get a chance to, you know, eat a real—well. What can you tell me?

DORCAS: Uh, well, there's—

JAN: Oh, God, I left my notepad out in the car. *(Hopping up)* Let me just go and get—

DORCAS: I really don't have much time.

JAN: Oh, well, um, could I borrow some paper then? Sorry.

DORCAS: *(Getting paper)* You don't tell them—I mean, I don't want any trouble.

JAN: Don't worry, you— *(Taking paper)* Thanks. *(Getting a pen out of her purse)* Okay. Go ahead.

DORCAS: Do you have any children, Miss —

JAN: Mrs. Mrs Malone.

DORCAS: Do you?

JAN: Well, to be honest with you—

DORCAS: Because my friend Norma says it's—perfectly natural—that babies cry all the time, but I don't believe it. Not like this baby. This baby just cries and cries and cries. It makes all the hair on the back of my neck stand up. I've been hearing this for so long now, that—and when this baby cries, I can't think straight, I can't sleep—

JAN: Have you seen the child? Observed any cuts or bruises?

DORCAS: No, I—

JAN: *(Writing)* Hmm. How old?

DORCAS: What?

JAN: The child. How old?

DORCAS: Oh, I don't know. Young. A baby. An infant. A little tiny infant.

JAN: And you hear the baby crying when?

DORCAS: At night, mostly. When everything else is quiet. Of course, I work during the day.

JAN: *(Writing this down)* Where?

DORCAS: I'm a secretary for Quality Processing, the film lab down on Pine. Do you know it?

JAN: Uh, I think that's where my husband and I had our honeymoon pictures developed. Which apartment does the crying come from?

DORCAS: *(Going over to wall)* From this one. Sometimes it's like the whole wall just—shakes with it, you know? I put my hands against it to keep the whole building from—

JAN: *(Folding up paper and putting it in her purse)* Well, thanks for your time, Miss Gibson. Let me look into this. *(Handing pen towards her)* Was this your pen?

DORCAS: No, it was yours.

JAN: Do you think there might be any other apartments available in this building? My husband and I are living with his parents and—

DORCAS: I really don't know. You could ask the landlord. Apartment 6G.

JAN: Thanks, thanks, I will. Oh, here, let me leave this with you. *(Pulling a pamphlet on child abuse out of her purse)* This will kind of tell you what you should be aware of—some of the reasons that parents abuse kids, that kind of stuff—you know, unrealistic expectations, immaturity, isolation. Also what kinds of signs the kids—

DORCAS: *(Handing pamphlet back to her)* I don't have time to read this kind of—here. I don't want it.

JAN: Oh. Okay. Your landlord, what's his name?

DORCAS: Mr Thompson.

JAN: I think I'll ask him about that apartment. Couldn't hurt. Oh, and Miss Gibson—you did the right thing to call. Bye.

DORCAS: Goodbye. *(She comes down to window and stares out. The sound of a baby's crying. Spot on DORCAS's face as she continues to stare out the window.)*

(Light/music cue. SHIRLEY sits at the table drinking a cup of tea. On the table in front of her is an old shoe box filled with photographs. DORCAS enters, wearing a coat, just getting home from work.)

DORCAS: Mama? What are you doing here?

SHIRLEY: Drinking tea. Peppermint tea. Looking through old pictures.
I kept thinking I'd get these put into an album someday, but—

DORCAS: But what?! What are you doing here? I had a long talk with your
doctor and he—

SHIRLEY: Dr Robertson? You believed anything that old pill pusher had to
say?

DORCAS: I'm just so surprised to see you here.

SHIRLEY: Surprised that I'd come see the light of my life, the apple of my eye?

DORCAS: *(Embarassed)* Mom—

SHIRLEY: You look tired, honey. Here, take your coat off, sit down.
Let me get you a cup of tea. Peppermint's good for your tummy.
How was work today?

DORCAS: Oh, it was—how are you? I mean you look so—

SHIRLEY: I feel great. Absolutely no pain. I don't understand it, last week I
felt so terrible, you know.

DORCAS: I know.

SHIRLEY: I didn't want to talk about it with you, I was afraid that.... I don't
want to be one of those little old ladies who are always complaining about
their bowel movements. Plus with my birthday coming up and you—

DORCAS: Oh my God! That's right, your birthday. I—I've got some stuff here
that I bought—oh, Mom, this is great. Wait, wait. I have it in this bag! *(Goes
to shopping bag by bed and pulls out some pointed birthday party hats like children
wear, and some noisemakers that you blow into)* Here, put one on!

SHIRLEY: Oh, no—c'mon now!

DORCAS: Mom, please! *(They both put hats on and blow noisemakers.)*

SHIRLEY: Well, that's done. *(Starts to take hat off)*

DORCAS: No, Mom, leave it on. We have to have some cake or something.
(Short pause) I don't have any cake. How about some bread and jam?

SHIRLEY: That sounds good. Strawberry?

DORCAS: Strawberry it is. Not as good as what you used to make,
but it'll have to do.

SHIRLEY: Your place looks nice, honey. You keep it nice and neat.

DORCAS: It's so small I have to—otherwise everything gets out of control.

SHIRLEY: I remember when you first moved here—what were you?
Nineteen?

DORCAS: Mom, please, It was a long time ago. Let's not go into it.

SHIRLEY: One day you were home, we were so happy, and the next you just packed and moved to the other side of town. Wouldn't even answer my—

DORCAS: That's not how it was. You know that. *(Referring to bread she's been preparing)* You want butter on it too?

SHIRLEY: No, no, I don't need the extra calories. I was having such a nice time sitting by this window, looking through these old pictures. Should have written on the back of them, though. Can't remember who half these people are.

DORCAS: Like who?

SHIRLEY: Like who the hell is this standing next to you?

DORCAS: Why were you looking at this photo?

SHIRLEY: It was in the box.

DORCAS: That...that was Sam Russell.

SHIRLEY: That's Sam Russell? My God, he—he looks so young. He looks like a kid.

DORCAS: He was a kid. We were all kids once. C'mon, that's enough old photos.

SHIRLEY: Isn't this tea good? My teabag broke though. I'm getting little leaves on the tip of my tongue.

DORCAS: Let me get you another.

SHIRLEY: No, that's okay. Makes it kind of chewy. *(Looking back at photo)* Whatever happened to Sam?

DORCAS: C'mon, Momma, let's —

SHIRLEY: I always kind of liked him.

DORCAS: Liked him?! How can you say that?

SHIRLEY: His hair was too long but—I thought the two of you would run away and get married, make me a grandmother.

DORCAS: Mother!

SHIRLEY: Well? What's wrong with that?

DORCAS: That's not what you told me when I was growing up—you said if I ever—

SHIRLEY: Oh, for heavens' sake, who can remember that far back?

DORCAS: Sam was the—you—he and I—well, God, Momma! Let's just have our bread and jam, okay?

SHIRLEY: Okay. Okay. Don't bite my head off.

DORCAS: You want more tea?

SHIRLEY: Please. *(Pulling another photo out of box)* Oh my gosh, look at this one.

DORCAS: Now, no more—

SHIRLEY: You and your Dad and that red trike you had. Boy, your dad was a handsome man, wasn't he? Holding you in his arms, his little deer. It was your Dad named you.

DORCAS: It's the only thing I haven't forgiven him for.

SHIRLEY: Oh honey, don't say that. He named you after his favorite Aunt Dorcas. It means deer in Greek.

DORCAS: Mother, I know that, and you know that, and daddy knew that. No one else knows it. It's just a weird name. I just wanted to be called Linda, or Julie, or Becky, or—

SHIRLEY: Becky?! Oh no. You were a deer. My dear deer. My reason for living. You were always so good. Never got into any trouble. I've always been so proud of you, you never once…oh, I used to feel so bad for Becky Schaffer's parents, her getting pregnant, she never did finish high school, and—

DORCAS: *(Attempting to change the subject, pulling photo out of box)* Here's a picture Daddy took of you singing to me. *(Laughing)* Look at the expression on your face! You used to really belt it out.

SHIRLEY: I always had a good voice.

DORCAS: Well—

SHIRLEY: I did! You always liked my singing.

DORCAS: It made me laugh!

SHIRLEY: That's because I sang funny songs! You're supposed to laugh.
(Launching into it)
Do your ears hang low, do they wobble to and fro?
Can you tie them in a knot, can you tie them in a bow?
(DORCAS joins in.)
Can you throw them over your shoulder
Like a Continental soldier?
Do your ears hang low?

SHIRLEY: *(Laughing)* Now that was one of my all-time greats! God, that felt good to sing that.

DORCAS: We're gonna have the neighbors pounding on the walls!

SHIRLEY: Admit it! I have a good voice!

DORCAS: *(Laughing)* Okay, okay, I admit it!

SHIRLEY: Oh, I loved sitting at the piano with you and singing.

DORCAS: I know, Momma.

SHIRLEY: You were always the perfect daughter. Once your father died... you're the only person who has never disappointed me. That year when you wouldn't even see me—I wanted—I've always loved you.

DORCAS: I know.

SHIRLEY: *(Feeling the top of her head)* Oh, look at us! We still have our birthday dunce caps on. This elastic string is starting to choke me, I'm gonna take it off.

DORCAS: No, wait! I haven't sung to you yet. Oh, I'm so glad you're here. You can't take it off until I sing to you.

SHIRLEY: Sing what?

DORCAS: Happy Birthday, of course. The special version. Wait, wait, let me get the tune:

Happy Birthday, Happy Birthday
I love you
Happy Birthday, Happy Birthday
Yes, it's true
When you blow out the candles
One light stays aglow
It's the love light in your eyes
Whereever you go —

SHIRLEY: *(Applauding)* Beautiful! Thank God you inherited my vocal powers. Your dad couldn't carry a tune in a bucket. Sing it again—wait, let me use the bathroom—all that tea, and my bladder's the size of a peanut. Sing it again! *(As she exits)* Boy, that bread and jam tasted delicious.

DORCAS: Happy Birthday, Happy Birthday—I love you *(The phone rings.)* I'll get it! *(Still singing as she goes to phone)* Happy Birthday, Happy Birthday— Yes it's true —*(Picking up phone)* Hello? Oh, hello, Nurse Hanson. How are you? Excuse me? *(Pause)* No, that can't be—she's right here, we're having a birthday...hold on. *(Calling out)* Momma? Momma, come on out here, there's— *(Back into phone)* Could you hang on a minute? Just a minute— *(Drops phone, runs into bathroom, quickly comes out visibly shaken. Fighting back the tears.)* Hello? Yes. What time did she die? No, no, I'm all right. Yes, thank you. No, thank you for calling me, for telling me. Thank you for telling me. No, I understand...I know she wasn't in any pain, I know. She told me. Thank you for letting me know. Thank you for letting me know.

(Light/music change. DORCAS's apartment. She is offstage. There is a loud knocking at the door.)

JAN: Miss Gibson? Hello? Anybody home? Miss Gibson? It's Jan Malone.

DORCAS: *(Entering from bathroom; she has her robe on)* Go away.

JAN: Miss Gibson—please! I really need to speak with you.

DORCAS: Please! I can't talk with anyone. Please go away. Go away.

JAN: It's crucial that I speak with you! Just for a minute.

DORCAS: *(Reluctantly opening door)* Mrs Malone, it's—oh, come in. Just for a minute.

JAN: *(Enters holding a large stack of newspapers)* These were all piled up outside your door.

DORCAS: *(Taking them)* Here, they can just go anywhere. *(Puts them down)*

JAN: I'm sorry to bother you again but I've called and never got any answer. Then when I tried contacting you at work—

DORCAS: I was fired. Isn't that something? To work for a company for nearly sixteen years and then—let me tell you. You know what's worse than being unemployed? Being an older woman and unemployed. No one tells you—

JAN: I'm sorry. About your job, I mean.

DORCAS: What are you sorry for? You didn't fire me, did you?

JAN: No.

DORCAS: Then don't be sorry. *(Pause)* Listen, I thought you were going to look into the crying. It's gotten worse, it goes on night and day now, I never get any sleep. You said you were going to investigate it.

JAN: Yes, that's why I'm here—you see *(Pause)* —do you mind if I sit down?

DORCAS: I — *(Trying to be gracious)* —do you want a cup of tea?

JAN: Thank you. That would be nice. *(She pulls out her notes and a small brown paper bag as DORCAS puts on the whistling tea pot.)* Here, I've got a maple bar in my bag we could split.

DORCAS: No, no thank you.

JAN: Okay. I want to go over the information you gave me several weeks ago, because—

DORCAS: Because what?

JAN: Well, I'm not sure, I—I think maybe I didn't get it all down correctly. *(Referring to notes)* Now, you said that you've never actually seen the child. Is that correct?

DORCAS: No, but I don't have to see it to know that something's very wrong. I mean, my God, if you heard it—

JAN: And you think this child is—what? Three years old?

DORCAS: Oh, no, I didn't say that. I said like a baby. Maybe an infant, like a newborn.

JAN: And you're sure you hear it from this wall?

DORCAS: Yes. Yes, from that wall.

JAN: Because— *(Looking at her notes and then up)* —no one lives on the other side of that wall.

DORCAS: What?

JAN: I spoke with your landlord and no one's lived in that apartment for the past six months. It's being renovated. So it's possible you've heard workmen in there, but no baby. So then I thought maybe you were just confused about the direction of the sound. That's when I found out that only one apartment on this floor has a child, and that child is three years old.

DORCAS: What—it's not like I...I don't know what I'm hearing!

JAN: So then I investigated the floor beneath you and— *(The tea kettle has started to whistle loudly.)* —your water's boiling.

DORCAS: You think you can just come in and tell me that I don't know what I'm—I'm not making this up! My God, why would I make such a thing up, why would anyone make—

(The sound of the tea kettle continues to pierce the room.)

JAN: Uh, do you want me to, to turn that off?

DORCAS: *(Ignoring her and the sound)* I'm not able to get any sleep. Do you think I'm making that up? Do you have any idea of how horrible it is to never be able to get any sleep, to lie there awake, night after night, and hear the sound of some poor little baby being—I don't know! Held by its thumbs and beaten because it won't shut up? Because it keeps crying and you know there's something you're supposed to be doing and it still won't shut up? So you, you—

(The sound of a baby's crying comes up under the tea kettle.)

JAN: *(Overlapping)* Wait, wait, what are you—

DORCAS: —want to scream back, because it's like someone is ripping the flesh right off your bone, like they're just tearing it off you, to hear this crying going on and on, and you think, I don't know—I'm gonna put you into the closet until you shut your mouth, until you—

JAN: Please, my God, that tea kettle is going to — (*She takes the kettle off and kettle whistle goes out while crying continues.*)

DORCAS: And this mouth just continues to scream and you scream back— I'm going to throw you against the wall! I am! What are you doing here? I never asked you to be here, and you're supposed to be soft and pink, not red like a lobster, and he still didn't want me, not even after he knew about you—shut up! No one's supposed to know about you and the neighbors will, Momma will, my God, she'd die if she ever—

JAN: Oh, God, please, you've got to sit down, I don't know—

DORCAS: Don't tell me you can't hear that!

JAN: No, I can't hear—

DORCAS: (*To crying infant*) Shut up! Why can't you ever just shut up! What do I have to do to make you shut up, my God, what to I have to do to just get some sleep, I'm gonna kill you, I'm gonna— (*The crying abruptly stops. Pause.*) Oh. Oh my God, I, there's something— (*Trying to pull herself together*) —Please, you have to go home. You have to go now, you have to leave—

JAN: I can't leave you like this, I can't—

DORCAS: You have to go! Oh my God, I was so sure it was the neighbors, I was—please, you have to go, my head is—

JAN: (*Going for phone*) I've got to call someone. You've got to have some—is there someone you want me to call, someone who could come be with you, who—

DORCAS: I'm going to be sick, I'm…God, my head! I just need to be left alone, please, I just need to get some sleep so that I can—

JAN: (*Crossing over to her*) Miss Gibson, you've got to let me know who I can call. Do you have a friend, a relative—

DORCAS: Oh, God. (*Calling out for her*) Momma?

JAN: Someone who could—

DORCAS: Momma?!

(*Music/light cue. SHIRLEY enters. JAN is oblivious to her presence.*)

JAN: What's her number? Is she somewhere I can—

DORCAS: (*To SHIRLEY*) I have the worst headache.

JAN: Maybe I can find some aspirin in my purse—

DORCAS: All I need, really, is some sleep. Oh God, Momma—all these years I wanted to tell you, but it made everything so awful—I mean—

JAN: *(Looking frantically in her purse)* I must have some aspirin here somewhere—

DORCAS: And then there was a baby, and I—I couldn't tell you, I couldn't tell anyone—

JAN: *(Looking at DORCAS with realization)* Oh my God. Oh my God.

DORCAS: I was so afraid that...I wouldn't be your deer anymore, that you wouldn't—oh God, my head.

JAN: Please, don't—are you? Please don't say anymore, I need to get someone here—

DORCAS: I thought I would wait until everything was good before I told you and it never got good.

SHIRLEY: *(Putting out her arms to DORCAS)* Dorcas.

DORCAS: He's safe, out by that tree. See, Momma? Your grandchild, you can see—

JAN: Someone to help you—

DORCAS: Sometimes I've just stood and looked...oh, my head.

SHIRLEY: *(Comforting her)* Shhh—

DORCAS: I don't deserve—

JAN: I've got to call the police. *(Going to phone and dialing)* I've got to call the police. *(Into receiver)* Hello? Yes, yes, I'd like to report—oh, God, I don't know, a murder? God, I don't know when—a baby—uh, I—wait, I've got the address right here—

DORCAS: It's 161 Tanglewood Drive. The name's on the box downstairs. Tell them it's a biblical name. It's Greek for deer. *(Softly)* It's Greek for deer.

CURTAIN

SPRINGTIME

Maria Irene Fornes

SPRINGTIME
© copyright 1989 by Maria Irene Fornes

Maria Irene Fornes is the author of more than two dozen works for the stage, among which are PROMENADE, THE SUCCESSFUL LIFE OF 3, FEFU AND HER FRIENDS, EYES ON THE HAREM, THE DANUBE, MUD, THE CONDUCT OF LIFE, ABINGDON SQUARE, WHAT OF THE NIGHT?, and ENTER THE NIGHT. These plays are performed throughout the United States and Europe.

She is the recipient of seven Obie awards, one of which was for Sustained Achievement. She is also the recipient of a Distinguished Artist Award from the National Endowment for the Arts; a New York State Governor's Arts Award; an Honorary Doctor of Letters degree, Bates College, Lewiston ME; a Distinguished Directors Award from the San Diego Theater Critics Circle; and an Award for Distinguished Achievements as an artist and educator from the Association for Theater in Higher Education. She has received grants and fellowships from the Rockefeller Foundation, the John Simon Guggenheim Memorial Foundation, C I N T A S, and the N E A among others. At present she is the recipient of a Lila Wallace-Readers Digest Literary Award.

Ms Fornes conducts playwriting workshops in theaters and universities throughout the U S, and abroad. From 1973 to 1979 she was managing director for the New York Theater Strategy. Beside most of her own plays, she has directed plays by Calderon, Ibsen, Chekhov, and several contemporary authors. Two volumes of her plays have been published by P A J Publications; other plays have been included in various anthologies. She is a member of the Dramatists Guild and the Society of Stage Directors and Choreographers.

SPRINGTIME was first performed as part of a quartet entitled WHAT OF THE NIGHT? by the Milwaukee Repertory Theater on 4 March 1989. The cast and creative contributors were:

RAINBOW ....Kelly Maurer
GRETA ....Catherine Lynn Davis
RAY ....Daniel Mooney

Director ....Maria Irene Fornes
Sets .... John Story
Costumes .... Cecelia Mason
Lights .... LeRoy Stoner

CHARACTERS

RAINBOW: *Twenty-nine years old. Slim and spirited.*

GRETA: *Twenty-six years old. Slim, handsome, and shy.*

RAY: *Twenty-seven years old. High-strung and handsome. He wears a dark suit.*

SETTING

A small city. The year is 1958.

RAINBOW's bedroom. A small room. On the left wall there is, upstage, a small door; downstage of the door there is a small window. Downstage of the window there is a chair. In the up right corner of the room there is a small bed with metal foot and headboard. To the left of the bed there is a night table. On the night table there is a book, a pitcher of water, and a glass. On the back wall hangs a painting of a landscape. On top of the bed there is a night gown.

SCENE 1: GRETA IS ILL

(RAINBOW *and* GRETA *have just entered.* GRETA *takes off her dress. She is in a slip. She sits on the bed and starts to put on the nightgown.*)

RAINBOW: Don't worry, Greta. I know what to do.

GRETA: What, Rainbow? What can you do?

RAINBOW: I'll find some money. Don't worry.

GRETA: How?

RAINBOW: I'll find money, Greta. I can't tell you how.

GRETA: Why not?

RAINBOW: You won't love me anymore if I tell you how.

GRETA: Tell me.

RAINBOW: Please don't make me tell you.

GRETA: I don't want you to do anything that would make you ashamed.

RAINBOW: I've been in jail.

GRETA: Why? What did you do?

(RAINBOW *helps* GRETA *lie down. She covers her with the sheet.*)

GRETA: Tell me.

RAINBOW: I've been in jail for stealing.

GRETA: Stealing?

RAINBOW: Yes. I haven't done it since I know you. But now I must do it again. You're ill, and we must take care of you.

GRETA: No! I don't want you to steal for me. You'll be arrested. You'll go to jail. You mustn't.

RAINBOW: I must, my darling.

(*There is a silence.* GRETA *puts her face on the pillow and sobs.*)

SCENE 2: STEALING FOR GRETA

(GRETA *is lying in bed.* RAINBOW *sits on the chair.*)

RAINBOW: I got it off his pocket. He came out of the store and put it in his pocket. I grabbed it and ran. He ran after me and grabbed me. He tripped. I yanked my arm off, and I threw him. Look. He tore my sleeve. *(Putting a wristwatch on* GRETA*'s hand)* He ran after me, but I was gone. Went in a building and hid. Saw him pass. Went to the back of the building and got out through the yard. I was afraid to go in the street. I was afraid he may have gone around the block. There's no one there. I walk to the corner and grab a bus. I didn't look like a thief. Would anyone think I'm a thief? Wasn't out of breath. Sat calmly. *(Getting the watch from* GRETA*)* It's a good watch.

GRETA: Get rid of it.

RAINBOW: I'll sell it.

GRETA: To whom?

RAINBOW: I'll find a buyer.

GRETA: I'm afraid.

RAINBOW: Don't be.

GRETA: Just get rid of it.

RAINBOW: We need the money. For you. To make you well.

SCENE 3: RAINBOW IS CAUGHT

(RAINBOW *sits on the chair. She turns her face away from* GRETA. *Her hand covers her cheek.* GRETA *lies on the bed.*)

GRETA: Look at me! Who hurt you like that?

(RAINBOW *turns to face* GRETA.)

GRETA: Who did that to you?

RAINBOW: The man whose watch I took.

GRETA: I knew you'd get hurt. I knew you couldn't do what you were doing and not get hurt.

RAINBOW: I got careless. I went back where I got the watch.

GRETA: Why?

RAINBOW: He grabbed me and he made me go with him.

GRETA: Where?

RAINBOW: To his place.

GRETA: Oh!

RAINBOW: I tried to get away. He forced me. I resisted, and he pushed me in. He said he'd put me in jail.

GRETA: What did he do to you!

RAINBOW: I had to agree.

GRETA: To what?

RAINBOW: To do something for him.

GRETA: What!

RAINBOW: Meet someone.

GRETA: Who!

RAINBOW: He didn't say.

GRETA: What for?

RAINBOW: He's nasty.

GRETA: Are you afraid?

RAINBOW: Yes.

SCENE 4: GRETA WONDERS IF RAINBOW LOVES RAY

(GRETA *lies in bed.* RAINBOW *stands left.*)

RAINBOW: He's like a snake.

GRETA: Do you love him?

RAINBOW: Love him? I hate him. He hates me. He hates me for no reason. Not because of the watch. He never cared about the watch. Just for no reason. He never cared about the watch. That was nothing for him. He hates me. Just because he wants to. I hate him but I have a reason. (*She goes to the chair.*) I understand him, though.

GRETA: You do?

RAINBOW: Yes.

GRETA How can you?

RAINBOW: I think in his heart of hearts he's not the way he appears to be.

GRETA: What is he like? He couldn't be good and do what he does.

RAINBOW: Well, he's not what he appears to be. *(Pause. GRETA is convinced.)*

GRETA: …Could I have some water?

(RAINBOW pours water. She lifts GRETA's head up and holds the glass to GRETA's lips. When GRETA is done, RAINBOW puts the glass down and sits.)

GRETA: Didn't you already do what you had to do for him? Didn't you already — pay for the watch? Why do you still have to work for him?

RAINBOW: He's a friend.

GRETA: If I die…will you love him then?

RAINBOW: …If you die? *(RAINBOW goes to the side of the bed and kneels.)* If you die I'll love you. Whether you live or die it's you I love. And if I ever loved anyone else, it would not be Ray. Not Ray. Never Ray. *(GRETA laughs.)*

SCENE 5: HEUTE SIND KLEIDER ENG

(RAINBOW sweeps the floor.)

GRETA: You never wear clothes that fit.

RAINBOW: This?

GRETA That's a size too small.

RAINBOW: It's my size.

GRETA: Clothes should be looser.

RAINBOW: Not anymore, Madam. Now clothes are tight. How do you say that in German?

GRETA: What.

RAINBOW: What I just said.

GRETA: What.

RAINBOW: Now clothes are tight.

GRETA: Heute sind Kleider eng.

RAINBOW: *(Mispronouncing)* Heute sind Kleider eng.

GRETA: *(Impatiently)* Heute sind Kleider eng.

RAINBOW: How do you say, "You lose your temper too easily?"

GRETA: Who?

RAINBOW: You.

GRETA: I lose my temper?

RAINBOW: Yes.

GRETA: I don't.

RAINBOW: How do you say it?

GRETA: That I lose my temper?

RAINBOW: Yes.

GRETA: I don't lose my temper.

RAINBOW: How do you say it?

GRETA: Ich werde niemals heftig.

RAINBOW: Ich werde niemals heftig…. I love German! *(She swoons to the floor.)* …I love German.

GRETA: That means "I don't lose my temper." *(As exiting:)* Ha!

SCENE 6: RAY GIVES ADVICE TO RAINBOW

(RAINBOW stands right, fluffing the pillow. GRETA sits up against the headboard.)

RAINBOW: Can you imagine? And I said to him, "It's you who places too much importance on whether I like men or I like women. For me it's not important. What's important is that since I met Greta it's only she I love." *(Placing the pillow behind GRETA)* That's what's important. *(Taking the bedspread off the bed)* Why should it be important whether I like men or women? Does it make any difference to anyone? *(Taking the bedspread out the door to shake it)* If it doesn't make any difference to anyone, why should anyone care? *(Turning to GRETA, still holding the bedspread)* He said, "If it doesn't make any difference, why don't you choose to love a man?" And I said, "It doesn't make a difference to anyone else, but, of course it makes a difference to me." *(Placing the cover over GRETA)* If I don't like men, why should I pretend that I do? And why should I try to love someone I don't love when I already love someone I love? And besides, do you think it makes a difference to anyone?

GRETA: I suppose it doesn't make any difference to anyone.

RAINBOW: That's right. Why should I force myself. *(Sitting next to GRETA)* And he said, "What difference does anything make? Live, die, it doesn't make any difference." And I said, "Live or die makes a difference. I want to live and I want to be happy, but I don't care about the things you care about." And he said, "What things?" And I said, *(Walking to the chair)* "The way you see things." And I said that I'm not going to pretend to see life the way he does. And he said, "Why not?" that he thought I should.

And he said that I should care about those things, and if I don't, I should pretend that I do. And I said *(Sitting)*, "Why?" And he said that he talks to me as a brother would, for my own good. And I said I thought he had some nerve, because I thought his life was far from impeccable—far from it. And I told him that.

GRETA: His life is far from impeccable.

RAINBOW: I told him he had some nerve.

GRETA: Your life is impeccable now. I don't see anything wrong with it.

RAINBOW: Neither do I.

GRETA: Your life was peccable when you were working for him. But now that you've paid your debt to him and you don't work for him anymore your life is impeccable. It was he who made your life peccable. *(RAINBOW laughs.)* Why do you laugh?

RAINBOW: How do you say peccable in German?

GRETA: Why?

SCENE 7: GRETA WONDERS HOW RAINBOW SEES THINGS

(GRETA lies in bed. RAINBOW sits by the window, looking out into the yard.)

RAINBOW: With time they look better and better.

GRETA: What, honey?

RAINBOW: The flowers.

GRETA: How could that be?

RAINBOW: Maybe it's the fertilizer I put on the soil.

GRETA: What looks better?

RAINBOW: The colors. They look healthier.

GRETA: How do you see things? Do you see things different from the way I see them?

RAINBOW: Why do you ask?

GRETA: *(Smiling)* I just wondered.

RAINBOW Why?

GRETA: I worried....

RAINBOW: That we see things differently... ?

GRETA: Yes.

RAINBOW: We don't.

SCENE 8:
GRETA DISCOVERS WHAT RAINBOW DOES FOR RAY

(GRETA *is standing on the chair. She is opening an envelope. She takes out some pictures and looks through them with alarm. She throws them on the floor and stares into space.* RAINBOW *enters. She looks at the pictures on the floor. Then she looks at* GRETA.)

GRETA: Is that what you do for him!

(RAINBOW *kneels down to get the pictures.* GRETA *tries to reach for the pictures.*)

GRETA: Why! Why!

(GRETA *starts pounding on* RAINBOW *and tries to hold her down.*)

GRETA: Why! Why are you doing that when I asked you not to! Why do you do that! Why do you do that! Why do you do that! You're lying naked with that man! Who is that man! What is he doing to you! Why do you do that! Why do you take your clothes off! Why do you take such pictures!

RAINBOW: I'm sorry! I'm sorry!

GRETA: Why do you do that!

RAINBOW: I have to.

GRETA: Why!

RAINBOW: Because you must have treatment. (GRETA *cries.*) I don't mind. (GRETA *sobs.*) It's for you.

SCENE 9: GRETA ADMIRES THE SUNLIGHT

(GRETA *sits upstage of the window. The chair faces front.* RAINBOW *stands next to her.*)

GRETA: Could you open the window? (RAINBOW *opens the shutter.*) I like to sit here and see the sun coming in. I like to let it come in through the open window. The sun is brighter that way—or so it seems to me. There are times when I feel disturbed. I feel restless. I feel nasty. And looking at the sun coming in makes me feel calm.

SCENE 10: GRETA THINKS THAT RAY IS IN LOVE

(GRETA *stands left of the bed, straightening it.* RAINBOW *sits on the chair.*)

GRETA: Ray was here this afternoon.

RAINBOW: What did he want?

GRETA: He didn't say. He waited for you and then he left. (*She starts moving down as she smooths the covers.*) Does he sound to you like he's in love?

RAINBOW: No.

GRETA: He sounds to me like he's in love.

RAINBOW: Who with?

GRETA: I don't know, but he sounds to me like he's in love.

RAINBOW: How does a person in love sound?

GRETA: (*Sits on the right side of the bed*)A person in love holds his breath a little after inhaling or while they inhale. They inhale, stop for a moment, and inhale a little more.

RAINBOW: I haven't seen him do that.

GRETA: (*She lies on the bed.*) I have.

RAINBOW: He seems preoccupied to me.

GRETA: Yes, I think he sounds preoccupied. Maybe he's lost money in the market.

RAINBOW: Maybe he has. Why are you concerned about him?

GRETA: I'm not.

RAINBOW: You sound concerned.

GRETA: He's preoccupied.

SCENE 11: RAINBOW DOESN'T FEEL LOVED ANYMORE

(GRETA *lies in bed.* RAINBOW *stands by the door facing her.*)

RAINBOW: Something's wrong. Something's wrong because you're not happy, because you have to keep things from me. I know you don't tell me what you think—not everything. Did you ever keep things from me before? Is this something new, or have you always kept things from me? (*Pause*) Is it that you don't love me anymore?

GRETA: *(Shaking her head)* No.

RAINBOW: For me to love is adoring. And to be loved is to be adored. So I never felt I was loved before. Till I met you. But I don't feel loved anymore.

SCENE 12:
RAY WANTS SOMETHING FROM GRETA

(GRETA lies in bed. RAY stands to the left of the bed by her feet, facing her.)

GRETA: I lash out at you because I can't deal with you. I can't even understand what you are.

(RAY moves closer to her and starts to lean toward her. She recoils.)

GRETA: You're like some kind of animal who comes to me with strange problems, to make strange demands on me. *(She pushes him off. He persists.)* You come in all sweaty and hungry, and you say you want this and you want that. Take your hands away from me! Not again! Not again! Never again! Don't touch me! Leave me be! I have nothing to give you. Don't tell me that you want these things. Talk about something else. What else can you talk about?

(RAINBOW enters. She is obviously alarmed. She looks at GRETA, then at RAY, then at GRETA again. GRETA turns her head away and sobs. RAINBOW and RAY look at each other.)

SCENE 13: RAINBOW LEAVES GRETA

(RAINBOW stands at the door looking out. GRETA sits on the bed looking at her. "Melancholy Baby" is heard.)

Come to me, my melancholy baby.
Just cuddle up and don't be blue.
All your fears are foolish fancy, baby.
You know, honey, I'm in love with you.

(GRETA moves to the chair. She sits facing RAINBOW. She looks down.)

Every cloud must have a silver lining.

(GRETA looks at RAINBOW.)

So wait until the sun shines through.
Smile, my honey, dear,
While I kiss away each tear.
Or else I shall be melancholy too.

(GRETA *reaches out and takes* RAINBOW'*s hand.* RAINBOW *allows her to hold her hand, but does not respond.*)

Come sweetheart mine.
Don't sit and pine.
Tell me all the cares
That made you feel so blue.
I'm sorry, hon.

(RAINBOW *faces* GRETA.)

What have I done.
Have I ever said
An unkind word to you.
My love is true.

(RAINBOW *leans over and puts her head next to* GRETA'*s.*)

And just for you.
I'll do almost anything
At any time.
Hear when you sigh
Or when you cry.
Something seems to grieve
This very heart of mine.

Come to me my melancholy baby.
Just cuddle up and don't be blue.

(RAINBOW *walks to the door slowly and exits while the song plays to the end.* GRETA *lowers her head. Then she turns to the right. After a while she looks up. As the song is ending, she looks down again.*)

SCENE 14:
GRETA READS RAINBOW'S LETTER

(GRETA *is sitting on the chair, opening a book. She takes an envelope from it. She opens the envelope, takes out a letter, and reads.*)

GRETA: My beloved, I'm sometimes obliged to do things that are dangerous, and to do things that I hate. To befriend people and then betray them. Someday I may be hurt. If this happens and I'm not able to tell you this, I hope one day you'll open this book and find this note. I love you more than anything in the world, and it is to you that I owe my happiness. I always felt that I didn't want to love only halfway, that I wanted to love with all my heart or not at all, and that I wanted to be loved the same way or not at all. With you, I had this, and if anything happens to me, I wanted you to remember this: That you are my angel and I will always love you. Even after death. Forever yours, Rainbow.

END OF PLAY

STEPPING OFF A CLOUD

Christina Cocek

STEPPING OFF A CLOUD
© copyright 1995 by Christina Cocek

A native of Houston, Texas Christina Cocek is a screenwriter, playwright, and actress who now lives in Los Angeles.

CHARACTER

MARSHA LYMAN

(A therapist's office. MARSHA, a client, stands alone next to an expensive, comfortable-looking chair. She wears a stylish, tailored suit and speaks directly out front.)

MARSHA: If I have to listen to one more person in one more support group sitting in one more insipidly low-lit, plaid-couched, hideous, styrofoam-cup-cluttered conference room whine about their dysfunctional past, I swear I'm going to piss fruit punch.

In the last three years, I've attended "Codependents-R-Us" meetings, "Fear of Intimacy" meetings, "Fear of Commitment" meetings, "Fear of Fear" meetings, twelve-step this, twelve-step that, twelve-steps forward, twelve-steps backwards, twelve-step any frigging direction you want to go in. And I am proclaiming right here before God, you, and my Anne Klein suit that I have reached my limit. I have reached my absolute pinnacle. My checkered flag. My coop de grass. Which means, in short, I cannot take it anymore.

A woman from my group actually called me the other night at two-thirty in the morning to tell me she was scared of the moths in her piano. Apparently there were these moths flying around in her piano. Don't ask. Anyway, she said she had this debilitating fear of moths in pianos that had something to do with her childhood in Marin County. Because of this, she told me she wanted to commit suicide. Commit suicide? Because of moths in her piano? And I mean, I want to be supportive, I want to reach my hand out to these people. But, I simply can't deal with it anymore. My ears physically cannot listen to another story. I want to stand up in the middle of one of those rooms and say quite frankly, quite succinctly, "Just get over it, honey. We've all got baggage. It's just that some of us choose to leave it in a locker at the bus station!" *(Beat)*

But, I don't mean to judge. Really I don't. I know what it's like. You know I know what it's like. I know what it's like to feel fragile and hopeless. To feel little. Really little. To feel like there's some big party going on next door and you weren't invited. And to be scared that if you were invited, you would, without a doubt, be attracted to the one guy in the room with the lampshade on his head. And to be talking on the phone and to hear yourself saying, "Just one more minute. Could we talk just one more minute, please?" Because you know that when you hang up there's going to be that silence and you're going to have to face the fact, once again, that you're not at all what you thought you were. And, worse yet, you just might never be.

(She's sitting in the chair now, holding tightly to its arms.)

My God. This is the most comfortable chair that ever was. Why is that? It's like gravity with cushions. Like liquid. Like it's just wrapping you in its arms and saying "Stay here. Stay here."

(She stays there, closing her eyes and lingering a moment. Then, suddenly, she pops out of the chair.)

But, even so, I think there comes a time when we've got to move on. We've just got to. We can sit around and talk about the assholes for just so long. There comes a point when you've just got to accept that this is what's on the end of your fork. This is it. Sorry, chump, but these are the materials you've been issued. Are you gonna sit there or are you gonna make a move? Maybe it does really come down to having the courage to not complain. Maybe my mother is right. God, what a frightening thought. And you know I don't mean that we should deny or stuff down our feelings like garbage we want to hide from the neighbors. That's not it at all. I know we have to look inside ourselves. We have to go inside. It's what makes us real people. It's what makes us human human beings. All I'm saying is that once you've seen the stuff, once you've viewed this merchandise in the display case of your past, I think you've got to have the guts to get on with it. To incorporate the information and move forward.

And it's difficult. Geez Louise, I know it's difficult. It's like stepping off a cloud with no parachute. But, I think it can be done. I know it can be done. Because I'm doing it. Whether you or anybody else thinks it's a good idea or not. Because I get these glimpses sometimes, these wonderful little hints of something beyond this. Like a peek over the edge. And, I mean, I don't get them very often, but I get them enough to know that there is something in here *(Touches heart)* besides all this struggling. Besides all this ache.

And it's scary to say it, but I think that what I'm seeing is greatness. I do. I mean, maybe not Leonardo da Vinci greatness but some kind of exceptional-ness, if that's such a word. Because we all have something that's great about us. Don't we? A flicker of light, a slight turn of the soul that makes us a little bit different from that person next to us. That makes us able to give something to the world. Something that others'll hold dear. And it's only when we're brave enough to see what that is that we can finally make that beautiful glide upward into a place of, I don't know, clarity. No. Grace. That's what it is. A state of grace. With no handrails, no excuses, no complaints. Just this tiny glimmer of faith.

(She sits in the chair again.)

It's like in that movie *2001*. At the end, when that astronaut is outside the spaceship and his cord breaks. Or maybe somebody cut it, I don't remember. Anyway, I remember that he just kinda floated backwards, away from the spaceship. And all you could hear inside his helmet, real loud, was the sound of his own breathing.

(She takes in a couple of slow, deliberate breaths as if she were that astronaut.)

And he just kept getting farther and farther away.

(She takes in another slow breath, then closes her eyes and holds tight to the arms of the chair.)

Just one more minute.

(After a moment, she opens her eyes and releases her grip on the chair. She calmly stands and takes a check from the pocket of her jacket.)

Anyway, I guess what I'm saying, Dr. Rosenthal, is I'd like you to accept my final check. Because, no matter what anyone says, I'm going to take that step off that cloud now. I think it's time I heard my own breathing.

(The light on the chair slowly fades, leaving MARSHA *alone in a pool of light. Then, after a moment, her light fades to black as well.)*

THE END

TRIPS

Sally Ordway

TRIPS

For all rights please contact Broadway Play Publishing Inc

Please see page 332 for a bio of Sally Ordway.

TRIPS was first produced in the Yale Showcase '89 (Yale Alumni Playwrights) in New York, New York.

MILLIE . . . . Georgia Boughton
PAT . . . . Joan Pape

CHARACTERS

MILLIE
PAT

(MILLIE and PAT, *two women in their seventies, are rocking on the enclosed porch of a retirement apartment complex. They are both holding notebooks and pencils and watching the road in front of them.*)

MILLIE: Well, I got a blue one on my side.

PAT: You sure did. Not much traffic on a Sunday afternoon. Looks like it's going to be a dull game.

MILLIE: *(Marking in her notebook)* One blue.

PAT: Oh, there goes a red one on my side.

MILLIE: *(Looking up)* I didn't see it.

PAT: You were too busy marking down your blue one. Anyway it was there. *(Marking it down)* One red Chevvie.

MILLIE: The make doesn't count, just the color. You know that.

PAT: I know that. I just like details.

MILLIE: You're a Virgo.

PAT: Millie, you always say I'm a Virgo to everything.

MILLIE: Well, you always act like a Virgo in everything.

PAT: I don't believe all that horoscope stuff.

MILLIE: I do. I read mine everyday.

PAT: I know you do. I watch you doing it.

MILLIE: Well then you'll know Pat that today it said I'd be doing some travelling soon.

PAT: Some chance.

MILLIE: Oh, I don't know. It could happen.

PAT: All the way to the super market or the dining room. Nobody goes anywhere interesting here. Just a lot of sit down old folks in a retirement home.

MILLIE: *(Looking out at the road)* I wonder where they were going?

PAT: Who?

MILLIE: The red car and the blue car.

PAT: In opposite directions.

MILLIE: No. I mean their final destinations. Maybe they were off on trips.

PAT: Not likely.

MILLIE: Why not? One could have been going to Nashville to hear the Ol' Opry and the other going to Memphis to lay flowers on Elvis's grave.

PAT: Nashville and Memphis. That's the same direction. The blue car and the red car were going in opposite directions.

MILLIE: Well, then they could have been going to two other towns. I don't know.

PAT: They were probably going nowhere, just a simple Sunday drive.

MILLIE: Hank and me used to take all kinds of car trips with the kids when they were growing up.

PAT: You told me.

MILLIE: Oh, there's a green one on my side. *(Marking it down)* One green one.

PAT: You're having all the luck.

MILLIE: *(Musing)* We used to play cow poker.

PAT: Cow poker?

MILLIE: On the car trips. You know cow poker. The game where you count the cows on your side of the car.

PAT: Oh yeah and a graveyard on your side wipes out all the cows you counted.

MILLIE: That's the game. Did you ever play it?

PAT: Yes I guess I did.

MILLIE: It passed the time and kept the kids busy. Car trips are real hard on kids.

PAT: They're hard on everybody.

MILLIE: Not on me. I loved going places in the car. We used to go all over. The beach, the mountains....

PAT: When I was in the WACS I did a bit of travelling but mostly on trains and planes. It was an exciting time.... All those bases... The war...

MILLIE: The war... We couldn't go on car trips much then with the gas rationing. I didn't like the war years.

PAT: I did since I spent the rest of my life being a social worker and taking care of Mama 'til she passed on. A spinster's life. Taking care.

MILLIE: Oh I see a black one. *(Marking it down)*

PAT: You really are having all the luck today.

MILLIE: Just nobody's going your way today. And then Sunday's such a slow day. Did you have lunch in the dining room?

PAT: Yes. I had to sit with Mrs Hansford. She keeps saying her husband's dead.

MILLIE: She's touched. He's just over there in the nursing home alive as can be.

PAT: 'Course he doesn't know much....

MILLIE: But at least he is alive. She shouldn't say he's dead. She'd know if he really was dead...like my Hank.... She should stop saying he's dead.

PAT: She should. She just wants people to feel sorry for her.

MILLIE: Well, that's not the way to do it. What did you have to eat?

PAT: Tough turkey and mushy dressing.

MILLIE: They always have that for Sunday lunch. That's why I never go. Besides I still like to cook.

PAT: I don't. Those apartment kitchens are too little.

MILLIE: You never did like to cook. You told me that. You fed your Mama out of cans.

PAT: Did I tell you that?

MILLIE: You certainly did. Oh there's another blue one. *(Marking it down with excitement)* I've got two blue ones.

PAT: You've had all the luck today.

MILLIE: See, maybe I will get to travel. Maybe the kids will invite me out to Oregon or to California to see them. I wish they didn't live so far away.

PAT: They never come down here to see you. What makes you think they'll invite you out there to see them?

MILLIE: I don't know. I was just thinking about my horoscope.

PAT: That silly thing.

MILLIE: *(Excited)* Oh, oh, oh. There goes another blue one. *(Marking it down)* That make three blue ones. Look, the blue car, it's stopping right in front of us, Pat. I'm going out and talk to the people in it.

PAT: You're what?

MILLIE: You heard me. I'm gonna ask them where they're going. I'm gonna ask them to let me ride with them.

PAT: You wouldn't.

MILLIE: Oh yes I am I'm going right out there. *(Closing her notebook)* Here's my notebook. I won the game. (MILLIE *walks out into the audience, which is the street.)*

PAT: *(Getting up)* Millie! You're crazy.

MILLIE: *(Yelling back)* I know, but I'm going places.

CURTAIN

WATCHING THE DOG

Sybille Pearson

WATCHING THE DOG
© copyright 1995 by Sybille Pearson

The live stage production rights to this play are represented by Broadway Play Publishing Inc. For all other rights please contact the Joyce Ketay Agency, 1501 Broadway, #1910, N Y N Y 10036, 212 354-6825.

Sybille Pearson is the author of PHANTASIE (published by Broadway Play Publishing Inc), SALLY AND MARSHA, UNFINISHED STORIES, and the librettist of the musical BABY, for which she received a Tony nomination. She is a recipient of a Rockefeller Playwrights fellowship and has been a participant at the O'Neill Playwrights Conference, the Sundance Playwrights Conference, and has been a playwright-in-residence at Virginia Tech. She is a teacher of musical theater at the Tisch School of the Arts at N Y U, and a member of the Dramatists Guild.

CHARACTERS

GERRI: *A fifty-year-old woman*
ARLENE: *A fifty-year-old woman*
BURT: *A fifty-year-old man*
SUSAN: *A thirty-year-old woman*
CINDY: *A female terrier played by a woman in her thirties*
CHARLES: *A male Doberman played by a man in his twenties*
RECEPTIONIST: *An offstage woman's voice*

TIME

The present, a cold morning in February

SETTING

A veterinarian's office waiting room in New York City. The furnishings consist of two mismatching plastic armchairs, one wooden bench, and a low coffee table. Posters of "Happy Families with Happy Dogs" decorate the walls. A guppy-filled fish tank stands to the side. The exit stage right is to the RECEPTIONIST's desk and the examining rooms. The exit stage left is to the street.

(Three women and a dog are in the waiting room. GERRI, aged fifty, soft spoken and distracted, sits on the bench; a new cat carrier case is beside her. A Siamese meow is occasionally heard from inside the case. GERRI is a well-dressed, reasonably sane woman who is in the midst of a life crisis which she, herself, finds slightly ridiculous. ARLENE, aged fifty, with an intense abrupt manner, sits in a chair. Her cat is in a well-used carrier case on the floor by her feet. ARLENE is dressed hastily in a silk blouse and sweatpants. She, too, is a reasonably sane woman caught in the midst of a life crisis which angers her and which she releases through anger. SUSAN, a thirty-year-old woman not in crisis, sits in the other chair. Her dog, CINDY, a terrier, sits well-behaved by her feet and eyes ARLENE.)

(ARLENE gets up and goes to the fish tank. CINDY goes to ARLENE's chair, jumps up on it, and sits.)

SUSAN: *(With pride)* She always sits in that chair.

(ARLENE addresses CINDY.)

ARLENE: Excuse me.

SUSAN: *(Calling dog)* Cindy. *(CINDY obeys quickly, returning to position by SUSAN.)* She doesn't mind the cold but she hates February. Fine about taking pills. I think she's a hypochondriac, but there isn't much for a city dog to do in February.

ARLENE: I don't like dogs. *(A beat of silence. ARLENE remains standing.)*

(GERRI systematically takes off her cardigan sweater, then her pullover sweater, till she is down to a cotton open-necked shirt. She takes a Baggie filled with tissue out of her purse and blots her neck and chest. She is going through a menopausal hot flash. The flash lasts for twenty counts which she counts, either aloud or by tapping her foot.)

GERRI: *(Removing sweaters)* One. Two. Three. *(She is aware of the other women watching her.)* It's a flash. Like labor pains. Not the feeling. Of course, not the feeling, but the same wavelike timing. Fifteen, sixteen, seventeen. *(She taps her foot for two more counts.)* *(She speaks to dog.)* All gone. Have to wait till you're my age. *(She hums for a beat, then speaks to herself.)* It's all ridiculous.

RECEPTIONIST: *(Offstage)* Miss Haynes, Dr Cornfield will see Cindy now.

(CINDY exits.)

(SUSAN slowly gathers her belongings.)

SUSAN: She likes her own moment with him first. She doesn't have much of a life of her own. *(She exits.)*

ARLENE: Age is a generality. The specific is death.

GERRI: Pardon?

ARLENE: *(As an apology)* Forget I'm here. *(She walks to fish tank.)* What kind of a person has fish for a pet?

GERRI: Oh yes.

(After a beat, ARLENE turns to GERRI.)

ARLENE: *(Pointing at GERRI's carrier)* Sick?

GERRI: She's going to be altered.

ARLENE: Males get altered. Females get spayed.

GERRI: Oh yes. *(She speaks to her cat in carrier in an effort to end the conversation with ARLENE.)* Yes, yes, yes.

ARLENE: There's enough to feel guilty about. You don't feel guilty about a cat! *(She walks back to fish tank.)* You don't buy a fish if you need warmth in your life, unless I don't know something which could easily be. *(She sits on a chair.)* Cornfield always runs late. You think he's a good doctor? Of course, you think he's a good doctor or you wouldn't be here. What I need is two Saturday seminars in small talk. Please excuse me.

GERRI: Please excuse me. I'm not able really to have a conversation anymore since I've started to hear myself while I'm talking. *(She hums for a beat.)* When I hum, it clears. It goes. It's absurd.

ARLENE: You have an echo?

GERRI: No, I hear what I say. It's hard to explain. Excuse me for seeming rude. *(There is a silent beat. GERRI's cat meows. She speaks to cat, putting her finger through an air hole for cat to smell.)* We're all here. *(To ARLENE, referring to her cat)* Yours likes his carrier.

ARLENE: He hates it.

GERRI: I just meant he's lying so still.

ARLENE: *(With intensity)* He hates it.

GERRI: Oh yes.

ARLENE: They're inventing the equivalent of C Ds for video tapes...obsoleting V C Rs. Who...who decides which movies get put on C D and which ones get put to sleep? Why sweat it, right?... You're ahead of me?

GERRI: *(Confused)* In which way?

ARLENE: Your appointment is before mine?

GERRI: Oh yes. You were here before me.

ARLENE: The hypochondriac was ahead of me.... Do you think he has more dog patients than cats?

GERRI: It's my first time. A friend with a dog, though, recommended the place. *(She hums softly.)*

ARLENE: I'm always here when a dog's here. Last week I waited an hour with a Doberman looking to eat my foot. Talk about extensions. *(She indicates a penile extension.)* Why can't men admit why they have Dobermans? *(Her attention is caught offstage left.)* Of course, it's a Doberman. Of course, I believe it. What is there not to believe in this week?

(BURT, a fifty-year-old man, a gentle soul who habitually takes a split second to edit his thoughts before he speaks, enters. He is led by his Doberman, CHARLES, who walks BURT through the waiting room to the RECEPTIONIST's area.)

BURT: Charles. *(CHARLES doesn't heed. BURT shortens the leash so that, at least, he can walk next to his dog.)*

(GERRI looks at BURT with surprise. BURT nods his head to her in silent greeting as he is pulled into reception area.)

BURT: *(Offstage)* I don't have an appointment.

RECEPTIONIST: *(Offstage)* One minute, Mr Somers.

(ARLENE sits on bench next to GERRI.)

ARLENE: He came 'cause I came.

GERRI: You know him?

ARLENE: Not the man. The dog.

GERRI: How do you know his dog?

ARLENE: I don't know either of them. I meant it was guaranteed a Doberman would be in my life this week which is the week my company, which I've worked for for seventeen years, relocated to Minnesota, which is the week the man I lived with for almost as long relocated out of the apartment, which is the same week... *(She points to her cat, but can't finish the thought.)* which is the same week I'm in the same room with a Doberman again. *(She speaks simply and truthfully.)* I'm very afraid of Dobermans. Can I sit here next to you?

GERRI: Please.

(BURT enters without dog. He talks generally to the room, referring to his dog and the RECEPTIONIST.)

BURT: *(Lighting cigarette)* He went with her. He likes her. He likes squirrels. He likes birds. *(He refers to cigarette.)* This bother anybody?

ARLENE: Yes.

(BURT *puts cigarette out in ashtray.*)

(*A beat of silence*)

GERRI: *(With emotion)* Did you have an appointment today?

BURT: *(With emotion)* And now I need an appointment?!

ARLENE: Dobermans don't need appointments?

(BURT, *so involved with* GERRI, *did not hear* ARLENE *clearly.*)

BURT: *(Turning to* ARLENE*)* Excuse me, were you asking me something?

ARLENE: Dobermans don't need appointments?!

BURT: *(Explaining)* Not for teeth cleaning.

ARLENE: Because they're lethal weapons? Because they have to be ever ready? Because they kill people ahead of them on line?

BURT: Does your cat need its teeth cleaned?

ARLENE: *(With pride)* My cats have never had their teeth cleaned.

BURT: Then you might not know that you don't need an appointment. If Alan's free, he'll take you.

ARLENE: I call him Dr Cornfield and I have an appointment.

BURT: Alan. The animal dentist in the basement.

(ARLENE *goes to fish tank.*)

(BURT *and* GERRI *mouth the next lines.*)

GERRI: *(Putting sweaters on)* You shouldn't have come.

BURT: Of course, I should have come.

(BURT *speaks out loud to* ARLENE.*)

BURT: I would be grateful.... Miss.... (ARLENE *is not paying attention.* ARLENE *turns.*) Would you mind if I took two puffs?

ARLENE: I don't need this power. I don't want this power. *(She turns back to fish tank.)*

RECEPTIONIST: *(Offstage)* Miss Sax, please.

(ARLENE *hears* RECEPTIONIST *call her name and intentionally ignores it. She walks to fish tank.*)

ARLENE: I've never seen a fish show emotion. Fear, yes. But I'd define fear as more an activity than an emotion. *(She turns to* GERRI *and* BURT.*)* What if all that was going to be left in the world was fish? I don't know how to relate to one.

GERRI: I think it's your turn.

ARLENE: What if we were all meant to end up back in the primordial sea and that one.... *(She points to fish in tank.)* had a message for me. Had the answer. The explanation. I would never get it! So why sweat, right?

RECEPTIONIST: *(Offstage)* Miss Sax, Dr Cornfield will see you and Alex now. *(After a beat, ARLENE picks up her carrier and exits stage right.)*

BURT: *(Loudly)* Of course, I should have come. There's no reason I shouldn't come—

(GERRI signals him to speak softer.)

GERRI: *(Pointing to RECEPTIONIST)* Burt.

BURT: Why?

GERRI: She can see us.

(BURT's speech pattern is to take a very slight hesitation before each thought as he finds the precise phrase he wishes.)

BURT: No one cares about affairs that are over! *(He takes a letter out of his pocket and lowers his voice a bit.)* I don't accept your letter. I don't take it seriously. *(He puts letter in GERRI's hand.)* I don't take it.

GERRI: It's simply impossible for me to be connected to anyone, because I'm not anyone I know right now.

BURT: That's completely ridiculous.

GERRI: *More* than that. It's an absurd situation.

BURT: What has changed? What has changed since Wednesday?

GERRI: It's not the flashes. They disorient, but they're the only thing left I can control.

BURT: You have flashes? Hot flashes?

GERRI: They are predictable and controllable. But the rest of my life? I have completely lost my sense of balance.

BURT: That could be an inner ear....

GERRI: It's not physical. It's symbolic. The balancing of my life. I can't do it. I was always able to balance you, Joe, my work, the children....

BURT: What did I say? Did I say something on Wednesday?

GERRI: No.

BURT: I upset you?

GERRI: I'll die if you think it's you.

BURT: What children? Your children are at college. You don't need to balance your children.

GERRI: They were there for balance, giving balance.

BURT: Is it someone else?

GERRI: Never. It's no one but me. While the world is in crisis, I'm hearing myself! It has to stop. *(She hums.)*

BURT: We've twenty-five years of knowing each other. A quarter of a century. Half our life if we died tomorrow. We are a life. So if it's nothing I said and nothing to do with us then there's nothing to change because nothing has changed.

(GERRI *undergoes a flash. She removes sweaters and counts to nineteen by counting aloud and tapping her foot.)*

GERRI: ...four, five....

BURT: You're hot? You're in a flash?

GERRI: It'll be over....Ten. Eleven.....

BURT: I feel helpless, useless....

GERRI: I have only two per hour. This is the second one. It's controllable.

BURT: *(Relieved)* For Christ sake, Gerri. That's what it is. A physical time of change. So it's a change of life. But it's not a change of life....

GERRI: ...Nineteen.

BURT: Our life. It's not a change of our life.

GERRI: It's not that simple. That sane. It didn't start with the flashes. It didn't start last week. It started when I realized that I was going to turn fifty....

BURT: I'm fifty. You're fifty. Paul Newman is over fifty. Jane Fonda is....

GERRI: And some people are humiliated and embarrassed that they haven't the strength, the grace, the dignity to turn fifty well. That they've flunked turning fifty and I've flunked. I've flunked basely, in the most vulgar and common ordinary way, and I won't accept that. I intend to return to being a woman in balance, and the only way to do that is to step out of my life, step out of the T V movie that my life has become.

BURT: What movie? Symbolic? What?

GERRI: It's as though I'm sitting over there. As though I'm watching my life as a movie. As though I am the movie. But it isn't as though my life were a foreign movie I'd want to see. It's a T V movie of the week, starring me, playing the part of a woman obsessed with aging in a surfer's world. But I live in New York where the young boys I see are not wearing flowered bathing suits but long coats in summer with pockets for selling crack. But I don't see them. I only see myself. I'm deeply aware that having a breakdown over turning fifty is vacuous and vain, but I can't get out of this mivie. I can't stop sticking my head into baby carriages wishing my house were full of babies again, knowing if my wish came true I would probably kill myself. When I look in the mirror, I see a crone, a barren, unneeded, without use woman. And what do I do? I go out and buy a healthy, perky, looking-forward-to-life, fertile girl-cat, child substitute, and the first thing I do is bring her here and have her made barren! I understand nothing about my life.

BURT: The doctor, the therapist...the one you saw....

GERRI: I'm seeing her. She still sleeps through my sessions which I find rejecting and difficult, but reassuring, because whatever I'm going through couldn't be that serious otherwise she wouldn't be sleeping through it. But the worst is that I've started hearing myself, which I am in fact doing right now. And the way to stop it is, of course, to not talk, which I can do at home by turning on the news. Since there's a news show on from five in the afternoon till eleven-thirty at night, no one thinks it's odd if you're watching the news. In fact, Joe thinks I've finally connected to the world now that the children are grown. He's happy not to talk with three tuitions on his mind, our rent constantly going up. We spend most of our time now watching the news. It feels like we're more together than we've ever been. On the couch together, sometimes sharing a bowl of strawberries, nodding to each other, shaking our heads over what we're seeing and passing the strawberries, while I know I'm going crazy in a benign sort of way. The balance is gone.

RECEPTIONIST: (Offstage) Mrs Stapleton, please.

(GERRI stands.)

BURT: I'll wait.

GERRI: No. Please don't.

(GERRI picks up the cat carrier and exits stage right as ARLENE enters without a cat carrier. She is close to tears but fights them by pacing.)

ARLENE: You have to know when to let go. Have to say, "That's it. No more. You're gone. Goodbye. It's over."

BURT: (To himself) No.

ARLENE: If we lived in the country, the cat would go down to the basement or take himself to the cave where old cats who've lived a good life...he's over eighteen...go to die. He wouldn't ever go to a doctor and pay another hundred dollars to be pumped up with fluids so he could live for another week so he can piss the fluid out on the rug and then come back to decide if he should die or not!

BURT: Your cat's dying?

ARLENE: *(Rejecting thought)* He eats. It's only when he's not eating that he looks dead. Every morning I put the can opener by his face to see if he's alive. He eats. He's stopped relating to people, to his environment. He's skin and bones, dehydrated, his fur sticks out like he's been plugged into an electric socket, he throws up his food, but he eats. He's ravenous. *(She demonstrates the cat eating, snorting while "inhaling" his food.)* He inhales because he has no working teeth. Then... *(She demonstrates how the cat jerks his head to the plate.)* Like one of those plastic birds next to a dish of water. But then... *(She leans over with her arms spread out as though she were a dead cat.)* back to looking dead. I wouldn't be here making this decision if he kept his eyes open. He'd make it. He's a vain cat. If he saw what he looked like, he'd overdose. But his eyes are always closed. I can't tell what he's thinking and I always knew. I know I'm talking about a cat, but I've told him more than I've told anybody else. And sure he spent most of the day washing and posing and sleeping, but when I felt a bleakness, not knowing what goddamn way I fit in the world, the cat knew. He'd get right in position, right into the curve here. *(She points to the back of her knees.)* And we'd both sleep until it passed. I've got to ask myself: Alright, Arlene, what are your motives? You brought him here. He didn't hop in his box and say take me here and decide my life... I'm not without agendas. When he pisses on the living room rug—which is the only place he wants—to get to it he has to totter through half the apartment bypassing four strategically placed litter boxes, and, since there is no door to the living room, a milk crate. I say a living thing has more value than a rug. But I want to kill him. Instead, I take a scissor and cut out the places he's hit,because a cat's urine knows when a cat is dying and transfers into a spot of immortality. How can I put down a new rug until the cat is dead? Who in his right mind would give a person in my situation a new rug as a present, then take it as a personal affront that she won't lay it down and moves out after twelve years of a life together? After twelve years, I'm sure Frank had other reasons but I don't find it valuable to sit down with people who leave and ask them why. I don't find rejection a learning experience. Maybe I am romanticizing the past. But it's harder. Harder when people leave you now.... Maybe not for men, but I feel it like a death now, on my way to that next level where living alone is the norm, joining the widows travelling alone, pulling their suitcases with leashes, their hair neat, not raging like harpies. Even though the ordinary act of going to the mailbox is a reminder of death. I saw it with my mother... the little pause before she put the key in the mailbox, wondering if there'd be a letter saying the next one of her friends had died. We're the only species that anticipates death. I'd yell at my mother: "You come to New York to visit me. The first thing you do every morning is open the *Times* and read the obituaries of people who died who you don't even know." And what do I do? The moment I turned fifty I started to look for the obituaries. I don't run into them while reading the *Times*. I look for them. I'd never even opened the D section before. It would go freshly pressed under the litter box. *(She walks to receptionist area.)* I'll give her a check. Tell Cornfield to do it and get the hell out of here. *(She stops. She allows herself to cry. A silent beat.)* My parents... My father's been dead for twenty years. My mother, five. And that asshole, that pissing puking sick dying cat... His going makes me feel an orphan. Like all the other deaths are finally true. *(She sits on bench next to* BURT.*)* Cornfield's not going to hold him, is he?

BURT: Hold him?

ARLENE: Cornfield's not going to hold him while he gives him the shot. Frank held the cats when they got the shot. Our relationship had death built into it. He moved in with me, a mature woman with four mature cats and a mature cat is a cat on its way out. Frank didn't give a shit about cats. They were there or they were not there. But he held them when it was time to die. He believed if you give them their death, you owe it to the cats to be there with them. I, the great cat lover, would say goodbye to them and go walk in the park. I'm talking crazy at you and I don't even know you. Would you do it?

BURT: *(Without hesitation)* I'll hold him for you.

ARLENE: I didn't mean that. I'm sorry....

BURT: I'm sorry...

ARLENE: I'm sorry. I meant have him put to....

BURT: Please forgive me.

ARLENE: Forgive me.

BURT: I misunderstood.

(After a beat)

ARLENE: I'm so moved.

BURT: I didn't... *(He stops himself.)*

(There is a moment of silence in which they are aware that something important has happened for each one. When they continue to speak, they are more aware of the emotion they feel than the logic of their words. BURT *and* ARLENE *refer to the posters of "Happy Dogs and Their Families" on the walls.)*

BURT: It's like saying without a dog you can't have a happy marriage.

ARLENE: Without a dog you have troubled children.

BURT: Or being around a happy marriage makes a dog happy.

ARLENE: Do you feel that to be true?

BURT: Or *only* dogs in happy marriages can be happy.

ARLENE: Your dog's married?

BURT: Married?

ARLENE: I meant....

BURT: I'm not married. Neither is my dog.

ARLENE: Is he happy? That's a very personal question. So you're not married but you have a dog.

BURT: Is he an unhappy dog because I'm not married?

ARLENE: Is he unhappy?

BURT: He likes the doorman. The man at the newstand.

ARLENE: Meaning he doesn't like you?

BURT: I don't have an answer.

ARLENE: Please, you don't have to answer.

BURT: I want to answer. It's...you can't buy company. Company comes. It's not the dog's fault that he doesn't acknowledge me. He watches television with me but when I turn the set off, he leaves the room. Who he likes is the high school girl who walks him during the day.

ARLENE: How does he show he likes her?

BURT: She says "Your dog likes me."

ARLENE: How does he show he likes the doorman?

BURT: He bounces. He bounces when he walks to him. *(After a beat)* I don't want this to pass. I want you to know that when I said I'd hold your cat I meant it.

ARLENE: I know. *(After a beat)* I *can* hold him if I knew I could be with someone afterward.

BURT: You'll be with me.

ARLENE: I don't like being coy.

BURT: I'm not used to being like this.

ARLENE: I want to say, I'd like to be with you afterwards.

BURT: I would like that too.

ARLENE: I never expected— In this goddamn week, I never expected you. *(She exits quickly stage right.)*

RECEPTIONIST: *(Offstage)* You can't walk in.

ARLENE: *(Offstage)* If I don't go in now I'm never going in.

RECEPTIONIST: *(Offstage, calling after ARLENE)* The Doctor's with....

ARLENE: *(Offstage)* My cat's in there and I'm in there!

(Door slam.)

RECEPTIONIST: *(Offstage)* Dr Cornfield. Miss Sax is in Room B.

(BURT *calls to* RECEPTIONIST.)

BURT: Excuse me.

RECEPTIONIST: *(Offstage, losing her cool)* What!?

BURT: Could you call down and see if Alan is finished with Charles. Thank you.

(BURT *whistles* "Fools Rush In.")

(After a beat, GERRI *enters with an empty cat carrier.)*

BURT: *(With excitement)* I said I would hold her cat while it died.

GERRI: You what?

BURT: I did it without thinking.

GERRI: You killed a cat?

BURT: I told her I would hold it while it died.

GERRI: Why would you want to hold a cat while it died?

BURT: It was unexpected. An act for her. Said with no hesitation. A moment unplanned.

(The actress playing GERRI *goes totally blank. Instead of panicking, she stands still. After an appropriate amount of time passes,* BURT *feeds her her line.)*

BURT: And I know you want to know who she is?

GERRI: Yes.

BURT: I don't know. I'm going out with a complete stranger!

(Another pause. GERRI *can't find her line.)*

GERRI: *(To* BURT, *as the actress)* Sorry, Dick.

BURT: That's right. The woman who couldn't talk to fish. *(He continues with his own lines.)* Gerri, I've never done anything until I understood my actions. Never acted without analyzing, without visualizing the pros, the cons. And just now, without a pause, I said "Yes." And when I first saw her I even thought she was odd.

GERRI: *(Softly, as the actress)* I'm afraid I can't finish.

(BURT *walks to fish tank.)*

BURT: *(Covering)* Hello, fish! *(Pulling himself together)* Yes, I know you thought she was odd too. But God, Gerri, it's been so long that I don't even know when I didn't have that pause— that hesitation before speaking, that hesitation in which a thousand possibilities can disappear....

(GERRI *speaks to* BURT, *as the actress, exploding with emotion. Once she starts, she is on a roll and can not stop. As she continues speaking, her own Southern inflections emerge.*)

(*During her monologue,* SUSAN, *the actress who doubles as a stage manager, takes command and runs across the stage while pulling an uncomfortable and startled* BURT *offstage. We can see but not hear the whispered conference between* CINDY, ARLENE, SUSAN, *and* BURT *through an opening in the wings. The dog,* CHARLES, *a young actor fascinated by the experience, stands at the other side of the wings, listening to* GERRI.)

GERRI: *(Explosive, to* BURT:*)* I can't get that damn dog out of my head. *(To audience)* I'm sorry. I'm truly sorry but I'm standing here thinking only about a damn dog. No. This is not part of the play. This is a real dog, a lost dog. That *I* saw, not Gerri. That I Kathy saw coming to work tonight and I can't get it out of my head. It may very well be that I've lost my mind, and it is true that I am severely depressed. But if you live in this city and you're *not* depressed, you're not paying attention. Maybe it's finally got to me. Thirty-two years of working inside theaters, inside dark rooms without windows, spending the whole day looking inside me for another part of me to use. That could make anybody stop seeing— The last time I looked into the face of this city was in the seventies, during the sudden death game between the Yankees and the Red Sox, which I had to stop watching to get to an audition for a part I wasn't going to get. All I could think of was get me out of the subway, get me up on the street so I can find out who won. I took one look at the faces on the street and I knew it. I saw it. New York had lost. I didn't have to ask anyone. The sadness going through to the back of the eyes was there. The Yankees had had it. And I turned past a Papaya stand and there were some men hunched around a radio. The damn game was still on. New York was up. Bucky Dent hits and we win! It wasn't 'till I got out of the audition that it hit me that the flat look of loss was just the look of the city. I'd never searched, never needed anything from those men's faces before. It wasn't that I hadn't looked at the city. When I first came here, I couldn't stop walking and looking. But I was a young Southern woman, who was no way a beauty, but young enough to be only looking at the world to see who's looking at her. And now? Now I can't walk down the street without the city searching out my face, checking me out, seeing if I'm the one who'll hand out a quarter. And I hate them. I hate them looking at me, hate walking past them, hate glancing quickly, making quick judgments, deciding who's homeless, who's addict, who's needy, who's conning me? That's where the theater is now. Out there. That's where who's got the best lines gets my quarter. Who's got the fullest character...the detail, the torn shoe, the crutch that looks used, gets the quarter. I'm the

walking reviewer, the critic of the poor, doling out my quarters to the
"stars" of the street. But tonight I'm watching a dog! A dog who might still
be on 41st Street or might have got hit or maybe turned into the miracle dog
and got found. But he wasn't a wild dog. Even though he was dirty from
the street, he had that residue, that indescribable look of home still on him.
He was trying to cross the avenue to get somewhere. And the cars and cabs
kept turning. The poor thing wasn't trained to be alone. He had no idea
how to deal with the city. What made it even sadder was that he was a big,
once proud—fierce on the leash—German shepherd. Helpless. Running
blindly up and down the street, too afraid to cross. I was too afraid to help
because I didn't know what he might do in his fear. And I watched and
wept. Next to me was a man pulling food out of the trash, inspecting a
tossed-off muffin with a bite taken out of it. I wouldn't have seen him if he
hadn't asked me for change. And I look at him, the tears still clouding my
eyes, find a quarter, and walk in here and say my lines which I can say in
my sleep. But the peace, the safety I always find in the theater, I can't find
it lately. I know something terrible has happened to me if what I'm doing
is only watching the dog. *(She takes a moment to collect herself.)* I sure as hell
am not Mother Theresa. I've never even played a nun. What a fifty-year-old
woman whose only skill is make believe can do for a city that doesn't need
any more make believe—I don't know. But she does something. I don't
know what something is, but I'm sure it has to do with looking, with
stopping and looking. Stopping and looking until I see what I can do.
As much as I would give anything to walk... *(With a dramatic gesture)* no,
to sweep up this aisle, go out that door, flinging it open wide so the theater
will fill with the sound of the city.... My purse is downstairs and my coat
and book. If I left without them, I'd have to come back and get them and, if I
walk back in here, I'm never going to leave. I know of every possible way of
not following through. Before this dog becomes an anecdote like every other
important moment of my life, I had best leave... And say goodbye. *(She
exits.)*

ARLENE: *(Shouts at the exiting* GERRI*)* The *Times* is here. The critic from
The New Yorker. This is opening night!

*(*SUSAN *enters. As the stage manager. She wears headphones.)*

SUSAN: We're going on. We're finishing. Places. *(To* ARLENE*)* Where's Burt?
Get Burt. *(To* CHARLES*)* Play something.

*(*SUSAN *crosses to* CINDY. *They huddle.)*

*(*CHARLES *plays Chicago-type blues on the harmonica. Within a few beats,*
CINDY *crosses downstage to the audience. The music underscores her speech.)*

CINDY: *(To audience)* Wow...for the whole cast I'd like to say we're sorry,
sorry this happened. Wow. Like E- Mo- Tion- Al. Like women over fifty,
isn't it? But like since we didn't have any understudy rehearsals yet,

because off-off-off-Broadway you can't pay understudies 'til you know you have the money, and you don't know that 'til the show's been reviewed, which is supposed to be like tonight. Tonight, wow. Well...so I'm going to tell you what happened with Gerri and we'll go from there and do it, finish the play. Gerri only had a couple of lines left anyway.

OK. Gerri comes on and Burt tells her he's waiting for Arlene, which makes Gerri jealous, like even though she was the one stopping their relationship, but feeling jealous makes her like feel happy because feeling any emotion in her life right now is a form of break-through and she goes out of the waiting room, and just as Gerri is leaving, Charles, who's like finished with the dentist, is brought into the waiting room, and he sits down, and ignores Burt. So Charles sits ignoring Burt and looks at the posters.

(SUSAN *gestures to* CHARLES *to get into position.* CHARLES *stops playing and gets into position.*)

CINDY: Burt...

SUSAN: Get Burt.

(CHARLES *exits.*)

CINDY: Burt like waits for Arlene, like he's standing alone, like he's thinking can I...do I have the guts, the nerve to change my life? And then Arlene...

(ARLENE *jumps her cue.*)

ARLENE: *(Offstage)* I don't give a damn if grief counseling is a part of the fee. I don't want it.

CINDY: Like embarrassing. *(She whispers offstage.)* Where's Burt?

CHARLES: *(Offstage)* Burt. Burt.

(BURT *enters, upset, unfocused.* CHARLES *enters behind him.* CINDY *exits.*)

BURT: I was waiting for the lights. I was waiting for the lights.

(CHARLES *puts his arm around him.*)

CHARLES: It's all right, man.

BURT: I need more time. I can't do this. I'm not ready.

(CHARLES *puts his arm around him.*)

CHARLES: Then take your time, man.

(CHARLES *gently "hushes"* BURT.)

BURT: Where do you stand? Where am I? Where...?

ARLENE: *(Offstage)* I don't give a damn if grief counseling is a part of the fee. I don't want it.

BURT: I need more time.

(CHARLES *holds* BURT.)

CHARLES: OK, man. Take your time, man. You'll get there. OK, man.

(*From the wings,* SUSAN *signals the lighting booth.*)

CINDY: (*Offstage*) There's been like homeless on the street half my life. Who'd stop an opening night for that?

(*The lights go down on the dog holding the man.*)

END OF PLAY

WATER PLAY

Sally Nemeth

WATER PLAY
© 1995 copyright by Sally Nemeth

Sally Nemeth was born in Chicago and worked extensively in the Off-Loop theaters there, founding Chicago New Plays, a playwrights' collective. She subsequently relocated to New York City, and now resides in Brooklyn.

Her play HOLY DAYS premiered at the Soho Poly Theater in London in 1988. Critically acclaimed, the production won three awards at the Fringe Theater Awards, and later was produced in Dublin, Ireland and Auckland, New Zealand. In 1990, it premiered in the U S at South Coast Repertory in Costa Mesa, California, and the production won four Los Angeles Drama Critics Circle Awards. The play has been published by Broadway Play Publishing, both in an acting edition and in the anthology PLAYS FROM SOUTH COAST REPERTORY.

Nemeth's play MILL FIRE premiered in 1989 at the Goodman Theater in Chicago, and later moved to New York under the auspices of the Women's Project. In 1990, it premiered in London at the Bush Theater at Riverside Hammersmith, and is included in the Women's Project/Applause Books anthology WOMENSWORK.

Nemeth's full-length SPINNING INTO BLUE, commissioned by South Coast Rep, was part of the 1990 Showcase of New Plays at Carnegie-Mellon and was produced in 1993 at Victory Gardens Theater in Chicago. In the summer of 1994, an evening of one-acts and monologues titled SALLY'S SHORTS was produced by One Dream Theater in New York.

She is a 1989 recipient of a National Endowment for the Arts grant, and a 1990 recipient of a New York Foundation for the Arts grant.

WATER PLAY was workshopped at the 1990 Taper Lab New Work Festival in Los Angeles, CA. The cast and creative contributors were:

EVANGELINE .... Marg Helgenberger
JACK .... Alan Rosenberg
DRESDEN .... Clancy Brown

Director .... Mel Marvin
Dramaturg .... Robin McKee
Stage manager .... Claire Syrett
Original music .... Lynn Anderson

WATER PLAY was subsequently produced in March 1992 in New York City by Road Theatre at Downtown Art Co, Barbara Bornmann, Producer. The cast and creative contributors were:

EVANGELINE .... Andrea Gallo
JACK .... Andrew Polk
DRESDEN .... Kevin Davis

Director .... Nancy Salomon Miranda
Dramaturg .... Victoria Abrash
Stage manager .... James Marr
Set design .... Richard Meyer
Lighting design .... Paul Clay
Music and sound design .... Ellen Mandel
Costume design .... Vibrina Coronado

CHARACTERS

EVANGELINE
JACK
DRESDEN, *all in their thirties*

SETTING

Not here

TIME

Not now

(Setting: a loft space. Very open, very high-tech feel. There is a large picture window up center with rain constantly running down it. Stage right is a sleek sofa with a streamlined industrial look. In front of it, a low table. To the left of the sofa is a lamp that looks like a skyscraper, emitting little slits of light. To stage left is a computer station that looks like a modern sculpture. It should emit that strange greenish V D T light. In fact, the whole space is dimly lit, as there is no natural light. Everything in the space looks waterproof as well. There are two entrance doorways: stage right goes to the outside of the building, and stage left to the interior of the apartment. Near the stage right entrance is a sculptural coat rack in Memphis style. Suspended above is a screen stretching the entire length of the playing area, onto which phrases can be projected.)

PROJECTION: WATER SEEKS ITS OWN LEVEL.

(EVANGELINE enters in a trenchcoat, dripping wet, carrying a small duffel suitcase, which is also dripping. She dumps the duffel next to the coat rack, unzips it and begins pulling soaked clothing out of it, hurling the clothing to the floor with a splat. She gets to the bottom of the bag and pulls out a notebook sealed in a Zip-loc bag. She makes her way across the room, removing her wet outer clothing and dropping it to the floor. She exits through the interior door. Moments later JACK enters from the interior door carrying a laundry basket. He is tidy, dressed in black Asian pajamas, Mandarin collar, black cloth shoes. He picks up EVANGELINE's wet clothing, and plunks it into the laundry basket. As he gets to the coat rack, EVANGELINE appears in the interior doorway toweling her hair dry, looking fetchingly disheveled. She carries the Zip-loc bag. JACK finishes tidying up by hanging EVANGELINE's trench coat on the rack. He turns and sees her.)

JACK: Well.

EVANGELINE: Well.

JACK: Well, iffen it don't rain it'll be a long dry spell.

EVANGELINE: That's droll. Considering.

JACK: I'm known for my arid wit.

EVANGELINE: Do tell.

JACK: Among other things.

EVANGELINE: What other things.

JACK: Just other things. You know. So.

EVANGELINE: *(Takes the notebook to the computer station, takes it out of the bag, opens it, sits)* Any calls?

JACK: They're all on there. Corps of Engineers, Red Cross, Coast Guard —

EVANGELINE: *(Types into terminal)* Uh-huh.

JACK: But not the call you want.

EVANGELINE: Which one is that.

JACK: You know which one. I take it you didn't find him.

EVANGELINE: I didn't.

JACK: I can't say I'm disappointed.

EVANGELINE: OK. OK.

JACK: You going to tell me about it.

EVANGELINE: Yeah, sure.

JACK: So tell me about it.

EVANGELINE: Well, what's to tell really. I went to the address I had for him. The last address. Water was up into the first floor—knee-deep already. No roof, slow rot. That smell.

JACK: Mildew.

EVANGELINE: Yes. I had a job on the East Coast once. Where the Intracoastal Waterway began—or ended, depending on how you look at it.

JACK: Middle Atlantic. I remember.

EVANGELINE: You would. Things like that. You have a memory for things like that.

JACK: Attention to detail.

EVANGELINE: That's a strength—a useful tool—that kind of memory.

JACK: But no great picture of the overall scheme of things. He says that, doesn't he.

EVANGELINE: And you remember the rest of it?

JACK: You know that I do. June. It was June, and had rained for two weeks solid. Your field report said. Not the kind of rain you get here. No downpour. Just constant. Lulling.

EVANGELINE: Yes. For two weeks. I was in the field. Working in the marshes. Water samples where fresh and salt met. Biological survey of new brackish areas in that specific area of coast.

JACK: I wrote the paper.

EVANGELINE: From there I went to New York. Shipped my trunk out here ahead of me. Charged new clothes in New York. Two weeks more. I come back and the trunk is here, unopened.

JACK: It was addressed to you. I never open things addressed to other people.

EVANGELINE: Everything in it mildewed. Ruined. That smell.

JACK: Everything had grown furry—and green and black.

EVANGELINE: Mold and mildew.

JACK: A science project.

EVANGELINE: What?

JACK: A science project. Like things left too long in the refrigerator. You should have done a biological survey. Written a paper.

EVANGELINE: It didn't occur to me at the time.

JACK: What *did*?

EVANGELINE: That you'd let them rot for a reason.

JACK: That's a bit oblique.

EVANGELINE: No. I thought it was pretty damn direct. *(Beat)* Do we have anything to eat or drink in this place?

JACK: No.

EVANGELINE: Could we get something?

JACK: We?

EVANGELINE: Could you?

JACK: What did you have in mind.

EVANGELINE: Whatever.

JACK: *(Getting a trenchcoat and fedora from the rack. He puts them on.)* Do you have money?

EVANGELINE: Just put it on our tab.

JACK: That limits our choices.

EVANGELINE: To what.

JACK: *(He steps into a pair of big buckled galoshes, sitting at the foot of the coat rack.)* Pizza or Chinese.

EVANGELINE: Pizza. With everything. *(He starts out.)* No, wait. No onions.

(He exits. There is music as she works at the terminal. She looks at the screen and begins to rock back and forth. The phone rings. She picks it up.)

EVANGELINE: Hello. *(There is no answer. She hangs up and resumes her typing, checking her notebook. The phone rings.)* Hello.

(No answer. She hangs up. She looks at the screen again and sits back, stroking her own arms, contemplating the screen. The phone rings again. She lets it ring a few times, then picks it up, hangs it up and takes it off the cradle. JACK re-enters with a pizza box in hand. He removes his hat and coat, hanging them on the rack, then steps out of the galoshes, moving the pizza from hand to hand. He heads for the interior door, wafting the pizza under EVANGELINE's nose. She looks up, smiling, as he exits, then looks back to the terminal. She stands, sliding her silk shirt from her shoulders and dropping it to the floor as she follows JACK. Underneath, she wears a camisole. DRESDEN, dressed in a full Sou'wester, inches along the window, walking the ledge, S L to S R. He stops at the center of the window for a moment, spreadeagled against the glass. He looks into the room, then moves on. The phone begins to beep. When he is through his cross, JACK comes out, replaces the phone on the hook, and picks up EVANGELINE's shirt. He holds it to himself, and looks out the window. The music should play out. The lights fade.)

PROJECTION: MOST OF OUR BODY IS WATER. MOST OF THE EARTH IS WATER.

(It is the next morning. EVANGELINE enters wearing different clothes and a long white overshirt that looks like a lab coat. She strikes a pad at the computer station and begins to talk, wandering the room.)

EVANGELINE: Pillow rock formations on the coast of California. A complete geological anomaly. Did not occur anywhere else. Limestone deposits along the San Andreas fault. Baja California. None of it made any sense until we looked below the surface of the ocean. Looked to the constantly shifting continental plates, and the subaquatic volcanic action.

(JACK enters from the outside, bright red rubber boots and a clear plastic raincoat over his black pajamas. He carries a white bakery bag inside his coat. He is, of course, wet.)

EVANGELINE: Stop tape. You were up early.

JACK: *(Removing outer garments and neatly hanging them on the rack)* I'm an early riser.

EVANGELINE: I suppose that you are.

JACK: Up to make the coffee, go to the bakery or deli or whatever. Fry the eggs.

EVANGELINE: You didn't wake me.

JACK: Did you need to be up early?

EVANGELINE: No. I'm just surprised that I didn't wake when you got out of bed.

JACK: I'm very quiet. Considerate.

EVANGELINE: I usually miss the body heat.

JACK: I'm a reptile.

EVANGELINE: Since when.

JACK: I'm devolving. Learning how to breathe through my skin.

EVANGELINE: And see with your tongue.

JACK: Gills are my next project. Danish? *(He holds out the bakery bag.)*

EVANGELINE: Any cheese?

JACK: One. The rest are prune.

EVANGELINE: I'll take the cheese. And coffee. *(JACK hands her the bakery bag and exits to the interior. She digs out the cheese danish.)* Playback. *(The computer starts to play back a tape of her musings on the West Coast. JACK re-enters with two cups of coffee and sits with her on the sofa, listening.)*

JACK: What's that.

EVANGELINE: Just thinking out loud. The West Coast.

JACK: Never did what it was supposed to do, did it?

EVANGELINE: And what was that?

JACK: It never broke off in the predicted cataclysmic seismic event. It just sank like everything else.

EVANGELINE: It didn't sink.

JACK: It's under water.

EVANGELINE: But it didn't sink. It was reclaimed by the sea.

JACK: That's a moot point.

EVANGELINE: No, it's a totally different dynamic.

JACK: Well it's still under water.

EVANGELINE: Listen to me. Sinking implies that the land went down. Deep six. Reclamation implies that the water was active, not the land. The water rose, the land did not sink. Different dynamic.

JACK: Same result.

EVANGELINE: I won't argue the point. It's different. That's that.

JACK: And we'll still be under water soon, whether we sink or the waters rise.

EVANGELINE: O K. Think about it like this. With the rising waters we stand more of a chance.

JACK: We do?

EVANGELINE: Rising waters can and do crest. And may have already.

JACK: Do you know that?

EVANGELINE: It's an educated guess.

JACK: Operating on intuition. Very sloppy.

EVANGELINE: Not everything is empirical. Neat and clean. As much as you'd like it to be, it hardly ever is.

JACK: Is this my lesson for the day?

EVANGELINE: Don't.

JACK: Don't what.

EVANGELINE: Don't read into it. Don't always think I'm talking about you. About me and you. Because I'm not always.

JACK: Then why do I always hear it?

EVANGELINE: You hear what you want. And you always have.

(She exits to the interior. JACK sits alone for a moment.)

JACK: Playback.

(The tape of EVANGELINE's voice begins to play. JACK listens for a moment, then goes to the computer terminal, types in something and gets a printout. He reads the printout, folds it carefully, and tucks it in his breast pocket. He stops the tape. He picks up the breakfast things and exits to the interior. Lights fade.)

PROJECTION: PRECIPITATION IS MORE THAN JUST RAIN.

(DRESDEN enters from the outside in a full Sou'wester with Wellingtons, carrying a bucket. He shakes the water from himself. There is music throughout this. He removes his hat and starts to wander the room, feeling it out. He finds his spot, then places the bucket beneath it. The ceiling begins to leak right where the bucket was placed. He looks up, satisfied, and goes off to the interior. He emerges with another bucket in his hands. JACK is hot on his heels carrying various pots, pans, bowls, buckets. DRESDEN wanders about, placing these vessels on the floor, table, etc. as JACK is handing them to him. Everywhere a vessel is placed a leak springs. They complete their task. DRESDEN removes his coat, and hands it to JACK, who hangs it on the rack. DRESDEN ambles to the computer station, removing a notebook in a Zip-loc bag from the waistband of his pants. JACK exits to the interior. DRESDEN removes the notebook from the bag, and begins to enter data into the computer. The lights fade slightly. A saxophone plays softly.)

PROJECTION: AT A CONFLUENCE IT IS CLEAR WHERE THE MUDDY MISSISSIPPI GETS ITS NAME.

(EVANGELINE *enters from the interior, wearing a silk robe, looking very film noir.* DRESDEN *continues to type.*)

EVANGELINE: It was cold and I was damp. I was in a taxi going from an airport to a place I'd never been, in a town I'd never been in, which is always a financial risk. You know. The cabbie gives you two choices and asks, "Which way do you usually go," and you say "I don't know, I'm not from around here." And he smiles and flips down the flag and takes the scenic route, all the while telling you why this is the best route. You know the story. Roads washed out, river on the rise. You know. Now this cabbie was quite a geezer and proceeded to tell me that this was quite a town in the forties. Yep, in the forties this was quite a town. If you couldn't make a buck here you couldn't make a buck nowhere. He told me about all the taverns I'd have liked back then, and how he'd build bridges for the conservation corps, and how the government sent twenty-five dollars of every thirty he made straight to his family. And how the town's changed since then, all while we're driving down a strip lined with defunct and marginal businesses. We get close to the address—the one I have for you—and the water is up into the street. He's to his hubcaps in water and refuses to go further. He flips down the meter at fourteen twenty-five. I give him a twenty and tell him to give me back three. Yammering away, he hands me two. I ask him for the third, and he yammers that he gets forgetful when his mouth gets to running. Not only does the gamey old fucker take me around my ass to get to my elbow and talk my ear off, but he tries to stiff me too. I don't like the looks of any of this. I give him the three singles, tell him to wait, and leave my bag in the back. He starts in about the water coming up, and if it rises any further he can't wait, and on and on, I'm cold and I'm wet and I'm standing in shin-deep water. I tell him there's a ten in it for him if he waits, and head off for the house that I see. (JACK *comes through wearing his boots, a long Australian rain coat, and a Chinese hat. The music abruptly stops, the mood shifts.*) Chinese?

JACK: We can still run a tab there.

DRESDEN: Szechuan?

JACK: Cantonese.

DRESDEN: That's a shame.

(JACK *exits to the exterior. The saxophone begins again.*)

EVANGELINE: I go to the door. The water is now knee-deep. I know you can't be here, but I knock. Call your name. Try to force the door against the rushing water The smell is atrocious. Bilge water. I return to the cab, tell the cabbie to take me back to the airport. He tells me that I came in on the last flight of the night. And doesn't volunteer any information regarding lodging.

DRESDEN: Backwater town.

EVANGELINE: So, where were you?

DRESDEN: I was there.

EVANGELINE: Not at that house

DRESDEN: For a while I was.

EVANGELINE: Well, you neglected to leave a forwarding address.

DRESDEN: How unlike me.

EVANGELINE: It is.

DRESDEN: Which is why you came after me.

EVANGELINE: I thought you'd left for good.

DRESDEN: You didn't think I'd be back.

EVANGELINE: No. I didn't.

DRESDEN: And that's why you came looking.

EVANGELINE: Among other reasons.

DRESDEN: One reason. You're only allowed one.

EVANGELINE: I don't know.

DRESDEN: One overwhelming reason. One that eclipses all others.

EVANGELINE: I came looking for you because I needed you.

DRESDEN: Needed or wanted.

EVANGELINE: Needed.

DRESDEN: Because there is a difference.

EVANGELINE: *(She sits on his lap, straddling him.)* Need.

DRESDEN: Because in the grand scheme of things there are very few that matter, and even fewer things that would get me to stay. That make sense?

EVANGELINE: Absolute.

DRESDEN: And I am needed. Makes me feel all warm inside.

EVANGELINE: Don't be a prick.

DRESDEN: I'm not meaning to be.

EVANGELINE: The hell you're not.

DRESDEN: If I were a prick, I wouldn't have come back at all.

EVANGELINE: Why did you come back?

DRESDEN: I sensed I was needed.

(They kiss, then he stands, holding her to him, and carries her into the interior. JACK enters from the exterior, carrying a bag of Chinese food in his hands. He removes his hat and coat and hangs them on the coat rack. He speaks to the audience.)

JACK: There is something in each and every one of us that fears the water—that fears the weather. I've seen—we've all seen rational adults screaming for help while standing in water three feet deep. We are the beasts who do not naturally swim. It is a learned skill. Something we lost with our dewclaws. Something we lost as the continents drifted. They say that Continental Drift is caused by the shifting plates of the earth's crust, and that that crust sits atop molten rock. But to you and me, Continental Drift says that we are afloat. It is the water we see that divides us, and the water that must have pushed the continents apart, rushing in to take what lowland it could. We could see it in action—whole parts of Africa being reclaimed to the sea. Fresh rivers turning brackish overnight. Marine beasts moving steadily inland where herds of land animals once grazed. Those land animals moving steadily inland and overgrazing already crowded grasslands. Famine, stampede, an upset of the ecosystem. An upset caused by water and by weather. Forces so large it takes the pull of the Moon, the orbit of the Earth around the Sun to have any effect on them. It is no wonder that we fear these things. Standing on the coastline of a continent and watching a storm blow in is a humbling sight. Facing a storm on the open sea even more so—tankers the size of cities being torn apart by the forces of nature. When the waters began to creep up on the coastlines many years ago, people raised their homes onto stilts and vowed to stay. There are those who want to face that power daily—to perch on its edge and face it. And they are the first to go, and maybe that is why they stay. Inland, through radical engineering and water management, we have stayed relatively dry. But the inland waters are on the rise, and the forces that can only be controlled by the pull of other heavenly bodies will prevail. And we are the beasts who do not naturally swim.

(He turns and walks offstage, towards the interior. The lights fade to almost black.)

PROJECTION: NO DIVING IN THE SHALLOW END

(JACK, EVANGELINE, and DRESDEN file in, carrying white Chinese carryout containers and chopsticks. They sit down on the sofa in that order and begin to eat. The lights rise. DRESDEN wears a white shirt, khaki pants, and deck shoes. EVANGELINE wears trousers and a blouse. JACK, as always, wears the black pajamas.)

JACK: I should have put it in the microwave.

EVANGELINE: I actually like it cold.

JACK: The sauces get gluey.

EVANGELINE: Well, you can always heat yours up. Nothing stopping you.

(JACK *gets up and exits to the interior, carrying his food.* DRESDEN *leans over and begins to nip at* EVANGELINE's *earlobe. She continues to eat.*)

EVANGELINE: Stop.

DRESDEN: Why?

EVANGELINE: Just do.

DRESDEN: Why?

EVANGELINE: Because it's like eating in front of starving people.

JACK: *(Entering, juggling container)* Hot, hot, hot.

(He sits and begins to eat. DRESDEN *glares at him, stops eating, then sits back.)*

DRESDEN: In the Mariana Trench, the ocean floor is some seven miles below the surface. At that depth, the pressure is tons to the square inch, the water near freezing and almost still. Light extends only three-hundred-fifty feet below the ocean surface, so the darkness at seven miles is absolute. And still, in this hostile place, there is life. Life that is so basic, so primeval that to see it is to step back in time. We look to the sky for the origin of the universe, and we look to the sea for the origin of man. The life at the depth of seven miles exists on carcasses: the carcasses of surface dwellers that float down to that depth to be picked clean by the crustaceans and eels and other scavengers. It can take months for a carcass to reach that depth. *(During this speech, both* EVANGELINE *and* JACK *slow their eating, and eventually stop, setting the containers down in unison.)* This *would* be better hot. *(He takes his container and exits.)*

JACK: You're not eating.

EVANGELINE: No. Neither are you.

JACK: You sure you don't want that heated?

EVANGELINE: If I do, I'll do it.

JACK: Dresden could just pop it in so long as he's up.

EVANGELINE: Jack.

JACK: All right. All right.

EVANGELINE: You're being frantic.

JACK: No. Not frantic. I don't feel at all frantic.

EVANGELINE: Well, you're being something.

JACK: Something is better than nothing.

EVANGELINE: It depends on what that something is.

DRESDEN: *(Appears in the doorway with an open bottle of wine and three glasses)* One for you, one for you, and one for me.

JACK: I'm just not thinking. I didn't ask if anyone wanted anything to drink.

DRESDEN: *(Pours a taste in* EVANGELINE's *glass)* Well, you can't be expected to think of everything.

EVANGELINE: *(Tasting and spitting)* Vinegar.

JACK: Let me see the bottle.

*(*DRESDEN *hands it over.)*

JACK: It is vinegar. Where did you get it?

DRESDEN: Kitchen shelf.

JACK: That's not where the wine is kept.

DRESDEN: Where is the wine kept?

JACK: In the wine rack. In the storage room. In the basement.

DRESDEN: Who'd have thought.

JACK: *(Fishing in his shirt for the keys around his neck)* I'll go get it.

EVANGELINE: I'll go.

JACK: You don't know....

EVANGELINE: I'll go. Give me the keys.

JACK: *(Pauses, holds up a key)* This one.

(She takes the key and exits. JACK *sits and begins to eat again.)*

DRESDEN: Ah, well.

JACK: It was a nice gesture.

DRESDEN: It said red wine.

JACK: Vinegar. Red wine vinegar.

DRESDEN: Didn't read that far.

JACK: No eye for detail.

DRESDEN: That's so.

JACK: But a good sense of the big picture. Isn't that so too.

DRESDEN: As a matter of fact.

JACK: The bird's eye view. The big picture.

DRESDEN: It all spreads out before me.

JACK: So what is it. That big picture. That vista.

DRESDEN: You want to know.

JACK: I'm asking you.

DRESDEN: What's in store.

JACK: Your perspective.

DRESDEN: I see dogs in trees and people perched on the peaks of their roofs. I see huge barges wrecked on the ruins of whole communities. I see dams and locks bursting with the rush of tons of water behind them. I see lines and lines of levees crumbling. People sandbagging in their sleep. I see cities that look like Venice—without the old-world charm.

JACK: You see, or have seen.

DRESDEN: What.

JACK: Is this actual sight, or vision.

DRESDEN: I don't follow.

JACK: Did you see these things, or did you make them up.

DRESDEN: What do you think.

EVANGELINE: (Enters with bottles of wine and champagne in her arms, her pants rolled to her knees and her shoes in her hand) The foundations have started to seep. The basement is ankle-deep in water.

DRESDEN: At least you saved the wine. There are some priorities.

EVANGELINE: These were floating. I was picking them up and a rat swam by. A huge rat.

DRESDEN: All rats are huge when they're swimming in your basement.

EVANGELINE: Well. Do something.

DRESDEN: About what. The water, the wine, the huge rat?

EVANGELINE: All of it.

DRESDEN: Right. Keys. (She hands them over.) Care to give me a hand?

JACK: I hate rats.

DRESDEN: You could save the wine rack. Singlehandedly.

JACK: If it's floating, it's probably all ruined.

DRESDEN: They bring up perfectly good bottles of wine from ancient wrecks.

JACK: I'll pass.

DRESDEN: Suit yourself. (He exits.)

EVANGELINE: *(Holds out a bottle of champagne)* You think this is ruined?

JACK: *(Takes it and starts to open it)* No.

EVANGELINE: You're not the least bit frantic, are you.

JACK: No.

EVANGELINE: In fact, I'd say you were somewhat measured in your manner.

JACK: You would.

EVANGELINE: I would.

JACK: Imagine that.

(He pops the cork and drinks from the bottle, exiting to the interior. EVANGELINE slowly begins to open her own bottle of champagne. The lights dim slightly.)

PROJECTION: THE ANCIENT MARINER WAS NO FOOL

DRESDEN: *(Enters with a small, brown rat in his hands. As he speaks, he will soothingly pet the rat.)* When the sun never set on the British Empire, the Navy carried cats to all the corners of the earth. They introduced cats to Tahiti, New Guinea, New Zealand to help the poor syphilitic islanders cope with the rats in their grain bins. The rats in their dark and vile huts. The British Navy had a seemingly endless supply of cats. Handed them out left and right, but always had some left for themselves. Why? Rats in the provision holds? Rats in the dark and vile cabins below decks? Yes, but I think the reason goes deeper than that. I think they kept cats in the hope that they would exterminate all rodents so the sailors would never know when that ship was going down. Because if there aren't any rats to leave a sinking ship you can always tell yourself that the water pouring over the gunwales is just a minor setback. Can't you. *(Receives no response)* Of course you can. And if a ship is not sinking there is no reason to jump. No reason to lash yourself to a spar and abandon the vessel. No reason whatsoever. Isn't that right. *(No response)* There is a glass in front of you. Fill it for me. *(EVANGELINE complies, leaving the glass where it sits.)* Put out your hands. *(She does. He places the rat in her hands.)* See. He's not going anywhere. *(He picks up his glass.)* Yet. *(He exits to the exterior.)*

EVANGELINE: *(Sits for a moment, stiffly holding the rat)* Jack? Jack, come here. I need you.

(JACK enters, sees the rat, exits again and enters carrying a plastic watertight box. She dumps the rat in, wiping her hands on her legs. JACK closes the lid and sets the box outside the exterior door. He starts back across the room.)

EVANGELINE: Can I ask you something?

JACK: You can ask me anything.

EVANGELINE: If tomorrow, everything came to an end—I mean everything. No dry perch anywhere for anyone—

JACK: This is hypothetical.

EVANGELINE: I said if.

JACK: So you did.

EVANGELINE: So, if tomorrow that happened—

JACK: I'd float. I'm a good floater.

EVANGELINE: Jack—

JACK: Then I guess I'd develop gills. I'm already working on that, you know.

EVANGELINE: I mean it, Jack.

JACK: So do I. I'm infinitely adaptable.

EVANGELINE: You are.

JACK: I am. And I know there are people who would say we had it coming. It was our turn to go. That mammals have had their day in the sun, as the dinosaurs had before us. But there are aquatic mammals. Highly successful aquatic mammals. And I plan to join the ranks.

EVANGELINE: Have you ever had a drowning dream?

JACK: Never. Have you?

EVANGELINE: All the time.

JACK: Well, they may not be prophesy. They may be something entirely different.

EVANGELINE: Like what.

JACK: You do amaze me.

EVANGELINE: Like what.

JACK: What do you dream. Exactly.

EVANGELINE: Usually I'm swimming. No land in sight. A huge wave moves toward me, churning, curling. A wall of water, blotting out the sky. I'm terrified and try to swim away from it, but get sucked toward it. The wave crashes over me—tons of water, and I tumble over and over so I don't know which way is up. Then I stop tumbling and start to claw my way back to what I think is the surface, my lungs bursting, I start to see what I believe to be light—the light of the surface, of the sky. Clawing, climbing for it, weakening as it seems farther away, and I've got no more breath to hold.

JACK: *(Pause)* Then what.

EVANGELINE: I wake up. What else?

JACK: Breathe.

EVANGELINE: I wake up gasping.

JACK: Before you wake up. Breathe.

EVANGELINE: Does that work for you?

JACK: I never have drowning dreams.

EVANGELINE: That's right.

JACK: I dream I can fly.

EVANGELINE: With an olive branch in your beak?

JACK: No. Why would I dream that?

DRESDEN: *(Enters, arms full of wine bottles)* Under the circumstances, it just seemed like the right thing to do.

(Blackout)

PROJECTION: A HARD COASTLINE IS NOT THE BEST MEANS OF DEFENSE

(EVANGELINE sits at the computer terminal, working. DRESDEN sits on the couch, drinking wine. JACK is nowhere to be seen.)

DRESDEN: In a feat of engineering more wondrous than the eighth wonder of the world, the Eastern Shelf Barrier was built in the North Sea to protect the Netherlands from a storm surge. One quarter of the Netherlands lay below sealevel, and it was theorized that the Barrier's safety margin would be null and void were the oceans to rise another three feet. And seeing as how the oceans had risen one foot in the past century, and that the rise was accelerating, the Netherlands figured they were buying another hundred years or so, tops, but it was better than nothing. When the Barrier gates were closed to the sea, inexplicably, wave heights in the North Sea grew, pounding at the Barrier. There was no rise in the water level—the water just grew more active. Alarming waves of frigid water, battering away. It was said you could hear the crashing of the monstrous waves hundreds of miles away from the Barrier gates. The Netherlands became a nation of insomniacs, the sound of their eventual demise constant in their ears. The nation mobilized in their sleepless stupor, moving the inhabitants of lowland cities and towns to higher ground. And once the lowland populace was high and dry, they opened the gates, and at once, the North Sea grew calm and placid.

EVANGELINE: You're anthropomorphizing.

DRESDEN: I love when you say that.

EVANGELINE: You are.

DRESDEN: Missing their homes and the familiar, the lowlanders gradually drifted back to the towns and cities of the delta. Surreptitiously, in groups of seven and ten, they'd slit the throat of a sheep or pig, and hurl the carcass into the sea. Blood sacrifice. Hopeful appeasement of the angry god. A popular front formed, demanding the destruction of the Barrier gates. The government, proud of their feat of engineering, refused. Guerilla bands of lowlanders began to zip out to the Barrier in fast boats, hurling explosives at the foundations. Over time, the bombings took their toll, the Barrier was weakened, and one day crumbled into the sea. That same night, a rogue wave hundreds of feet high wiped out the lowlands, and the sea rushed in, taking the land forever.

EVANGELINE: If there's a lesson here I don't like it.

DRESDEN: You don't have to.

EVANGELINE: Well good, because I don't. Not a bit.

DRESDEN: Not your kind of story. Not the sort of story to lull you into a dreamless sleep.

EVANGELINE: As a matter of fact, no.

DRESDEN: (Strokes her hair as he speaks) And we all spend our waking days waiting to sleep the sweet dreamless sleep. The sleep where our psyche does no overtime, where we could care less if we discover we were weaned too early. The sleep that lasts the whole night through, uninterrupted by waking, startled, gasping for air, clawing at the covers. Sleep, pure and simple. You want it. I've got it.

EVANGELINE: Why do you do these things to me?

DRESDEN: I think mostly because I can. Because you let me.

EVANGELINE: I don't.

DRESDEN: You don't? Then why do I do these things to you? (He reaches over her shoulder and hits the print button. The machine spits out a sheet of paper. He hands it to her.)

EVANGELINE: It's blank. You did something wrong.

DRESDEN: Like what.

(He kisses her and exits to the interior. She wads up the sheet of paper and throws it to the floor. She types something into the terminal, prints it, gets a blank sheet, wads it up, tosses it to the floor. She repeats this a couple of times, growing more agitated. As she does this, JACK enters quietly and stands by her.)

PROJECTION: NOAH'S WIFE HAD NO NAME

EVANGELINE: Jack?

(JACK *reaches into his breast pocket and hands her the folded piece of paper he put there earlier. She unfolds and reads it.*)

EVANGELINE: "Look on the bright side—at least it's not fire and pestilence. Best of luck to you all—Headquarters." (*She smooths the paper.*) Jack.

JACK: Yes.

EVANGELINE: Where did you get this.

JACK: Hot off the wire.

EVANGELINE: How long have you had it.

JACK: A while.

EVANGELINE: Why didn't you let me in on this.

JACK: I thought you had enough on your mind.

EVANGELINE: Well, Jack, that was thoughtful, but hardly appropriate, considering.

JACK: Considering what.

EVANGELINE: The nature of the news.

JACK: Can you change it? Exert some influence? Some force? Can you, in the eleventh hour, raise your hands to the sky, part the thunderclouds, and send the sun streaming in to dry the sodden plains? Is that within the realm of possibility?

EVANGELINE: I'd like to think that it is.

JACK: It's not.

EVANGELINE: So far we've managed.

JACK: Let it go, Evangeline.

EVANGELINE: Just like that?

JACK: Just like that.

EVANGELINE: I don't think that I can.

JACK: Then at least appreciate your few hours of ignorance. My gift to you

DRESDEN: (*Entering, carrying three orange life jackets*) So. Time to dress for success. (*He puts a jacket on the chair in front of* EVANGELINE.)

EVANGELINE: How long have you known?

DRESDEN: Longer than you.

EVANGELINE: How long.

DRESDEN: Longer than Jack.

EVANGELINE: How could you.

DRESDEN: *(Putting on his Sou'wester)* How could I *what?* How could I know? How could I not tell you?

EVANGELINE: How could you let me hope.

DRESDEN: Nothing I could do about that.

EVANGELINE: You could have.

DRESDEN: With everything you know, everything you've always known, you still have hope. Don't you?

EVANGELINE: I suppose that I do.

DRESDEN: And what do you hope for.

EVANGELINE: I don't know.

DRESDEN   I don't believe that. *(Holds a coat open for her)* Allow me. *(She is unresponsive)* A little help here. *(She puts her arm into the coat. He puts the coat on her and places the life jacket around her neck.)* Hope for the best, Evangeline. The best is yet to come.

JACK: What's the plan?

DRESDEN: Move to higher ground.

JACK: Where.

DRESDEN: A taller building.

JACK: Better picture of the deluge.

DRESDEN: The big picture. *(Holds out a life jacket)*

JACK: Thanks. I won't be needing that.

DRESDEN: You're welcome to come along.

JACK: Thanks just the same.

DRESDEN: Well, all right. *(He heads for the exterior door, and hangs the life jacket on the coat rack.)* I'll leave it here in case you change your mind. Evangeline?

EVANGELINE: *(Standing by the computer, stroking the keys.)* Yes?

DRESDEN: Time to go. *(He exits.)*

EVANGELINE: *(Walks to door, turns, faces JACK)* Bye Jack.

JACK: Bye.

EVANGELINE: Thanks for the gift.

JACK: Anytime.

(She exits. JACK slowly walks to the doorway, as though following, then turns back and looks at the room. The ceiling springs a new leak. And another, and another— the sound of drips proliferate. JACK watches the room rain, then walks to a large steel bowl, already full of water from the ceiling. He sits behind the bowl, facing out. He scoops some water into his hands, watching it trickle out. He splashes water in his face. He takes a deep breath and goes face first into the bowl of water, his hands stretched out before him, as if in supplication. As he stays down longer and longer, his hands start to clutch and grasp and pound the floor. He comes up gasping. He takes some deep breaths and plunges in again. His hands claw and scrape and it seems he stays down a little longer, but he comes up for air again, red-faced and gasping. He collects himself, takes a couple deep breaths, and dives in again. His hands pound and clutch and claw, but eventually stop, relax, and go limp. He lies face down and prone, spread-eagled, face in the water. EVANGELINE enters, bursting through the doorway, runs to JACK, takes a handful of hair at the back of his head, and hauls him out of the water.)

EVANGELINE: BREATHE!

JACK: *(Looking at her calmly, without gasping at all)* I was breathing. I was. *(He laughs delightedly, and strokes her cheek. The lights fade.)*

PROJECTION: WHEN YOU START TO SIGHT BIRDS, LAND IS NOT FAR AHEAD

(Blackout)

END OF PLAY

WELL DONE POETS

Laura Quinn

WELL DONE POETS
© copyright 1993 by Laura Quinn

For all rights please contact Broadway Play Publishing Inc.

Laura Quinn was born in Washington, D C; raised in Northern Virginia; and spent a lot of time on the Outer Banks of North Carolina. At an early age she decided to become a writer because it seemed like a neat thing to be. For a few years she got sidetracked, and tried to be an actress, but after taking a playwrighting class at the University of Virginia, she decided writing plays was much less stressful than auditioning. Quinn graduated from U V A in 1988 with a B A in English and drama and received her M F A from The Playwrights Workshop at the University of Iowa. Her work has been produced by Source Theatre Co of Washington, D C; the Zena Group Theatre, for W B A I Radio's Soundscape Series; Love Creek productions; and The Offstage Theatre Co. She currently lives in New York City.

WELL DONE POETS was originally commissioned by The Offstage Theatre Company of Charlottesville, Virginia, for Barhoppers III, and was presented at Miller's Bar in April 1992 with the following cast and director:

BETH .... Julie Lynn
CARRIE ....Bambi Chapin
AARON .... Thadd McQuade
Director .... Tom Coash

A subsequent version tied for first place at the Love Creek Fifth Annual One-Act Festival at the Nat Horne Theater, N Y, N Y, in January and February 1993 with the following cast and director:

BETH ....Sarah Bass
CARRIE ....Doria DeSerio
AARON .... Robert Dubec
Director .... Loris Diran

CHARACTERS

BETH: *An economics major at a prestigious university. Very drunk.*

CARRIE: *A biology major at the same university. Also drunk.*

AARON: *A math major at the same university working as a waittron. He is not drunk, but he wishes he was.*

(Scene: A college bar. It's the kind of night where the staff outnumbers the customers. BETH and CARRIE, two drunk college students, sit at a table. Their beer glasses are full, but the two beer pitchers in evidence are empty. There is a small book, still in the bookstore bag on the table. CARRIE holds a can of red spray paint. BETH and CARRIE are arguing, not passionately, but stubbornly.)

BETH: Plath.

CARRIE: Sexton.

BETH: Plath.

CARRIE: Sexton.

BETH: Plath.

CARRIE: Sexton.

(CARRIE knocks over a beer glass with the can of spray paint.)

BETH: Whoops. *(She goes after the glass.)*

CARRIE: Sexton.

BETH: *(From under the table)* Plath.

(CARRIE tries to wipe up the beer on the table with her hands, and only succeeds in sloshing it off the table.)

CARRIE: I'm getting everything all wet.

BETH: Huh? *(Some beer drips on her head.)* Oh.

(BETH crawls back into her chair. CARRIE continues to wipe the beer off the table onto the floor.)

CARRIE: And there's a wave. And another.

BETH: Oh no.

CARRIE: And another. And another.

BETH: Hey!

CARRIE: What?

BETH: You're getting the floor all wet.

CARRIE: You're drunk.

BETH: Look at all these puddles on the floor.

CARRIE: I didn't do that.

BETH: You did too.

CARRIE: How could I? It's your glass that spilled.

BETH: It's your spray paint.

CARRIE: We need another pitcher.

BETH: Waiter! Waiter!

CARRIE: Nope! That's gender specific.

BETH: Right. Wait! Waitron!

CARRIE: Tron. Tron.

BETH: Tron.

CARRIE and BETH: Tron, tron, tron, tron, tron, tron...

(They dissolve into snorty giggles.)

CARRIE: *(Whispering)* Sexton.

BETH: *(Whispering)* Plath.

(CARRIE and BETH alternate "Sexton" and "Plath" rapidly. They grow louder and louder and start overlapping each other.)

(Enter AARON the waitron. He wipes the table off with a rag, gathers up the empty pitchers, and waits.)

CARRIE:	BETH:
SEXTONNNNN!	PLAAAAATHHHHH!

AARON: Dickey.

CARRIE: Excuse me?

AARON: Dickey. The poet. James Dickey You know, "We have all been in rooms/We cannot die in, and they are odd places and sad."

CARRIE: Excuse me, but we are discussing women poets.

AARON: Oh. Sorry.

BETH: Could you just do your job and bring us another pitcher please?

AARON: Same kind?

BETH: The cheapest.

AARON: Right.

BETH: Thank you so much.

(AARON exits.)

CARRIE: You shouldn't have been so nice to him.

BETH: Was I too nice?

CARRIE: You're too tenderhearted, and while I do not advocate separatism...

BETH: Boo separatism.

CARRIE: I must agree with.... I don't know, who should I agree with?

BETH: Virginia Woolf?

CARRIE: What did she say?

BETH: I have no idea.

CARRIE: Sure, I'll agree with her. Why not?

(BETH *and* CARRIE *toast and drink.* AARON *reenters, carrying a pitcher.*)

AARON: Here you go.

BETH: Thank you.

AARON: Sorry about the women poets thing.

BETH: Huh?

AARON: I mentioned a man poet and you glared at me.

CARRIE: We did glare at him.

BETH: But we don't hate you.

AARON: Glad to hear it. What do you two think about Kumin?

BETH: Who?

AARON: Kumin. You know, won the Pulitzer prize. Used Anne Sexton's pool.

BETH: Oh. Kumin. Pool.

CARRIE: We considered Kumin, but her name does not have the correct ring.

BETH: Besides, we've never heard of her so she couldn't have committed suicide. (*Putting her all into it for* AARON) Plath. Thylvia...Sylvia Plath. It bursts from your lips like an uncontrollable sneeze. Like a hair ball. To Plath!

(BETH *tries to drink out of her empty glass.* AARON *grabs* BETH's *weaving hand and fills up the glass for her.*)

AARON: To Plath.

BETH: Thank you.

AARON: You're welcome. You like Plath, huh?

BETH: Yep.

AARON: "Every woman adores a fascist."

BETH: Huh?

AARON: "You stand at the blackboard, Daddy/In the picture I have of you/A cleft in your chin instead of your foot." It's *Daddy. Daddy.*

BETH: Who's Daddy?

AARON: Plath's *Daddy.*

BETH: Plath's father wrote poetry too?

AARON: No.

CARRIE: Beth, I think that's a Sylvia Plath poem.

BETH: It is? Oh! Thank you.

CARRIE: Do you know any Anne Sexton?

AARON: Do you?

CARRIE: Not a word.

BETH: But we're going to!

CARRIE: We're going to educate ourselves.

BETH: Just as soon as we decide on a name. Cheers.

CARRIE: Cheers!

(BETH *and* CARRIE *clink glasses and drink.*)

BETH: My goodness, can you fill this up for me again? (AARON *fills up her glass.*) Thank you. You are so nice. He is so nice.

CARRIE: That's why I'm not a radical separatist.

BETH: We should tip him. I've got plenty of change.

CARRIE: I think you spent it on the book.

BETH: Hey, do some Sexton.

AARON: Do some Sexton?

CARRIE: Yes, please, recite some Sexton. Sexton. Sex. Ton. Ton. Sex. A ton of sex.

BETH: The tongue of sex?

AARON: It was her nickname.

CARRIE: We are going to educate ourselves. (*She and* BETH *toast and drink.*) We are going to start a poetry reading society for people who know nothing about it. Perhaps you could be our first speaker. A person who "knows" poems. It would be very exciting.

AARON: I couldn't be your first speaker.

CARRIE: And why not? We'd pay well.

BETH: Yes... *(She searches for change.)*

CARRIE: Not astronomical amounts mind you. After all, you're no Saul Bellow...

AARON: He's not a poet.

CARRIE: Of course not. You're no... famous, alive, male poet. Still, we would love to have you.

BETH: *(Digging out a coin)* Here. Here's some money.

CARRIE: Our lives have been shallow.

AARON: No.

BETH: Yes. Really. I'm an economics major.

CARRIE: And I'm a biologist.

BETH: Not very deep careers.

AARON: But lucrative.

CARRIE: But we realize that now.

BETH: We know who we are.

CARRIE: And we're going to change.

BETH: We're considering killing ourselves.

CARRIE: But only as a form of political protest.

BETH: Here's some more money.

AARON: Should I call you two a cab?

BETH: O K. We're a cab.

(BETH *laughs so hard at her joke she nearly falls out of her chair.* AARON *struggles to help her back into it.)*

CARRIE: Liberal arts, ah, how we have neglected thee. When I think of all the years I wasted studying science. Now, how many years is that? Let's see, I won my junior high science fair in... seventh grade. That was 19... O K, it's 1992. 92-91. 91-90. 90-89. 89-88. 88-87. 87-86. Did I just say that twice? Well, anyway, science is safer because in science you die by accident. You know, you get poisoned like Marie Curie did. But you just don't have the passion. The fervor.

AARON: The alcoholism.

BETH: That too.

CARRIE: For all women there is the option of the sweet oblivion of sleeping pills.

BETH: Just like Sylvia and Anne.

CARRIE Cheers.

BETH: Cheers.

(BETH *and* CARRIE *toast.*)

AARON: They didn't use pills.

BETH: No?

CARRIE: I told you we shouldn't assume things.

BETH: Well, at least we won't have to rob a pharmacy.

CARRIE: True. Could you tell us how they killed themselves, please? We're seeking to emulate great poets.

AARON: Sexton asphyxiated herself in her garage.

BETH: Was it a mistake?

AARON: Gee, I don't know. Who would sit in their car with the engine running and the garage door closed?

BETH: Anne Sexton.

CARRIE: Touché.

BETH: Thank you. Do you have a car?

CARRIE: Yes, but I don't have a garage.

BETH: Damn. What about Sylvia?

AARON: What about her?

BETH: Garage?

AARON: Oven.

BETH: She fried herself to death?

CARRIE: For God's sake, Beth, if Sylvia Plath had wanted to fry herself to death she would have used the stove. Not the oven. Remember? The oven is the thing with the door. Sylvia Plath baked herself to death. (*To* AARON) I'm sorry if Beth is a little slow.

AARON: Is that her name?

CARRIE: Yes, and I'm Carrie. Short for Caroline. Like the song. That's Beth.

AARON: Short for Elizabeth.

CARRIE: Very good. And you are?

AARON: Aaron with two a's.

BETH: Was it gas or electric?

AARON: It must have been gas. You can't asphyxiate on electric.

BETH: How sad. How sad. Poor Sylvia...we'll never know why you chose to die.

AARON: Actually we do. Her husband was having an affair.

CARRIE: There you go. It was a man. We'll have to find a garage.

AARON: You girls aren't serious about this, are you?

CARRIE: Define serious.

AARON: You're not really going to kill yourselves? On my shift?

BETH: We wouldn't do anything so private in a public place.

CARRIE: We're interested in forms of protest. Suicide is quite popular as a protest method.

AARON: Where? In Japan? We're not in Japan.

CARRIE: Suicide was often the only form of expression left to women crushed by male society.

BETH: In their fascist boots.

AARON: O K, fine. I think the bar's closing.

BETH: Oh no.

CARRIE: Aaron, before the bar closes, will you do us a favor?

AARON: What?

CARRIE: Would you please do some Anne Sexton for us?

BETH: Oh yes, please do.

CARRIE: The Plath was just lovely.

AARON: If I do some Sexton for you will you let me put you in a cab?

BETH: You'll have to be pretty good.

AARON: I'll be phenomenal, believe me.

BETH: I hope I like Sexton.

CARRIE: We got a book of hers. *(She pats the book, still in its bag.)*

BETH: It was on sale.

AARON: Terrific. You're on your way to poetry appreciation. *(He reaches for the book, but BETH pulls his hand back.)*

BETH: Do you know any poems by heart?

AARON: I know bits and pieces.

BETH: Can you do a whole poem?

AARON: Maybe.

BETH: Carrie can. She's got a photographic memory.

CARRIE: I do.

BETH: She does.

CARRIE: It's not automatic.

BETH: She has to turn it on. We'll prove it. Turn it on Carrie.

CARRIE: O K. It's on now.

BETH: Now, Aaron with two a's, go.

AARON: Go? Just like that? O K. Ah... "I have gone out.... I have gone out." A "possessed witch," or "not a woman quite." Something, something, something, "I have been her kind."

BETH: That is so good.

CARRIE: I like the Plath a lot better.

BETH: It's so incredibly good!

AARON: It's not done.

BETH: There's more?

CARRIE: Well then, we need more beer.

AARON: You certainly do. *(He exits with the empty pitcher.)*

BETH: I have been her kind. I have. Carrie. I have been her kind. I have been Anne Sexton's kind. In fascist boots.

CARRIE: I thought he said the bar was closed.

BETH: He's making an exception for us.

(AARON comes back with a glass of beer for himself.)

AARON: The reenforcements are here.

CARRIE: Should you be drinking, tron?

AARON: It's a slow night.

BETH: Hey, this is a bicentennial quarter.

AARON: Pay attention.

CARRIE: Why?

AARON: Because you're women and this is a woman poet. This is a real woman poet. This isn't some bimbo flouncing around writing flowery shit.This is two-fisted-drinking, chain-smoking, bad love-affair-having Anne Sexton who was as self-destructive as any man. More so!

BETH and CARRIE: More so!

(All three toast and drink.)

AARON: Here's to a woman's woman!

(They drink.)

AARON: Here's to the type of human being who could take tranquilizers, drink red stingers—

BETH: Slingers.

CARRIE: Stingers.

AARON: Whatever. *Her Kind,* by Anne Sexton.

CARRIE: *(Bellowing)* "I have gone out.... I have gone out." A "possessed witch," or "not a woman quite." Something, something, something, "I have been her kind."

AARON: Wow.

BETH: I told you she could do that.

AARON: Ah, O K, stanza two. *(A tad more enthusiastic than the first time)* Ah, in stanza two, Sexton deals with ah…earth goddess imagery. Portraying women as the caretakers of the darker side of nature. Oh God, I wrote an eight-page paper on this poem, and I'm drawing a complete blank.

BETH: Does it end the same way the first stanza does?

AARON: Yes.

BETH and CARRIE: I have been her kind. *(They clink glasses and drink.)*

AARON: All right. O K, in stanza three, if I'm remembering this right, Sexton talks about being a woman, condemned as a witch, forced to ride in this cart from village to village where she's tortured. You know, as an example to other women.

CARRIE: Gross.

AARON: Yeah, it is. But it isn't. She's sort of saying, go ahead! Whip me, burn me, break my back on the rack. You're not going to scare anybody. Women get put through this kind of Hell everyday. Women are not afraid to die.

BETH: And Anne Sexton has been her kind!

AARON: Exactly.

CARRIE: Very good, Beth!

BETH: Well, die and kind rhyme. Sort of.

AARON: "Not ashamed to die." That's the line.

BETH: Not ashamed to die!

CARRIE: Not ever ashamed to die!

(The three toast.)

AARON: You know what we should do? We should really learn that poem, road trip up to Sexton's grave and dance around it singing that.

BETH: It could be our first club activity.

CARRIE: But Aaron couldn't participate.

AARON: Why not?

BETH: We're not letting men in.

AARON: But I'm going to be your first speaker.

CARRIE: A speaker is not a member.

BETH: It's policy.

AARON: Who made the policy?

CARRIE: Beth.

AARON: Beth, your policy sucks and barring men from clubs is sexist.

CARRIE: You haven't known Beth very long or you'd understand the pain she's suffered.

AARON: I haven't caused her any pain.

BETH: You cause me pain just by sitting at this table.

CARRIE: I must say that alcohol is a wonderful thing. Beth, I feel I know you.

BETH: You do know me.

CARRIE: More than the actual time-span of our acquaintance.

BETH: How long has it been?

CARRIE: Well... *(Checks watch.)* ...I got here at, let's see....

AARON: Five-thirty. You got here just in time for the free popcorn.

CARRIE: Thank you, Aaron. Beth, I've known you since 5:30.

BETH: P M?

CARRIE: P M.

AARON: You've known Beth since happy hour?

BETH: Quality time!

CARRIE: She recruited me.

BETH: To follow the drum!

CARRIE: To be the first member in her...well, we're still arguing over the name. The fill-in-the-suicidal-woman-poet Memorial Self-Educating Poet Appreciators Society. Is that right Beth?

BETH: I'm so drunk.

AARON: That's the first sensible thing I've heard all night.

BETH: Hey, do you have any spoons we can hang off our noses?

CARRIE: Beth, I want you to know, I love you like a sister, but I'm worried about your drinking. Do you do this often?

BETH: Please, don't ask me to think.

AARON: O K, I'm going to take this pitcher away, mop up the floor, and then I'm going to call the Women's Transit Authority.

BETH: Carrie has a car.

(CARRIE *has fallen asleep.*)

AARON: God I hope their number's in the phone book.

BETH: Aaron?

AARON: What?

BETH: What is wrong with you?

AARON: Me?

BETH: Your race. Men. I hate men. I really do.

AARON: Thanks.

BETH: But not you. You're trying at least. You know poetry.

AARON: You know money.

BETH: Huh?

AARON: You're an economics major.

BETH: Economics majors know nothing about money. Economics majors are bozos.

AARON: You're not a bozo.

BETH: No, of course not. But all the rest of them are. Do you want to know why?

AARON: Why?

BETH: Because they're men. I spit on men. *(She tries to spit.)*

AARON: Ew. Here, let's wipe your mouth.

BETH: See, I don't even spit well. If I could spit well, I would spit on them.

AARON: Men?

BETH: Yeah. But I can't spit well. I can't hold my beer well. I can't even walk well right now. The only thing I can do well is...whine.

AARON: Anne Sexton whined a lot.

BETH: No.

AARON: It's in the latest biography.

BETH: I have been her kind, huh?

AARON: I don't think you're suicidal.

BETH: No. But haven't you ever thought, "If I killed myself then they'd all be sorry?"

AARON: Yeah, but logic usually comes screaming in to stop me.

BETH: Logic. I know a lot about logic. I'm very confident. I'm very smart. About money. Not about words. I never know what to say and that's why I want to study great women poets because they have great things to say and if I said what they said then I might have something better to say than what I do say. Right?

AARON: It depends. What do you want to say?

BETH: I'm not sure.

AARON: What's the situation?

BETH: I've gotten a really big award to study economics in London.

AARON: Good for you.

BETH: Damn right good for me. I had stiff competition.

AARON: Men?

BETH: I wouldn't go that far. Let's just say...

AARON: Males.

BETH: Y-chromosomally challenged.

AARON: I like that.

BETH: Thank you.

AARON: Very politically correct.

BETH: Thank you. So, some of these y-chromosome carriers, some of these y-chromosome carriers in positions of power, namely my professors, namely one professor with a y-chromosome...told me that the only reason I got this award was because there was pressure to give it to a woman. And didn't I think that I should decline the award so some y-chromosome who really deserved to go could go.

AARON: What a shit-head.

BETH: That's what I thought.

AARON: Did you tell him that?

BETH: No. I didn't say anything. I couldn't think of anything to say. No, that's not true. I did think of one thing to say. I thought of saying, "I am woman, hear me roar."

AARON: You didn't say that, did you?

BETH: Of course not! Do you think I'd yell a tampon commercial at the chairman of the economics department? I might as well have yelled, "Hey, y-chromosome! Do you ever feel, you know, not so fresh?" I wanted to say something noble. I wanted to think of a great quote, but all I could think of was Helen Reddy.

AARON: That's tough.

BETH: Nobody likes Helen Reddy.

AARON: He can't take the award away from you, can he?

BETH: No, that's decided by a bunch of English chromosomes. Carrie's been to England, and she said that the y-chromosomes there are worse than the y-chromosomes here. And they're English, and I'm not an English major. I bet they just sit around and quote Tolstoy all the time.

AARON: He's Russian.

BETH: Whatever.

CARRIE: *(Who has woken up)* He's a man.

BETH: Exactly.

CARRIE: I'll protect you in England.

AARON: You're going too?

CARRIE: We can get drunk in pubs.

BETH: Biochemistry award.

CARRIE: We'll get drunk in the dorm.

BETH: Hey Carrie, can we use anything in that poem? Can you do it again?

(BETH *shakes* CARRIE *by the hair.*)

CARRIE: "Every woman adores a fascist."

BETH: Is that Plath?

AARON: Plath.

BETH: That won't do. I don't adore fascists.

CARRIE: It's poetic irony.

BETH: Is it?

CARRIE: Yes. Most decidedly so.

BETH: What does that mean?

CARRIE: That a poet is being ironic.

BETH: Really?

AARON: That about sums it up.

CARRIE: Irony does not look good in spray paint. *(She begins shaking the can of spray paint.)*

AARON: What are you going to do with that?

BETH: *(To* CARRIE*)* We should wait until after the bar closes. *(To* AARON*)* Hey, Aaron with two a's, you want to come?

AARON: What are you going to hit?

CARRIE: Chairman's office.

BETH: You should drive us. We're drunk.

CARRIE: Beth has a key, but no one knows she has it.

BETH: I worked in the econ office my freshman year and they never asked for the key back. Sometimes I use it to get in there after hours to use the stapler and the copy machine. I feel bad about the copy machine.

AARON: Look, Beth, you have a right to be angry with this twerp—

CARRIE: Y-twerp.

AARON: Whatever, but you cannot spray paint his office. That kind of behavior can get you in real trouble.

CARRIE: Who insinuated that we were going to spray paint his office?

AARON: You did.

CARRIE: I most certainly did not. We are simply going to spray paint an appropriate message on one wall.

AARON: You'll lose your award.

BETH: No.

AARON: You might get kicked out of school.

BETH: Possibly.

AARON: Look, he only did this to hurt you...

BETH: He succeeded. I'm going to get him back.

CARRIE: Blood red all over his white walls and white leather couch.

BETH: Our blood.

CARRIE: Women's blood.

BETH: Menstrual blood.

AARON: Oh, gross.

BETH: Don't make fun of me.

AARON: Don't reduce yourself to his level.

CARRIE: Don't tell her she doesn't have a right to be angry.

AARON: I never said....

CARRIE: You implied....

AARON: Nothing.

CARRIE: Oh, right.

BETH: He made me hate myself. He made me feel dumb. I thought of everything I should have said, but I realized he'd never listen to me. I just want to make him listen to me. I needed some good words, and the bookstore guy said I should get Sexton or Plath.

AARON: Sexton's a good choice.

CARRIE: She was on sale.

(AARON *takes the book out of the bag.*)

AARON: *Love Poems.*

CARRIE: Is that the type or the title?

AARON: Both.

BETH: No.

CARRIE: We shouldn't have shopped inebriated.

AARON: It's a good book.

CARRIE: Figures he'd like it. These 90s-type ys are all alike. No spine.

AARON: I have a spine and I also have some taste when it comes to poetry.

CARRIE: I'm sure you do, muffin, but, *Love Poems* does not suggest—oh how should I say it?—the intense male-castrating anger we feel.

BETH: Maybe we should have bought Plath.

CARRIE: Too expensive.

BETH: But angry.

AARON: Look, there's a lot of anger in these poems. They're not typical love poems. They're not about loving y-chromosomes. They're more about loving your own xs.

CARRIE: X-chromosome?

BETH: Anne Sexton was a lesbian?

CARRIE: Did she sleep with Sylvia Plath?

AARON: I don't know and I don't care.

BETH: You should know these things. You're a poetry major.

AARON: I'm a math major. I write poetry.

BETH: Why?

AARON: Because I'm insane and suicidal. Now, I think this is what you should spray on bozo's wall. You want to hear this or not?

BETH: I want another beer.

AARON: Okey-dokey. *In Celebration of My Uterus.* "Everyone…"

BETH: Come again?

AARON: *In Celebration of My Uterus.*

CARRIE: You've got to be kidding,

BETH: What's it about? (*She takes the book away from* AARON *and reads the poem.*)

CARRIE: I think it's about her uterus.

AARON: It's more than just her uterus.

CARRIE: If that were the case wouldn't she have called it, *In Celebration of My Uterus and More"*?

BETH: Why would anyone want to celebrate having a uterus?

AARON: It's a poem celebrating her x-chromosomeness. The one great thing that is woman. The belief that the destiny of women is life.

BETH: But she committed suicide.

AARON: She didn't write these poems from the grave.

CARRIE: Look, muffin, I'm a biologist. I know what a uterus is.

AARON: And I know poetry, and I'm telling you that the uterus is a metaphor for more than just whatever it is a uterus does, and stop calling me muffin.

CARRIE: You got great shoulders, you know that?

AARON: That's it. You two are out of here.

(AARON *starts to head for the phone.* BETH *grabs* AARON's *arm.*)

BETH: Pen. Aaron, can I use your pen?

(BETH *takes* AARON's *pen, and a few other things out of his apron, dropping them on the floor.* BETH *begins to busily write in the book.*)

CARRIE: Get his phone number.

AARON: *(Picking up his things)* I don't want you calling me.

CARRIE: You're cute when you're angry.

AARON: You're annoying when you're drunk.

CARRIE: Are your eyes going to be that sparkly when I'm sober?

AARON: You'll never know.

CARRIE: Want to go out?

AARON: No. Give me back my pen.

BETH: In a second.

CARRIE: Are you writing in that book? That book is half mine.

BETH: I'll pay you back. Listen. *(She reads.)* Dear Professor Carney: After careful consideration of your suggestion concerning my award I issue my reply. I will not bake myself because you don't like me. I will not wrap my lips around a tailpipe because you are narrow-minded. That time is over. Instead, I give you this book because it is a time for believing that people and society can change. Sincerely, Elizabeth Dawson.

AARON: That's beautiful.

CARRIE: I don't get it. He won't get it. I think "Fuck you" would be much more clear.

AARON: It's not exactly subtle.

CARRIE: You can't be subtle when you're talking spray paint.

BETH: P.S., I hate you.

CARRIE: I like that part.

BETH: Carrie, I don't think I'm going to spray paint.

CARRIE: What are we going to do then? Get his car?

AARON: *(To* BETH*)* You're going to send him the book.

BETH: I think that's the right thing to do. Now, Aaron, as our first guest speaker would you kindly read to us please? *(She hands him the book.)*

AARON: The whole book?

BETH: Yes, please. You see, I really don't know her kind, and before I can expect Professor Carney to understand her, I think I should understand her myself.

(Lights down)

END OF PLAY

WORKOUT
Wendy Wasserstein

WORKOUT
©copyright 1995 by Wendy Wasserstein

The live stage production rights to this play are represented by Broadway Play Publishing Inc. For all other rights please contact Arlene Donovan, I C M, 40 W 57th St, N Y N Y 10019.

Wendy Wasserstein was born in Brooklyn and raised in Manhattan. She received a B A from Mount Holyoke College and an M F A from the Yale School of Drama. Her Off-Broadway play UNCOMMON WOMEN AND OTHERS was produced at the Phoenix Theater in 1978. In 1989, Wendy Wasserstein was awarded the Pulitzer Prize, the New York Drama Critics Circle Prize, the Drama Desk Award, the Outer Critics Circle Award, the Susan Smith Blackburn Prize, and the Tony Award for her play, THE HEIDI CHRONICLES. Her other credits include ISN'T IT ROMANTIC and MIAMI. For P B S' *Great Performances* series, she has written DRIVE, SHE SAID, and adapted John Cheever's THE SORROWS OF GIN, as well as her own UNCOMMON WOMEN AND OTHERS.

Wendy Wasserstein's publication credits include a collection of essays, *Bachelor Girls* (Knopf); *The Heidi Chronicles and Other Plays* (Harcourt Brace Jovanovich); and *The Sisters Rosensweig* (Harcourt Brace Jovanovich). She serves on the council of the Dramatists Guild, on the board of the British American Arts Association, and The MacDowell Colony board. She has taught at Columbia University and New York University, and holds an Honorary Doctorate from Mount Holyoke College. She served as a contributing editor of *New York Woman* magazine, and currently serves as a contributing editor of *Harper's Bazaar*. Her latest play, THE SISTERS ROSENSWEIG, opened at Lincoln Center in October 1992, and moved to Broadway in March of 1993.

CHARACTER

WOMAN

(A woman enters a small room wearing leotards and a midi sweattop. She turns on disco music and lies on the floor. She begins to exercise, and begins to talk.)

Ready for your workout? We'll start with buttock tucks. These are my favorite. Now lie back, breathe deep. Big breath. Mmmmmm. Relax, feet forward. Remember, make the muscles burn.

(She begins to bounce her buttocks.)

And lift and lower. And lift and lower. Squeeze it. Squeeze it. Push up, release. Push up and release. Really squeeze it, Denise. Lift up, lift up and bounce bounce bounce.

(She begins doing leg lifts.)

This is what I like to think about when I'm doing my workout. I think about how I got up at four-thirty in the morning and ran for five miles. And how great that run felt. Keep bouncing, up down up down. I like to think about the brewer's yeast I gave my children for breakfast. Squeeze it! Squeeze it! And how proud I am that the words "french toast" are never used in our house. I think about my husband's stamina. It's better now than when we first got married because we're organized. Work deep. Work deep!

(She does lifts in fire hydrant position.)

And I think about the novel I'm writing between nine and eleven this morning. And the chain of appliance stores I'm opening at twelve. I just think it's so important that we take charge of our own appliances. Last week I restored the electricity for the city of Fresno. And a year ago I couldn't use a can opener. Just keep bouncing, Denise. And one, and two. And this afternoon after my yoghurt shake...

(She goes into a split.)

Oooooooooooooh I felt the burn that time. I'm going to learn Serbo-Croatian so I can star in the Marshall Tito story, which I am also producing, directing, writing, editing, and distributing. I'll need all my strength. Let's do twenty more. Denise, put the gun down. Your life isn't my fault! Be angry with your buttocks. Let them know your feelings.

(She squats, elbow to knee.)

At five o'clock I'm going to my daughter's dance recital, where my husband will announce his candidacy for governor—I hope you all will vote for him—and I will announce the publication of my new workout book for children under six and their pets. On our way home, the entire family will stop at the home of a woman friend of mine for women's friendship and tofutti ice cream. Release, release, we're almost there. Don't give in. Push it. Push it.

(She begins doing jumping jacks.)

And then my very favorite part of the day. Tuck in. Feel it all over. The children are outside playing nonviolent baseball with radishes and zucchinis, my husband is preparing his part of the family meal and debating with Connie Chung and the six o'clock news team by satellite. Just two more. Get ready to release. And it is time for my moment. Just me.

(She stops exercising for the first time.)

And I sit for the first time in the day. On my favorite chair, with my favorite quilt. And I take a deep breath, and I cry. *(She pauses.)* But just a little.

(She stands up.)

And then I tuck in my stomach and pull up from the chair. Vertebra by vertebra. And I take a deep inhalation and exhale. And now we're ready for fifty more jumping jacks. And one, and two, and three, let's go, Denise.

(She continues jumping happily.)

END